SOCIETY AND POLITICS IN SOUTHEAST ASIA

SOCIETY AND POLITICS IN SOUTHEAST ASIA

Ganganath Jha

Anamika Publishers & Distributors (Pvt.) Ltd.
4697/3, 21-A, Ansari Road, Daryaganj
New Delhi-110 002
Phone : 23281655

First Published, 2009

ISBN : 978-81-7975-195-4

Printed in India

by **Anamika Publishers & Distributors (Pvt.) Ltd.,** 4697/3, 21-A, Ansari Road, Daryaganj, New Delhi-110002, Laser Typesetting by Arpit Printographers, Shahdara Delhi-32 and Printed at Nagri Printers, Delhi.

To

Professor Parimal Kumar Das

(1936–2001)

My teacher, mentor and guide

at

Jawaharlal Nehru University

Preface

Socio-political development of Southeast Asia in the past few decades have been interesting. We find dictatorial systems are gradually withering away and democratic polity being embraced. This tendency is not because of the outside pressures but due to the internal demands. The information media are very active and political parties and pressure groups are strengthening democratic institutions. Wherever or whenever military usurps power, they are criticized, and hence the military tries to restore democratic norms as happened in Thailand. Although the military rulers in Myanmar are not bothered to accomodate the demands of the democratic forces, but it is an exceptional case. Southeast Asians are rapidly adapting to changes in the national environment, economic situation and strategic areas. The developments in Indonesia, Philippines, Thailand and Vietnam suggest that authoritarianism of the system are not sustainable. Indonesia and the Philippines disowned authoritarianism because of the pressures of "peoples power". The communist Vietnam and Laos have introduced reforms in the system and have transformed from command economy to market economy. Political changes are introduced to reduce the gap between rich and poor and fulfil popular aspirations and long-term interests of the country. Southeast Asian leaders—Mahathir Mohammad, Lee Kuan Yew, Fidel Ramos, Chartchai Choonhavan—have talked about "Asian values", common market and East Asian Community to attain higher levels of development and prosperity. The visions of Asian leaders are to bring about qualitative changes in the technological and other aspects of life so that the dream of "Asian Century" in 21st century becomes a reality, but in that endeavour regional peace and solidarity is a pre-requisite.

Although Southeast Asia is much more developed in comparison with South Asia and they have higher levels of integration and co-operation, yet there are some issues and problems that needs to be understood properly and addressed carefully. I have touched some of them in this book. Most of the writings included had been written in due course of time for seminars or workshops and the topics include an analysis of ethnic assertion, society and politics in Cambodia, Laos, Vietnam, Thailand, Indonesia and their evolving political system. Ethnic identity and their regional dynamics, minority rights and rapidly changing politics, the rise of religious extremism and the struggle for democracy in Myanmar has been analysed. Besides there is also a section about Indian diaspora in Southeast Asian region. A glance over the book will certainly provide an understanding of socio-political life of Southeast Asians and existing and emerging problems on the path of their developments.

Finally I will like to say a few words in acknowledgement. As I was not satisfied with what I had written in these articles, I was hesitant to approach a publisher. Mr. Anupam Banerji, who met me in the chamber of Prof. D. Gopal in IGNOU persuaded me for publication of all these articles. Thus I am grateful to him for his efforts and to Anamika Publishers and Distributors for the publication. I am also indebted to my colleagues and doctoral students in the centre for their good wishes, but I am always beholden to Dr. Kaul, Dr. Shankari and Prof. Sahadevan for their kind words. Lastly I owe sole responsibility for any errors committed in this book.

Ganganath Jha

Contents

1

Politics of Ethnic Assertion in Southeast Asia

There are ten countries in Southeast Asia, namely Brunei, Cambodia, Indonesia, Malaysia, Laos, Myanmar, the Philippines, Singapore, Thailand and Vietnam. Some of them are very prosperous and have nearly 8 to 9 per cent annual rate of growth. Singapore has NIE (Newly Industrialised Economy) and developed status and Malaysia, Thailand, Vietnam and Indonesia are rapidly moving in that direction. Situated between Indic and Sinic civilisations, politically none of them are fundamentalist. They have evolved their social and political institutions in such a way, which can reflect their traditional customs and moorings. Located in the middle of East Asia and South Pacific and endowed with tremendous potentials to be "Asian Tigers", this area is considered very important in any strategic calculations of the Asia-Pacific. In order to examine their politics, it is imperative to understand their ethnicity as reflected through the behaviour of these states.

Ethnic Identity

Ethnic groups always try to protect their identities. If they are in a dominant position in a given society, their task is not difficult. But if they are in a minority, they have to face problems in retaining their separate cultural identities. It becomes more difficult if the size of the state is small and an ethnic group adversial. Most of the states in Southeast Asia, except Indonesia, are territorially small. Therefore the question of ethnic and cultural identities are very intense.

Southeast Asian countries became independent after 1945, except Thailand, which was never colonised. Their existing boundaries were drawn by the colonial masters. Most of the states are multiethnic, multi-racial and multi-religious. Their sense of common nationalism developed during their fight against the western colonial masters and the Japanese invaders. After gaining independence, they tried to promote their sense of nationalism based on culture, literature and epics of the dominant ethnic groups. National symbols and anthem that they accepted mostly were related to dominant ethnic groups.

Dominant ethnic groups began to assert their perception very effectively in the initial stage of their nation building. As the government is run by the support of the dominant ethnic groups, no ruler whether charismatic or otherwise could refuse to obey assertion by the dominant groups over other ethnic groups. The minority ethnic groups, interested in preserving their distinct identity, thus suffered setbacks, and subsequently developed some grievances. During the colonial period, they had enjoyed equal privileges and they were considered important tools to neutralize the demands of the dominant ethnic groups or in the policy of "divide and rule". When the indigenous rulers took over, they gave more importance to national integration and thus evolved national guidelines to be obeyed universally. As most of the countries in Southeast Asia remained under authoritarian rule for several decades, national guidelines were pursued constantly and rigorously.

Dominant Ethnic Groups

There are four prominent ethnic groups in this region, whose identities have been well established even beyond their borders. The ethnic Malays are dominant in Malaysia, Indonesia, Brunei and the Philippines.[1] The Philippines is a Christian state, but other countries dominated by the Malays are Islamic. The ethnic Thais are spread into Thailand and also in Laos and parts of Myanmar and Vietnam. The Viets are spread into Vietnam and parts of Thailand, Laos and Cambodia. The ethnic Burmans are dominant in Myanmar. Majority of the people in Thailand, Laos and Myanmar are Buddhists. Besides aforementioned four ethnic groups, there are thousands of small ethnic groups in Southeast Asian countries. Some of them have integrated with the mainstream of socio-economic life, but some are still struggling hard to preserve their separate identity, i.e., Moro , Patani, Rohingyas, Hoas, Karen, Shans and Irianese and Timorese of Melanesians groups. Politicisation of the masses in the post-independence era and modern education provokes them to treated equally with the dominant ethnic groups. If politics is the study of who gets what, when and how, it is pertinent to know what, when and how these ethnic groups are striving to achieve their objectives under the prevailing system.

Hans J. Morgenthau, an eminent Political Scientist, suggests that politics, like society in general, is governed by objective laws that have their roots in human nature. In order to improve society, it is first necessary to understand the laws by which society lives. The operation of these laws being impervious to our preferences, men will challenge them only at the risk of failure.[2] Thus it is necessary for every party or group to take into account the laws governing the society before launching any movement. Generally, movements without the active support of the majority do not succeed.

A number of minority ethnic groups have resorted to extra constitutional methods and adopted violent means to attain independence or autonomy. Though they had initial success in some areas, i.e., Mindanao and East Timor, they were overwhelmed by the superior forces of the state subsequently. Now as the pace of development and modernisation have gained momentum in the entire region and as the states are equipped with sophisticated weapons, the insurgents face a dilemma either to surrender or remain isolated. The imperatives of power politics suggest that they should compromise and get away with the share of spoils that the state can offer. The political masters know well that "power is the essence of politics", are unwilling to come forward to accommodate the grievances of the insurgents, because it may complicate their leadership at the helm of affairs. The adverse propaganda against insurgent ethnic groups have been conducted in such a way that the leaders espousing compromise with them would be perceived critically by the media and politicians alike. For instance, U Nu, the Prime Minister of Burma (1948-62) wanted to sign an accord with the insurgent ethnic groups, but that proved the major cause of his downfall.

The dominant ethnic groups do display the sense of ethnocentricity on occasions and they have geared their powers to project that distinctive characteristics of their religion, culture and historical personalities are regarded as the features of their nationalism. For instance, Thailand prefers its ethnic minorities to assume Thai names and observe Buddhist festivals as national festivals. Similar is the case with Laos and Myanmar. On the other hand, ethnic Viets have been under the impact of Confucianism and Buddhism and traits of Sinic culture are ingrained in their character. Their sense of nationalism emerged in course of their war against France, Japan and the United States. Their communist ideology inspired them to go for an egalitarian society and in the process, the business class of Haos suffered. On the other hand, in the Islamic countries of Southeast Asia— Brunei, Malaysia and Indonesia— Islamic cultural heroes and religious symbols are considered national symbols. Though Indonesia has no state religion and it believes in secularism, the impact of Islam is omnipotent.

Problems of Minorities

The minority ethnic groups espouse and advocate the inclusion of their cultural symbols in the national category side by side the dominant ethnic groups. They thus voice their concerns and in the process express their own sense of ethnocentricity. The expression of such ideas are disliked under the existing political system in entire Southeast Asia. Such an attitude is projected against national harmony because this provokes the organised and influential groups of minority ethnic community to oppose the system. The opposition of a section of the minority ethnic groups invites the wrath of the state which finally leads to omission and commission. The western type parliamentary system is non-existent in Southeast Asia and therefore the channels of grievance redressal are very thin. The minority ethnic groups might like to find a forum to voice their grievances to affect changes in the system, but their options are limited.

The peaceful transformation of a society and government are preconditioned by the following factors:

(*i*) the ability of public opinion to express itself freely;

(*ii*) the ability of social and political institutions to absorb the pressure of public opinion; and

(*iii*) the ability of the state to protect the new status quo against violent change.[3]

There has been widespread censorship of the press irrespective of the fact that they are under communism, dictatorship or democracy. Thus the freedom of speech and expression is extremely limited in all the countries in the region. The ruling elite gives top priority to development and the media is geared to highlight the problems of development and modernisation. They, however try to avoid to indulge in political polemics. They believe that if the fruits of development reach to the deprived ones, other rights would automatically follow. They are acquainted with the UN Declaration of Universal Civil and Political Rights and believe in paving the way to that goal through economic development. In the meanwhile the insurgents are increasingly getting isolated and restive. Some of them are engaged in the subvertive activities or guerilla war. Therefore, the state perceives them as fifth columns and the insurgents reciprocate in the same fashion. As a result the leadership of the dominant ethnic groups are biased and turn protagonists of strong arm methods, ushering into untold miseries to innocent people.

It is a reality that some enlightened section of the dominant ethnic groups would like to share power with the minority leaders. They do think in the long-term interests but they cannot ignore the imperatives of power for ones own existence. In the political context, G. Schwarzenberger has rightly observed power as the capacity to impose ones will on others by reliance on effective sanctions in case of non-compliance. The demonstration of powers of the dominant ethnic groups over the minority and certain conditions, thus provoke the reactions of the ethnic minorities. In the absence of a proper forum—fully elected legislature, free mass media, effective political parties—they are left with little options, but to indulge in acts of sabotage. In the process, they loose public sympathy and support.

There were thousands of kingdoms, sultenates and principalities before the advent of the colonial rule in Southeast Asia. Colonial masters had distinct language, dress, religion, food habits and cultural ethos. Sri Vijaya and Majapahit rulers of Indonesia were forerunners of Malay identity and culture. Their empire extended widely in Southeast Asia, extending from the tip of Thai border to the peninsular Malaya and various islands of Southeast Asia. Again the Sultanate of Sulu and Patani were great centres of Islamic culture and civilisation in the medieval period. They were prosperous and strong but internecine warfare with the neighbouring states weakened them. When the Spanish colonial rulers arrived, Sulu was merged with the Philippines and Patani was divided into two parts integrated with—British Malaya and Thailand respectively. As the people of Patani were ruled by two different countries, their movement for nationhood was also diluted. The ethnic Thais and Viets were martial races immigrating from Yunnan to Southeast Asia and they captured the territories of the Khmer kingdom to establish their own empires. They ruled with an iron hand for centuries and dominated the politics of the region. Laos was the vassal state of Thailand for centuries and Thailand and Burma fought wars for 300 years on one pretext or the other.

Thailand has evolved its own sense of nationalism and they do not permit their citizens to speak anything against nation, religion and the king. On the other hand, Indonesia is a believer and practitioner of *Pancasila* principles and nobody is allowed to be critical of those ideologies. Five principles of Pancasila are following:

(*i*) Belief in God Almighty
(*ii*) The principle of just and civilised humanity
(*iii*) Indonesian unity
(*iv*) The principle of democracy guided by the wisdom of representatives
(*v*) Principle of Social Justice.[4]

Malaysia, on the other hand, has provided constitutional guarantees to protect the rights of the Bhumiputras, that is ethnic Malays. Some important and sensitive posts have been reserved for the people of the dominant ethnic group and Brunei situated along Malaysian borders, also upholds the principles of special privileges to the Bhumiputras. Myanmar has also provisions to protect the rights of the ethnic Burmans. In order to prove that point, they have even changed the name of the country—from Burma to Myanmar. This process of Burmanisation of the country (Myanmar) ever since 1962 has antagonised the minority ethnic groups. Likewise, the Philippines attaches great importance to the Christian population of Luzon and has proved unfriendly with the Moro Muslims. The Christians were offered advantages advertently ever since independence and the Moro Muslims were reduced to a minority status in Sulu and Mindanao areas during the regime of President Ferdinand E. Marcos. A section of the Moro Muslims began to organise themselves to fight against the state, and in this endeavour they had sympathy and support of their co-religionists initially in the neighbouring countries, but only for a brief period.

In fact, Southeast Asian countries realised that if they encouraged secessionist tendencies of ethnic minority groups, it would rebound and prove counter-productive. Every country has a sizable section of the minority ethnic groups and this factor compelled them to develop common security concerns and subsequently retracted their steps and showed greater understanding of the problems of each other. Such a perception proved conducive to regional solidarity. This feeling of commonality was re-envigorated by the signing of the Treaty of Amity, Cooperation and Friendship in 1976, under the aegis of the Association of Southeast Asian Nations (ASEAN). This agreement paved the way for creation of friendly environment in this region. This also contained effectively any transnational support to terrorist/subversive activities. Later on, the ASEAN countries forged very friendly relations with China in the wake of China's four modernisation drives. Trade and commercial relations with these countries developed so rapidly, that China had to close the chapter on proletarian revolution or communist fraternity. China had the potentials to destabilise or sabotage the political system in the region. However, better trade relations demanded stability and prosperity in Southeast Asia. The Chinese almost ignored their earlier ideological commitments in favour of the realistic benefits. They made considerable investments in the economy of Southeast Asia and it was suitably reciprocated. Now the entire region is booming based on the principles of market economy and free trade.

Thus, the sources of external threats were contained, but they have yet to cope with the internal challenges of nation building and modernisation. The challenges do emanate from the imbalanced relationship in power politics and that is a two-edged weapon. The parties or groups in pursuit of power, try to use ethnicity or religion to advance their positions against their adversaries. This has more often been the root cause of the rise of fundamentalist ideas. Though this is a sensitive issue because none of the states in question would admit standing on the fundamentalist course, yet this is an emerging problem of the growing politicisation.

Constitutional Provisions

Here it would be pertinent to analyse the constitutional provisions affecting different sections of population in these countries. Brunei Darrussalam, where 66 per cent of the population are Muslims, 12 per cent Buddhists and 9 per cent Christians, has declared Islam as the official religion. Its legislature—33 member

Legislative Council—was dissolved in February 1984 and since then Brunei has no legislature. The supreme political powers are vested in the Sultan. Though this country has 25 per cent Chinese population; they are classified as non-citizens and are excluded from state benefits. There is ban on alcohol import and Christmas cannot be celebrated publicly.

There is a ban on Muslims too-eating in restaurants, because they think that the cooks are non-Muslims invariably. Malay Islam and the institution of monarchy is a compulsory subject to be taught in the secondary schools.[5] However, all citizens enjoy free medical care and education, government housing loans and full employment. The ethnic Malays have reasons to be happy with the system and therefore Brunei National Democratic Party (PKDB) has been unable to find an independent base.

The Indonesian political system is based on *Pancasila*, in which deliberations lead to a consensus. They have a legislature—House of People's Representatives—with elected and nominated members. Though there are 87 per cent Muslims and 9 per cent Christians, they have offered religious liberty to all. It is an archipelagic country with more than 17000 islands and has striven for "unity in diversity". Indonesia, ever since its independence in 1945 to 1998, witnessed only two Presidents, namely Sukarno and Suharto. It was very difficult to contain the influence of Suharto, firmly entrenched in power. Therefore, some religion-based parties were trying to exploit the religious sentiments. An Islamic organisation, Nahdalatul Ulama, under the leadership of Abdurrahaman Wahid became popular in 1990s. It advocated constructive role of religion in politics and had been highly critical of the professional politicians.[6] They also expressed their concern privately that the country's four million ethnic Chinese were getting richer and the indigenous people poorer. Thus Muhammdiyah Muslim Movement under the leadership of Samsyuddin was getting a tacit support. It advocated bigger share for Indonesia's 164 million Muslims in decision-making within Golkar and its influence was growing. The government was greatly concerned for all those developments.

Malaysia, on the other hand, has declared Islam as the official religion as more than half of its population are Muslims. It has a bi-cameral legislature—Senate and House of Representatives and a democratic polity. It has also allowed the emergence of a multi-party system and had a charismatic leadership of Mahathir Mohamed, with a strong mass support. Therefore, it was difficult to oust him from power. Some Islamic organisations, such as Pertai Islam Se-Malaysia (PAS) was trying to challenge his authority by preaching the role of Islamic religion in the politics of the nation. The political masters are aware of their demands and trying to offer as much advantages to the ethnic Malays as possible. The government is trying to project that the ethnic Malays can fulfil their aspirations under the rule of UMNO led by Malays only. Malaysia under Mahathir embarked on 20-year new economic policy during 1970-90 and offered substantial reservations for the Bhumiputras.[7] Though the government tried to improve the economic conditions of the Malays vis-a-vis the Chinese constituting about 37 per cent of the population. However, it could not fulfil the desired objectives. The Chinese population remains affluent and dominant in business and trade.

Singapore, situated in the middle of the Malay world offers an excellent example of inter-ethnic harmony. It has uni-cameral legislative assembly called Parliament. It has 81 members elected by secret ballot with the customary exception of those serving criminal sentences, all citizens over 21 years are eligible to vote. Voting in an election is compulsory. There is a common roll without communal electorates and they have tried to make sure that representatives from all the communities are elected to the parliament. They have also established Presidential Council for minority rights which is authorised to consider and report on matters affecting persons of any racial or religious community as referred to it by parliament or the government. The Council is authorised to draw attention to any bill or subsidiary legislation which in its opinion is a differentiating measure. Though overwhelming number of the population are ethnic Chinese, Singapore has four official languages, i.e., Malay, Chinese (Mandarin), Tamil and English. They consider Malay as the national language and English as the language of administration. The system of grievance redressal is effective and the people are generally happy.

Thailand is in the process of democratic experiments. It adopted a new constitution in 1991 which provided for a bi-cameral legislature—270 member Senate and 360 member House of Representatives—multi-party system and greater avenues for popular participation in decision making. Thailand with more than 47,049,223 Buddhists and 1,869,427 Muslims, has declared Bhasa

Thai as the official language. It has been a great campaigner of the policy of ethnic assimilation and it has admirably resolved its disputes with the ethnic Chinese. The latter has been allowed to play their traditional role in business and trade and in the meanwhile the integration through intermarriage and other measures have yielded satisfying results. However, there are some other ethnic groups which have shown defiance, such as ethnic Malays in the South and ethnic Viets in the Northeast. In fact Thai government insists on adherence to the basic tenets of Thai nationalism—nation, religion and the king. Minority ethnic groups have options either to integrate or remain isolated perpetually.

The Philippines has been witnessing momentous changes ever since the Marcos regime was overthrown and Corazon Aquino took over on 25 February 1986. Filipinos adopted a new constitution in 1987 through which a bi-cameral legislature—24-member Senate and 200-member House of Representatives was established. It has a population of more than 31,169,488 Roman Catholics; 14,33,688 Anglipayans; 15,84,963 Muslims; 33,639 Buddhists; 11,22,999 Protestants; 4,75,407 Iglesia in Cristo and they are scattered on several islands. The Government of the Philippines has been facing the problems of national integration and it was therefore that Marcos had proclaimed martial law in 1972.[8] English is the official language. Majority of the population are Christians and are determined to pursue secular polity. However, the system offered more benefits to the Christians compared to the Muslims in the past few decades.

Myanmar has been under authoritarian rule for several decades. In last few years it is facing the threat of insurgency. The problems of national integration are intricate. This country with 68 per cent Buddhists, tried to promote integration by force which ultimately proved counter productive. It has a sizable number of minority ethnic groups, i.e., Shans, Karens and Rohingyas who are organised to offer opposition. Under the leadership of General Ne Win (1962-88) the regime pursued a policy of Burmanisation.

The government adopted dictatorial means to subdue the dissenting ethnic leaders and as a result the minorities were persecuted, executed and isolated. The Rohingya Muslims were treated very harshly and their nightmarish trauma compelled them to flee to Bangladesh.

Besides Rohingyas, Karens (Christians) and Shans (Buddhists) also suffered immensely. In fact, they demonstrated that the country belonged to ethnic Burmans only and other ethnic groups in Myanmar could survive only at their mercy. The military usurped the power in the name of Burmans. As a result, there were great upheavals and the resentment grew. When General Saw Maung came to power on 18 September 1988 and State's Law and Order Restoration Council (SLORC) was created to administer the country; Burmese became the official language and remained medium of instruction in all the schools. Though religious freedom and use of English were permitted, no substantial concession was given to attract the support of the minority ethnic groups.[9]

Likewise, Indochinese countries—Vietnam, Laos and Cambodia—have also to grapple with their ethnic problems. The *raison d'etre* of the Khmer Rouge in Cambodia is based against ethnic Vietnamese, who migrated to that area in the historical past or in the post-1978 period. In 1975, when Khmer Rouge had come into power, it had pursued anti Vietnamese policies and had driven out 50,000 ethnic Vietnamese from Cambodia. At present when it is out of power and increasingly isolated, its legitimacy is based on rights of Khmers against the Vietnamese. It is willing to drive out Vietnamese population and influence on Cambodia. The ruling coalition of Cambodian People's Party and Funcinpec, led by Norodom Ranaridh and Hun Sen, however, is trying to offer equal rights to all the ethnic groups.

Vietnam is also multi-ethnic society comprised of ethnic Viets, Chams, Khmer, Thais, Hoas and tribal people. It has adopted a unicameral legislature called National Assembly and has introduced "multi-candidate election system" to encourage popular leaders to participate in the decision-making. The Communist Party of Vietnam no longer decides the panel of candidates but it depends on personality and social base of the candidate.

In fact, the Vietnamese abolished private trade in South Vietnam in 1978 and closed 30,000 private shops which had been allowed to function in the post-unification era. As most of these businesses were run by the ethnic Chinese (Hoas), it affected them exclusively.[10] This development was given an anti-Chinese colour at the cost of Hoas. The Chinese government expressed solidarity with the Hoas and hostility broke out against Vietnam. It repeatedly talked of war and naturally Sino-Vietnam relations soured. Faced with difficulties in leading a normal life, Hoas started deserting their homes in boats and rafts and thereby known as "boat people". Their number increased in thousands during 1978-81 and their plight shook the conscience of the civilised world. As a result, the international community criticised Vietnam and it had a desirable impact. Vietnam retraced its steps and helped the rehabilitation of the Hoas subsequently, but this event inflicted great harms to the cause of inter-ethnic solidarity which had developed in course of their wars against the external invaders.

Besides Hoas, Moro Muslims have also suffered due to their assertive attitude in the Philippines. Moros demanded independence or autonomy for themselves based on distinct history, cultural identity, religion and geography.[11] They fought fierce wars to attain their objectives and finally the Aquino government agreed to grant limited autonomy through the formation of Autonomous Region of Muslim Mindanao (ARMM) in July 1988. Four provinces out of 13 in Mindanao—Lanao del Sur, Magindanao, Sulu and Tawi Tawi—approved the proposal and thereafter the elections to appoint the Governor and other office bearers of ARMM was also held. The democratic leaders in the Philippines are trying to forget the legacies of the Marcos era and Moros are being encouraged to participate in decision-making. Thus the resolution of the Moro problem was in sight. But Abu Sayyaf and other terrorist outfits have their own agenda. Presently Acehnese model may be applied for conflict resolution of ethnic problems in other parts of Southeast Asia.

The most difficult and complicated example of ethnic assertion and dispute in entire Southeast Asia can be traced in East Timor, formerly a Portuguese colony and subsequently 27th province of Indonesia. This problem was more or less like Kashmir (India), and equally internationalised. The indigenous population are Christians of Melanesian descent. They are also known as Topasses in Indonesia. They sought secession on the ground that they are different from the Malay Muslims and also because they were subjected to a different colonial master than other parts of Indonesian archipelago.[12] They did enjoy the traditional support of Portugal in particular, and had posed problems to the Indonesian government to integrate. The U.N. was seized of the matter which had not legitimated integration of East Timor with Indonesia. Insurgency activities in East Timor was accelerated by an organisation called Fretilin, and innocent people were the victims of internecine warfare.

Indonesia claimed East Timor because it was a part of Indonesia before the advent of the European colonial rulers. When it got independence from the Dutch rule, East Timor like Goa (India) remained the only area outside its control. It was clearly in possession of Western half of Timor and the surrounding areas of East Timor. It was expected of Portugal to concede the claims of Indonesia as France did in case of Pondicherry and Mahe vis-a-vis India. The Portuguese proved different. India too had to fight to integrate Goa, Daman and Diu. Similarly, Indonesia was compelled to fight and integrate East Timor. But the Portuguese succeeded in internationalising the issue and effectively created international opinion against Indonesia's integration of East Timor. However, the situation has changed after the 1999 referendum, when East Timor decided to separate from Indonesia. Now East Timor is a sovereign independent state and grappling with pathetic economic situation.

Conclusions

To conclude, it can be stated that the minority ethnic groups are concerned about preserving their distinct identity and cultural symbols side by side the majority community. Some ethnic groups, such as Moro, Patani and Rohingyas emphasise the importance of their religion (Islam) above all other things, but Timorese attach prime importance to ethnicity to prove their distinctiveness. It is necessary for the dominant community to be considerate and sympathetic to understand the sentiments of the minority to have a fruitful dialogue. The minority ethnic groups would prefer significant changes in the academic curriculum to accommodate knowledge about their religion and cultural identity at par with that of the dominant groups. They would like shares in the civil service and overall decision-making. Above all confidence-building measures are sufficiently required to inspire them to participate in nation-building and modernisation.

Problem of ethnic assertion (group solidarity in conflict or cooperation) is as old as human civilization. Ethnicity was one of the potent instruments to strengthen the position of political masters in their societies. Rulers used to evolve policies to boost the morale of their followers through ethnic appeals and the chiefs were regarded as the custodian of ethnic rights. Gradually ethnicity did not remain the reserved prerogative of the rulers, but it was sought to be used politically by the people. This was also used against the rulers and such a trend was disliked. This gave birth to power struggle. Under the circumstances if ethnic assertion took place through the political rulers astutely, it was welcomed by the majority. If it was attempted by the minority against the state, it was condemned as sabotage and invited ruthless use of force. Hence thesis and anti-thesis between dominant and dominated ethnic groups originated. Thus the competition for assertion and counter-assertion continued.

The important point is that if the feeling of nationalism is high, the capacity of understanding and resilience can develop under that parameter. On the other hand, if the activities of any ethnic group is directed against the existence of the state without caring for the opinion of the majority, it would be checkmated by the superior force of the state.

There is an increasing urge for democratic government and polity in the entire Southeast Asian region. The various regimes are trying to fulfil the aspiration of all sections of the people and have been evolving innovative methods of development. The cooperation with the system at this stage in the long-run would definitely help the divergent ethnic groups to retain their cultural identity and due assertion in future. The politics of ethnic assertion is an eternal phenomenon and should be viewed not in a negative but in a positive and constructive way.

REFERENCES

1. For a detailed study, see J.M. Gullick and Maxwell William, "The Study of Malay Society", *Journal of the Malaysia Branch of the Royal Asiatic Society*, Vol. 64, No. 2, 1991, pp. 7-46.
2. Hans J. Morgenthau, *Politics Among Nations : The Struggle for Power and Peace*, Calcutta, 1967, p. 4.
3. *Ibid.*, p. 418.
4. Republic of Indonesia Armed Forces Manual on the Dual Functions of the Armed Forces, Jakarta, Department of Defence and Security, 1 June 1982, pp. 125-27.
5. K.U. Menon, "Brunei Darrussalam in 1988 : Aging in the Wood", *Asian Survey*, Vol. 29, No. 2, February 1989, pp. 140-44.
6. R. William Liddle, "Indonesia's Threefold Crisis", *Journal of Democracy*, Vol. 3, No. 4, October 1992, pp. 60-74.
7. "Analysis and Appraisal on Malaysia's New Economic Policy, 1971-90", *Developing Economics*, Vol. 29, No. 4, December 1991, pp. 281-454, and also see, William Case, "Semi-democracy in Malaysia : Understanding

the Pressures for Regime Change", *Pacific Affairs*, Vol. 66, No. 2, Summer 1993, pp. 183-205.

8. For further details, see, J. Bresnan, ed., *Crisis in the Philippines : The Marcos Era and Beyond*, Princeton University Press, 1986.
9. For Burmese Politics, see B. Lintner, *Outrage : Burma's Struggle for Democracy*, London, 1990 and J. Silverstein, *Burmese Politics : The Dilemma of National Unity*, Rutgers University Press, 1980.
10. Lewis M. Stern, "The Overseas Chinese in the Socialist Republic of Vietnam, 1979-82", *Asian Survey*, Vol. 25, No. 5, May 1985, pp. 521-36.
11. For further details, see, T.J.S. George, *Revolt in Mindanao : The Rise of Islam in Philippino Politics*, Kuala Lumpur, 1980.
12. For a comprehensive analysis of this aspect, see Jill Jollife, *East Timor : Nationalism and Colonialism*, St. Lucia, 1978.

2

Thai Society and Politics

The Kingdom of Thailand, also known as Siam in the past, lies in the centre of the Indochina Peninsula (Vietnam, Cambodia and Laos) and the northen part of the Malay Peninsula. In the north and the northeast Thailand borders on Laos, in the east on Cambodia, in the West and northwest on Burma and in the South on Malaysia. The country was known till 1939 as Siam. Thailand occupies area of 514,000 sq. km. which is slightly higher than France. The country is geographically divided into four regions—Northern, Northeastern, Central Basin and Southern Peninsula. The economy of each region develops on the bases of the resources available in the concerning areas. According to the estimate of 1969, Thailand has a population of more than 34 millions. Now in 2007, the estimated population of the country is 64 million. Thailand is a plural society consisting of nearly thirty sub-nationalities. Among them Thais (Siamese) and the Lao constitute about 85 per cent of the total population. Thai, a language originated from Sino-Tibetan group, is the national language. Buddhism which plays an important part in the life of the country, and is professed by nearly 90 per cent of the total population, has been the official religion since long.

Thailand had never experienced colonial rule and consequently did not follow the traditional pattern of civil military relations; i.e., military subordination to civilian authority. After the 1932 coup that ended the period of absolute monarchy, the military established its primacy in Thai politics. It extended its influence on vital institutions of government and rationalized participation on the basis of its tradition of leadership provided in times of crisis. The only civilian leader who had some popular support among the masses, Pridi Phanomyong and who is also an important leader of the coup of 1932, was branded a communist and not allowed by the military elites to establish his roots in Thai politics. Other civilian leaders did not have the required charisma and thus, the military entrenched itself in the country's politics. At the same time, the military leaders could not establish institutions and norms to facilitate transition of power in a peaceful manner. The net result has been a succession of military rulers in the past 60 years who could assume power only through coups and counter-coups, making the Thai political system extremely volatile and unstable. There have been intermittent attempts at establishing a civilian government and nurturing democratic institutions, but they were thwarted by military coups or political manoeuvring on the ground that they were unable to protect the honour of the King, nation or religion, the three emotive issues in Thai politics. Recent events have, however, showed that while clockwork coups are a part of Thailand's old world they have no place in the modern age, where a growing middle class, especially in Bangkok, insists on making its own destiny. 'Mobile Phone Mob' or middle class demonstrators joined by a rainbow coalition from all walks of life insist that their politics be finally freed from an overdose of military involvement.

While the appointment of Chuan Leekpai as Prime Minister of Thailand following the national elections in 1992 signified a triumph for democratic forces, this victory can hardly be seen as ushering in a new political era. Although pro-democratic forces, comprising Chuan's *Democratic Party*, the *New Aspiration Party* (NAP), the *Palang Dharma Party* and Solidarity won the election, they did so with only a small margin of five seats. As a result one cannot expect anything except a fragile and shaky government despite their decision to bring in the pro-military *Social Action Party* to strengthen the coalition. Thailand is also bound to face political instability, mainly because of a lack of cohesion within the coalition. Bickering and clash of interests will become inevitable as the coalition partners seek to expand their bases of support. Political corruption is another problem which may weaken the government, as short-term personal or group interests emerge. The new government's relationship with the military is also crucial. The 1991 coup against Chatichai Choonhavan's administration was triggered by a lack of mutual trust between the government and the military. Underlying the question of the military's reaction to its changed circumstances is the prevailing public mood of democratic awareness. The military's brutal suppression of the pro-democracy demonstrations in May '92 served to raise public political consciousness. Many Thais, particularly of the urban middle class, are now demanding a truly representative government that belongs to the people and not to small groups within the military elite. The economy's dramatic growth in recent years has strengthened the nonbureaucratic forces, including the business community, the media and other professional groups. These influential groups are now looking for an efficient, honest and elected government to move the country's economy forward. During 1978-1991 in forcing Vietnam to move out of Cambodia, Thailand provided strategic support to Cambodian rebels and that proved a crucial factor in Vietnam's withdrawal from Cambodia.

Land and People of Thailand

Thailand, is strategically situated in the centre of Southeast Asian mainland and spread over 513, 115 square kilometers. It was due to its strategic location that Japan occupied it first before advancing further in the rest of southeast Asia. Japan infact used Thailand as a spring-board to invade Burma, Java, Malaya and Singapore (during 1942-1945). It was again due to its location that it was chosen as the headquarters of Southeast Asia Treaty Organisation (SEATO). Thai air bases at Udon Thani, Nakhon Phanom, Ubon, Nakhon Ratchasima, Takhli and U-Tapao and the naval base at Sattahip were developed by the United States in order to contain communism in the region. Thailand once again played a strategic role during 1978-1991 in deterring Vietnam from staying in Cambodia. Thailand provided strategic support to Cambodian rebels and this proved a crucial factor in Vietnam's eventual withdrawal from Cambodia.

How Thailand Escaped Colonial Rule

Thailand is the only country in Southeast Asia to have escaped colonial rule. The enlightened monarchy of Thailand was solely responsible for maintaining the independence of the country. The conduct of diplomacy and foreign relations, particularly under the leadership of King Mongkut (1851-68) and Chulalongkorn (1868-1910), was very realistic. Thai kings had a clear perception of the security environment of the region and had the capabilities to tackle France and Great Britain's colonial ambitions vis-a-vis Thailand. They had the necessary command over English language as well as the sophistication needed to solve the emerging problems. They were polite and respectful while dealing with Western emissaries and tried to accommodate their demands in a suitable manner. The British emissary, Sir John Bowring was so happy with the behaviour and hospitality of the then King Mongkut that he wrote a famous memoir, "The Kingdom and People of Siam, with a Narrative of the Mission in 1855". He was a great advocate of Thai interests in Great Britain.

Thailand had evolved effective instruments to conduct its foreign policy. It had introduced foreign advisors for framing suitable policies vis-a-vis Western powers. Thus there was a British advisor to suggest policies concerning Great Britain, a French advisor to deal with France and a Dutch to deal with Netherlands and so on.

For a proper understanding of the society and politics of Western powers and for enlisting their cooperation, King Chulalongkorn astutely established a personal rapport with some monarchs in the West. He sent some of his sons for education under the care of prominent European monarchs of the time. This also helped him to build a team of indigenous experts for handling diplomacy with competence and sophistication. Indeed, King Chulalongkorn's attempts to get international recognition were remarkable.

As a result of proper conduct of Thai diplomacy, an understanding developed between Great Britain and France for mintaining a buffer state between British Burma and French Indochina. Historical records testify that in 1889, M. Waddington, the French Ambassador in London, called on the British Prime Minister, Lord Salisbury, with the suggestion that it would be advantageous for both countries to declare Thailand a buffer state between their respective empires. The response of the British Prime Minister was positive and thereafter both the countries evolved a strategy to treat Thailand as a buffer area.

This is not to suggest that these colonial powers did not create any difficulties for the sovereignty of Thailand. In 1893, French gunboats came up to Menam Chao Phraya to press their claims over Laos. France looked for the natural border line for demarcating the boundary between Thailand and the Union of Indochina and it pressed its claims on the areas situated on the left bank of the Mekong River. Thai rulers, after some reservations, conceded the French demands and vacated the territories known as Laos today. Thereafter, France looked for the natural border line to demarcate Thai-Cambodian border also and chose Cardamom mountain ranges for the same. Thus, France subsequently pressurized Thailand to forsake its claims over Battambang, Siemrip and Sisophon. Thailand knew its strategic weaknesses in relation to France and therefore, instead of a confrontation chose to hand over disputed areas to the latter in 1907. These developments had their impact on the attitude of Great Britain also. It also wished to extend its colonial areas on the Malayan frontier. In 1909 Britain demanded the jurisdiction over Kedah, Perlis, Kelantan and Trengganu and Thailand agreed to do so. Thailand maintained its balance even in the face of great provocation from Western powers and thus manage to protect its sovereignty.

The Institution of Monarchy

When Thais defeated the Khmer government at Sukhothai under the leadership of King Indraditya in 1253 A.D., they laid the foundation of the Kingdom of Thailand. Indraditya's successor King Ramakhamheng the great (1270-1317) was a great warrior and statesman. He fought to combine several principalities into his Kingdom. His jurisdiction spread from Mekong River in the north to Malayan penisula in the south and from Burma in the west to Cambodia in the east. He established tributary relations with the Han emperors in China and received their support for subduing the Khmer and Annamite rulers in the region. Thailand with its capital at Sukhothai, under the stewardship of Ramakhambeng, became the most powerful state in the Southeast Asian region. His successors were also powerful and fought several wars against the Burmese, Khmer and Vietnamese rulers.

The security and geo-political environment of the Southeast Asian region became disturbed in the 19th century. There was an imperialist race amongst European countries and the various Southeast Asian states began to succumb to colonial rule. The Dutch had already consolidated their rule over Indonesia. The French empire had entrenched itself in Indochina. Great Britain was consolidating its hold over Burma and Malaya. The colonial powers were focussing their attention now on Thailand. In the situation Thai rulers displayed tremendous understanding and searched avenues to escape colonial yoke.

The Kings of Thailand provided worthwhile leadership in an endeavour to deter Western powers from indulging in gunboats diplomacy against it. King Mongkut introduced reforms in domestic policies and adopted a liberal outlook towards the Western world. He stopped paying tributes to China and began to attach importance to Great Britain from 1851 onwards. In 1855, he signed a Treaty of Friendship and Commerce with Great Britain and conceded some trade benefits. He also offered extraterritorial rights to British subjects residing in Thailand to enable them to pursue trade interests in Thailand. Such a policy suited the Britishers interested mainly in business and commerce. Thus, Britain sought friendly relations with Thailand and never challenged its sovereignty. Though Britain was in a position to create problems for Thailand because one, it was controlling Malaya, Burma and the Indian sub-continent and second, it had geo-political compulsions to check French expansion in the region, yet it desisted from doing so.

The successor of King Mongkut was Chulalongkorn the great, who was popular with his subjects. He was more liberal and shrewd than his predecessor. He searched avenues for establishing personal rapport with monarchs in the European continent with a view to enhance Thailand's national interests. The successors of King Chulalongkorn however were not so capable and strong to handle the domestic situation. King Vajiralongkorn (1910-1925) and King Prajadhipok (1925-1935) were educated and trained in Great Britain and were impressed with the British model of government and polity. They were liberal in their outlook and this made a section of the Sakdina class (aristocracy), unhappy. There were some misunderstandings about the character of King Prajadhipok. Under the circumstances, a group of civil and military men led by Pridi Phanomyong and General Phibun Songgram hastily formed a group that supported a coup in the name of Peoples Party for overthrowing the system of absolute monarchy.

The promoters of the coup surrounded the capital on 24 June 1932 on all sides and presented an ultimatum to King Prajadhipok. The coup leaders demanded that the King either accept the position of a constitutional head, resign or face for bloodshed. The King was thus faced with a delicate situation. He abhorred bloodshed and thought that any delay on his part would result in unnecessary bloodshed. So he agreed to constitutional monarchy.

Constitutional Monarchy

Several constitutions have been framed since 1932 to suit the needs of the changing political order and subsequently abandoned for a new one. But there is a factor common to all the constitutions is that they regard monarchy as a revered institution. The King is the ceremonial head of the state and of the armed forces. The sovereignty, technically, rests with the people and the King exercises those powers only which are in conformity with the provisions of the constitution. The person of the king is sacred and cannot be violated, accused or sued in any way. He leads the nation on ceremonial occasions and is revered by the people of Thailand. He is the symbol of Thai nationalism and people are still loyal to him.

The present King Bhumibol Aduldej is very influential. He has helped the leaders of different political parties with sincere advice for resolving conflicts and crisis. Thus, in the wake of students revolution in October 1973, he advised Field Marshal Thanom Kittikachorn to resign. This diffused the tension and paved the way for democratic experiments. The King once again displayed his great diplomatic skill in 1992 when he advised General Suchinda Kraprayoon to hand over power to his successor in view of the civil unrest against his leadership.

Military Leadership

Thailand has had a tradition of military leadership right since the end of absolute monarchy. The military established its primacy in Thai politics immediately after 1932 coup d'etat. It extended its influence on vital institutions of government and pleaded justification for its presence. The civilian leader, Pridi Phanomyong, who had some popular support, was projected as a communist. Though Pridi became the Prime Minister of the country, he failed to lay the foundations of civilian rule. When he came out with his idealistic proposals to introduce radical changes in the socio-economic structure, it was disliked and opposed by the political elite. His proposal was to nationalize all agricultural lands for better distribution and production. While nationalizing, he did not propose to pay compensation immediately. The acquisition of lands were to be through the issue of bonds and not by cash. He also advocatd evolving a public distribution system of rice and other essential commodities and elimination of the role of middlemen in business. His proposals won him more enemies than friends and he was portrayed as an enemy of the prevailing political system. His political career was really doomed when in 1946, King Anand Mahidol was assassinated in mysterious circumstances. Pridi was somehow implicated in the case. The situation became so bad for Pridi that he had to leave the country and stay in exile for years in France.

Thus, the most important civilian leader of 1932 coup was eliminated. Other civilian leaders did not have the required charisma and the military eventually entrenched itself in Thai politics.

There has been a succession of military rulers in Thailand in the past 60 years. General Phraya Pahol ruled Thailand from 1933 to 1938, Field Marshal Phibun Songgram from 1938 to 1944 and then from 1947 to 1957, Field Marshal Sarit Thanarat from 1957 to 1963, Field Marshal Thanom Kikkikachorn from 1963 to 1973, Admiral Sangad Cholorya from 1976 to 1977, General Kriengsak Chomanan from 1977 to 1980, General Prem Tilsulanand from 1980 to 1988 and General Chatchai Choonhavan from 1988 to 1991. The last two military leaders came into power through democratic elections but the prime minister, General Sunthorn Kongsompong came into power after a coup d'etate in February, 1991.

Here it will be appropriate to mention the role of Phibun Songgram in earmarking the strategies aimed at establishing the fact that military leaders are indispensable for bringing stability and progress to Thailand, Phibun Songgram dominated Thai Politics from 1932 to 1957 and was able to lay solid foundations for the primacy of military in Thai political system. Besides Pridi, he was supporter of democracy for his country but when he became the Prime Minister, he supported only a semblance of it. There was a unicameral legislature and provisions for elected representatives throughout his tenure, but all the powers of the government were concentrated in the hands of the centre. Concerning foreign policy, he was flexible. Till the end of the Second World War, Phibun was a close ally of Japan, but when he came back to power in 1947, he supported the policy of alignment with the United States. The friendship with Japan was used to recover territories lost to France in 1907 and to Britain in 1909. This pleased his people immensely and he received their backing.

Phibun also campaigned for "Asia for the Asians" and actually declared war against Western colonial powers. He backed up independence movements in the region and provided bases to Indian National Army of Subhas Chandra Bose among others. But after 1947 his priorities changed. He perceived a threat from China and the emerging communist movement in Vietnam. Thus, he joined the crusade against communism and became an ally of the United States in this regard. At the domestic level, Phibun tried to introduce socio-economic reforms to reduce the hold of the overseas Chinese on the Thai economic system. He tried to evolve such ventures as textile, paper, sugar, tobacco and distillery industries under the state, which was being run by military men and this strengthened their economic power. He astutely encouraged the military to take interests in business and trade. He extended all the necessary facilities and built canals and roads and means of communication. This way he was able to secure popular support for the military leadership.

The successors of Phibun tried to strengthen their support base and were eventually able to establish their presence in the socio-economic structure. As a result the military has emerged as the major agent of social change and political engineering in contemporary Thailand. They are key leaders of major political parties and cannot be marginalized even in democratic experiments.

An assessment of Thai politics suggest that no government can be stable in Thailand without the backing and participation of military elites. A soldier in Thai armed forces thinks that it is his bounden duty not only to defend the country, but also to provide leadership. They are greatly respected by the common people. Talented people in Thailand are attracted to defence services because they are lucrative and prestigeous. However, there has been some decline in the role of military in the country's polity ever since the rise of Chuan Leekpai to power.

Democratic Experiments

There have been intermittent attempts at establishing civilian government and nurturing democratic institutions in Thailand ever since 1932. Popular civilian leaders like Pridi Panomyong (1930s), Seni Pramoj (1940s), Sanya Thammasak and Kukrit Pramoj (1970s) tried to eliminate military elements and establish civilian democracy but could not succeed. They were either removed through military coup d'etat or on the alleged ground that they were unable to protect the honour of the King, the nation or religion, the three emotive issues. In October 1973 a student led revolution ousted the military dictatorship and established civilian rule. Dr. Sanya Thammasak, the new prime minister was immensely popular. Under his stewardship, a new constituion was adopted and elections were held. But the coalition government, which emerged thereafter was not stable and thus the coup of October 1976 took place. The military once again emerged as the most powerful force. A new constitution was adopted in December 1978 but it became null and void in February 1991 after a coup d'etat. However, there have been some landmark developments in Thailand during 1991-92 which have weakened the hold of military in power politics of the country and brightened the prospects for democracy. In order to have a proper understanding of the prospects for democracy, a brief appraisal of the current developments will be in order.

There was a coup d'etat led by General Sunthorn and General Suchinda Kraprayoon on 23 February 1991 to oust the popularly elected government of General Chatichai Choonhavan. This ushered in an era of military dicatorship in Thailand. The military sought legitimacy for the coup by stating that the Chatichai government was corrupt and that they were willing to restore democracy and a clean government to Thailand. They installed a civilian leader, Anand Panyarchun as interim prime minister and promised to hold elections as early as possible.

However, as is well known General Chatichai was ousted because of his strained relationship with the top leadership in the armed forces. Chatichai tried to induct the former army chief General Arthit Kamlang Ek in the defence ministry for neutralising the military's influence in politics. The military moved in on the eve of the swearing in of General Arthit and thus there was a bloodless coup. Now the military tried to neutralize the influence of Chatichai and his colleagues. It instituted Assets Verification Committee (AVC) to prove corruption charges against Chatichai and his former cabinet colleagues. The AVC started investigations in right earnest and some of the ministers in Chatichai cabinet were declared "unusually rich". But by the end of 1991 strange developments took place whereby Chatichai and his Thai Party was included into the pro-military coalition. When the election were held on 22 March 1992, the pro-military coalition got a majority. In this election most of the so-called corrupt colleagues of Chatichai became victorious on a pro-military platform. General Suchinda Kraprayoon who emerged the unelected Prime Minister, selected 11 such ministers whom the AVC had declared corrupt. This development was disliked by the people. This also exposed the fact that corruption which was a basic charge against General Chatichai was concotted. Thus, the popular legitimacy that the military had gained from the 1991 coup was diluted. This created a feeling of revulsion against the government and caused civil unrest.

Another reason for the unrest was the selection of the unelected prime minister. *Samakhi Tham Party* which was the largest partner of the pro-military coalition was led by Narong Wongwan. He became controversial immediately after his name was proposed for the post of prime minister. The pro-democracy parties argued that he was corrupt. On 25 March 1992, the *New Aspiration Party, Palang Dharma Ekkaparb* and *Democrats* addressed a joint press conference and called into question the credibility of Narong in the light of the US State Department allegation that he had been denied a visa to the US in mid-1991, because of his suspected ties with drug trafficking. The following day the US State Department spokeswoman Ms Margaret Tutwiler confirmed that it had in July 1991 denied a visa to Narong because of suspicions over his role in heroin trading. The impact of such a revelation was disatrous. The military thus withdrew their support in favour of Narong. The Next powerful contender was Air Chief Marshal Samboon Rahong of *Chat Thai*. He too did not have a clean image and was accused of dubious duty-free business deals. He was afraid about the public outcry and refused to be considered for the post. Under the circumstances, the candidature of General Suchinda who had not fought the elections on the plea that he was not willing to be the Prime Minister, was proposed. The pro-military coalition accepted his leadership and the King approved the appointment. Suchinda while accepting the post of prime minister said, "I pledge that I will be loyal to the King and provide protection to your majesty and the royal family with my life, and will carry out my responsibilities with honesty for the national and public interest without any regard for the special interests of individuals or certain groups."

But subsequent events were traumatic for Suchinda. He became the target of demonstrations as soon as he stepped into power. On 20 April 1992, thousands of protestors staged demonstrations opposite Parliament House and the Supreme Commander headquarters. The number of demonstrators started growing and the protest picked up momentum. When parliament was convened on 23 April, the opposition members of parliament wore black to mourn the demise of democracy. Outside a *Palang Dharma* Party leader sat on hunger strike, who was subsequently joined by 40 others. Chamlong Srimuang led the protestors with enthusiasm and spirits. By the end of April the situation began to deteriorate. In the beginning of May 1992, thousands of demonstrators sat down in central Bangkok surrounded by riot police. On 9 May, more than 150,000 people poured into the streets with a demand to force Suchinda to quit. They filled a park and spilled over into surrounding streets. Thus, the anti-Suchinda protest climaxed. The display of enthusiasm and spirits were similar to that witnessed in October 1973, when the Thanom Prapas clique was forced to quit making way for democratic experiments. The protestors demanded the resignation of the unelected premier and suitable amendments in the constitution so that there was no recurrence of the unelected prime minister in Thailand. They were unwilling to disperse unless their demands were accepted. Though efforts were made to assure to pro-democracy leaders about suitable amendments in the constitution, but it was not successful. The protestors continued to demonstrate and the military rulers lost their patience. They decided to tackle the demonstrators by force. The army crackdown started on 17 May 1992 and an emergency was declared the following day. About 50 people died as a result of the crackdown and hundreds were injured. The leader of the protest movements, Major General Chamlong Srimuang was handcuffed and arrested and thus the streets were cleared.

The backlash of the police action was devastating. Premier Suchinda and his supreme army commander, Issarapong Noonpakdi were held responsible for the bloodshed. This was not liked even by other leaders of the pro-military coalition. The opposition to Suchinda was being felt by his supporters. Thus, there was a rumour of another coup in the offing. At this juncture the King Bhumibol Aduldej intervened to solve the constitutional crisis. He advised General Suchinda to resign in view of the mounting pressure from the public and factions in the military. Thus Suchinda resigned on 24 May 1992. He was succeeded by the interim Prime Minister, Anand Panyarchun. This time Anand was entrusted the task of introducing necessary reforms in the constitution for making the system more democratic and ready for another election.

Anand's ascendance as a premier provided a healing touch to the people who suffered loss of lives and casualties in the May bloodshed. It neutralised the antipathy that Suchinda had masterminded. Anand's government tried to convince people that it would do justice to them and also try to punish culprits of the May bloodshed. The House of Representatives Committee was established to pin responsibility for the May bloodshed. Suchinda supported the constitutional amendments for more democracy. The parliament approved four important amendments to the constitution and on 10 June 1992 they were incorporated. They had great implications for the Thai political system. The amendments were as follows:

(*a*) The prime minister must be an elected member of parliament
(*b*) The power of the senate be limited to scrutinizing and passing laws
(*c*) Open debates be allowed in the second annual parliamentary session and
(*d*) The House Speaker be made president of the parliament.

After these amendments, general elections were held for the second time in Thailand on 13 September 1992. There were two important coalitions vying for power. The pro-democracy coalition was projected as "Angles" and the pro-military one as "devils" by the media. The pro-democracy parties became victorious and under the leadership of Chuan Leekpai a new government was established. The pro-military parties are demoralised at the moment while the new government has shown interest in strengthening democratic structures.

Thailand practiced democratic governance for a decade thereafter. When Prime Minister Thaksin Shinawatra became victorious for the second term in 2005, there were certain developments in the country which offended the military and the political elites. He sold out his Shin Corporation to a Singapore firm at the cost US 2 billion dollars and did not pay income tax to the government. Hence, he was criticized as corrupt. He was also charged of indulging in les majeste and cronysm. The military staged a coup to oust him in 2006. Thaksin was forced to seek asylum outside the country. The military leaders abrogated the constitution and now a new constitution has been made. The efforts are made to malign the leadership of Thaksin, but he remains popular amongst the rural people in the countryside.

Religion and Politics

Religion is one of the most important and emotive issues in Thai society. The state religion of Thailand is Buddhism. The interactions between political elites and the Buddhist Sangha over the years have been influencing the political system of Thailand deeply. The different social and ethnic groups vie amongst each other to attract the support of the Sangha without which they cannot claim proper legitimacy. There is a wide spectrum of religio-political phenomenon, i.e., the interaction of Buddhism and modern political ideologies, the use of religion in the politics of democracy or dictatorship, the efforts of some ambitious politicians in promoting religious revival and the use of Buddhism in fighting against communism and separatism in Thailand. All these underscore the importance of religion in government and polity.

It is a historical reality that in order to promote the causes of Thai nationalism, King Ramakhamheng in the 13th century, King Mongkut in the 19th century and his successors in the 20th century, considered Buddhism an important vehicle of this goal. Rama VIth had introduced Buddhist prayers in various public institutions, government schools, police forces and the army on the eve of the First World War. The prime minister, Field Marshal Phibun Songgram, provided special significance to religious aspects during the Second World War era with a view to promote the cause of nationalism.

The operation and role of the Buddhist Sangha, however, is different from its Islamic counterparts. It believes in discourses, persuasion and in arousing moral virtues. It has tried to reconcile differences amongst different social and ethnic groups and has paved the path for national integration and assimilation.

Economic Policy

Thailand has been pursuing a liberal economic policy and has been a champion of free enterprise in the region. Though Field Marshal Phibun Songgram had brought some industries under the public sector, not much should be read into it as these endeavours were purely expedient. His successors always gave priorities for the development of the private sector, but it was under the stewardship of prime minister Prem Tilsuanand (1980-1988) that the private sector was really given incentives and required facilities. This boosted the production of agricultural and industrial outputs and presently, the GNP per capita is $1,418.

General Prem found innovative avenues to earn foreign exchange for the country and thus, modern technologies were acquired for promoting fishing, gems, textiles and tourist industries. These efforts were successful and indeed the rise of these sectors has been largely responsible for the phenomenal rise of Thailand's economy in the past few years, if the present rate of growth continues. Thailand will be at par with the NIEs, i.e., Singapore, South Korea, Taiwan and Hong Kong.

It is relevant to point out here that Thailand was an ally of the United States. From the signing of the economic assistance agreement to the end of Vietnam war in 1975, American influence on Thailand's economic management continued. A large number of American advisors were posted in Thailand. A great bulk of American loans, grants and direct investments flowed into Thailand to finance infrastructures with strategic implications. The US poured enormous economic and military assistance to Thailand for its role in containment of communism in the region. From 1963 to 1978, Baht (Thai currency) was tied to the US dollar.

However, the strategic importance of Thailand for the United States was reduced with the end of the Vietnam war in 1975. Thailand was facing a grim economic situation as well as unstable regimes from 1973 to 1978. When the political order got restored, the rulers tried to improve economic management. It was felt that the spread of communism could be contained only with acceleration of economic growth. They, thus, began to review the functioning of various instruments of economic policy. Thus, the apex body of economic planning, National Economic Development Board (NEDB) began inviting fresh ideas to accelerate development. NEDB founded initially in 1959 endeavoured to coordinate and stimulate development, took charge of economic reforms and formulated "five year plans" accordingly.

The NEDB came out with fresh ideas during the presentation of the Sixth Five Year Plan (1986-1991). Before 1986 the NEDB accorded priorities to rural development and communication schemes. It took measures for raising the productivity and income of the farmers. Thus, the emphasis was on construction of roads, dams, irrigation canals, health schemes etc. But during the sixth plan period, it gave urgent priorities to develop private sectors. The private sector was projected as the prime engine for pulling the growth locomotive. As a result, the role of public sectors was transformed from one of regulating and controlling to supporting and promoting private business. The NEDB evolved liberal policies to attract foreign enterprises and promised incentives to them to invest in Thailand. Subsequently foreign owned enterprises were exempted from restrictions on repatriating profits and capital, and on foreign ownership of land, import duties and taxes on equipment.

The Thai government gave guarantees against nationalisation or competition from state enterprises. As a result about 1,037 companies started operations during 1987-1990. The largest foreign investors were Japan (27.4 per cent), followed by Taiwan (11.2 per cent) and the United States (10.9 per cent). The promotional programmes are giving emphasis on industries for export priorities, i.e., biotechnology, computer software, solar cells and microwave insulators.

The qualitative changes in the policies of the government towards private sectors have activated the Joint Public-Private Consultative Committee (JPPCC) which had been established in 1981 for the sole purpose of conducting dialogue between government and business representatives. JPPCC is playing the role of a think tank to promote business interests and to effectively lobby for private business ever since 1986.

JPPCC is also credited with influencing the decision makers in giving due importance to export-oriented economic strategy. The business representatives in the national JPPCC point out obstacles in production and marketization of several goods. Tourism and gem exports, two well known items of earning foeign exchange in recent years, were promoted due to the tireless efforts of the JPPCC. In the past both the government and the public viewed tourism and gems as luxuries for a handful of rich people but now that image is changed. These sectors were heavily taxed in the past, but now they understand the export value of such items. The government reduced utility rates, cut down sales tax for hotels and gave facilities for the import of precious gems resulting in tariff, customs and tax concessions. This helped the gem merchants of Thailand to be the leading gem exporters in Southeast Asia. On the other hand, there was better management of hotels and transportation system. This attracted the foreign tourists to Thailand and currently, the average arrival of tourists are around 2.4 million every year. Tourism has thus become the largest source of foreign exchange.

The performance of other export-oriented industries notably textiles and garments, processed food, jewellery and light manufacturers are remarkable. Since 1986, fish exports increased in volume by 35 per cent. Again tinned and frozen sea food represented 8.3 per cent of export earnings. The textiles contributed 13.5 per cent of export earnings, thereby superseding rice as the largest item for the same. The manufacturing sectors as a whole increased its share of GDP from 6.8 per cent in 1960 to 23.0 per cent in 1986 and subsequently showed buoyant trends.

Thailand is the second largest rice exporter of the world after the United States. It produces about 20.6 million tonnes of rice every year. It also produces about 5 million tonnes of Maize, 19.3 million tonnes of cassava roots and 2.3 million tonnes of fish. It has timber, sugar, rubber, teak and other potentials.

It is producing cement on a commercial level (7.9 million tonnes), half of which is purchased by Malaysia. It is also producing automobile assembly, integrated circuits and such other items for exports.

Thai Foreign Policy

The makers of Thai foreign policy have generally been flexible in their approach to various issues always taking care to meet the everchanging demands of international diplomacy. From its birth in the 13th century to the end of the opium war in the 19th century, it cultivated friendship of the Han emperors of China. In return China helped Thai rulers to consolidate their powers and grab a vast area of Southeast Asia under their control. When Britain's power increased substantially in 19th century Southeast Asia, Thailand shifted over its emphasis and gave priority to cultivating relations with Britain. It provided trade facilities and extra-territorial rights to Britain and thereby, placed British subjects beyond the purview of Thai courts. In return Britain respected the sovereignty of Thailand deterring France from creating troubles for Thailand. During the Second World War Thailand sided with Japan and in return Japan helped Thailand to regain the territories lost during the colonial period. But after the War, the US emerged as the most influential country in the region and Thailand true to its tradition moved fast to forge closer relations with the Americans. Thailand agreed to co-operate with US in pursuing the policy of containment of communism and adopted an anti-China, anti-Vietnam stand. Thailand joined the military pact of SEATO in 1954 and agreed to offer its bases as a springboard for anti-Communist operations.

Thailand was infact the headquarter of SEATO and a major base for the American forces during the Vietnam war. In return, the US gave enormous economic and military aids. It helped in the construction of roads, dams and bridges. It also strengthened the security postures of Thailand vis-a-vis its neighbours.

With the end of the Vietnam war in 1975, the strategic environment of Southeast Asia changed. China was eager to strengthen its relations with ASEAN countries. Thailand took the initiative to forge closer relations with China. Prime Minister Kukrit Pramoj paid a visit to China in 1975 to break the ice and the endeavour was fruitful. Thailand received oil from China on friendly terms. China paid a higher price for Thai rice in order to strengthen the latter's economy. Thus, Sino-Thai relations improved rapidly and were consolidated after Vietnam's military intervention in Cambodia in December 1978. Thailand became a conduit for the supply of Chinese arms to Cambodian rebels. Thailand provided sanctuaries to Khmer Rouge which was backed by China. It also provided shelter to KPNLF and Funcinpec guerrilla forces. The Cambodian rebels raised their guerrilla forces in Thailand and were supplied arms and ammunitions from China, the US and other sources via Thailand. China was very happy with Thailand for cooperating in the endeavour to isolate Vietnam.

Thailand, thus, was projected as a frontline state to deter Vietnamese expansion in the region. However, with the signing of the Cambodian Peace Accord in Paris in October 1991 and the dismantlement of the communist bloc, the situation has drastically changed.

Thai rulers are presently evolving a policy to convert Indochina from a battleground to a market place. Thailand is planning big investments in other Indochinese countries. It is eager to take their keep in the Mekong River Development Project and on the other hand, it is trying to revive rail links from Bangkok to Ho Chi Minh city via Phnom Penh.

Thailand is a leading campaigner for regional cooperation in the region. It took active interest in the formation of ASEAN, which comprised Brunei, Indonesia, Malaysia, Philippines, Singapore and Thailand. ASEAN cooperation embraces varied fields, i.e., industry and commerce, tourism, finance, food production and supply, fisheries, shipping, communications, air traffic services, meteorology, transportation, telecommunication, science and technologies etc. The ASEAN is also cooperating in strategic and political matters and has presently seven "dialogue partners", i.e., Japan, the US, Canada, Australia, New Zealand, South Korea and EU.

Thailand has successfully mediated in resolving some of the intricate disputes in Southeast Asia. In 1966 Thailand was the venue for talks between the foreign ministers of Malaysia and Indonesia for termination of the "Crush Malaysia Plan". Thailand also arranged a meeting amongst Malaysia and the Philippines to end the conflict over Sabah. Again Thailand, through ASEAN, deterred Vietnamese penetration in Cambodia.

Thailand today is one of the few countries to maintain good relations with military regime in Burma. It does not encourage Burmese refugees to come towards Thailand. Thai businessmen have taken contracts to cut teak woods in the Shan and Karen areas and there is a close commercial relationship between the two regimes.

Finally, it can be said that the Thai foreign policy has proved successful in achieving its goals. To summarise the developments of the past four decades, it can be said that strategic considerations guided its policies in the past but now side by side business interests are getting priorities. Thai government enlists the cooperation of businessmen at all levels of decision-making, particularly in the realm of foreign policy and thus its business interests are promoted.

To summarize, it can be stated that the Thai political system has four important pillars, i.e., the nation, its religion, the King and the army. Any arrangement for a new political order cannot be successful without attaching due importance to them. For survival of a leader, it is essential that he establishes a balance amongst these pillars.

In the realm of external relations, dynamism and flexibility have been the hallmark. Thais say that "like a bamboo, we bend with the wind". This aptly explains their behaviour and attitudes while determining foreign policy and dipolmacy.

REFERENCES

Chakrabongse, Prince Chula, *Lords of Life, the Paternal Monarchy of Bangkok, 1782-1932*, London, Alvin Redman, 1960.

Elliott, David, *Thailand; Origins of Military Rule*, Zed Press, 1978.
Girling, J.L.S., *Thailand: Society and Politics*, Ithaca, N.Y., Cornell University Press, 1981.
Jha, Ganganath, *Foreign Policy of Thailand*, New Delhi, Radiant Publishers, 1979.
Morrell, D. and Samudavanija, C., *Political Conflict in Thailand*, Cambridge, Mass., 1981.
Neher, C.D., *Modern Thai Politics: From Village to Nation*, Cambridge, Mass., Schenkman, 1979.
Wyatt, D.K., *Thailand: A Short History*, New Haven, Conn., Yale University Press, 1984.
Xuto, Somsakdi, ed., *Government and Politics of Thailand*, Hong Kong, Oxford University Press, 1987.

3

Ethnic and Territorial Issues between Laos and Thailand

Thailand and Laos are centrally located in the Southeast Asian region. They were part and parcel of Subarnabhumi where Sona and Uttara had gone to spread the gospel of Buddhism in the third century B.C. Thailand is bigger in size compared to Laos, a landlocked state. Presently both the states are members of the Association of Southeast Asian Nations (ASEAN) and considered by each other as friendly. After the construction of the Lao-Thai Friendship Bridge over Mekong River, links have been established between Vientiane and Thailand directly. Both Laos and Thailand have had ethnic and territorial issues to address in their bilateral relations but in order to have a proper perspective of that issue, a brief introduction to the geopolitical setting of the two countries are in order.

Laos has a landed territory of 236,800 kilometers. It shares contiguous border with five countries, namely China, Vietnam, Cambodia, Thailand and Myanmar. Its population is 4.5 million, which is mainly divided into three ethnic groups, namely Lao-Lum, Lao-Theung and Lao-Xoung.[1] Lao-Lum, being the largest of the three, inhabits the plains along the rivers. Lao-Theung inhabits the marginal zones of the forests and mountain ranges and Lao-Xoung lives mostly in the hills.[2] There are 60 per cent ethnic Lao, 35 per cent tribal groups (Hmong, Meo, Yao, Nung, and Shans) and 5 per cent ethnic Chinese, Vietnamese and Indians.

On the other hand, Thailand occupies 513,115 sq.km of the territory and a long coastline of 960 km facing the Gulf of Siam and another facing the Andaman sea. Between the two, the peninsula narrows at the Isthmus of Kra to a straitline distance of only 56 km.

Thailand has a contiguous border with four countries, namely Malaysia, Cambodia, Laos and Myanmar. The total population of the country is 58 million of which 94 per cent are Buddhists, 4 per cent Muslims and two per cent Hindus, Christian and hill people, namely Meo, Lahu, Yao, Lisu, Lawa, Lolo and Karens.[3] Though there are a significant number of ethnic Chinese also, they have been integrated in Thai social life through intermarriage and customs. Again there are some ethnic Vietnamese too, who have lived in the Northeast for the past six decades.

Strategically, Thailand has great regional importance. It was on account of its location that Japan occupied it first before invading other countries of Southeast Asia during the Second World War. K.M. Panikkar has noted that because of their participation in the war, the fall of Singapore became inevitable and the Japanese occupation of Burma possible. Without Thailand as a solid rear, Japan would not have been able to advance its troops through the Malayan peninsula.[4]

The US attached due importance to it in the containment drive and war against communism. In February 1950, Phillip C. Jessup, US Ambassador-at-large came to Bangkok for a three-day conference with US Ambassadors accredited to the region. They discussed the strategies to contain communism and in that endeavour the strategic significance of Thailand was stressed.[5]

The US later established Southeast Asia Treaty Organization (SEATO) and based its headquarters in Thailand which proved the kingpin and springboard for US military operations in Indochina States. Thai air bases at Udon Thani, Nakhon Phanom, Ubon, Nakhon Ratchasima. Takhli, U-Tapao and a naval base at Sattahip had been established and used by the US for decades at the time of Vietnam War.

When Vietnam militarily intervened in Cambodia in December 1978 and regional efforts were made to isolate and "bleed Vietnam white". Thailand once again played a key role. Thai support to Cambodian rebels proved strategic and Vietnam could not sustain its activities for too long. The guerilla warfare was too costly. Vietnam ultimately reviewed its Cambodian policies in view of the regional pressures and decided to withdraw lock, stock and barrel.

On the other hand, Laos too is strategically significant, particularly in the context of security threat to Southeast Asia emanating through China. The US understood this point long ago and tried to enlist its cooperation in the containment drive. It had extended SEATO's protective umbrella to Laos and unsuccessfully tried to win it as an anti-communist bastion. They presumed that if Cuba could prosper as a communist state in spite of its location in the midst of powerful anti-communist regimes, there was no reason why Laos could not survive in the midst of powerful communist states.[6]

The US was supporting its activities in Laos clandestinely during 1964-1975. The Central Intelligence Agency (CIA) had its regional headquarters in Laos. The US had also organised the groups of Meo and Thai Dan tribesmen for military training and thereby established the battalions of "Meo Irregulars" and "Thai irregulars", to be engaged in counter-insurgency operations and offensives against Pathet Lao in Laos and National Liberation front in Vietnam. Meo and Thai irrigulars ultimately proved to be the main nucleus of the American operations in Indochina States. Prince Souphanouvong, the leader of the Pathet Lao movement, understood this and he expressed it in the following words, "Meo and Thai irregulars were the main force units in Laos. Till 1968, their function was to back up the hill tribe forces, but by 1972, they were serving in lieu of Laotian nationals against Pathet Lao forces. Their leader was Vang Pao, who had about 30,000 forces at his command".[7]

The regional headquarters of CIA at Long Cheng also known as "Alternative" or "Happy Valley", was a major centre for anti–communist operations in Laos and other Indochinese countries. Long Cheng had also one air strip to facilitate landing and take off of the helicopters, transport planes and T-28 fighters.[8]

As Laos was dragged into the Vietnam war by the United States, the majority of the Laotians felt unhappy and hostile against America. But Thailand was an alliance partner of the US and fully cooperated with the American War efforts. Thus there was a vast difference in the perception of Laos and Thailand vis-a-vis the containment drive. In short, Laos and Thailand continued to remain adversaries in the days of the cold war. Both were on the opposite sides indulging in unfriendly acts against one another.

However, the security environment of the region changed after the dissolution of the Soviet Union in 1991. The US announced its decisions to withdraw from Southeast Asia and vacate Subic Bay naval base. The inevitability of a power vacuum became a matter of great security concern. The assertion of Chinese claims of sovereignty over South China sea has also disturbed the regional power centres.

In the meanwhile, the ASEAN felt concern about Chinese naval manoeuvres which has endeavoured to expand its territories and sphere of influence in the Pacific and Indian ocean around Southeast Asia. It has forcefully advocated its sovereignty claims over the Spratlys and proclaimed its law of the sea unilaterally. It has built naval bases at the Paracels in the South China sea and Coco and Haingii in the Indian ocean. Its aim is to bring entire Malacca Straits under its sphere of influence. The ASEAN states do believes that the Chinese manoeuvres in the region would surely prove detrimental in their long-term interests.

Hence the strategic importance of Laos in that context cannot be overlooked. The ASEAN partners, including Thailand, are aware that partnership with Laos is necessary to project Southeast Asia's collective voice and regional consensus. In this context, it is necessary to understand Laotian problems and this is an exercise in that direction. Needless to say that Thailand and Laos have had ethnic and territorial issues in their bilateral relations which have been influencing the conduct of their foreign policies from time immemorial. They have assumed fundamental importance now and this paper is aimed at analysing them.

Ethnic Issue

The ethnic Thais and Laotians are related to each other by the same decend, culture and religion. Both had originally migrated from the same area of Yunnan Plateau of China. They migrated towards Menam Chaopraya and Mekong River basins and settled down there. In the beginning, it was difficult to disinguish them from one another. The ethnic Thais and Laotians were cooperating with each other in their war with neighbours and had evolved close and equal partnership based on marriage, beliefs and common interests.[9]

However when the Kingdom of Lan Xang was estabished in 1353 and King Fa Ngum began to expand his kingdom, clash of interests were unavoidable. Both Laos and Thailand then were expanding their territories by annexing or conquering areas of the Khmers. They demarcated their domains from one another and evolved separate identity for themselves.

The Laotians while evolving a separate identity, gave new meaning and content to "blood-brother-friendship" relations with the Thais.[10] King Fa Ngum, being directly related to the king of Angkor (regarded as the incarnation of Lord Vishnu) through marriage and early socialization, wanted to establish a niche for himself in Laos in history. He preferred distancing themselves from ethnic Thais in order to strengthen the power-base of the Laotian society.[11] Having given birth to a separate nation, he wanted to evolve a distinct culture and his successors tried to emulate him. Laotians in the process somehow displayed the feeling of ethnocentricity in the context of their relations with the Thais, which ultimately proved the genesis of their tussles.

The ethnic Thais, after laying the foundation of Thai Kingdom in 1238, had attempted to evolve a superior culture. They had tried to emulate and assimilate the essence of Khmer culture in Thailand. During the reign of King Ramakhamheng the Great (1270-1317), Brahmin priests in thousands came from Cambodia to Sukhothai to provide a distinct outlook to Thai culture and religion King Ramakhamheng had also invited Buddhist priests from Sri Lanka to settle in his kingdom to enrich Thai culture and civilization.[12] In short, Thais had given utmost care to important religion and indigeneous beliefs to evolve a distinct culture.

The Khmer culture, however, was symbolised as a superior culture and king Fa Ngum and his successors considered themselves their true representatives because of their blood relations with the Angkor royalty. This factor subsequently shaped the socio-political outlook of ethnic Laotians for centuries.

The dominant factor for discord between ethnic Thais and Laotians however was on the issue of territorial claims. Thais and Laotians began to strengthen their power projections and in that endeavour they aligned themselves with two opposite poles in regional power politics. Thai Kingdom cultivated closer relations with the Han rulers in China and on the other hand Laos gave emphasis on their relations with the Angkor.

The power and glory of Angkor however could not be sustained for too long. There was a rapid downfall of that kingdom in the 15th century. Laos suffered setbacks with the downfall of the Angkor empire and Thailand emerged very strong. It was Thailand under King Boromoraja II that inflicted decisive defeat to Angkor in 1430 and thereafter Thailand began influencing court decisions in Laos too.[13] Every coronations in the following period was with consent and support of the respective monarchs in Thailand.

After 1700 A.D. Lan Xang disintegrated into three principalities which eventually became subject to intervention from the Thais and the Vietnamese. These two competitive forces pulled Laos in two opposite directions and subdued Laos to be a tributary of both. Thus Vientiane and Xieng Khouang had adversarial relations for some decades. Vietnam emerged as a strong and unified state after Gia Long ascended the throne and unified the country in 1802. Gia Long subsequently took active interests in Laotian affairs. Chao Anou, the ruler of Vientiane was thus projected as an ally and supported to eliminate Thai domination over Laos.

Chao Anou was nationalistic in his outlook. He wanted independence for his country and was ready to take assistance from the Vietnamese in that endeavour. He waged war against Thailand in 1826 and was defeated. He then fled to Vietnam and with the help of the Vietnamese troops attacked Thailand once again. He was captured and humiliated. He was then taken to Bangkok where he died in captivity. Thailand thereafter established complete dominance over Vientiane and other Laotian principalities. This move antagonised Vietnam which sent its forces and captured Xieng Khouang in retaliation.[14] Vietnam controlled that area only for a very brief period as the French came and started challenging the sovereignty of Vietnam. However, that did not inhibit Vietnamese cultural influence in mountain principalities of Laos.

It is a historical fact that Laos remained subdued for long by Thailand. This facilitated and promoted ethnic and family connections between the Laotians and the Thais. This was because ethnic Lao and ethnic Thais were related to each other originally and both had migrated south from the Yunnan Plateau in China. They had subsequently formed two states and had maintained a close and equal relationship based on marriage alliances or common interests. Ethnic Burmans had posed security threats to both and they collaborated very often to face Burmese invasions.[15] The participation in wars against common enemies gave strength to their ethnic connections from time to time.

Laotian interaction with ethnic Viets, on the other hand, began in the fifteenth century, but it was not as close as with Thai counterparts. History says that Lan Xang included the areas of

Mekong Valley region of present day Laos as well as northeastern Thailand. Again Xieng Khouang (Sam Neua and Phong Saly), a highland principality was the nucleus of Sipsong Chau Thai, a federation of several highland principalities, which had originally been established by the Thai people inhabiting present day Laos to demonstrate their ethnic and cultural solidarity.

Thai-Laotian relations began to change after the arrival of the French Colonial forces in Vietnam in 1850s. The French began to establish their firm foothold and developed colonial interests in Laos and Cambodia. This was because they wanted natural frontiers for their colonial possessions. Hence they broke Thai monopoly over Laos and Cambodia subsequently.

After the war against Laotian forces led by Chao Anou in 1826, Thailand had integrated the areas of lowland principalities of Laos with their own territory. They had not done so vis-a-vis mountain principalities, which were by and large inhabited by the tribal groups.[16] The French had no difficulties in annexing the territories of mountain principalities of Xieng Khouang and Sipsong Chau Thai, but as far as lowland principalities were concerned, they were under Thailand. The French exercised their gunboat diplomacy to pressurize Thailand to cede the territories of Luang Prabang, Vientiane and Champassak. Thailand was forced to concede and accepted French demands and withdrew from Laotian territories in 1893. Hence Indochinese Union was established and France became the unquestioned ruler of Laos too. But they could not dilute the deep-rooted cultural influence of Thailand in Laos. The ethnic bonds continued to remain strong.

Laos and Thailand have linguistic similarities. As average Thai can understand Laotian language and dialects. Their folklore have similarities and their epic—Ramakien and Ramakirti—extolls the virtue of Rama. Both profess in Theravada Buddhism and their dress, diet, culture, customs, traditions and festivals have striking similarities. The festival of Sonkran or Loi Krathong are still popular in both countries and Lord Buddha is the most revered God.

Both Laos and Thailand consider religious institutions as major centres for their distinct identity. Thais consider nation, religion and the king as the three sacred institutions of their society and allow a lot of public service activities to be performed by the Buddhist Sangha. Some of the Buddhist Sangha is involved in public welfare activities. They provide shelter to old and disabled people and have been helping sick people suffering from HIVs. The Buddhist temples provides a forum for social congregation and opinion makers and emerging leaders cannot ignore the importance of Sangha.

Laos too had been attaching importance to Sangha traditionally but when communist Pathet Lao came into power in 1975, they abolished monarchy and restricted the role of Buddhist Sangha. The Laotians approved the end of monarchy because the Kings of Laos in the post-Second World War era played a dubious role. They did not allow freedom to popular political organisations and remained a silent spectator to American bombing over Laotian territories. But as far as the role of Sangha was concerned, the popular opinion was always to maintain it intact without any dilution. Though religion was regarded as the opium of the society by orthodox communists, the Communist Party of Laos realized the importance and role of the Sangha even in the changed context. They gradually rehabilitated Buddhist priests and allowed activities of the Buddhist Sangha subsequently. It was natural because important rituals at the time of birth, death or ceremonial occasions could be performed only by the Buddhist priests. Moreover they had not obstructed the spread of communist movement in the region.

Today Buddhist temples are once again vibrant in Laos. The Buddhist Bhikhus are to be found in large numbers and Sangha is performing their traditional role. Buddhist monasteries and temples are major tourist attractions and one can get a taste of traditional Laotian culture by visiting them. If the temple of Emerald Buddha is considered most sacred and revered in Bangkok, so is the temple of That Luang in Vientiane. Though the political system in Thailand and Laos are completely different, Buddhism continues to be the common link of friendship, and Laotians are aware that there is no substitute to the role of Sangha as far as their socio-cultural activities are concerned. Again if the virtues of Buddhism is treated as the guiding spirits, Laotians have to look towards Thailand.

However it is a matter of grave concern that ethnic connections are often used for negative purposes. During the Cold War Year, "Meo irregulars" had been organised with the help of the US and Thailand against Pathet Lao. After the American withdrawal groups of exiled and non-resident Laotians in Thailand have been organised to pressurize and challenge the fundamentals of Laotian government. Again Lao exiles have formed Free Democratic Lao

National Salvation Force, (FDLNSF) allegedly based in Thailand, which propagates violent means to transform political system in Laos. As Thailand has been claiming sovereignty rights on some Laotian territories adjoining Sayabouri Province and very often concentrated troops on disputed border areas, illegal activities of Lao rebels in that area have proved intermittent. When crowned Thai prince Maha Vajiralongkorn visited Vientiane for the first time in June 1992, Lao rebels led by FDLNSF, attacked three Laotian government posts, killing two people and causing significant damage.[17] Lao rebels, which accused their government of using chemical weapons to subdue them were encouraged that a senior military officer then stated that a Lao government unit was receiving training in chemical warfare from Cuban and Vietnamese experts. On the other hand, Laos refused to accept such allegations and urged Thai government to stop subversive activities of the rebels. Hence Thailand did arrest 11 Lao exiles accused of planning subversive activities in July and further arrests were made in October that year. These steps proved useful in promoting bilateral relations.

It is in order to state that there are thousands of Laotians in Thailand even now who came to Thailand as refugees in course of the protracted civil war in Laos. Their number was 90,000 in 1989. At a meeting held in Laos in June 1991 between the representatives of the United Nations High Commissioner for Refugees (UNHCR), Laos and Thailand, an accord was signed, whereby it had been decided that 60,000 Lao refugees in Thailand would be repatriated or resettled in third countries by the end of 1994.[18] Despite this accord, Laotian refugees could not be repatriated as envisaged. In July 1992, Thailand in order to accelerate the repatriation process, announced that any refugee remaining in Thailand beyond the end of 1994 would have their status altered to that of illegal immigrant and would be deported. Again in 1993 Thailand announced its plans to close several camps to encourage refugees to return to Laos. Despite these statements, a chunk of the refugees did not go back to Laos.

At present the activities of ethnic Hmong living in Thailand are regarded sensitive and unfriendly by the Laotian authorities. Advocating a rightist agenda and centred at Thamkrabok monastery of Sayabouri province, ethnic Hmongs are critical of Lao People's Revolutionary Party (LPRP). They distribute leaflets against Lao People's Democratic Republic (LPDR) and engage themselves in propaganda drives against Laotian leaders. Laotian governments have reasons to feel concerned and Thailand is aware of it. Thai Foreign Minister, Surin Pitsuwan has assured his Laotian counterpart, Somsavat Lengsavad that Thailand was serious in solving the Hmong problem in order to eliminate suspicion between the two countries. He conveyed that Thailand would, as the UNHCR try to screen the Hmongs in Thamkrabok monastery.[19]

Thus we find ethnic issues are still relevant to bedevil or upgrade relations of the two countries. The history shows that tribal ethnic groups fought against one another and they had been promoted to do so by influencial powers in the post-independence era. Though Thailand was never colonised, but it was not immune from being influenced by political developments in adjacent neighbouring countries. Again Thailand is regarded as a safe sanctuary for the Laotian rebels traditionally. Laotian leaders used to cross over to Thailand when they were fighting for their indepedence and the French colonial forces were trying to arrest them. Both Souphanouvong and Souvanna Phouma were in Thailand in the post-Second World War era to escape from French persecution.

Territorial Issue

Laos and Thailand have territorial claims against each other, and it is contentious to resolve them. Though Thailand was never colonised but Laos experienced French colonial rule for sixty years. The colonial masters treated Thailand as a buffer zone between French Indochina and British Burma and they were dictating their terms to Southeast Asians. The demarcation of the territorial boundaries had been negotiated amongst the colonial powers and this had been done as per their convenience and not on historical or linguistic basis. Laos was under Thailand when the French colonial masters took over and they made their territorial adjustments according to their geo-strategic considerations. When Laos became independent, it began to claim certain territories on the other side of the border. In order to understand the rationale of Laotian claims and counterclaims of Thailand, it is necessary to give a brief glance over the historical developments in Lao-Thai relations.

The dominant factor for discord between ethnic Thais and Laotians have been the issue of territorial claims. Thais and

Laotians began to strengthen their power projections and in that endeavour they aligned themselves with two opposite poles in regional power politics. Thai Kingdom cultivated closer relations with the Han rulers in China and on the other hand Laos gave emphasis on their relations with the Angkor.[20]

The power and glory of Angkor, however, could not be sustained for too long. There was a rapid downfall of that kingdom in the 15th century. Laos suffered setbacks with the downfall of the Angkor empire and Thailand emerged very strong. It was Thailand under King Boromoraja II that inflicted decisive defeat to Angkor in 1430 and thereafter Thailand began influencing court decisions in Laos too. Every coronation in the following period was with consent and support of the respective monarchs in Thailand.

After the downfall of the Angkor empire, Laos became weak and Thailand became assertive in regional politics. When Laotian King Souligna Vongsa died in 1694, Laos began to disintegrate. There was a dispute over the succession to the throne, which resulted in the partition of the kingdom into three parts. The first was Vientiane situated in the centre, and which went to a prince supported by the Kingdom of Hue. The second and third parts were Luang Prabang in the north and Champassak in the south respectively, supported by the King of Thailand. The palace intrigue and conspiracies increased thereafter amongst the Laotian rulers, which invited foreign intervention and subjugation in the following years. Finally Thailand asserted its dominance and turned Laos as one of its vassals.

Thai King Taksin took full advantage of the internal division of Laos in the 18th Century. He attacked Laos in 1778 because the latter had cooperated with the Burmese in attacking Ayuthia. Laos was defeated and was turned as a dependency of Thailand.

King Chao-Anou, who ascended the throne in 1805 tried to resurrect Laotian nationalism. He was an outstanding warrior with remarkable abilities. He had opened dialogues with Annamite rulers and tried to gain independence from Thailand. He was defeated by the Thais at war front in 1827. He was finally captured and kept in captivity in Thailand. He died in 1835 and hence it was the end of Laotian resistance for decades. However, his efforts to regain independence were exemplary and, therefore, he is still regarded as a symbol of Laotian nationalism, who had been humiliated and insulted by the Thais, who continued to dominate Laos till the arrival of French colonial masters in the region.

It is noteworthy to point out here that the Thais continued to believe Laotian territories as their own till the end of the Second World War. Thai premier Phibun Songgram had envisaged to integrate Laos in Thailand after the departure of the French Colonial masters in the post-1945 era. Thailand claimed Laotian territories on historical and archeological grounds.

In 1882, France urged Thailand to withdraw from the territories on left side of the Mekong, including Luang Prabang and sent its gunboats to pursue its claims. As Great Britain was not interested to protect Thai claims and Thailand was not strong enough to answer France militarily, it accepted French demands and withdrew from Trans-Mekong territories. Thus France got 50,000 square miles of the territory, besides Chentabun to ensure Thai compliance of the agreement.[21]

However, France was not satisfied with the newly gained territories and some more areas were demanded in adjoining areas. In 1907 Franco-Siam treaty was signed and as a result Thailand vacated Battambang, Siemreap and Sisophone. Thus France got natural frontiers for Indochina along with a chunk of territories as buffer zones.

It is understandable that the boundaries between Thailand and French Indochina had been dictated and demarcated by force and Thailand continued to have a grudge against it. Thai grievances were revealed on the eve of the Second World War, when Thailand joined on the side of the Axis Powers. One of the conditions of Thailand to join Axis Powers was to get back all those territories lost on the Laotian, Malayan and Cambodian frontiers.

Japan indeed helped Thailand to regain control over Battambang, Siemreap and Sisophone temporarily during 1942-45. It also obliged Thailand by recognizing Thai sovereignty over Lao territory west of the Mekong River, including Sayabouri. Thailand also got part of the Shan state (Keng Tung and Mong Pan) in Burma and Kedah, Perlis, Kelantan and Trengganu at the Malayan frontiers.[21] However, when the World War II was over, Thailand had to withdraw from those territories once again. Its boundaries were limited and reverted to the areas which was under its control before 1942.

Laos in the post-world war era, has been claiming its rights over certain territories in Thailand. It is not acceptable to Thailand which nurses counterclaims over Laos. History indicates that Champassak included the areas of Northeast Thailand in the seventeenth century and when Franco-Siamese Treaty (1907) was signed, France did not claim Northeast Thailand and therefore this area was left under Thailand. The areas contested by Laos in Thailand are Nongkhai, Loi, Udon Thani, Sakhon Nakhon, Nakhon Phanom, Khone, Kaen, Kalasin, Maharakham, Roi Et, Yosothon, Ubon, Chaiyafum, Nakhon Ratchasima, Buriram, Surin and Sisakhet.[22]

On the other hand, Thailand is claiming to exercise sovereignty over Tasseng Na Bo Noi of Sayabouri province. Thailand has been flexing its military muscles to bring the contested areas under its control. It believes that according to the map drawn after the Franco-Siam treaty (1907), the contested area was the part of Chattakarn district of Pitsanulok province. In mid-1980s, Thailand succeeded in taking control over three villages of Tasseng Na Bo Noi, namely Bane May, Bane Kong and Bane Savang.[23] Thailand thereafter removed the border marks and placed the territory under its control. Laos objected to Thai incursions and sent aide-Memoire. It raised the issue in the Security Council of the UN. It has advocated resolution of the territorial disputes through dialogue and peaceful means.

The history of claims and counterclaims between Laos and Thailand are too long. Thais do display the feeling of superiority vis-a-vis Laos and they have not yet forgotten that they ruled over that territory for too long. Again they stand for different interpretations of the Franco-Siamese Treaty (1907). In this respect the statement of former Thai Premier, Kukrit Pramoj is worthwhile to mention. He spoke on Bangkok Radio in December 1975 that "If we return to the agreement signed before 1946, both Sayabouri and Champassak will belong to Thailand. If we return to still previous agreements, then the whole of present day Laos will be in Thailand.[24]

Despite strains amongst ethnic Thai and Laotians, the interactions between the two have continued. The people have been crossing the common borders, spreading into 1,650 kilometers and family relations on the two sides are welcome. The ethnic Laotians do find similarities with Thai counterparts and this has facilitated trade and commercial relations between the two.

Thailand has over the years realized the importance of Laos for bilateral and regional cooperation and regional stability. The past one decade has witnessed phenomenal rise in Lao-Thai trade and investment relations. In 1988 Thai Prime Minister, Chatichai Choonhavan visited Laos with a constructive agenda on cooperation i.e., a bridge over the Mekong River to link Laos and

Thailand by roadways, opening up of trading points on their common borders, the production of hydro-electric power and tourism, etc. He was extremely successful in confidence-building and striking a rapport with Laotian leaders. While in Vientiane, he announced his determination to transform Indochina from a "battlefield" into a "market place".

Chatichai's visit was extremely successful and as a result Laos decided to cooperate more closely with Thailand. Thus a series of agreements have been signed between the two in the years following, which shows an attempt for revival of friendship that had existed in the past.

In 1988, both countries established Joint Border Demarcation Committee (JBDC) for sttlement of border disputes and withdrawal of troops from the disputed areas. Thai government also assured that it would suppress subversive activities of Lao exiles in Thailand and as a part of confidence-building measure, Thai police arrested 11 Lao exiles in Thailand in 1992, who were alleged to be planning subversive activities against LPDR. Again JBDC delineated the common frontier to the satisfaction of both sides in 1993 and the troops of the two sides were withdrawn.[25]

There has been growing collaboration between the two to promote economic ties. Thailand is an important partner in producing hydro-electricity and the two signed major agreements on this collaboration during the visit of Thai Prime Minister, Chuan Leekpai to Vientiane in 1993. Thus Xeset dam has been planned to be constructed. In this connection, it is important to know that the first phase of Nam Ngum dam (1971), generating 30,000 KW, provided a surplus of energy that was purchased by Thailand. Its second phase (1987) had a capacity to generate 150,000 KW, which exported 90 per cent of the output to Thailand. As and when the new dams start production, it has a ready market in the neighbouring countries.

Thailand is ranked topmost as a foreign investor in Laotian economy, which also acts as conduit for capital inflows from their parties. Thai currency (Baht) is acceptable in Laos and between 1988-93, about 112 Thai firms pledged US $150 million for various projects. In 1993 Thailand invested $20 million to collaborate in the brewery sector, in which it has got monopoly.[26]

Thailand has also collaborated in improving communication network on 1650 km Lao-Thai border and 13 border checkpoints have been opened. Thailand is supporting regional efforts to improve roads and bridges in Laos with the support of China and Vietnam, and this endeavour is backed by the Asian Development Bank (ADB). The proposal is to build a road linking Northeast Thailand, Laos and Vietnam with one another. Again the construction of another road is planned in the "golden triangle", at the confluence of Lao-Thai-Myanmar and China borders.

The road communication between Thailand and Laos has improved tremendously with the inauguration of Lao-Thai Friendship Bridge on 8th April 1994. This 1,170 metre long bridge built by the Australians at the cost of US $30 million, facilitates Lao-Thai commercial and cultural ties. This bridge directly links Vientiane to Nongkhai.[27]

Laotians are always aware of the fact that they are a landlocked state and that Thailand provides them access to the sea. Though Vietnam has also provided them access to their ports, but that is difficult, time consuming and costly. Thai ports are modern and road and rail connections to that area are smooth and quick. Friendship Bridge over Mekong connects the two and rail services are available. Besides Friendship Bridge, connecting Nong Khai and Vientiane, other bridges over Mekong are being constructed with a view to connect other towns of Laos with Thailand. Again Laotians do not feel language barriers in Thailand and they prefer to pass through Thailand than any other neighbouring country.

The government of Laos has been facilitating movement of vehicles to promote cultural interaction with the Thais. In 1998, it agreed to allow Thai-registered vehicles to enter Vientiane instead of parking at the foot of the Lao-Thai Friendship bridge. On the other hand, Laotian vehicles from Laos could enter Thailand's Udon Thani province. This agreement had been signed by Thai Foreign Minister Surin Pitsuwan and his Lao counterpart, Somsavant Lengsavad when the Thai Foreign Minister paid a three-day official visit to Vientiane in June 1998.[28]

Surin Pitsuwan had come to Laos with a long-term agenda for friendship whereby he proposed a new framework for Thai-Lao relations called "Interdependence Partnership" towards 2003 and aimed at greater bilateral prosperity.[29]

It is a reality that Laotian infrastructure is underdeveloped and many roads are waterlogged during the rainy season. The three main Laotian cities, namely Vientiane, Luang Prabang and

Savannakhet , become almost isolated and they have to evolve their own ways and means of communication during the rainy season. If there is.food stortage in Vientiane, it is quicker to import from Thailand than to take surplus rice by road from Savannakhet.

The developments in the region suggest that Laos is considered important for the ASEAN states. It was therefore that immediately after the end of the Cold War, it was offered observer status in the ASEAN. Laos thus enthusiastically signed the Treaty of Amity and Cooperation in 1992 and welcomed ASEAN investments in the Laotian economy. Further Laos introduced economic reforms in the name of (New Economic Mechanism) and enacted a new constitution in August 1991 which defined the powers of the legislature, executive and judiciary.[30] These developments were in tune with the demands of the ASEAN. Again Laotians enacted laws on private direct investment by stating that "the state protects and develops all forms of state, collective and individual ownership, including the private ownership of domestic and foreign enterpreneurs who have invested in Laos". It further stated that "the state encourages all economic sectors (Public and Private) to compete and cooperate with one another in expanding their production and business. All such sectors are equal before the law".[31] As a result, Laos discarded centrally planned economy and adopted the policy of market economy. Thus Laos has proved a good partner of the ASEAN. In short, Laos has been supporting regional ethos and consensus and proved a good partner in ASEAN.

Laos, on its part, is sincere to prove herself a worthy partner of the ASEAN and besides signing the Treaty of Amity and Cooperation, it has recently signed "Protocol on Dispute Settlement Mechanism". It has agreed to abide by the ASEAN mediation and is pursuing friendly relations with all its neighbours. It has allowed greater interaction with Thailand and reduced its dependence on Vietnam. If both sides cooperate in trade, investment and cultural areas, it would bridge the communication gap in ethnic and territorial matters as well.

REFERENCES

1. *Tenth Anniversary of the founding of Lao People's Democratic Republic : Land and its People*, Vientiane, Ministry of Foreign Affairs, 2 December 1985, p. 8.

2. Harvey Demaine, "Laos : Physical and Social Geography", *Far East and Australasia*, Hong Kong, 1995, p. 488, and Joseph J. Zasloff, *The Pathet Lao : Leadership and Organisation*, London, 1973, p.1.
3. D.K. Wyatt, *Thailand : A Short History*, New Haven; Conn, 1984, p. 1.
4. K.M. Panikkar, *The Future of Southeast Asia : An Indian View*, New York, 1946, pp. 66-67.
5. Donald E. Nuechterlein, *Thailand and the Struggle for Southeast Asia*, New York, 1967, p. 8 and Frank, C. Darling, *Thailand and the United States*, Washington, D.C., 1965, p. 69.
6. For a detailed analysis, see Martin E. Goldstein, *American Policy Towards Laos*, Rutherford, 1973, and Robert Shaplen, "Our involvement in Laos", *Foreign Affairs*, New York, April 1970, pp. 478-93 and Chester Bowles, *Mission to India: A Search for Alternatives in Asia*, Delhi, 1974, pp. 18-28.
7. Ganganath Jha, *Foreign Policy of Thailand*, New Delhi, 1977, pp. 106-13.
8. Frances Starner, "Laos : Watch Your Neighbour", *Far Eastern Economic Review*, Hong Kong, 18 June, 1973, pp. 31-32.
9. Usha Mahajani, "US intervention in Laos and its impact on Laotian relations with Thailand and Vietnam", in Mark W. Zacher and R. Stephen Milne (ed.), *Conflict and Stability in South Asia*, New York, 1974, p. 239.
10. When the Burmese empire of Pagan fell to the Mongols in 1253, three powerful rulers in the region, namely King Ramakhamheng of Sukhothai, King Mangrai of Chiengrai and Ngam Muang of Payao concluded a pact of friendship in 1287, which is known as "Blood-Brother-Friendship Treaty". This grouping was led by King Ramakhamheng the Great, and it enlisted the support of powerful ethnic leaders and tribal chiefs in the region. For details, see D.G.E. Hall, *A History of Southeast Asia*, London, 1968, p. 123.
11. For further analysis, see M. Stuart - Fox, *Laos : Politics, Economics and Society*, London, 1986, and Viravong Mahasila, *History of Laos*, New York, 1964.
12. For an understanding of this aspect, see, Chula Chakrabongse, *Lords of Life: The Paternal Monarchy of Bangkok, 1782-1932*, London, 1960.
13. D.G.E. Hall, n. 10, pp. 110-39.
14. Usha Mahajani, n. 9, pp. 238-59.
15. *Ibid.*, pp. 238-39.
16. *Ibid.*
17. *Demaine*, n. 2, p. 492.
18. *Ibid.*
19. *Nation*, Bangkok, 4 June 1998.
20. Usha Mahajani, n. 9, pp. 239-59.
21. For further analysis, see *The Truth About Lao - Thai Relations*, Vientiane,

Ministry of Foreign Affairs, September 1984, pp. 1-33.
22. *Bangkok Post*, 24 February 1974.
23. Lao People's Democratic Republic Memorandum on the Thai nibbling attacks against the Lao PDR Territory in the Area of Tasseng Na Bo Noi, Botene District, Sayabouri Province, Vientiane, Ministry of Foreign Affairs, 29 February 1988, pp. 1-28.
24. *The Truth About Lao - Thai Relations*, Vientiane, Ministry of Foreign Affairs, 1984, p. 30.
25. *Demaine*, n. 2, pp. 492-93.
26. Ralph Smith, "Laos : History", *Far East and Australasia*, 1995, p. 492.
27. *Bangkok Post*, 8 & 9 April 1994.
28. *Nation*, 4 June 1998.
29. *Ibid.*
30. New Economic Mechanism (NEM) of Laos is aimed at market-oriented reforms. It is planned towards decentralization of economic decision-making, more accountability for public enterprises, fiscal and financial reforms, deregulation of prices, removal of trade barriers, implementation of new investment laws and overall greater reliance on market forces. For further elaboration, see Caroline Hong : "Laos sets out to woo investors", *The Straits Times*, Singapore, 4 January 1997 and Jean-Claude Pomonte, "Winds of Change in Laos", *Le Monde*, 3-4 January 1995.
31. Investing in Laos, *PDRL Newsletter*, Vientiane, Ministry of Foreign Affairs 1997.

4

Dimensions in Thailand's China Policy, 1972-1979

The rapidity of political developments in China, Vietnam, Laos, Kampuchea and Korea surprised many well-known observers of the area. The Sino-US detente, the secret visit of Henry Kissinger to Beijing, the de-Maoization and adoption of modernization schemes in China, the US pull-out from Indochina, the split in the communist camp, the murder of President Park Chung-Hee in South Korea have all added to the tumult and turmoil in an already disturbed regional politics. The decision of oil cartels to increase the oil prices since 1973 have caused strains in the economic systems of most of these countries. The spill-over of the crisis in the regional politics has polluted their strategic environment to such an extent that they find their security threatened on all sides.

Thailand, strategically located in the middle of Southeast Asia mainland, falls in this category. It was a launching pad for US activities in Vietnam, Laos and Cambodia. Situated at the very door-step of the Indo-Chinese countries the fear has been often expressed that it may become the next domino. The political culture of Thai monarchy is antagonistic to the communist political culture.

In the last few decades the Thai information media always described communism as the enemy of the free world. To contain it Thailand entered into military agreements with the western bloc. Thailand had provided naval and air bases to the US to be used against communist insurgents in the region. The Thais were so hawkish in their attitude that when the US decided to withdraw its troops from Thailand in view of the Vietnamization programme, there were demonstrations against it in Bangkok.

In the October Revolution of 1973, the students expressed their disenchantment with Thailand's internal and external policies to such an extent that the military rule was replaced by a democratic one. The revolution was directed against the US presence in Thailand as well as the then constitutional set-up. The brief constitutional experiment during 1975-76 saw three prime ministers in all. The military leaders came back to power in October 1976. They reverted to the policy of strengthening ties with the US, but also with the neighbouring socialist bloc. But the events in Kampuchea since 1975 posed a dilemma to Thai policy makers. China and Vietnam were involved in toppling successive regimes in Kampuchea. The Pol Pot-Ieng Sary regime was supported by China and opposed by the Socialist Republic of Vietnam. The Heng Samrin group supported by Vietnam ousted the Pol Pot regime. It was vehemently opposed by China. Initially, Thailand was not willing to offend either of the warring communist neighbours. But due to geopolitical factors, Thailand could not keep aloof from the happenings in Indochina. Finally, it took a position which may be interpreted as being in favour of the Chinese stand in Kampuchea. This paper will, therefore, analyse the compulsions for Thai foreign policy to lean towards China and the developments in their bilateral relations since 1975, and evaluate the prospects.

I

The visit of Thai Premier Kukrit Pramoj to China in June 1975 was a landmark in Sino-Thai relations. Thailand snapped its relations with Formosa. The Formosan Embassy which was second in size only to that of the US in Bangkok was closed down. Though the communist regime had been established in mainland China in 1949 and it had been recognized by most countries, Thailand was one of the neighbouring countries which had not recognized it till 1975.

The Thai Prime Minister met Chairman Mao on the very day of his arrival in Beijing. Mao received him warmly and gave him some private advice regarding the CPT (Communist Party of Thailand) for which Kukrit was grateful. The *People's Daily* assured Thailand that China would not interfere in its internal affairs.[1] The joint communique published on 1 July 1975 endorsed the principle of non-interference by 'any country' in the internal affairs of another country. China recognized that the Chinese living in Thailand who opted for Thai citizenship would forfeit any claim to Chinese nationality.[2]

After assuring their friendship China is known to have requested Thailand to allow the US forces to stay in Thailand. It was pleaded that the presence of the US forces in Thailand would play a useful role in countering the growing Soviet threat to the peace and security of various countries in the region.

Since the establishment of communist rule in China, both these countries had involved themselves in polemics. China was the headquarters of subversive organizations such as the Thai Patriotic Front (TPF). On the other hand, Thailand as the headquarters of SEATO provided facilities to the US to carry out anti-Chinese activities. Their respective mass media accused each other of interfering in its internal affairs. Kukrit's visit brought the dawn of a new era in Sino-Thai relations. Kukrit expressed his heartfelt appreciation for the Chinese reception and pleasure at the end of their mutual estrangement for over a quarter century.[3]

The detente in Sino-Thai relations made a good impact on the deteriorating economy of Thailand. The immediate effect was felt in the stabilization of their main source of income, rice. In the wake of the fall of Indo-China into communist hands, the US had decided to release about 500,000 tons of rice (destined for its aid programmes in Cambodia and South Vietnam) to rice dealers in Singapore at $200 a ton. This caused a rapid fall in the price of rice in the Asian markets. Thailand which had 3000,000 tons of surplus rice in 1974 (much of which had remained unsold) expected to have 1.5 million tons of surplus rice in 1975. The arrival of the US rice into the Asian markets caused a fall in the prices from $625 to $350 a ton. This worried Thailand. China understood this problem and made a friendly gesture immediately by buying up 200,000 tons of Thai rice, even though it had a substantial surplus of rice. This gesture pleased the Thai Government to a great extent as it helped stabilize the Price of their rice.

The visit of Kukrit paved the way for greater cooperation in the economic sphere. Thailand which had exported nearly $113,000 worth of goods to China (mainly rice) and imported $4.5 million worth of Chinese goods (mostly crude and diesel oil) further increased their quantum.[4] China decided to buy Thai maize, beans, tapioca, jute bags and tobacco.[5] Thailand faced an acute shortage of oil and was assured that China would try to supply crude oil, diesel and bunker fuel. China even agreed to export a minimum of 600,000 tons of crude per year.

The visit of Kukrit Pramoj thus provided a solid foundation for the improvement of Sino-Thai relations. However, it could not check the growing soviet influence in that country. In spite of China's strong opposition to growing Soviet contacts in the region, Thailand expanded its trade with the Soviet Union. According to the Department of Business Economic figures, the value of imports from the Soviet Union was Baht 222.8 million (US $11 million) while that of exports was Baht 148.3 million. The leading Thai exports were rubber and fluoride. The major Soviet products imported were cotton, optical equipment, organic chemicals and paper products. Recently the two countries signed a private sector agreement for trade in economic, scientific and technological co-operation. The Soviet Union placed an order with Thai Hua for 50,000 tons of maize worth about Baht 176 million to be shipped to Vietnam. Thailand is also willing to expand its trade with the COMECON countries and to open its embassies in Romania, Hungary, and Czechoslovakia.[7]

II

Sino-Thai relations were also affected by the Kampuchean crisis which was aggravated after the victory of the Khmer Rouge forces over the Americans. The Pol Pot-Ieng Sary regime adopted inhuman and unrealistic internal and external policies. It exterminated about half of the country's population and suppressed human rights and norms of international law. Its aggressive policy towards neighbours alienated even the fellow communists in the region. It maintained friendly relations with China alone. The immediate neighbours, Vietnam, Thailand and Laos, always felt uncomfortable about the developments in Kampuchea. History shows that major socio-political changes in one Indochinese country have affected the other countries in the region. Vietnam could not remain a passive spectator to the situation in Kampuchea. The questions often asked are: whether Vietnam should involve itself to this extent in Kampuchea? If yes, what should be the role of Thailand, Laos and other neighbouring countries? To what extent China should interfere in the situation? What should be the role of the former head of state, Prince Norodom Sihanouk, or of General Lon Nol or Pol Pot in the solution of the Kampuchean crisis? What should be the place of the Heng Samrin government in the international community? Whether ASEAN (Association of Southeast Asian Nations) or the UN (United Nations) should recognize the new regime in Kampuchea? Who should form the future government and on what criteria?

In order to get a correct perspective of the Kampuchean crisis, the different factors in it may be divided into three categories: national, regional and extra-regional. Since the downfall of Sihanouk, not a single government in Kampuchea has enjoyed national consensus. Every one of them adopted repressive policies and only represented a particular segment of the society. They never paid any attention to the attitudes of the foreign countries. General Lon Nol offended North Vietnam and the NLF in South Vietnam. Similarly, as soon as the Pol Pot group came to power it challenged the US by seizing their merchantship, *The Mayaguez*, off Kampuchean waters in May 1975 on espionage charges. The situation worsened to such an extent that the US had to undertake military action to rescue their ship. At that time many South-east Asian experts believed that such a strong US reaction was uncalled for. However, later developments have revealed Kampuchea's aggressive policies in internal and external affairs which aggrieved their comrades in the region. It began to antagonize and provoke Vietnam, its most powerful neighbour. Pol Pot offended the Vietnamese to such an extent that the latter became very active in overthrowing his regime.

Kampuchea and Laos are strategically located in such a way that they cannot remain happy by antagonizing Vietnam. When Sihanouk was the head of state, he maintained friendly relations with Vietnam and China both. He even allowed the NLF forces to supply arms and ammunitions through his country and thus provided a passage to the Ho Chi Minh Trail. When he was overthrown by a coup, his successor, General Lon Nol reversed his policy and strongly supported US policy in the region. His successor Pol Pot came to power with much enthusiasm in the wake of the defeat of the US forces in the region. He wanted to regain the glory that the Khmers once enjoyed in the region. However, his choice of means to attain it was wrong. He tried to flatter China and preferred to accentuate the rift in the communist camp. He, too, therefore, was overthrown. For a government to be stable in Kampuchea it is not only necessary that it be formed by national consensus but it has to strike a proper balance in its foreign policy.

However, regional politics in Southeast Asia have often been caused by extra-regional factors. The Sino-Vietnam rift has greatly aggravated the Kampuchean crisis. Their rift, the causes of which are both historical and contemporary, has led them to fight it out on their common border in 1979 with no clear victory to either. Thereafter they turned Kampuchea into a battleground for another trial of strength. China incited the Pol Pot regime to pursue anti-Vietnam policies. Pol Pot had already ordered the Vietnamese minorities to leave the country. Next, his government charged that Vietnam was threatening Kampuchea's national independence. The situation worsened to such an extent that Vietnam helped in the formation of KNUFNS (Kampuchea National United Front for National Salvation) and in collusion with it attacked Kampuchea and brought down the regime. Heng Samrin, the leader of KNUFNS, was installed as the head of state in Kampuchea who pledged to pursue friendly relations with the neighbouring countries. China did not recognize the new regime and used its diplomatic influence against it. With the exception of the Soviet bloc, none recognized the new regime. The ASEAN states supported the Chinese stand. The UN also did not recognize the new government.

The ASEAN and the UN still recognize the regime of Pol Pot. But Pol Pot out of Pnom Penh. The majority of Kampucheans are believed to be against him. The Pol Pot group has been driven out of Pnom Penh to a small strip of land on the Thai-Kampuchean border. Probably they are concentrated around the Cardamom mountain ranges with Thai sympathy. If Thailand were to close the sanctuaries, their activities will come to an end.

III

China has been encouraging Thailand to support the Pol Pot group. Though officially describing its position as neutral, Thailand in fact supports the Pol Pot forces against the government of Heng Samrin. The Pol Pot group has been organizing itself in those areas militarily to challenge the regime of Heng Samrin. They have engaged in guerrilla activities and on many occasions have inflicted damages on the government forces. As Vietnam can control the Kampuchean border areas on all sides except from Thailand side, it is the only area for the militant dissidents to operate from. That communist Vietnam could be so influential near its borders, was repugnant to Thailand. This is because historically it has been observed that whenever Vietnam dominated Khmer politics, there were security problems to Thailand. In the middle of the seventeenth century Vietnam had defeated the kingdom of Champa and had entrenched itself on the eastern side of Kampuchea. At that time the Khmer kings expected that the Vietnamese will be a counterpoise to Thailand in colonial objectives and hence the cause of Khmer independence will be enhanced. But the result was just the opposite. Sometimes on the pretext of aiding pretenders to the Khmer throne, and at other times for the ostensible purpose of aiding the Khmers against Thailand, it started interfering in the internal affairs of the kingdom. It even threatened to disrupt the very bases of Khmer life and institutions, tradition and history.[8] From time to time Vietnamese rulers incited the Khmer kings to engage in hostile acts against the kingdom of Thailand. In the present context, we find that the political system of Vietnam has changed. They believe and practice in the communist ideology. They have struggled hard against the US to preserve their system. On the other hand, Thailand is a monarchy and adheres to the Buddhist way of life. They are distinct in the region because they have never been colonized. With a brief interregnum, the military has been in power since 1932. The political elite is averse to the communist system. They have set up a special command force to contain communist activities. Only three countries supply arms and ammunition to communist insurgents in the region: Vietnam, China and the Soviet Union. Since China has embraced the US and sought solidarity and goodwill of the ASEAN, it is no longer feared in the region. Chinese leaders have verbally assured ASEAN leaders that they will not aid and abet local insurgents anywhere in the region. On the other hand, the Soviet Union has been handling its relations with communist insurgents in the region with much care. The Soviets are in search of breaking new ground of friendship in the region to face the Chinese threat. Again, it is situated at a great distance from the region and is therefore feared less. It is only Vietnam whose intentions towards the rest of the Southeast Asian countries are doubted. Since the dismantling of the Pol Pot regime, Vietnamese policy towards its neighbours has been a matter of much criticism. It is feared that Vietnam will immediately threaten its neighbours if they offended it in the least. Repeated assurances by Vietnamese leaders could not convince the ASEAN group that Vietnam has no aggressive designs against any of them. They do not believe that Vietnam will not aid and assist communist rebels. Their apprehensions surfaced at the summit of non-aligned countries in Havana and in the UN meeting in 1979.

Thailand allowed the Pol Pot forces to have some supply bases to continue their activities.[9] It was through Thailand that China had been supplying economic and military assistance to Pol Pot forces. China was known to be trying to have direct access to the Pol Pot forces through direct landing facilities in Thailand. It is not known whether such a request will be accepted by Thailand. But China could use economic pressures against Thailand to further its objectives in the region.

China was the main supplier of crude to Thailand in the post-1975 era. At the beginning of 1979 China agreed to supply 600,000 tons of crude to Thailand per year for five years at 'friendship price'. Subsequently, the latter was informed that the price will float up to OPEC levels by the middle of that year. Some Chinese officials even told a visiting Thai trade delegation in October 1979 that there would be no more oil until Thailand signed a civil aviation agreement allowing regular Chinese commercial flight to land in Thailand.[10] Thus it is clear that the Chinese wanted closer alignment of Thailand with China in regard to foreign policy. A number of officials in Thailand expressed the view that the Chinese may demand a higher political price for their oil.[11]

The Chinese liked to have communication facilities in Thailand to help Pol Pot forces. They wanted to have uninterrupted passage to supply aid and assistance to Pol Pot guerrillas. Is it possible for Thailand to provide such facilities? The contemporary history of Thailand shows that they can go to any extent in helping their allies in return for economic benefits. For example, it allowed the US to use its various air and naval bases for containment of communism in the region. The present regime in Thailand is quite friendly with the US and China both. Therefore, it may be expected that Thailand will openly support Chinese activities against the Heng Samrin government. Thailand obviously cannot do without Chinese oil which is the cheapest they can get. As the shortage of oil causes the rise in prices in Thailand and elsewhere, it is always desirable to get them at cheaper rate. If China continued to supply oil to Thailand at the 'friendship price', some of its leaders may like to align their country with China. But this is not as easy as it seems. Vietnam is a powerful country and it has demoralized the French, the American and even the Chinese forces militarily. It has a large veteran army filled with patriotism and courage. It has the potential to retaliate against unfriendly acts by neighbours.

IV

Thailand was a frontline ASEAN state in the post-1975 era. It was geopolitically important and any ambitious nation will try to have influence over that country. There was a wide gap in the life-styles of the rich and poor in Thailand. The condition of the poor was deteriorating every day as in other developing countries. There was disenchantment with their political system in large sections. The communist philosophy of equal distribution and right to work may well appeal to them to support CPT. If Vietnam finds Thailand unfriendly for long, it may organize the disenchanted and disgrunted element in the CPT cadre. In the event of a government assault against them, Vietnam may intervene on their behalf. In such an eventuality, Thailand's neighbours may not be able to face the Vietnamese challenge. Except China, the rest of the countries may not even like to offend the Vietnamese. But China could not stop the fall of Pol Pot in Kampuchea. China was unable to save its only ally in Indochina from falling into the hands of the rebels. Since the fall of Pol Pot, the Chinese leaders have been assuring its Southeast Asian friends that it will help them militarily in case of Vietnamese aggression. Chang Weilieh, China's Ambassador in Thailand, spoke in an interview to Theh Chongkhadikij, editor, *Bangkok Post*, in May 1979 that his country was ready to guarantee Thailand's security in the event of Vietnamese aggression. If the Vietnamese attack Thailand, the Chinese people will be on the side of Thai people and would help them in their struggle against the aggression. He promised Chinese aid to all countries threatened with aggression.

Vice-Premier Deng Xiaoping during his visit to Thailand in November 1978 assured Thailand of Chinese help. He cautioned

Thailand against the Soviet Union and Vietnam and said: 'Vietnam is a Trojan horse of the Soviet Union. There is a hooligan in the East. I am sure that we all understand the word Cuba and "Cuba of the East". We must be alert to this.'[12]

Commenting on Vietnamese Premier, Pham Van Dong's assurance that Vietnam will not support communist insurgencies, Deng said: 'Please do not force me to refer to Mr. Pham Van Dong. If China followed what Pham Van Dong said it would bring disaster to Asia and the Pacific'.[13]

V

The Chinese evidently consider that Vietnam is the enemy of Southeast Asia and want to use all their influence to contain the Vietnamese in the region. But is it rational for the Southeast Asian countries to do what the Chinese want them to do? Is it only Vietnam which accentuates the crisis in the region? Is it not a fact that the Pol Pot regime has completely disregarded human rights and killed millions of Kampuchean people? Can it be overlooked that Kampuchea is geopolitically very important to peace and progress in Vietnam? Can any country ignore revolution in a neighbouring country which is favourable to it?

The Heng Samrin forces are in possession of almost all of Kampuchea except a few miles on the Thai-Kampuchean border. Their urgent need is to get the recognition of the outside world. Thailand is certainly a hurdle in the way of recognition. China and some other countries claim that Pol Pot forces still control a large area of Kampuchean territory. The fact is that their control is limited to the forests and mountains on the Thai-Kampuchean border. As Thailand provides sanctuary to Pol Pot forces, it is extremely difficult to contain their activities. The supporters of the Pol Pot group are able to prove that they are still in Kampuchea, though they do not possess Phnom Penh. They say that Heng Samrin is a usurper and runs a puppet regime in Phnom Penh.

It is no exaggeration to say that the Pol Pot forces cannot operate if Thailand withdraws its support to them. Vietnam has been trying hard that Thailand should close the sanctuaries to Pol Pot forces. Many Vietnamese leaders including Pham Van Dong have paid visits to Thailand in this connection, and Thailand has assured them to remain neutral; however, the government of Thailand acts otherwise.

VI

Right since the fall of Pol Pot forces Thailand has been emphasizing the need of strengthening their security system. Prime Minister General Kriangsak Chomanan has visited China, the US, Japan and the Soviet Union and emphasized the importance of strengthening Thai security. Thailand has even pleaded for the location of a UN Peace Keeping Force on its border with Kampuchea. This is only to avoid a spill-over of the hostilities now taking place in Kampuchea. The Vietnamese, on the other hand, have time and again offered to sign a non-aggression treaty with Thailand. The Soviet leader Leonid Brezhnev has also assured on behalf of Vietnam that Veitnam will not violate the borders of any ASEAN country. Brezhnev wanted to dispel the anxiety of ASEAN over the possibility of the war in Kampuchea spilling over into Thailand.[14] Vietnamese Foreign Minister Ngyuen Co Thach declared on 20 October 1979 in a press conference that Vietnamese troops then operating in Kampuchea would not cross into Thai territory.[15] However, these assurance are not believed in fully by Thai leaders. Nor has Thailand accepted the non-aggression pact offered by the Vietnamese. They continue to speak about their security problems in the light of the turmoil in Indochina even now. This may be because Thailand is continuously engaging in anti-Vietnam activities by providing sanctuaries to Pol Pot forces. It is reported that by the end of November 1979 Thailand had opened its borders to Kampuchean refugees numbering about 700,000. Vietnam sees in all this a more immediate danger. It finds that the refugee programme of Thailand is only a cover for giving the China-backed Pol Pot guerrillas food, shelter and logistic support in Thailand.[16] The Vietnamese are willing to contain them and in order to do so it is necessary to have control over their hideouts and sanctuary. For this they will have to go and attack inside Thai territory

Vietnam has a long way to go towards nation-building and modernization. It needs a peaceful environment to pursue developmental activities. Vietnam has defeated the French and American colonial masters. Presently, the Pol Pot forces are the main obstacle in the Indochinese states troubling Vietnam. Therefore, Vietnam wants to use every resource at its command to contain Pol Pot forces.

However, the emergence of Vietnam as a strong power is a challenge to the Chinese superiority in the region. The Chinese have adopted a strategy to put such intolerable burdens on Vietnam that it might collapse from within.[17] Dilip Mukerji observes that China will, in any foreseeable circumstances, resist with all its power the emergence of regimes inimical to it in countries on or near its borders.[18] If so, the Chinese will time and again cause problems for Vietnam. Thailand, too, needs to handle its relations with China with great care and caution. Though the ASEAN partners are identical in their attitude towards Pol Pot and Vietnam, the other partners do not assist the anti-Vietnam forces as Thailand does. Philippines, Indonesia, Singapore and Malaysia are applying diplomatic pressures against the Heng Samrin government, but Thailand is accentuating the Kampuchean crisis. In order to bring about a healthy political climate in the region, it is necessary for the countries concerned to pursue a policy of non-involvement in the internal affairs of one another. Regarding Kampuchea, it seems a principle that the administration that rules over the capital and other important towns should be recognized. As a well-known expert in Southeast Asian studies, Anthony Barnett, puts it: 'By supporting Pol Pot and thereby refusing to allow the Vietnamese army to withdraw, ASEAN may be helping to dig more than the graves of a million Khmers.'[19]

VII

It is reported that Thailand's attitude towards Kampuchea may not be fully endorsed by the ASEAN partners. Recently Indonesian Foreign Minister, Mochtar Kusumatmadja, said that ASEAN should avoid giving the impression that it is in confrontation with Vietnam over Kampuchea. He opined that Vietnam should be considered a buffer between China and the rest of South-east Asia.[20] There is a recent change of attitude in Malaysia and the Philippines also. Only Thailand and Singapore favour a stiff attitude against Vietnam but they seem to be in a minority. The majority opinion of ASEAN favours a conciliatory policy, which is bound to impact Thailand too. As soon as Thailand changes its present attitude towards Vietnam, it is bound to add a new dimension to Thailand's China policy.

REFERENCES

1. *People's Daily*, Beijing, 30 June 1975.
2. For details of the joint communique published on the occasion of the recognition, see *Foreign Affairs Bulletin*, Bangkok, Vol. 15, No. 3, July-September 1975, pp. 68-70. Also see Ross Munro, 'China Denies Support to Rebels', *Hindustan Standard*, Calcutta, 17 July 1975.
3. See the statement of Premier Kukrit Pramoj at a state banquet in the Great Hall in Beijing, *Foreign Affairs Bulletin*, Vol. 15, No. 3, July-September 1975, pp. 67-68.
4. Ganganath Jha, 'Thailand's China Policy', *China Report*, Delhi, Vol. 14, No. 2, March-April 1978, p. 10.
5. This was decided when a Thai delegation led by Commerce Minister Nam Phoonwathu visited Beijing in mid-1978.
6. Anthony Rowley, 'Kriangsak's Other Battlefront', *Far Eastern Economic Review*, Hong Kong, Vol. 105, No. 38, 21 September 1979, p. 100.
7. K. Sonsomsook, 'Thailand : Goodwill has its Limits', *Far Eastern Economic Review*, Vol. 105, No. 36, 7 September 1979, p. 51.
8. V.M. Reddi, *A History of Cambodian Independence Movement 1863-1955*, Tirupati, 1970, pp. 16-17.
9. Ban Laem, some 500 metres inside Thailand, is one of those supply camps to Pol Pot forces, *The Times of India*, New Delhi, 19 November 1979.
10. The principle for Civil Aviation Agreement between China and Thailand had been agreed upon during the visit of Chinese Vice-Premier Deng Xiaoping to Thailand in November 1978. But the Thais have been reluctant to ink the final accord for fear that Chinese flights could prove another conduit of material aid to Pol Pot insurgents in Kampuchea. For details see *Far Eastern Economic Review*, Vol. 106, No. 41, 12 October 1979, p. 5.
11. Rowley, n. 6, p. 100.
12. *Straits Times*, Singapore, 5 November 1978. Also see *Bangkok Post*, 4 November 1978.
13. *Straits Times*, 4 November 1978.
14. Brezhnev gave this assurance at a meeting in Moscow with Datuk Hussein Onn, the Malaysian Prime Minister, *The Times of India*, New Delhi, 8 October 1979.
15. *The Times of India*, New Delhi, 22 October 1979.
16. Dilip Mukerji, 'Rift in ASEAN over Kampuchea', *The Times of India*, New Delhi, 12 December 1979.
17. Gargi Dutt, 'China Revisited : Hanoi a Bugbear', *The Times of India*, 23 November 1979.
18. Dilip Mukerji, 'Australia and the Third World,' *The Times of India*, New Delhi, 24 November 1979.
19. *Far Eastern Economic Review*, Vol. 106, No. 43, 26 October 1979, p. 4.
20. Mukerji, n. 16.

5

Thailand and Vietnam: A Frontline States' Perception of an Adversary, 1975-1985

Thailand, a front-line state, is directly affected by Vietnam's Indo-China policy. It has played a key role in the affairs of the region ever since the ouster of the Khmer Rouge Government from power in December 1978. Formerly the staunchest supporter of the American policy of 'Containment of Communism,'[1] Thailand adopted a two-pronged foreign policy after the withdrawal of the American forces in 1975 from Indo-China to retain its regional importance and national interests. On the one hand, it took the initiative to strengthen relations with the People's Republic of China with which it was involved in polemics and disputes ever since 1945.[2] On the other hand, Thailand tried to stop Vietnam to have a foothold next door. Though China and Vietnam are both communist countries and neighbours, Thailand's attitude towards them was not the same. Though, the Prime Minister of Thailand, Kukrit Pramoj, was not against Vietnam, he looked towards the ASEAN to evolve a common consensus on Indo-China. In October 1976, there was a military coup d'état in Thailand. The new government appreciated the policy of rapprochement with China, because the Thais were apprehensive of Vietnam. Thai rulers were concerned about the influence of the Vietnamese communists in the region, who were held in high profile and lived in burgeoning morale.

China, on the other hand, understood and appreciated Thai susceptibilities of Vietnam. China wanted North and South Vietnam to remain divided. But the Vietnamese comrades did not pay heed to the Chinese advice and instead got the two parts unified. China was unhappy about this development as it viewed the emergence of a strong state on its southern frontier with misgivings. It felt that the unification of the two parts of Vietnam would result in a strong step towards the formation of the 'Indo-Chinese federation'.[3] China became active and worked to thwart Vietnamese political ambitions and thus attempted to break the solidarity of the Indo-Chinese countries. It found a desirable ally in the government of the Khmer Rouge in Kampuchea. China promoted Democratic Kampuchea to act as a 'trouble shooter' against Vietnam. At the same time Chinese rulers were astute enough to forge an understanding with Thailand on this issue.

On the other hand, the Democratic Kampuchean Government was lukewarm in its attitude towards Vietnam. Its strategy was to delink itself with Vietnam as soon as possible. It wanted to maintain a distinct identity vis-a-vis the Vietnamese communists. Its policy included the abolition of the currency system and forcefully bridging the gap between rich and poor. It had initiated a 'Resettlement Plan' to transfer the urban population to the rural areas and *vice versa*. In the realm of foreign policy, it attached great importance to China. It laid claim to the Vietnamese territories and adopted a harsh attitude towards the overseas Vietnamese in that country. It was least concerned about Vietnam's sensitivity. Vietnam was greatly disturbed by these developments and subsequently it helped the forces led by Heng Samrin to overthrow the Khmer Rouge Government. The removal of the Khmer Rouge from power with the help of the Vietnamese forces in league with the National United Front for National Liberation, according to some, established a bad precedent in Southeast Asia. The new government known as the People's Republic of Kampuchea (PRK) was headed by Heng Samrin. This government abolished the 'Resettlement Plan' and reintroduced the currency (Riel Notes) system. It concluded friendship treaties with Vietnam. It soon extended its hand of friendship to Laos as well. The three countries entered into agreements with security implications.[4]

The Vietnamese military action in Kampuchea led to adverse reaction from the ASEAN countries not because of their sympathy for the Khmer Rouge, but because of armed intervention in the affairs of another country. They challenged the legitimacy of the new government and campaigned massively against Vietnamese penetration. It was in this endeavour that Thailand's role as a front-line state became significant. Henceforth, Thailand tried further to thwart consolidation of the Vietnamese strength in Kampuchea. Thailand sheltered the fugitive forces of the Khmer Rouge, including Pol Pot and provided them all possible assistance to fight against the People's Republic of Kampuchea. It also provided training facilities and other strategic assistance.[5] It became a channel to receive arms and ammunitions from China, the United States and other countries destined for the Kampuchean rebels. Thailand became a safe sanctuary for the rebels from where they could easily enter into Kampuchea to confront the Vietnamese forces and return. Prior to 1975, the American servicemen had used Thai territories for regular bombing missions to Indo-China. Now Kampuchean rebels were using Thai territories for guerilla activities in Kampuchea and returning to Thai camps after these missions. But earlier there was a section of the Thais who were opposed to American policies. In the present case, there has been no organised opposition to the activities of the Kampuchean rebels on the Thai soil.

At the international level, Thailand has been most vociferous against the Vietnamese action. Whether at the ASEAN or at the United Nations, the Vietnamese action has been criticised. The United Nations did not accord recognition to the People's Republic of Kampuchea. Neither the Non-Aligned Movement (NAM) nor the Association of the South East Asian Nations (ASEAN) recognised the new government. The United States, China, Japan and the West European countries did not accord recognition, in spite of the fact that the PRK was in effective control of the country. On the other hand, the Soviet Union and East European countries recognised the government of the PRK. India did not recognise the new government immediately but members of the Indian Parliament voiced their concern for the people of Kampuchea and pleaded for recognition. The government led by Indira Gandhi accorded recognition to the PRK in July 1980.

Kampuchean adventures posed a great dilemma for Vietnam, it probably had not envisaged that its action in Kampuchea would provoke international opposition to the extent existing today. Moreover, it feels uncomfortable about the challenges posed by the Kampuchean rebels on the Thai soil. Vietnam found it agonising to return to the pavilion. On the other hand, Thailand was seriously concerned about the Vietnamese presence next door. History is testimony to the fact, that whenever Vietnam expanded its influence and control in Kampuchea, it had posed a security threat to Thailand.[6]

In order to have a proper perspective of Thailand's Vietnam policy, it is necessary to briefly review its contemporary past. Since the end of the Second World War, Thailand consistently supported the United States in its efforts to annihilate the communists in China and Vietnam. Thailand entered into military and economic agreements with the United States bilaterally and multilaterally and subsequently joined the South East Asia Treaty Organisation (SEATO) in 1954. Thailand became the headquarters of the SEATO whose main preoccupation was to contain communist movements in Vietnam.[7] Thailand was the only country from the mainland to join the American security system. It allowed the United States to develop several air and naval bases in Thailand to be used against Vietnam. The air bases at Udon, Ubon, Nakhon Phanom, Takhli and Utapao were extensively used for operations against Vietnam and other Indo-Chinese countries from 1964 to 1975. The American servicemen were utilising the Thai bases to bombard the Vietnamese territories. As Thailand was the Rest and Recreation Centre (R&R) for the Americans, even those stationed in South Vietnam would come to Thailand for recreation and enjoyment. Thailand had even offered contingents of Thai troops to the United States to fight against the National Liberation Front (NLF) of South Vietnam. Thailand provided all possible assistance to the American cold warriors to contain communism in Vietnam but all those efforts proved abortive. The final outcome of the years of American exploits was its defeat in April 1975. The Americans withdrew militarily from South Vietnam, Kampuchea and Laos for good.

The failure of the American adventures in Indo-China affected its image and morale. At the same time, the end of the war in Vietnam reduced the strategic importance of Thailand for the United States. On the eve of the American withdrawal from Indo-China Thailand was experiencing democratic rule. Democracy had come to Thailand after years of military rule in October 1973, but it was only for a brief period, i.e., till October 1976. The democratic rulers were willing to maintain an equidistance in their relations with all the major powers. There was an effort to change the pro-American bias characteristic of the early period and, therefore, the American withdrawal from Indo-China did not disturb them. As a matter of fact, the withdrawal provided an opportunity to the democratic rulers to reappraise Thai-American relations more easily. Kukrit Pramoj, the then Prime Minister of Thailand visited China in 1975 in search of a rapprochement. He was the first Thai Prime Minister to visit the People's Republic of China. Kukrit was given a warm welcome by the Chinese leaders including Chairman Mao Tse Dong. He was assured that the Chinese government would not provide any sort of assistance to the Thai Communist Party.[8] A series of agreements and treaties were signed between the two countries. China was eager to supply all the oil requirements of Thailand. Kukrit Pramoj and his colleagues were happy at the outcome of their talks with the Chinese leaders.[9]

Kukrit Pramoj advocated for a thaw in Thai-Vietnam relations as well. He broached the idea to include Vietnam into the ASEAN fold. But his idea could not materialise because of the coup d'etat in October 1976. His successor, Thanin Kraivichian wanted to revive the policies of the military rulers in the pre-1973 period with some modifications. He gave priority to strengthening relations with the People's Republic of China and the old ally, the United States of America. As far as Vietnam was concerned, he was cautious.

In December 1973, when Vietnam intervened in Kampuchea, the Thai rulers got a ready pretext to oppose. Thailand was the first country to raise its voice against the Vietnamese aggression. Though Thailand is a monarchy and the victims in Kampuchea were a set of communists, the former did not hesitate to express wholehearted support to the latter. The rebels, as stated earlier, were provided facilities to be stationed at Thai-Kampuchean frontiers, and to sustain guerilla warfare against the Vietnamese forces.

The rebels subsequently increased their strength and fought against the Vietnamese forces repeatedly. Their activities led to perpetual tension in Thai-Vietnam relations. Both the countries adopted almost irreversible policies against each other. While Thailand demanded total withdrawal of Vietnamese soldiers from Kampuchea, Vietnam demanded a total disarming soldiers from Kampuchea, Vietnam demanded a total disarming of the rebels in Thailand. But Thailand was not alone in its demand for withdrawal. The entire ASEAN group of countries, including Thailand, Malaysia, Singapore, Indonesia and the Philippines, shared an identity of outlook on the Kampuchean issue.[10] The nations opposing Vietnamese policy in Kampuchea have had their own compulsions and objectives.

There are several factors influencing Thailand's anti-Vietnam postures. Historical and geo-political factors form the backdrop for the arousal of mutual suspicions and antipathy. Ever since 1253 when the foundation of Thai Kingdom was laid after defeating the Khmer governor at Sukhothai, Thailand posed a challenge to the Vietnamese rulers. The interests of the Thai Kingdom and those of the Vietnamese clashed with each other. Both sides wanted to acquire the territories of the Khmer empire which had grown weak. The two countries acquired the Khmer territories situated near their frontiers. The kings of the two countries wanted to annex all the Khmer territories. The clash of interests resulted in perpetual warfare between the two. These wars were not conclusive, sometimes one side secured a greater chunk of Khmer territories and sometimes the other. The Khmer rulers in order to face aggression had no option but to choose the friendship of either Thailand or Vietnam.[11] However, these two countries continued to exploit the Khmer resources.

When the colonial masters from Europe came to Southeast Asia, the politics of mutual antagonism in the region were subdued. The end of the Second World War marked the end of the era of Western colonialism in Southeast Asia. It is from this point onwards that we can find a difference in the Thailand and Vietnamese outlook once again. When the Japanese aggressors came to Vietnam, the Viet Minh decided to fight against them but when the Japanese invaded the Thai territory, the Thai decision-makers decided to cooperate with the invaders. After the war, the Viet Minh opposed Western interference in the internal affairs of the Southeast Asian countries, but Thailand promoted it by joining the SEATO. Thailand became a kingpin in a drive against communism and subsequently Vietnam became its chosen target. But the Vietnamese communists emerged victorious and formed their government in 1975. Thus, it was difficult for the government of Thailand to trust its adversary given the historical background.

It is a fact that Thailand perceives a threat to its long-term interests if Vietnam consolidates its position and power in Kampuchea. If Vietnam consolidates its position in Kampuchea, it will be fulfilling its historical dream, but for Thailand it will be a historical loss. The Vietnamese presence in Kampuchea poses other dilemmas as well. The political elite in Thailand—aristocrats, landlords, businessmen, military strongmen and owners of the hotel industry—has its own stakes and interests. These elements find a real challenge, if the winds of communism next door will overtake them. The multinational corporations, Japanese business, the landlords and the powerful military elements have a stake in the progress of Vietnam even if the latter does not interfere in the affairs of other nations. The poor, who are in majority, would like to improve their socio-economic condition under any political system.

Thailand is projected as a 'Domino' and the 'prophets of doom' have their own predictions. Some analysts have emphasised that after South Vietnam, Thailand is the next target of communism. Such an eventuality could be contained only if Vietnam remained involved in the quagmire of Kampuchea for years. Hence they canvass support in their 'attempts to let Vietnam bleed'.

It is noteworthy that China, a communist country and much more powerful than Vietnam which poses a threat to the governments in the ASEAN region, is no longer feared. After the visit of President Richard Nixon to China in 1972, the Chinese successfully handled their American and Southeast Asian policy. The Chinese leaders visited the capitals of the ASEAN countries and these visits were reciprocated. In all these meetings the Chinese leaders assured their counterparts in the ASEAN region that no assistance would be given to the communist parties in the ASEAN region, China forged cordial relations with all the six countries of the ASEAN through economic, military and cultural exchanges and treaties.

China has yet another reason to withdraw support to the communists in the ASEAN region. All the six countries of the ASEAN have a good number of overseas Chinese. These people are in control of the business sector in almost all the ASEAN countries.[12] Efforts to replace them with Bhumiputras in Malaysia and Indonesia have not yet succeeded. A change in the political system of the ASEAN countries would adversely affect the business of the overseas Chinese. China has every sympathy and support for its overseas population and, therefore, it does not want to harm their interests. The Chinese support for its overseas population was taken for granted in the event that Vietnam precipitated matters between the two countries. This factor finally led to the outbreak of the Sino-Vietnam war in January 1979.

Vietnam, on the other hand, is not handicapped by such inhibitions in its relations with Southeast Asia. Vietnam would not like to engage itself in supporting the revolutionary activities in the ASEAN region for some time to come. At present, it is interested in establishing a clean image in the Southeast Asian region. It wants to survive and prosper as a civilised and peace-loving nation. It is willing to follow the concept of 'communism in one country', instead of 'proletariats of the world unite'. The rulers in Vietnam have repeatedly expressed their desire to confine their activities to Vietnam alone. If they seek cordial relations with Laos and Kampuchea, it is primarily to strengthen the security outlook of the country. Vietnam is economically weak and it will take years to reconstruct the entire infrastructure of development. At the moment, it needs peace for progress. The history of Vietnam shows that since the beginning of the Second World War, it has tried to avoid war but war has always been thrust upon Vietnam. Whether it was the Japanese or the French, the Americans of the Chinese, Vietnam had no option but to fight.

Time has come when efforts are needed to understand the problems and compulsions of the Vietnamese. If the international community could help engage Vietnam both bilaterally and multilaterally in socio-economic activities, there would be a greater possibility of developing understanding. This may reduce the revolutionary image of Vietnam as it has done in the case of the People's Republic of China. But a survey of the politics of the ASEAN countries indicates a different outlook. They are instead supporting the Kampuchean rebels against Vietnam. The superpowers are fishing in the troubled waters of the region.

The Kampuchean rebels in Thailand are operating against the Vietnamese forces with the open support of Thailand, China, the United States and some other countries. They are operating in different groups. According to Bernard Gwertzman, a journalist, there are at present three important groups of Kampuchean rebels. The first group is the Khmer Rouge faction led by Pol Pot and Ieng Sary. It has an armed militia of 35,000 guerillas. The second group of rebels is led by Son Sann and has 17,000 guerillas. The third group operates under the leadership of Norodom Sihanouk and has an estimated number of 8,000 guerillas.[13] The second and third groups are mainly financed by the United States. The activities of the first group are largely financed by China. This is the largest group of all the rebels stationed in Thailand. Vietnam is specially concerned about the activities of this group. A white book, published by the

PRK on 10 July 1984 and entitled 'The Chinese Rulers' Crime against Kampuchea', blamed Thailand's complicity in the following words:

> Taking advantage of Thai ambitions over Kampuchea, Beijing tried to cajole and draw Thailand into a state of confrontation with Vietnam and the other Indo-Chinese countries. After the overthrow of the Pol Pot gang, the Beijing leaders tried hard to get Thailand to come to the former's rescue by allowing them sanctuary on Thai territory. They urged the Thai authorities to open the Thai border to the Pol Pot remnants and give them refuge on Thai territory, and allow Chinese supplies to them to cross Thai territory. Deng Xiaoping made these proposals to Thai Vice Premier, Sunthorn Hongladdarom. More effective cooperation with China against the Soviet Union and Vietnam, continued support to the Government of Democratic Kampuchea; recognition of its legitimacy; granting it permission to have an office—either legal, semi-legal, or clandestine—somewhere on the Thai border; continued permisson to the citizens; and party; administration and army cadres of Democratic Kampuchea to ask for political asylum or authorization to go to China or any other country through Thai territory.[14]

The Thai representatives are believed to have accepted the Chinese advice. Subsequently, Kampuchean rebels were well protected in Thailand. The ASEAN as an organisation supported Thailand and on its part spearheaded the 'sanctions programme' against Vietnam to punish it economically. The entire Western Europe including the United States and Japan called off their commitments to Vietnam until Vietnamese forces were withdrawn from Kampuchea. They not only supported the 'sanctions programme', but also refused to accord recognition to the PRK government. This led to a situation where Vietnam had no option but to seek more and more aid and cooperation from the Soviet Union. It is indeed pathetic that a country which is a symbol of Afro-Asian power and prestige is cornered so as to be dependent on Soviet aid and assistance. Vietnam is not at all happy with the prevailing situation. It is willing to improve its relations with the United States. But the Americans have repeatedly raised the issue of 2500 MIAs (Americans Missing in Action) in Vietnam. It is not easy to trace their whereabouts. Vietnam may be eager to cooperate with the United States in tracing MIAs but this is not enough to satisfy the Americans. The withdrawal from Kampuchea and a change in attitude towards the Soviet Union are some of the agonising demands.

In order to bring about a change in the situation in Indo-China, Chinese rulers have tried 'to teach lessons' to Vietnam. In January 1979, the Chinese forces fought the Vietnamese forces on their common frontiers. The war ended in a stalemate. China took recourse to economic and diplomatic manoeuvers to check Vietnam. In 1982 China helped in the formation of a coalition government of Kampuchea in exile and offered military assistance and cooperation to them. Prince Norodom Sihanouk was once again chosen to lead the government in exile. Sihanouk and other leaders of the coalition shuttled from one capital to another and called for an international conference on the pattern of the Geneva Conference on Indo-China to solve the Kampuchean imbroglio. But his credibility was challenged by Vietnam and his diplomatic offensives did not attract the desired support.[15]

Kampuchean rebels have been posing a serious challenge to Vietnam. Since the formation of the Kampuchean People's National Liberation Front (KPNLF), the armed militia of the rebels have inflicted heavy blows upon the Vietnamese forces. The rebels are confronting the Vietnamese forces intermittently in Kampuchea. It has become very difficult to contain their guerilla activities. The rebels have the freedom to return to Thai sanctuaries. In order to contain the activities of the Khmer rebels, the cooperation of Thailand is extremely vital. There is no indication of a change in the Thai attitude. Thus, it is a diplomatic challenge for Vietnam to reach an understanding with Thailand as far as the future of Kampuchea is concerned. The military measures could be counter-productive. A few Thai leaders and the Western media have on various occasions accused Vietnam of chauvinism and to harbouring intentions to annex Thai territories. Though Vietnam's military measures are directed only to subdue the Kampuchean rebels in Thailand. Resorts to hot pursuit have serious implications for Thailand.

Vietnam has, time and again, tried to destroy the rebel bases on the common borders. In December 1984, there was a serious offensive to destroy the KPNLF bases at Nong Samet, Nong Chan, Ampil and Rithisen. This led to destruction of the enemy forces. The civilian population in the area had to flee to Thai territories on a massive scale.[16] The situation had worsened and Vietnam and Thailand were almost on the verge of a large-scale armed conflict.

Vietnam has made numerous attempts to forge agreements with Thailand. Vietnam has been offering 'no-war' pacts to Thailand since 1979. Through Kampuchea it proposed the establishment of a 'demilitarised zone' along the Kampuchean-Thai border. Thailand did not entertain the proposal and said that it could not withdraw its troops from a part of its own territory.[17]

Thailand has raised the question of its security in view of the Kampuchean crisis. It is not ready to rely on the Vietnamese overtures. It has rejected the peace proposals of Vietnam consistently, and has demanded instead the withdrawal of the Vietnamese forces from Kampuchea. Vietnam has expressed its willingness to withdraw if certain conditions are fulfilled. Vietnamese withdrawal may be possible if the rebels in Thailand are disarmed and the security of Kampuchea is assured. Vietnam has modified its policy in view of the pressures that have been mounted by the international community.

Vietnam has tried for a rapprochement with Thailand without losing its face in Kampuchea. It has repeatedly offered to Thailand the proposal of signing treaties for non-aggression and non-interference but Thai response has not been positive. Vietnam has also tried to involve Laos and Kampuchea in the search for a rapprochement vis-a-vis Thailand. Vietnam even called a conference of the Indo-Chinese Foreign Ministers on 7 July 1982 to discuss the possibilities for a rapprochement with Thailand.[18] This conference discussed Thai susceptibilities and relations in great depth. It viewed Thailand's stand that its troops could not be withdrawn from a part of its own territory.

It proposed to Thailand to set up a 'safety zone' along the Thai-Kampuchean borders. In this proposal it also demanded the withdrawal of forces which did not belong to either Thailand or the PRK from the safety zone. The three Indo-Chinese countries expressed their readiness to discuss and reach an agreement with. Thailand on such concrete matters as the width of the 'safety zone', the scope of the withdrawal of the Vietnamese troops from the Kampuchean-Thai border, as well as the removal of the Pol Potist and other Khmer reactionaries and refugee camps away from the border.[19] The Indo-Chinese countries deemed it necessary that an agreement could be reached on a form of international supervision on the 'safety zone'. The proposal further requested that

> to show their goodwill, the PRK and Vietnam will unilaterally withdraw some units of the Vietnamese troops from Kampuchea. If the Thai side gave positive response to that action, Vietnam will withdraw more troops from Kampuchea. In case Thailand refused to establish a safety zone, the Indo-Chinese were ready even then to discuss and reach [an] agreement with the Thai side on any measure likely to ensure strict respect of the Kampuchean-Thai border as well as any measure, including a form of international supervision, to ensure peace and stability there.[20]

Indo-Chinese proposal was much detailed, but it had a catch. The acceptance to the proposal could provide Thai recognition and legitimacy to the PRK. Thailand, therefore, did not accept this proposal. The United States and China were elated at the Thai refusal of the Indo-Chinese proposal. The United States and China increased their quantum of aid to Thailand. The aid in the name of 'Kampuchean refugees' from different sources continued to flow into Thailand.

The Kampuchean factor is a mere pretext for the United States to provide strategic assistance to Thailand. The United States is in agreement with Thailand about the seriousness of the security environment of Southeast Asia, and it is ready to supply even some of the sophisticated weapons. It signed an agreement to supply 12F-16 Falcon jet fighters to Thailand and promised to supplement these with some more lethal weapons.[21] The Pentagon treats the case of Thailand vis-a-vis Kampuchea at par with that of Pakistan vis-a-vis Afghanistan. They attach importance to Thailand for halting the Soviet/Vietnamese expansion in Southeast Asia. Thailand as front-line state is willing to play that role.

Thailand continues to regard the presence of Vietnam in Kampuchea as a perpetual threat to its security. On the other hand, Vietnam maintains that the presence of Kampuchean rebels in Thailand is a constant danger to its security. Vietnam has been trying to project that the Chinese policy in Indo-China threatens the security of Southeast Asia as a whole, and Vietnam should be treated as a shield against China. It has been arguing that the three Indo-Chinese countries and the six ASEAN countries should sit together and discuss their common concerns and legitimate interests. It has, time and again, pledged to accelerate the process of unilateral withdrawal from Kampuchea, if the security of the three Indo-Chinese countries is assured. Vietnam has proposed to Thailand and the other ASEAN countries to sign treaties of non-aggression and non-intervention. The Vietnamese leaders have visited the ASEAN countries for better understanding and cordial relations. But these efforts have not produced the desired results.

The policy of Thailand vis-a-vis Vietnam is guided by the perception of an adversary. These two countries have indulged in polemics resolution in increasing tension in their mutual relations for long. The oft-quoted Thai saying, 'Like a bamboo, we bend with the wind,' is not being applied in relation to Vietnam. However, a thaw in the Thai-Vietnam relations, is the prerequisite for a long-term solution of the crisis in contemporary Indo-China.

REFERENCES

1. For a perspective of this aspect, see Frank C. Darling, *Thailand and the United States*, Washington, D.C., 1965. Donald E. Nuechterlein, *Thailand and the Struggle for Southeast Asia*, New York, 1967.
2. Ganganath Jha, *Southeast Asia and India: A Political Perspective*, New Delhi, 1986, pp. 76-88.
3. Ho Chi Minh, the father of the Communist Party in Vietnam, had conceived of an idea to form the aforesaid federation with the inclusion of Laos, Kampuchea and Vietnam. In 1947 Ho Chi Minh had appealed to the UN about the same. D.G.E. Hall, *A History of Southeast Asia*, London, 1968, p. 849, also see *Ho Chi Minh: Selected Writing and Speeches*, New Delhi, People's Publishing House, 1975, pp.1-2.
4. For a proper treatment of these developments, see Bernard K. Gordon, 'The Third Indo-China Conflict', *Foreign Affairs*, New York, Vol. 65. No.1, 1986, p. 66.
5. Bernard Gwertzman, 'US May Aid Rebels in Kampuchea', *The Times of India*, New Delhi, also see *op. cit.*, pp. 83-85.
6. V. M. Reddi, *A History of the Cambodian Independence Movement, 1863-1955*, Tirupati, 1970. See also, D.G.E. Hall, *op. cit .*, pp. 123-30.
7. For details see, Prince Wan Waithayakorn, *The Story of SEATO*, Bangkok, 1968. George Modelski, *Southeast Asia Treaty Organization: Six Studies*, London, 1962. Ganganath Jha, *Foreign Policy of Thailand 1954-1971*, New Delhi, 1979.
8. *People's Daily*, 30 June 1975.

9. For details see Joint Communique, *Foreign Affairs Bulletin*, Vol.15, No. 3, July-September 1975, pp. 4-8, 68-70. Also see, *Bangkok Post*, 1 and 2 July 1975.
10. See, *Vietnam Courier*, Hanoi, Vol. 20, 1984, pp. 10-11.
11. Reddi, *op. cit.*, pp. 15-16.
12. For a detailed treatment of this problem see, William Skinner, *Chinese Society in Thailand*, Ithaca, N.Y., 1957; and Victor Purcell, *The Chinese in Southeast Asia*, London, 1951.
13. Bernard Gwertzman, 'US May Aid Rebels in Kampuchea', *The Times of India*, New Delhi, 13 April 1985.
14. 'Chinese Rulers' Crimes against Kampuchea', *Vietnam Courier*, Hanoi, Vol. 20, No. 9, 1984, p. 8.
15. For further elaboration on this aspect, see Nguyen Co Thach, 'Note to Foreign Ministers of NAM on 4 December, 1982', *Vietnam Courier*, Vol. 14, No. 2, 1983, pp. 7-8; also see Parimal Kumar Das, 'Vietnamese Perception of Non-alignment' in K.P. Misra, ed., *Non-Alignment: Frontiers and Dynamics*, New Delhi, 1982, pp. 293-98.
16. *Bangkok Post*, 26 and 31 December 1984; *The Times of India*, 26 December 1984.
17. *Vietnam Courier*, Vol. 18, No. 2, 1982, p. 9.
18. *Ibid.*, pp. 9-10. See also, *Bangkok Post*, 9 July 1982.
19. *Vietnam Courier*, pp. 9-10.
20. *Ibid.*; see also, *New York Times*, 8 and 9 July 1982.
21. *The Times of India*, 6 April 1985.

6

Muslim Minorities in the Philippines and Thailand

A significant characteristic of the Muslim[1] minorities in the Southeast Asian region has been that they have tried their best to maintain their distinct identity. In some cases, the majority community has even blamed the Muslim minorities for posing a threat to the unity of the country and for generally being a potential constraint in the way of nation-building. But any conflict is bound to be bilateral; the differences between the two communities get further accentuated when the dominant community does not wish to listen to the demands of the minority community. The indifference of the majority community towards the grievances of the minority generates a feeling of deprivation in the latter, provoking their militant groups to agitate. These become violent sometimes and thereafter the relations between them become further strained. It is thus clear that it is not only the activities of the Muslim minorities but that of the respective majority community also which lead to intensification of socio-political and religious conflicts in the region.

Throughout Southeast Asia, the Muslim minorities are feeling deprived of certain rights *vis-a-vis* the majority community. But in the case of the Philippines and Thailand, the existence of such a feeling has posed a serious challenge even in the way of nation-building. Muslim population in these two countries is quite substantial, and it is organized enough to have resorted to violent means to gain an autonomous status. It is in this context that the present paper seeks to analyse the role and behaviour of the Muslim minorities *vis-a-vis* their relations with the governments in the Philippines and Thailand and their impact on the politics of these countries.

Muslims in Philippines

Muslims constitute about 10 per cent of the total population of the Philippines, and these are located mostly on the island of Mindanao and Sulu archipelago. These areas are well-known for agriculture, fishing, forestry and mining. There are gold deposits at Davao and Zamboanga on Mindanao, while Cotabato river basin is famous for producing rice, and Sultan Kudarat is renowned for its copper deposits. There are prospects of oil being found in Palawan, a long island to the northwest of Mindanao, South Cotabato and Davao del Sur.

Muslims in these areas are generally unhappy with the central government which is dominated by the Christians, and feel that they are being treated as second class citizens. This seems to be confirmed by a recent survey conducted by the Philippine sociologist, Dr. Rudolfo Bulatao. Bulatao interviewed about 1,700 people from eight ethnic groups (Bicolanos, Cebuanos, Tagalogs, Ilocanos, Warays, Chinese, Ilonggos and Muslims) to determine how ethnic groups feel about themselves and each other, and the degree of prejudice and social distance between various groups. This survey found that the Muslims were the least favoured by employers, neighbours and sons-in-law.[2]

For some years now, the Muslims have been demanding preferential economic treatment for the community. They have been pressing for the establishment of a personal law system which would recognize the Muslims' right to practise Islamic law in full—enabling them legally to practise polygamy, obtain divorce, settle inheritances and set up their own religious courts. They also want greater participation in the local government through the establishment of a more federalized republic.[3] Senator Mamintal Tamano, the former head of the Philippine Commission on National Integration and the President's former Adviser on Muslim Affairs, urged the Philippine Government in April 1973 to embark upon a massive land settlement programme for the landless Muslims, establish a Muslim Development Bank, and provide legal recognition to Islamic laws. The Senator emphasized that whereas the Muslims traditionally owned most of the landed areas of Mindanao, Palawan and Sulu archipelago, they currently owned only 17 per cent of it. He suggested that the Muslims should be represented in all branches of government services—a quota being fixed for the government departments—and that more Muslims should be taken into the army. A lasting solution to the Muslim problem, it was generally held among the Muslims, could be achieved only if the following fears were erased:

(*i*) fear of being unable to practise their religion;
(*ii*) fear of being displaced from their ancestral homes;
(*iii*) fear of having no future in the country, having been excluded from participation in government service and deprived of any benefit from the fruits of economic development; and
(*iv*) fear of losing their cherished values, customs and traditions.[4]

Muslims are actively championing the cause of establishing Bangsa Moro Islamic region, with their own flag, seal, security forces and language (Arabic)). To achieve that objective, they have founded the "Moro National Liberation Front" (MNLF) under the leadership of Nurulhadji Misuari. MNLF has a central committee, a political bureau, a propaganda system, an internal bureau, and a regular army called the Bangsa Moro Army. There are also local defence contingents and a reserve force. The Philippine army has even claimed that the rebels possess arms as good as its own, including American-made M-16s, Belgian G-2s and small rockets.[5] MNLF not only supports armed struggle against the central government to gain their autonomy, but also demands specifically that the areas located at Region IX and XII of the Philippine Republic be placed under its control. Region IX, it may be pointed out, consists of the provinces of Zamboanga del Sur, Zamboanga del Norte, Sulu, Basilan, and Tawi-Tawi; it has 980 islands and altogether 19,000 square kilometres of area. It is rich in iron ore (11.5 million tons), copper and gold, palm oil, plywood, fishing etc.[6] Region XII covers an area of 23,000 square kilometres and comprises the provinces of Maguindanao, North Cotabato, Sultan Kudarat, Lanao del Norte and Lanao del Sur, an area of rugged mountain ranges, fertile valleys and plains. MNLF also demands Palawan, where oil exploration is currently in process.

The Government of the Philippines is predictably allergic to the demand for Bangsa Moro Islamic region. It holds that the Muslims are not eligible to demand autonomy for all the provinces falling under region IX and XII. According to government sources, the

Muslim minority constitutes a majority community only in five provinces, namely; Sulu, Basilan, Tawi-Tawi, Maguindanao and Lanao del Sur. As these five provinces lack geographical homogeneity, the government, it is put forward, does not find it feasible and desirable to grant an autonomous status to them.

The MNLF, however, continues to claim that the Muslims are in majority in 13 provinces of the Philippines, viz; Basilan, Davao del Sur, Lanao del Norte, Lanao del Sur, Maguindanao, North Cotabato, Palawan, South Cotabato, Sulu, Sultan Kudarat, Tawi-Tawi, Zamboanga del Norte and Zamboanga del Sur, and hence all these 13 provinces should constitute the Bangsa Moro Islamic Region and be granted an autonomous status.

The Philippine government is also apprehensive that the grant of autonomy to the MNLF would go against the interests of the majority community in many ways. Christians own much of the land and operate nearly all the industry and commerce that there is in the Southern Philippines. (In 1973, Muslims possessed only 17 per cent of the total cultivable lands in the island of Mindanao and Sulu archipelago). Many Christian businessmen, military and civil officials, and, of course, the Christian priests, do not take kindly to the idea of living in an autonomous Muslim region. Many Christians also retain a lingering distrust of their Muslim neighbours and feel that being backward the Muslims do not understand land ownership and management, or business ethics.[7]

Such an uncompromising attitude has only embittered the relations between the Christian and the Muslim communities. MNLF has intensified guerrilla warfare and it is reported that 100 Philippine soldiers are killed every day in action against the MNLF forces.[8] Early in January 1977, President Marcos himself admitted that there had been 10,000 civilian casualties in the last four years, with 500,000 people having been rendered homeless. Casualties among armed personnel are estimated at between 4,000 and 5,000. It is difficult to quantify losses in fiscal terms, but one estimate puts the cost of the conflict to the government at Peso 2 million (US $272,000) a day. The present conflict has tied down about 10,000 Philippine troops, including the civil home defence forces. The Philippine army has even been using 105 millimetre and 155 millimetre Howitzers and Patton tanks, backed by bombing and strafing raids by the air force, to control the hostile activities of the MNLF.[9] Indeed, the relations between the two communities have worsened to an extent where return to normalcy seems to be nowhere in sight. Many factors are responsible for this problem and for examining its genesis, it is necessary to discuss its historical perspective.

Muslims, who have a cultural gap with the Christians and have different religion, history, customs and traditions, have been resisting the Christian domination of the Philippines for the last several centuries.[10] The United States, which had colonized the Philippines, had exploited the existence of such sentiments to its advantage, and tried to divide the two traditional communities of the Philippines into two groups. With that express object in mind, the United States signed a treaty with the Sultan of Sulu and offered him the status of a separate power. Accordingly, a special "Moro Province" was created for the Muslim Filipinos. The Muslim community gradually began to follow the American line and began to oppose the idea of independence for the Philippines on the ground that the Muslims would never submit to the rule of a government led by the Christians in the Philippines. In 1926, Robert Bacon, the member of the House of Representatives in the United States, introduced a bill in the US Congress, proposing to separate Sulu and Mindanao from the Philippines and have the United States permanently retain those islands under American sovereignty. However, those bills could not secure the approval of the US Congress. At the end of the Second World War, when the United States indicated its readiness to grant independence to the Philippines, the Filipino Muslims again raised their voice against such a decision. Even on the eve of the US Congressional Act granting independence to the Philippines, a mass meeting of the Muslim Datus (leaders) sent a petition to the US President and Congress which said:

> Because we have learned that the US is going to give the Philippines independence, we want to tell you that the Philippines is populated by two different peoples with different religious practices and traditions. The Christian Filipinos occupy the islands of Luzon and the Visayas. The Moros predominate in the islands of Mindanao and Sulu. With regard to the forthcoming independence, we foresee what condition we and our children who shall come after us will be in. This condition will be characterised by unrest, suffering and misery. Our Christian associates have for many years shown their

> desire to be the only ones blessed with leadership and with progressive towns, without sharing with us the advantage of having good towns and cities. Their provinces progress by leaps and bounds while ours are left behind.
>
> Should the American people grant the Philippine independence, the islands of Mindanao and Sulu must not be included in such grant. Our public lands must not be given to the people other than the Moros. We should be given time to acquire them because most of us have no lands.[11]

This petition had little impact on majority of the members of the US Congress which approved the bill to grant independence to the Philippines. The leaders of the newly-independent Philippines were mostly Christians who were more than willing to uproot the very foundations on which the Muslim claims for autonomy were based. During the tenure of President Magsaysay, a Resettlement Act was passed, its primary aim being to help the Christian community to settle in the areas dominated by the Muslims. The Philippine government not only encouraged mass emigration of the Christians from the overcrowded north to outnumber the Muslims in the south, but also provided massive aid and assistance to the Christian community to settle in the areas where the Muslims were in the majority. The continuous influx of the Christian settlers in the south soon upset the political power balance in the region. In 1960, there were 370,000 Christians and 650,000 Muslims in the Cotabato area (Mindanao); by 1970, the number of Christians swelled to over 750,000. It is in this context that the Mindanao Development Authority held that the continuing dispossession of their ancestral landholdings by the Christian migrant groups was the main reason for the Muslim unrest in that region.[12]

By the end of the sixties, Muslims began to pose a serious threat to the government. In 1968, the Muslims of Mindanao founded Mindanao Independence Movement, at the initiative of former Muslim Governor of Cotabato, Datu Udtog Matalam. Subsequently, there followed a spate of atrocities and massacres in Mindanao perpetrated by both the Muslim and Christian extremists and security forces.[13]

Around this period, Muslim discontent got aggravated by the widely circulated story of the Jabidah massacre when a Muslim military unit, allegedly being trained by Manila for operations in neighbouring Sabah, was said to have been machinegunned to death by the government troops. The Muslims now accused the Government of the Philippines of supporting genocide against the community.[14] Many established Muslim leaders advocated strongly the Muslim independence movement, and openly encouraged their supporters to fight for secession. In 1970, the "blackshirts" movement—openly believing in acts of violence—was launched in Mindanao to oppose the emigration of numerous Roman Catholics from the north who were believed to have taken over lands from the Muslims in the south. The confrontation became so serious that President Marcos had to order a ceasefire on 26 February 1971, in order to find a peaceful solution to the conflict which threatened to lead to a demand for secession. However, the situation took an ugly turn on 19 June, when an armed group of Christians massacred 61 Muslims, including 29 women and 13 children in a mosque in Cotabato province where the Muslims had been made to assemble to await the beginning of a peace conference with Christians. Consequently, the Muslim organizations sent a memorandum to the United Nations accusing their own government of perpetrating genocide and persecution of religious minorities.[15] This only infuriated the government forces, and on 10 August 1971, the military command sent an ultimatum to the followers of the "blackshirts" movement to surrender within a week. Though Baugon Atatuk, the spokesman of the "blackshirts", agreed to negotiate, the unrest continued, and regular skirmishes between the Muslims and the government forces were reported.

In September 1972, President Marcos declared martial law; the situation in the southern Philippines, however, deteriorated further. By November, evidence was mounting that considerable supplies of arms were arriving on the island of Jolo as well as Tawi-Tawi group of islands.[16] In December a full scale attack was launched by the Muslim rebels at Jolo and Tawi-Tawi. On 26 December, Francisco S. Tatad, the Secretary of Information, conceded that the authorities were faced with a secessionist movement which controlled several villages in Mindanao. In Sulu, Zamboanga Del Sur, Zamboanga del Norte, Lanao del Sur and in Cotabato del Norte, the rebels seized control of most of the countryside and used classic guerrilla tactics of encircling the urban centres and cutting the roads, of ambush and withdrawal, of surprise attack and mobility. They had a vital underground supplementary force among their sympathizers, whom the armed forces were unable to isolate. The confrontations were always uneven as the rebels knew the terrain and could exploit that to their strategic advantage. On the other hand, most of the government soldiers were strangers from other islands who had little knowledge of the local dialect.[17]

President Marcos called some 300 Muslim leaders at the Presidential Palace on 3 January 1973 to settle the Muslim problem. These included Muslim members of the Congress and the members of the constitutional convention, Governors, Mayors and representatives of prominent Muslim groups, among them the Udtog Matalam faction. Marcos proposed to promote tourism in southern Philippines by extending the Zamboanga airport runway to accommodate commercial jet airliners, directing the Economic Development Authority to shift industries from northern Philippines, which are exposed to frequent typhoons, to the south, lifting of customs restrictions and offering credit facilities to encourage barter trade with Malaysian and Indonesian Borneo.[18] He also offered selective amnesty for the Muslim rebels, and urged the Muslim leaders to eschew violence and adopt peaceful means to solve their problems. Further, he agreed to divert a substantial portion of the US $200 million foreign loans for social development to Mindanao and Sulu. A total of 68 million pesos was budgeted for public works projects in the two provinces during the fiscal year 1972-73. An Associated Press report of 13 April 1973 stated that the Government was seeking US $524 million in international aid for the rehabilitation of Muslim areas.[19]

However, these measures failed to pacify the militant Muslims. Following the failure of President Marcos' efforts to find an amicable solution to the Muslim problem, the Philippine armed forces deployed the army and navy against the dissidents. The Chief of Staff, General Romeo Espino, criticized the soft attitude of President Marcos towards the Muslim rebels and expressed his willingness to seek a military solution to the problem.[20] It was now decided by the government that a special task force should be formed to assess the situation in the south. Consequently, a task force, headed by Alejandro Melchor, Presidential Executive Secretary, was formed and entrusted with carrying out the following functions:

(*i*) To make an immediate assessment of the damage brought on private property and government facilities, services and establishments;

(*ii*) To identify and mobilize all resources of funds, and prepare an integrated plan for the reconstruction and rehabilitation of Mindanao in the context of the national development programme; and

(*iii*) To restore peace and order by military operations, apprehend rebellious leaders and implement a selective amnesty and rehabilitation programme.[21]

The establishment of such a task force only served to intensify the militant mood of the Muslims. In September 1973, the Defence Secretary, Juan Ponce Enrile, gave official figures for one year of fighting in southern Mindanao as 3,560 rebels killed, 341 wounded and 195 captured, while government lossess were given as 271 dead, 424 wounded and 32 missing. In December 1973, the rebels launched a massive attack on the town of Cotabato. Consequently, about 10,000 people were reported to have fled their homes and according to the Philippine Red Cross, about 4,000 people had been evacuated from Tuluman and Colombio while 2,000 people were said to have left M'lang and President Roxas for the Red Cross Centres.[22] Subsequently, there were pitched battles between the MNLF and government forces at Jolo, Cotabato, Zamboanga, Dinaig, Upi, Malabagan and Basilan. The Government was able to partially retrieve the situation by calling its armed forces and resorting to severe measures like bombing and strafing of areas under the MNLF control. Hostilities, however, continued unabated.

In yet another bid to appease the MNLF, President Marcos agreed on 21 April 1975 to integrate the Muslim rebels into the nation's armed forces, and ordered the formation of a Muslim engineer's battalion. He also announced the establishment of two regional offices in Mindanao and Sulu under Muslims who would take over government administration in the area, the dismissal of three provincial governors and two mayors in the south, and the allocation of US $27,000,000 for development projects in Mindanao.[23] On 17 October 1975, President Marcos ordered that regular army units be moved out of Lanao province to placate the Muslims who were angry at the assassination of a mayor and some other citizens.[24]

These conciliatory gestures failed to defuse the tense situation, as any government measure aimed at reforms in the south continued to be viewed with great suspicion by the Muslims. As the major part of the national resources, which are so vital for modernization programmes, are spent in controlling the Muslim rebels, the government is anxious to find out a long-term solution of this crisis. Therefore, when some of the West Asian countries showed their eagerness to solve this problem, President Marcos readily agreed to negotiate with the MNFL leaders. The talks started on 15 December 1976 in Tripoli (Libya) between the Philippine delegation led by Carmelo Barbero, under secretary of Defence for Civil Affairs, and Nur Misuari, the MNLF chairman, under the auspices of Libya, Somalia, Senegal and Saudi Arabia. A tentative peace agreement in principle was reached on 23 December 1976 and a cease-fire ordered on the next day.[25] A copy of the agreement published on 5 January 1977 stated that immediately after the signing of the final agreement in Manila, a provisional government, to be appointed by the President of the Philippines, would be established in the autonomous area. It would be charged with the task of paving the way for the conduct of elections to a legislative assembly in the autonomous territory, and administering the area until a government was formed by the elected legislative assembly.[26] The document also laid down that the questions to be discussed at future talks would be: the relationship between the Muslim and national administrations and economic and financial systems; Muslim representation in the central government; the regional security force; the question of a Muslim section in the national armed forces; Muslim education; and sharing of revenue from the region's resources between the regional and central government.[27] President Marcos stated on 24 December that the ceasefire which would be gradually implemented by 20 January 1977, would be supervised by a commission comprising equal number of members of the Philippine and MNLF representatives as well as by a four-nation committee from Libya, Somalia, Senegal and Saudi Arabia. He further stated in a Press conference on 27 December 1976 that it was proposed to establish a regional legislative assembly, an executive council and special Muslim courts, all of which would, however, remain under the overall control of the national government. Preliminary agreement had also been reached on the formation of a regional security force which would remain under the supervision of the national security forces. The President added further that the talks on the details of the Tripoli which would remain under the supervision of the national security forces. The President added further that the talks on the details of the Tripoli agreement would be held in Libya in early February 1977, with a view to a final settlement.[28]

Meanwhile, a dramatic development took place in the Philippines. The Government in a surprise move decided to hold a plebiscite in the southern part of the country, which President Marcos claimed was constitutionally valid, to know whether the people of the area wanted to be under MNLF control or not. President Marcos ordered the plebiscite to be held in all the 13 southern provinces for which there was a demand for autonomy. Initially, he gave only one week's time to the election commission to hold the plebiscite. Marcos indicated that the plebiscite would be held on a province-by-province basis, but made it clear that if the results showed that only the five Muslim provinces (Basilan, Lanao del Sur, Maguindanao, Sulu and Tawi-Tawi) wanted autonomy, it would be difficult for the governement to co-ordinate the region administratively, because Lanao del Sur and Maguindanao on the island of Mindanao were to the northeast of the other three provinces, which encompassed scattered groups of islands.[29]

The MNLF leaders took strong objection to the government's sudden call for a plebiscite. As the Christians outnumber the Muslims in the provinces of the south (excluding five provinces), the leaders of the MNLF were not willing to accept such a measure. The MNLF said that it would boycott the plebiscite, because such a measure had not been discussed by them at the Tripoli peace talks. Misuari, the MNLF Chairman, further declared that if Marcos went ahead with a plebiscite, fighting in the south would recommence.[30]

The government went ahead with its plan to hold a plebiscite. The Philippine panel leader at the peace talks in Tripoli, Carmelo Barbero, now included the provision for plebiscite in the proposal for autonomous Muslim provinces that he submitted in February 1977. This said that an autonomous region including the 13 southern provinces would be set up provided that, in accordance with the provisions of the Constitution, the organization of the said provinces, cities and villages into one autonomous region was ratified by the majority of the qualified voters in the region in a referendum which would be called for the purpose. It was for the first time in Tripoli that the Manila panel stipulated that the controversial plebiscite was a prerequisite to the formation of a single autonomous region. This proposal explained that if the majority of the voters were against the idea, the two existing administrative regions covering 10 of the

13 provinces would remain, but with a limited degree of autonomy. This autonomy, in line with President Marcos' earlier announced plans for nation-wide autonomy, would entail an elected regional assembly with powers mainly to legislate on development within the national framework. The government's proposal was that a regional executive council would be recommended to the President for appointment. Taxation would be monitored by the central government, which would also be responsible for defence and security—although members of the local front groups (presumably the MNLF) could become members of the Philippines' armed forces and police, subject to control by Manila.[31] On the other hand, Tevetoglu, the spokesman of the MNLF, put forward his counter-proposal calling for virtually a separate state in the south. It called for an autonomous Islamic region with Zamboanga city as the capital and a provisional autonomous government organized by the central committee. This government would decide on representation in a *Majlis As-shura* (regional assembly) which would then elect a *Majilis Al-Tanfeezi* (regional executive council) and a Chief Minister who would then appoint a cabinet. But the appointment of the Chief Minister, it was made clear, would require the agreement of the MNLF central committee. Tevetoglu's proposal also recommended a regional security force headed by a Major-General, comprising members of the MNLF's Bangsa Moro Army and absorbing Philippine constabulary and other para-military units on a selective basis.[32]

Tevetoglu's proposal was not acceptable to the Philippine Government team and the talks ended in a virtual stalemate. The Government of the Philippines after postponing the holding of a plebiscite twice, finally went ahead with it in all the 13 provinces of the south on 17 April 1977. Voters were asked whether they wished to merge into the autonomous region and also to approve or reject proposals for the following on an accompanying "remark sheet":

(*i*) complete control by the MNLF of the administration in the autonomous area;

(*ii*) the region's own flag and official language;

(*iii*) the naming of the region as the autonomous Bangsa Moro Islamic Region and its inhabitants as the Bangsa Moro;

(*iv*) the granting to the region the power of legislation on general matters including taxation, similar to that of the national government;

(*v*) the region's own court of appeals and supreme court;
(*vi*) organizing of a security force by the MNLF separate from and outside the supervision of the national security forces;
(*vii*) the election of Chief Minister and Deputy Chief Minister of the executive council of the region by the regional legislative assembly with the agreement of the MNLF central committee, the Chief Minister to be also commander of the regional security force;
(*viii*) the auditing of the region's accounts by a regional commission only, and not by the national commission on audit as provided by the Constitution; and
(*ix*) supervision of the regional administration by the national government.

The MNLF predictably boycotted the referendum, on the ground that no such consultation had been provided under the first Tripoli agreement. The results of the plebiscite showed that a great majority of the southern population rejected the plea for autonomy. The official results issued by the Commission on Election on 23 April showed that 97.93 per cent of the total votes cast in the 13 provinces rejected autonomy for the region under MNLF rule (about 75 per cent of the 4,025,000 registered voters had cast their votes). According to official figures, only about 3,000,000 out of the total population of some 6,500,000 in the 13 provinces were Muslims, whereas the MNLF put the Muslim population at 5,000,000.[33]

The leaders of the MNLF criticized the manner in which the plebiscite was held. In a separate Press conference on 1 May 1977, Islamic Conference Secretary-General, Amadoe Karim Gaye, and the Philippine Foreign Secretary, Carlos Romulo, announced that the talks between the MNLF and the Philippine Government had collapsed.

Since the breakdown of the negotiations, the Defence Secretary, Juan Ponce Enrile, and many of the generals have been pressing for a military solution to the conflict in the south. He has stated:

> It is futile to hope for a negotiated settlement to the conflict. The time has passed for new talks with either rebel leader Nur Misuari or with former mediators from the Islamic Conference, at least in the foreseeable future. Knowing the intentions of Misuari and his group, I believe that it is futile to expect a peaceful settlement of this problem, although, of course, we will still

> attempt to exhaust all possible peaceful approaches. I am not optimistic. I consider it a very dim possibility.[34]

The Muslim insurgency has meanwhile continued to linger in the south. The Government of the Philippines has accused the MNLF of violating the so-called ceasefire agreement 300 times from December 1976 to December 1977. On the other hand, the MNLF has claimed that the army had broken the agreement 703 times in which over 600 people had been killed.

It is a well-known fact that the Philippine Government is determined to suppress the Muslim rebellion in the south by any means. As the number of the Christians exceeds that of the Muslims and as business, industries and agriculture in the south are in the hands of the Christians, no government in power in the Philippines will go out of its way to support the demands of the MNLF. Some of the Muslim, leaders are aware of this. Abulkayer Alonto, the first vice-chairman of the MNLF, and Hashim Salamat of the same organization as well as Rashid Lucman, former Philippine Congressmen from the Muslim community, are some of the people who are not supporting the hard-line followed by Misuari.[35] Hashim Salamat is belived to have been supported by Egypt, which favours a negotiated settlement of the Muslim problem. Salamat is in contact with Rashid Lucman, the head of Bangsa Moro Liberation Organization (BMLO), based in Saudi Arabia.[36] However, Misuari, who is strongly backed by Libya, does not see eye to eye with the leaders advocating a moderate line to solve the problem. In April 1978, he proposed to the Philippine Government the following four conditions for the reopening of the peace talks:

(*i*) The Tripoli Agreement of December 1976 regarding Muslim autonomy and cease-fire should be implemented;

(*ii*) The peace talks between the MNLF and the Philippine Government should be held under the auspices of the Islamic Conference;

(*iii*) Those talks should be held outside the Philippines;

(*iv*) The peace talks should be preceded by the ending of military operations against the MNLF in the southern Philippines.[37]

At present, there is no likelihood of any of these conditions being accepted by the Government of the Philippines, and there is thus every possibility that the insurgency in the south will continue unabated for the foreseeable future.

Muslims in Thailand

Muslims constitute about four per cent of the total population of Thailand. Thai Muslims may be divided into two categories, the Malays and the non-Malays; Malays form the majority, while the Thai, Pakistanis, Indians and Chinese and others of Muslim faith constitute roughly 20 per cent of the Thai Islamic population. About four-fifths of Thailand's Muslims are Malays living in South Thailand. The smallest region, with 27,000 square miles in 14 peninsular provinces, South Thailand contains somewhat less than 14 per cent of the country's area and about 12 per cent of its people. This region, however, produces over 90 per cent of the country's natural rubber and practically all of its tin. Muslims also grow rice and fruits such as coconut, rambustan, and durian. Most of the Thai Muslims earn their livelihood through some combination of rice farming and coconut growing (this region grows two thirds of the country's coconut palms). Most of them are self-employed, working on their small land holdings where they frequently plant rubber; some also work as tappers on the rubber plantations owned by the Chinese.

The great bulk of the Muslims are concentrated in the Changwats (provinces) of Pattani, Yala, Setul and Narathiwat, directly adjacent to the northern part of peninsular Malaysia. The Muslims constitute 78 per cent of the total population of Pattani, 61 per cent of the total population of Yala, 78 per cent of the total population of Narathiwat and 83 per cent of the total population of Setul.[38] Their history, language and culture are different from those of the Thai Buddhists, but match closely to those of the Malays situated across the border in the peninsular Malaysia.

The pattern of society in the four southern Changwats is such that the Muslims feel alienated from the Thai mainstream. Muslims are separately situated, away from the Buddhist inhabitation. The Thais and the Chinese are mainly situated in the cities, whereas the Muslims are situated in the countryside. They are mainly farmers and labourers. Their social activities, till recently, were confined to a visit to the mosque and the Islamic schools known as *pawno* (there are 335 *pawnos* in Pattani, 83 in Yala, 16 in Setul and 78 in Narathiwat). Study of Islam, Malay and Arabic offered by the village *pawno* takes precedence over secular education which is run by the government schools.[39]

The Thai kingdom, where about 93 per cent of the population is Buddhist, has not proved sufficiently sympathetic towards the religious and linguistic differences with the Muslims in the south. Muslims are very much interested in retaining the essence of their traditional culture and fear that the Thai Government is trying to assimilate them by changing their local systems, institutions, language and religion. It was in this context that on 3 April 1947, the Malays in Pattani, headed by Haji Sulong and a few others, presented a set of seven demands to the Interior Minister, with a copy to the Premier, Luang Thamrong Navaswasdi. These demands included, *inter alia:*

(*i*) The appointment of a single individual with full powers to govern the four provinces of Pattani, Yala, Narathiwat and Setul and in particular having authority to dismiss any individual, to be local in one of the four provinces and to be elected by the people;
(*ii*) Eighty per cent of the government servants in the four provinces to be Muslims;
(*iii*) Malay and Thai to be the official languages;
(*iv*) Malay to be the medium of instruction in the primary schools;
(*v*) Muslim law to be recognized and enforced in a separate Muslim court other than the civil court where the one time Kathi sat as born assessor;
(*vi*) All revenue and income derived from the four provinces to be utilised within them; and
(*vii*) The formation of a Muslim Board having full powers to direct all Muslim affairs under the supreme authority of the head of state mentioned in (*i*).[40]

The immediate reaction of the government was cool, but the then Prime Minister showed some sympathy for the problems of Muslims in the south. The government was not, however, ready to sit with the Muslims and seek a solution to their grievances. The Muslims went on emphasizing the importance of the knowledge of Islamic religion, the history of Muslim Sultenates, and the Malay language. They continued to refer to the grandeur of the history of Pattani, and made great efforts to cultivate a sense of nationalism in the minds of the four southern Changwats by underlining the fact that their forefathers (including their Muslim rulers) had been defeated and humiliated by the Thai kings and that they had consequently been deprived of their freedom. They also used Islam, their religion, for making a common cause to struggle with the Thai administration for attaining autonomy or complete independence.

The majority of the Muslims are now advocating secession from Thailand. By and large, the Muslim secessionists base their claims mainly on their legitimacy as a separate ethnic community. They are broadly divided into three categories. One group favours a separate administrative unit within a federation with Thailand. The other group wants an independent state under a Sultan, and the third advocates a single independent state of Pattani. The first group seems to be popular among the older generation of the Thai Muslims, whereas the second and the third group is popular among the younger generation.

The second and the third separatist group maintain that they must have full independence, for they constitute a separate race with their own religion. These two groups view the Thai administration as a colonial institution which exploits them and their natural resources. They argue that there is no basis for a compromise with the Thai central government; and stress upon gaining independence through armed struggle, including guerrilla warfare. In 1969, the rebellion in the four southern provinces gathered a new momentum, when the Muslims established "Barisan National Pembebasan Republik Patani," BNPRP (National Liberation Front of the Pattani Republic), under the leadership of Tengku Abdul Jalal, which in turn launched "Tentera National Pembebasan Rak'yet Patani" TNPRP (National Liberation Army of the Pattani People). According to Bapa Idris, the official leader of the TNPRP, the struggle to free Pattani cannot be achieved by spreading flowers, but only by flying bullets.[41] TNPRP was divided into groups of 10 to 25 men, each under different leaders. It consists of people recruited from Pattani, Yala, Narathiwat and Setul. TNPRP has been making Press statements and distributing messages and newsletters in the villages. It has also tried to indoctrinate the inhabitants with a spirit of nationalism and urges hostility against the Thai rule.

The guerrillas of the Pattani Liberation Front are mostly located in the Pesisir Gunong Budo Hill area in the tri-border region of Yala, Narathiwat and Pattani provinces. The Front occasionally conducts ambushes and attacks police installations to obtain weapons, and sometimes uses terrorism to remind both the government and the villages of their existence. But routine operations seem confined to extortion, conducting road blocks, kidnapping for ransom, and closing the rubber plantations in order to collect funds for further strengthening of the organization.[42]

The Communist Party of Thailand (CPT) has recently announced the formation of the Muslim Liberation Army of Thailand (MLAT) under CPT leadership. The Party's clandestine radio station has said that the MLAT endorsed Marxism, Leninism and Mao Tse-tung's thoughts, advocated the rights of nationalities and autonomy under the big family of the Thai nation, and would work towards the Thai revolution.[43]

The Thai Government has so far failed to curb effectively the activities of the Pattani Liberation Front. At the same time, it has taken some decisions which has led to further reservations about the Thai rule in the minds of the Muslims in the south. The nature and functioning of the Thai bureaucracy in the south may be cited as an example. The administrators who rule over the Muslim provinces in the south are recruited and trained in Bangkok. They are ignorant of the local language, culture and customs, and as they are transferred to other provinces every three years, they care even less to know much about them. On the other hand, the Government of Thailand installs several huge Buddha images in the Muslim areas which is suspected to be a ploy to lead those areas towards religious assimilation. Though the centre exploits the huge resources of the area, it has done comparatively little for improving the lifestyle of the people in the south.[44] While it is a fact that the Thai Government is not as aggressive against the Muslim rebels as the Government of the Philippines is against the Filipino Muslims, there is no doubt that the determination of the Thai Government to annihilate secessionist movements is just as pronounced as that of the Philippine Government.

Some Conclusions

The Muslim problem in the Philippines and Thailand poses threats to the process of nation-building in those countries. The genesis of this problem might be traced to the orthodox nature of the Islamic religion. The human agents of change and institutions of social engineering that impart direction to the process of nation-building, include two sets of variables. It embraces the actions and attitudes of political leaders, including political activists operating at lower levels as commuters between society and polity, and other specialized elites and publicmen who participate in the process of nation-building. Relevant here are the strategies and styles that these various agents devise in response to different exigencies of support mobilization, involving, on the one hand, reconciliation between the dominant developmental aspirations of the national community at large as perceived by them, and, on the other hand, the aspirations and interests of the strata they themselves represent, as exemplified by their values and their perception of their own roles. Secondly, this includes deliberately enacted organizational forms and institutions through which goals of national development are to be achieved. These deliberately devised agencies of change refer to the institutional apparatuses of centralized planning, structures of local governmental administration, political parties and the like.[45]

The motivation of the human agents of change and social engineering is basically to protect the interests of the people at large. If a small minority threatens the interests of the majority community, it will be the occupation of those agents to protect the interests of the victims. They will try to contain the sources of strength available to the rebels. In this process, they may adopt either democratic or dictatorial measures. In the case of the Philippines and Thailand, the Muslim minority appears to have threatened the interests of the majority community. Thus, the main concern of the human agents of change and social engineering has been to protect the interests of the majority community; that means the protection of the interests of the Christians in the Philippines and that of the Buddhists in Thailand, who constitute more than 90 per cent of the total population in both the countries, respectively.

It is natural that the majority community will enjoy certain privileges in any society. Those privileges are constitutional and also extra-constitutional. For instance, take the case of Malaysia, an Islamic state. Its 1957 Constitution safeguards the future economic and political position of the Malay population. It says that the head of the Malayan federation would be known as the Yang di-Pertuan Agong. He would be elected for a term of 5 years by the Malay Rulers from among their numbers. He would appoint the Perdana Mentri (Prime Minister). He would also appoint the Cabinet on the advice of the Perdana Mentri. It is also mentioned that the head of state, acting on the advice of the Cabinet, would have responsibility for reserving to the Malays a reasonable number of positions in the public service, education, business life, etc. It would rest with the various state rulers to keep just balance between the Malays and the non-Malays. Moreover, the Constitution had further laid down that the Malay land reservations could only be cancelled if the Legislative Assembly agreed to such action by a majority of its members and by votes of not less than two-thirds of the members present and voting.

The Constitution of the Philippines is secular in outlook and Thailand's state religion is Buddhism. As such, in both these countries, there is no constitutional discrimination between the majority and minority communities unlike Malaysia, an Islamic State, where the rights of the Malays have been safeguarded by its Constitution. Thus, the important factor for generating Muslim discontent in these countries may be the slow pace of modernization in the areas inhabited by them in the Philippines and Thailand. As a matter of fact, there is not only paucity of roads, a shortage of schools and hospitals and inadequate transport facilities, but there is also a weak infrastructure to support the day-to-day needs in the southern parts of both the countries. But this alone may not be a compulsion for launching rebellion against the government. In this context, the support of some Islamic countries to the Muslims minorities is quite pertinent. The appeal of the Islamic brotherhood is so strong that some of the Islamic countries do not hesitate to meddle in the affairs of other states to protect the interests of Islamic faith. In recent years, Libya has come out openly to aid and assist the Muslim secessionist movement in the Philippines and Thailand.

If the MNLF in the Philippines or PLF in Thailand at some point attain their objective through the means that they have adopted, it may have its impact on the region as a whole. Almost every country in the region has some problems regarding their minorities, who may then get moral strength to raise their voice for secessionist movements. It is natural that the minorities will be having a separate history, religion, customs, and traditions, but it need not be used as a pretext for secessionist movements. Moreover, the division of the country on the basis of religion need not necessarily lead to the ideal solution of such type of problems.

To sum up, Muslim insurgency in the Philippines and Thailand is likely to continue in the coming future, and unless there is a revision in the demands of the rebels and a readjustment of their conflicting interests, there is a bleak prospect indeed for finding a long-term solution of this crisis.

REFERENCES

1. An integral part of the medieval Muslim belief system which continues to receive fervent adherence in our own time is that the Muslims, as recipients of God's guidance through the Prophet, constitute a chosen community charged with the task of living according to divine injunctions and spreading the message of God among the non-Muslim humanity, who have forgotten, misread or distorted it. The Muslims, according to their self-view, constitute a charismatic community. Since their religion is perfect, they have been declared the best community and their Prophet is the last messenger of God. See Gopal Krishna, "Piety and Politics in Indian Islam," in T.N. Madan, ed., *Muslim Communities of South Asia,* New Delhi, 1975, p. 144. For the study of Muslims, see Watt W. Montgomery, *Islam and the Integration of Society,* London, 1961 and *Islamic Political Thought,* Edinburg, 1968, and F. Rahman, *Islam,* London, 1966, E.I.J., Rosenthal, *Political Thought in Medieval Islam,* Cambridge, 1958, A.J. Wensinck, *The Muslim Creed,* London, 1965, Clifford Geertz, *Islam Observed,* London, 1968, H.A.R. Gibb, *Studies on the Civilisation of Islam,* London, 1962 and T. Izutsu, *God and Men in the Koran,* Tokyo, 1964.
2. *Far Eastern Economic Review,* Hong Kong, Vol. 84, No. 25, 24 June 1974, p. 32.
3. Brian Phelan, "The Philippines : Spectre of Jihad," *ibid.,* Vol. 80, No. 19, 14 May 1973, p. 29.
4. "Continued Muslim Unrest in the Philippines," *Asia Research Bulletin,* Singapore, Vol. 2, No. 12, May 1973, p. 1758.
5. J.S. Barry, "The Philippines : Why the Roads are not safe Anymore," *Far Eastern Economic Review,* Vol. 81, No. 26, 2 July 1973, p. 22.
6. Rodney Tasker, "The Philippines : Autonomy Telethon," *ibid.,* Vol. 96, No. 14, 8 April 1977, pp. 8-9.
7. Rodney Tasker, "Peace Pact : Christians Concerned," *ibid.,* Vol. 95, No. 6, 11 April 1977, p. 13.
8. Abul Khyr Alonto, Vice-Chairman of the MNLF, said this in an interview, *ibid.,* Vol. 88, No. 26, 27 June 1975, pp. 22-23.
9. Fabio Mucci and Massimo Quinque, "Minorities : Manila's Misery," *ibid.,* p. 21, and Rodney Tasker, "The Moro Rebellion : Who calls the Shots," *ibid.,* Vol. 95, No. 2, 14 January 1977, pp. 18-19.
10. Wilfredo F. Arce, "Social Organisation of the Muslim People in Sulu," in Frank Lynch, ed., *Sulu's People and Their Art,* Quezon city, 1963, p. 17 and also see, Peter Gowing. *Mosque and Moro : A Study of Muslims in the Philippines,* Manila, 1964 and Delor F. Angeles, *Mindanao : the Story of an Island,* Davao City, 1964 and Leon M. Guerrero, *Encounter of Cultures : The Muslims in the Philippines,* Manila, 1972.
11. T.J.S. George, "The Philippines: A Good Idea at the Time," *Far Eastern Economic Review,* Vol. 79, No. 12, 26 March 1973, pp. 14-15.

12. Hans Luther, "Background to the Muslim Secessionist Movement in the Philippines," *Asia Research Bulletin*, Vol. 3, No. 10, 3 March 1974, pp. 2519-22 and also see Man Mohini Kaul, "Muslims in the Philippines," *Institute of Defence Studies and Analysis Journal*, New Delhi, Vol. X, No. 1, July-September 1977, pp. 26-37; Pushpesh Pant, "Communal Violence and Secessionist Insurgency in the Philippines," *ibid.*, Vol. V, No. 4, April 1973, pp. 528-42; Chester L. Hunt, "Muslim and Christian in the Philippines," *Pacific Affairs*, Richmond, Va., Vol. 28, No. 4, December 1955, pp. 331-49 and Bhagwan Das Arora, "Insurgency in the Southern Philippines: Domestic and Foreign Implications," *Foreign Affairs Reports*, New Delhi, Vol. 24, No. 11, November 1975, pp. 179-94.
13. Tasker, n. 9.
14. *Ibid.*
15. *New York Times* and *Time*, London, as cited in *Keesing's Contemporary Archives*, Bristol, 1-8 May 1971, p. 24580.
16. Judy Stowe, "The Philippines: Three Dimensional Muslims," *Far Eastern Economic Review*, Vol. 80, No. 24, 18 June 1973, p. 25.
17. Phelan, n. 3, p. 29.
18. *New York Times*, 14 April 1973 and also see, *Keesing's Contemporary Archives*, 5-11 March 1973, p. 25763.
19. *Asia Research Bulletin*, n. 4, p. 1758.
20. *Ibid.*
21. *Ibid.*
22. *Far Eastern Economic Review*, Vol. 83, No. 12, 25 March 1974, pp. 12-13.
23. *New York Times*, 22 April 1975 and *Bulletin Today*, Manila, 22 April 1975.
24. *Philippine Daily Express*, Manila, 18 October 1975 and *New York Times*, 18 October 1975.
25. Rodney Tasker, "The Philippines: Marcos Moves closer to a Southern Peace," *Far Eastern Economic Review*, Vol. 95, No. 1, 7 January 1977, pp. 24-28, and *Philippine Daily Express*, 6 January 1977.
26. *Ibid.*
27. *Ibid.*
28. *New York Times*, 28 December 1976.
29. Rodney Tasker, "The Philippines: Plebiscite for the South," *Far Eastern Economic Review*, Vol. 95, No. 8, 25 February 1977, p. 23.
30. Rodney Tasker, "Muslim Peace Talks Run Aground," *ibid.*, Vol. 95, No. 1, 4 March 1977, p. 8.
31. *Ibid.*, "Imelda Tries to Keep Peace," *ibid.*, Vol. 96, No. 13, 1 April 1977, p. 12.
32. *Ibid.*
33. *Bulletin Today*, Manila, 24 April 1977, and Rodney Tasker, "The Philippines: Uneasy Peace After the Plebiscite," *ibid.*, Vol. 96, No. 17, 29 April 1977, p. 9.

34. Rodney Tasker, "The Philippines: Words of Peace Futile," *Far Eastern Economic Review,* Vol. 98, No. 47, 25 November 1977, p. 27.
35. Rodney Tasker, "Marcos Tries to Split the Rebels," *Far Eastern Economic Review,* Vol. 99, No. 6, 19 February 1978, pp. 21-22 and *ibid.,* Vol. 100, No. 15, 14 April 1978, p. 5.
36. *Ibid.*
37. Rodney Tasker, "The Philippines: A New Peace Initiative," *ibid.,* Vol. 100, No. 14, 7 April 1978, pp. 16-17.
38. Nantawan Haemindra, "The Problem of Thai Muslims in the Four Southern Provinces of Thailand (Part one)," *Journal of Southeast Aisan Studies* (Singapore), Vol. VII, No. 2, September 1976, p. 198.
39. For details see Police Colonel Gampanat Chintavirot, *Notes on the Separatist Movement in the South,* Bangkok, 1974.
40. Haemindra, n. 38, p. 208.
41. Nantawan Haemindra, "The Problem of Thai Muslims in the Four Southern Provinces of Thailand (Part 2)," *Journal of Southeast Asian Studies,* Vol. VIII, No. 1, March 1977, pp. 85-105.
42. *Ibid.,* pp. 85-105.
43. *Far Eastern Economic Review,* Vol. 100, No. 15, 14 April 1978, p. 5.
44. A team of Thai Scholars, including Dr. Chai Anan Samudvaniji, Dr. Suchit Boonbongkorn and Dr. Sombat Chantounwongse, of the Faculty of Political Science, Chulalongkorn University, Bangkok, spoke about these problems in a talk at the School of International Studies, Jawaharlal Nehru University, New Delhi, 20 April 1978.
45. D.L. Sheth, "Application of Comparative Political Analysis to the study of Nation Building," in Rajni Kothari, ed., *State and Nation Building: A Third World Perspective,* New Delhi, 1976, pp. 86-87.

7

Vietnam Politics and Society

Vietnam, located adjacent of South China Sea, is an important partner in the Association of Southeast Asian Nations (ASEAN). It is one of the few countries which retains communism as the basic principle of governance but the ideology is not allowed to obstruct the path of economic liberalisation. There is constant reviewing of economic policies to suit the needs of trade, investment and open market. The economic reforms have paid dividends and hence it is a major rice exporting country of the world at par with Thailand and the United States. It is a major force to be reckoned within the calculations of the ASEAN Regional Forum (ARF) and considered important actor to inspire regional cooperation.

Vietnamese Society

Vietnam has a population of about 80 milion people in which ethnic Viets comprise the majority (87 per cent) but Chams, Khmers, Tais, Hoas and Hmongs are also in considerable numbers. Official statistics indicate that there are 53 minority groups thinly spread in the extensive mountanous regions. As Vietnam had been arbitrarily partitioned (1954-1975) into North and South and as they were governed by different ideologies and objectives, the life-style of the people in North and South became incongruous to one another. When the two parts were integrated in 1976, differences at the socio-economic level were apparent. Although the efforts were aimed at socialistic drives in the newly liberated South, but there were little success. The ethnic Chinese (Hoas) in Ho Chi Minh city resisted the policy of nationalisation and resettlement programmes. Thus Hoas were targeted as hostile elements and forced to live at par with the people in the north. Hoas did not accept government orders and decided to quit Vietnam. Hence there was a Hoa exodus to China and ASEAN countries. This was one of the important reasons for Sino-Vietnam War (1979). It is found that southern part of Vietnam is more fertile and has larger concentration of population, and higher level of urbanisation. The largest town of Vietnam is Ho Chi Minh city, followed by Hanoi and Haiphong in terms of population despite the execution of resettlement programme (1975–76). Although 3.5 million people were moved from Saigon to Central Vietnam in 1975–77, the cartography could not change. The greater section of the people in and around Ho Chi Minh city are business-oriented whereas the people in Hanoi are more conscious of ideology. They tend to equate communism with their nationalism and their mindset about their political system are yet to change. However, a section of the people in the south have displayed their preference for liberal democracy to the annoyance of the Communist Party of Vietnam.

Vietnamese Religion

Religionwise Vietnam is influenced by both China and India. Mahayana Buddhism, Taoism and Confucianism have been influencing the society since time immemorial, but the impact of Christianity and Islam have also touched Vietnamese heartlands in the past few centuries. As the government has guaranteed complete freedom of religious beliefs, the places of worship have emerged in different parts of the country. The cult of ancestor worship, practiced in individual households and clan temples had been allowed even when the doctrines of Marxism and Leninism were vigorously implemented. The Unified Buddhist Organisation of Vietnam, the Roman Catholic Church and the Protestent Church have played creative role in the nation-building activities. The religious organisations have also played prominent role in the mass mobilisation for nationalist endeavours. It was the main centre for primary education for decades and it was Vietnamese Buddhist Bhikhus who first had started self-immolation against religious policies of Ngo Dinh Diem and American intervention in Vietnam in 1960s.

Present Politics

The contemporary history of Southeast Asia has testified that the Vietnamese are dynamic in their approach and realistic in their policies. They are pursuing the policy of Doi Moi in their system and consequently political institutions are rapidly reformed to keep pace with the changing world. Hence, the role of the Party, National Assembly, Army, Bureaucracy and the Press have undergone transformations in tune with the democratic trends in the region. Though, the nature and function of the major political institutions are changing but the scrutiny of the changes suggest that the Vietnamese believe in continuity and change. One-party rule of the Communist Party remains but the evolving system has endeavoured to promote democratic way of life without diluting the principle of "dictatorship of the Communist Party."

Nobody can deny that Vietnam remains a communist country, but at the same time they cannot deny that they are cultivating democratic way of life by introducing the features of liberal society, i.e., decentralization, privatization, free trade, etc., to prove that Vietnam is an ideal partner of the Association of Southeast Asian Nations (ASEAN).

Historical Overview

Vietnam has a history of warfare against the Chinese for one thousand years from 111 B.C. till 939 AD. It emerged as a powerful Kingdom in the 13th Century AD after annexing Champa and subduing the Khmers. It lost its sovereignty only after the end of the opium war (1842), when France, as a colonial power, emerged on the Southeast Asian horizon with British support. France colonised Vietnam in 1858, and expanded their rule over Cambodia and Laos, but the Vietnamese did not accept colonial rule gracefully, and continued to struggle against it. Hence, it has a long and chequered history of struggle and warfare against colonialist forces.

The communists under the banner of the Indochina Communist Party (1930-42) and the Vietminh (1942-54) led the freedom movement and defeated the colonial powers. The United States in pursuance of the policy of containment of communism, replaced the French to oppose freedom, and independence of Vietnam in 1954. Ignoring the nationalist nature of the communist movement, the Americans helped the process of temporary partition of Vietnam. It organised and aided anti-communist forces and sent its security forces to defeat communist guerrillas. The US involvement in Vietnam thus started growing and between 1964-75, 7 million tonnes of bombs, three times the tonnage used in World War II, had been dropped on Vietnam. Besides, napalm and phosphorus bombs were also used.

The tragedy of this phenomenon for the US was its defeat. It had to withdraw its forces lock, stock and barrel in April, 1975. Besides, it had to accommodate thousands of Vietnamese refugees in the US. Vietnam war indeed proved very costly for the US, in which the US lost the lives of 56,559 servicemen and an expenditure of US $150 billion. Though millions of Vietnamese also died, but they were victorious finally in defeating the colonial forces and in uniting the two parts of Vietnam under a common political system. The communist ideology worked as a cementing force to unite the people of North and South Vietnam against external enemies.

The Communist Party of Vietnam (CPV) has special status because it led the nationalist movement against France and anti–colonial struggle against the U.S. successfully. Whether it was Indo-China Communist Party (ICP) or National Liberation Front (NLF), their mobilisation and strategies were decided by the communist cadres. The role played by the communists were so much nationalistic that communism began to be equated with nationalism, and communist endeavours were projected as nationalist goals.

The victory over the US in 1975 boosted the morale of the Vietnamese. As it was under the stewardship of the CPV, the then leaders attached prime importance to it in the political system. Hence, they adopted one-party rule and the Constitution adopted in 1980, entrusted it with supreme powers of rule-making and rule-application. That did not work properly and therefore, there were some modifications when in 1992, a new Constitution was passed. Now the attempt was made to separate the legislative, executive and judicial powers of the Government and thereby moderate the powers of the CPV. Though the consensus continues to be in favour of one-party rule of the CPV, but the Constitution enacted in 1992, has definitely curtailed the role of the party to a great extent. Article four states that "CPV, the vanguard of Vietnamese working class, the faithful representative of the interests of working class, the working people and the whole nation, following Marxism-Leninism and Ho Chi Minh's thought, is the force leading the state and society."

At the same time, the reforms are accelerated under the slogan of "we the people are fundamental". All party organisations including Communist Party, operate within the framework of the Constitution and the law. The people, therefore, exercise power through the National Assembly and the People's Councils. The new Constitution, though, recognises the leadership of CPV, and guarantees that it is the one and only legitimate political party, but the overall situation is changing.

Mentioning the continued leadership of the Communist Party, however, is unique, because other socialist countries in the process of reorganisation and reform in the post-Cold War era, particularly in Eastern Europe left out the provisions dealing with the role of the Party, Vietnam has shown its courage by attaching importance to the CPV constitutionally even in the changed context and it continues to project it as a vehicle for development and modernisation.

The critics of the Vietnamese political system have been very active. They believe that Vietnam is unchanged as far as Doi Moi in Political matters are concerned. They are unable to understand the rationale of one-party domination. They have been saying that the CPV conservatively clings to the right of leadership role and unless this situation is changed, Vietnam cannot evolve a democratic way of life. Notwithstanding, an objective assessment of Vietnamese politics that the leading position and role of the CPV has been agreed by the Vietnamese revolutionaries in the past five decades. The CPV leadership has been acceptable to the masses and without it, it is difficult to promote nation-building and at the same time promote reforms with efficiency and legitimacy. The CPV is relevant even in the changed context and plays its part in promoting liberalism and market economy.

Vietnam has accelerated the process of development and endeavoured to be a "market place". It wants foreign collaboration and investments and this factor was realized first by the CPV, which in its Sixth Party Congress, in December 1986, took momentous decisions that were beyond the scope of conservative communist thinking. The CPV, under the leadership of Nguyen Van Linh, adopted the policy of Doi Moi. This accelerated the reform process to open Vietnam to the outside world while projecting credentials of Vietnam as a peaceful country.

Doi Moi

Doi Moi is a unique way of bringing changes in the socio-economic life of socialist country and revolutionary in its own way. It is a means to social change and economic development, to the introduction of certain aspects of liberal democracy. The various steps under Doi Moi have paved the path of development and the undergoing changes are appreciated at the global level.

Doi Moi has a wide meaning and it is being defined in various ways. Japan's Tetsusaburo Kimura analysed that Doi Moi has a wide range of contents, but it can be understood in three parts. The first is market opening measures including the abolition of the Central Government's monopoly of trade, encouragement of foreign investment and a shift to floating exchange rate system. The second part of Doi Moi is through which autonomy has been given to farmers, merchants, and enterprises in terms of manufacturing and sales. The third is the abolition of price control and use of interest as macro-economic variable.

On the other hand Akie Ishida has said that Doi Moi is a legal reform in conformity with policy changes from a centrally planned economy to market-oriented economy. It is aimed at recognising multi-sector structure in the economy, operation of market mechanism and expansion of external economic relations.

Ishida and Kimura both have stated that the emphasis of Doi Moi is reforms in the economic system, but its long-term impact on politics is a subject of speculation. Thus, Kimura says that Doi Moi is not to renovate everything in the short-term, but it is a process to study and experience trial and error. It is a repetition of an advance and retreat. It is different from Perestroika and Glasnost in meaning and texture, and a unique contribution of Vietnam under a communist order.

Doi Moi has proved advantageous in accelerating economic growth rate which has been around eight per cent since 1992. The measures under Doi Moi have enabled the government to control inflation rates and Vietnam is exporting 1.5 to 2 million tonnes of rice to the outside world. It has emerged as a third biggest rice exporting country. Besides, it is exporting crude oil, coal, tin and marine processed products. Agricultural exports also include groundnuts, wine, rubber, coffee and tea. Again textiles and handicrafts production are rapidly rising. Thus, it has contributed to the factors for regional stability and prosperity.

While attending economic restructuring, Vietnam also looked towards some political institutions which have interconnections with management and economy. Hence, the role of the party, National Assembly, army and the press are changing. These transformations are complimenting the effectiveness of the economic institutions and helping the process of liberalisation and market economy. Here an attempt is made to analyse briefly the changes in the role of the Party, National Assembly, Army and the Press to prove that the political system too is in the transitional phase, and it is changing to cope with the challenges of economic development and globalisation.

Communist Party

Though, the new Constitution of Vietnam says that the CPV is the force leading the state and society, its powers have been reviewed as a result of the corresponding increase in the powers of National Assembly. Now it is not necessary to be a member of the Communist Party to be a member of the National Assembly. Nguyen Xuan Oanh, a member of the Vietnam's National Assembly spoke to International Herald Tribune that the election for National Assembly in 1987, brought major change: 60 per cent of those elected were new to the legislature. They came from a variety of backgrounds. About 10 per cent of those did not belong to the Communist Party. Independent candidates are encouraged to fight and as they have opted for multi-candidate election, the electorates have choice of alternative.

The 1992, Constitution has attempted to define the limits of the role of the Party by stating that the people are the master, the state is the manager and the party is the leader. While affirming the leadership in the CPV, the Constitution has pointed out its obligations to the state and society. For the party to lead does not mean, "try to impose its will", or "to do everything in place of the state bodies and social organisations." All party organisations should carry out activities in the framework of the Constitution and law.

The CPV has thus set for itself the reformative measures for the daunting tasks ahead. It has sought to raise the standard of its leadership and for building and developing an economy along the line of market mechanism. The Party's guidance is designed to promote people's right of mastership, to raise the managerial skill and effectiveness of the state and role of the Front along with that of the people's organisations and social bodies, to mobilise the whole political system in society, thereby creating the strength of social democracy.

Though, the style of functioning of the CPV is changing, yet the demands for introduction of multi-party system have cropped up. This is because of the pluralist culture and historical legacies of

Vietnam. Tonking, Annam and Cochin-China had three separate systems and there were cultural differences between the people inhabiting in the north and south. Saigon was the centre of business and trade during the Colonial period. The Americans propped up business culture of Saigon further and it was considered an ideal trading centre during 1954-75. When the two parts of Vietnam were united in 1975-76, Saigon (Ho Chi Minh City) had medium sized factories for production of consumer goods. It had a large service industry and an efficient commercial banking system. On the other hand, northern areas had communist infrastructure, where collectivisation of agriculture and a weak industrial base existed. With the unification, socialist drives started everywhere for integration of the economies as well. The CPV leadership ignored the ground realities in the process. Centralisation came in place of privatisation and collectivisation of agriculture was promoted in the south as existing in the north. It disturbed the entrepreneurial initiative of the people. Hoas the business class of Chinese origin felt victimised so much so that they began to desert their homes to seek asylum elsewhere.

Vietnam soon became one of the poorest countries of the world. With rapid deterioration in the economy, people felt restless. They started questioning the leadership of the country and this tendency was witnessed at various forums of the government in due course. By 1986, the situation deteriorated to an extent that a number of leaders including Prime Minister Pham Van Dong resigned, to pave the path for reformists to take over. Hence Doi Moi process began.

Though, review of the existing rules and overhauling of the system have been promoted, Vietnam is not yet prepared to nurture a culture to tolerate dissent. Ross Range of New York Times reported in May 1995, that harsh sentences are meted out for the slightest show of dissent, such as "15 years sentence" given to a man, named Phan Van Quang for waving the flag of the former South Vietnam during the Ho Chi Minh City international marathon in 1992. Rose Range, at the same time has reported that "although government controlled, the press is relatively uppity, reporting all manners of corruption, scandal and general incompetence local television is heavily westernised. On my first night in the town, I was stunned to see 'Apocalypse Now' showing on the main channel followed by Operah, Popeye, the Master's tournament and the NCAA final etc.

Thus, the western culture through media is welcomed and this would gradually influence the people. A number of westernised Vietnamese who have been doing business overseas are returning back. They have new thinking and new awakening and they symbolise new culture. They are interested in restoring Vietnam as an ideal trading centre and hence they would like to promote democracy and free trade. As multi-party system is an important element of democracy, it would naturally be encouraged advertently or inadvertently.

There are indeed some Vietnamese leaders who advocate the case for multi-party system and demanding more democratisation in the political process. Prominent amongst them are Tram Xuan Bach (former Politburo member), Bui Trinh (former Vice-Editor, Nhan Dan), Phan Dinh Dieu (mathematician), Duong Thu Huon (Novelist) and the Club of Resistance Fighters (an organisation of Veterans in the southern part of Vietnam). Again some pressure groups in the name of the Scientific Socialist Party (1990), the Form of Freedom (1993), the United Buddhist Church, and the Organisation of Catholic Church have time and again criticized the leadership and the system. The influence of these groups are, however, confined to certain areas only and nationwide support is required to transform one-party rule to multiparty system.

National Assembly

Prime Minister Nguyen Van Linh and Vo Chi Cong strengthened the powers of the National Assembly. They believed that it was wrong to turn it as a rubber stamp and therefore while restructuring the system paid particular attention to make National Assembly vibrant and a strong institution of the government. Vo Chi Cong stated that "it is necessary to allow the National Assembly to represent the people and to give it responsibility for solving important problems in the life of the people".

The powers and functions of the National Assembly have been effective in the Doi Moi era. Though, the old Constitution had also projected National Assembly as the highest organ of state power and the sole organ to legislate laws, it was virtually a rubber stamp till the adoption of new Constitution in 1992.

The new Constitution says that the National Assembly is the people's highest representative agency, and the highest organ of state power, exercising its supreme right of supervision over all operations of the state. It elects the President and Vice-President, the Prime Minister and senior judicial officers, and ratifies the Prime Minister's proposals for appointing members of the government. It decides the country's socio-economic development plans, national financial and monetary policies and foreign policy. The term of each legislature is five years. The National Assembly Standing Committee supervises the enforcement of laws and the activities of the government Amendments to the Constitution may only be made by a majority vote of at least two-thirds of the Assembly's members.

Again the Prime Minister has to be a member of the National Assembly, but this is not necessary for other ministers. The Prime Minister is responsible to the National Assembly and his term of office is the same as that of National Assembly. Again the term of office of the presiding judge of the Supreme People's Court corresponds to the term of the National Assembly and he or she is responsible to the National Assembly. The important point to be noted is that the National Assembly has started asserting its powers and this trend is encouraged.

The National Assembly before 1992, was ineffective because it was convened semi-annually merely for five days and its representatives merely raised their hands in favour of proposals made by the Council of Ministers. This practice was changed in 1993 and now each session continues for at least 29 days. As a result of the extended session, the time for discussion is longer and substantial. The representatives express their opinions and reservations freely and authorities have to answer their questions. If any bill is not discussed in the house, the representatives are empowered to reject it. The members of the National Assembly are also empowered to voice the concern of their respective constituencies and make important resolutions for consideration of the government.

The changes in the nature of National Assembly is not only due to the powers that the new constitution has given but also because of the electoral reforms through which non-party and independent members depend on their performance in the National Assembly. So, they have to be vocal and fearless to voice the opinion of the people. They are not afraid to express their concern for the omissions and commissions committed by the government officials. They are playing important role in the nation-building and modernisation processes.

Armed Forces

Vietnam is trying to impress that it is not chauvinistic as projected in the past. It has peaceful intentions. It fought wars in the past because it was compelled to fight. Now that there is crusade for economic development at the regional level and Doi Moi is the desirable goal, Vietnam abolished conscription under which men between 18 and 35 years and women between 18 and 25 years had to go compulsorily for military training. Vietnam also reduced the number of its armed forces by 50 per cent in 1987 and it further reduced it in conformity with peace time needs. In 1988, the strength of the Vietnamese armed forces comprised eight per cent of the total population, but the government endeavoured to reduce it to one per cent of the total population. The military spokesman, Lt. General Nguyen Quyet is stated as saying that the military have undertaken a basic change in both direction and strategy. It is being streamlined into a defensive force consistent with peace time needs. The ultimate aim is to have an army numerically small but high in quality.

Vietnam has thus succeeded in creating a new image and the world view regarding Vietnam has become positive. The Vietnamese no longer see the world in terms of two mutually antagonistic camps, but endeavouring to link Vietnam's economy with global economy. Foreign Minister, Nguyen Co Thach (1986-91), talked about interdependence in international matters and in May 1988, he was instrumental in passing a resolution which had deep-rooted impact on strategic thinking of Vietnam. The CPV politburo passed resolution 13 which officially accepted interdependence factor in international relations. While explaining resolution 13, Zachary Abuza says that it provided a new holistic paradigm for national security: One that included 'a strong economy, a peaceful international situation, "sufficient defence" and an increase in bilateral relations with countries in all three worlds.

Thus, Vietnam adopted comprehensive security approach which included three components:

(*a*) to foster good bilateral relations with all countries, including former enemies, i.e., the U.S. and China,
(*b*) to have no alliances, nor a reliance on a superpower, and
(*c*) to maintain a peaceful external environment so that all resources can be spent on developing the economy.

The Press

The outlook of the Vietnamese press has changed in the past one decade. Though, censorship has altogether not been relaxed, the journalists are encouraged to report investigative articles and about wrong-doing of the officials. They keep a watch on bureaucrats and ministers. This development has irked some CPV stallwards. The government has given directives to the press to reflect not merely "the voice of the party" but also the "voice of the people". It has permitted the press to expose dark areas of socio-economic life and investigative pieces are given incentives.

Premier Nguyen Van Linh had set a new tone of the press by stating that they should not bend their pens in order to please officials. He said that "if a person is unable to write as the wish, they should do research and enhance their knowledge, till the suitable time comes for free and fair reporting". He clearly said that the press should not write opportunistic pieces. His successors also promoted investigative articles and this has helped in the better performance of the government and better image of media.

It is noteworthy that the changes in the political system have long-term implications on Vietnam's foreign policy and relations. It has been unique on the part of Vietnam to diversify its relationship from the erstwhile Sovit Union to the countries in Asia-Pacific. After the break up of the Soviet Union, with which it had cultivated intimate relations for decades, it adjusted astutely as a trustworthy partner of the countries in Asia-Pacific. Hence, the polemics of the cold war era was forgotten and realistic assessment of the international situation began. As trade with former communist allies declined, Vietnam was quick to forge new commercial links with Asian tigers. At the same time initiatives were taken to promote trade links with the countries in the European Union and the United States. Murray Hiebert reported in Far Eastern Economic Review in May 1992, that Vietnam escaped the clutches of economic disaster by turning to its Asian neighbours to replace the collapsing Soviet Union, its major trading partner so far.

Singapore, Japan and Hong Kong, which together accounted for half of Vietnam's trade in 1991, were the biggest beneficiaries of the Soviet collapse. Official Vietnamese statistics in mid-1992 showed that two-way trade with Singapore shot up from $111 million to $868 million, with Japan from $309 million to $709 million and with Hong Kong from $182 to $502 million. Thus, Singapore emerged Vietnam's biggest trading partner in 1992, accounting for 26.7 per cent of imports and 33.7 per cent of exports. Vietnam and Singapore thus granted "most favoured nation" status to each other and signed a series of agreements to boost trade and investment relations. Other ASEAN countries also came forward to forge commercial links with Vietnam and subsequently became important trade partners and investors in Vietnam.

Moscow, for decades, had controlled more than half of Vietnam's foreign trade and had provided Hanoi with more than $1 billion in aid and concessionary trade arrangements. It was difficult to envisage anything without the Soviet aid and assistance in Vietnam for decades, but it was smooth and admirable effort to diversify it. Vietnam succeeded in finding new markets, new allies and new donors in the post-1991 era.

The widespread changes in Vietnamese politics had implications on the attitudes of the US also. The Americans, which proved the stubborn enemy of Vietnam from 1945 to 1991, began to review its policies and adopted a favourable posture. President Clinton decided to remove the US veto on Multilateral lending to Vietnam in 1993 and paved the way for IMF, World Bank and ADB lending and operations. In 1994, the US lifted trade embargo and evinced interests in resuming diplomatic ties. In August 1995, Secretary of State, Warren Christopher initiated the resumption of diplomatic ties at the level of charge d'affairs and full diplomatic relations were established in May 1997.

Vietnam has earned the friendship of the ASEAN also due to changes in its system. This grouping, which had adopted anti-communist postures right since its inception, and had ostensibly worked for isolating Vietnam for decades, changed their attitudes rapidly. The ASEAN as a group was advertently supporting "bleed Vietnam white" policy ever since December 1978 and was critical of Vietnamese intervention in Cambodia. The Communist system was being ridiculed and they were projected as barbaric monsters. But changes in the Vietnamese political system, followed by the dissolution of the Soviet Union, changed the attitudes of the ASEAN countries. Hence, the ASEAN first offered observer status to Vietnam in 1992 and thereafter full membership in 1995. Though, Vietnam remains a communist country, but this reality does not inhibit its relations with the ASEAN partners.

The ASEAN leaders have very positive opinion regarding Vietnam and they admire the latter for worthwhile partnership. They are genuinely interested in Vietnam's locational advantages, mineral resources and its cheap and relatively well-educated labour force. Above all, Vietnam is considered important for ASEAN solidarity and regional consensus.

It is noteworthy that ideology, which perennially proved an irritant in Vietnam's interaction with the ASEAN and East Asian neighbours, is not considered a threat in the present context. The Communist Party of Vietnam is working as a facilitator to promote business and trade with the outside world. It is not at all interested in exporting revolution and does not talk of Indo-Chinese federation. Hence, it is unwilling to interfere in the affairs of Laos and Cambodia. It voluntarily withdrew its forces from Cambodia (1988) and is a silent spectator in view of the anti-Vietnamese rhetoric of the Khmer Rouge.

Vietnam now believes in peaceful resolution of the conflicts and is acting as a trustworthy and responsible neighbour. Above all, it has displayed good understanding of regional realities and simultaneously introduced structural changes to accommodate regional interests in tune with regional consensus. To conclude in the words of Vietnamese ambassador, Pham Sytam,

> the objective of reforms in Vietnam is indeed the policy of openness and integration into the world, selecting and adapting the world's essence with due regards to the trends and spirits of the present time. It is also a process in which whatever attained by modern science and technology is useful for his people and country would be taken in. The previous policy of "closed door" resulted in stagnation. International cooperation has become a common trend of the time now and an important condition for development too. The Doi Moi process is to befriend all nations for peace, independence, and development.

To conclude at the end, the following observations are important :

(*a*) The politics in Vietnam is in the transition phase from orthodox communist system to a liberal society.

(*b*) Rapid transformation is taking place in the name of Doi Moi (renovation). Although renovation of the political system in

Eastern Europe resulted in the end of Communist Party monopoly over national politics, Vietnam leadership has retained it recognising its constructive role.

(*c*) Vietnam is regarded pivotal in the success of certain projects for regional cooperation, i.e., Ganga-Mekong Project, Greater Mekong Sub-regional (GMS) Project, East Asian Growth Tringle and above all ASEAN Region Forum (ARF). All matters concerning security to the region needs the cooperation of Vietnam and there can be no consensus towards resolution of the Spratlys unless Vietnam is recognised as an important regional actor.

(*d*) Vietnam attaches utmost importance to normalisation of relations with the United States and People's Republic of China, although they pursued the policy of "bleeding Vietnam white", for more than a decade.

REFERENCES

Buttinger, J., *Vietnam, a Political History,* London, 1969.

Chanda, Nayan, *Brother Enemy: The War After the War: A History of Indochina since the Fall of Aigon,* San Diego, 1986.

Duiker, William J., *The Rise of Nationalism in Vietnam, 1900-1941,* Ithaca, New York, 1976.

Kahin, M.G., *Intervention: How American Became Involved in Vietnam,* New York, 1986.

Than Mya & Tan, Joseph, (ed.), *Vietnam's Dilemmas and Options: The Challenge of Economic Transition in the 1990s,* Singapore, 1993.

Turner, Robert F., *Vietnamese Communism: Its Origin and Development,* Stanford, 1975.

Vu Tuan Anh, *Development in Vietnam: Policy Reforms and Economic Growth,* Singapore, 1994.

8

Vietnam-China Dispute over the Spratlys, 1975-1991

The question of sovereignty over the Spratlys is a subject of bitter contest and confrontation between China and Vietnam[1]. China claims jurisdiction over the entire Spratlys area and wants Vietnam to withdraw. Vietnam on the other hand, claims jurisdiction over that area on the basis of its actual possession. It has advocated multilateral negotiations to resolve any dispute over the occupation of the area, and is fighting to protect its claims. This dispute assumed a new dimension recently after a naval clash with China on March 14, 1988. The Vietnamese side suffered casualties but could not be driven out.[2] While the clash did not alter the existing occupation and situation, it resulted in arousing old tensions, tirades, adverse propaganda and exchange of protest notes. Both sides have been citing historical evidence to seek legitimacy to rule over the Spratlys. Both are trying to strengthen their strategic postures.

Sino-Vietnamese competition in the Spratlys is having an adverse impact on the security environment of the Southeast Asian region. This study is an analysis of the geopolitics and strategic dimensions of the Spratlys dispute. It makes an appraisal of the location, natural resources, and genesis of the Sino-Vietnamese conflict over the Spratlys and reviews rival claims. At the end, there are some concluding observations.

The Chinese claim that Vietnam forcibly occupied the Spratlys in April 1975. But this allegation is factually wrong on two grounds. First, a brief history of Vietnam suggests that it ruled over that area even when it was under French colonial rule. Second, Vietnam is not the sole master of the Spratlys. It is in possession of some areas along with Taiwan, the Philippines, Malaysia and China. Some of the major islets and reefs under the possession of Vietnam are the Spratly Island (Truong Sa), Song Tu Tay (Pugad), Nam Yet (Tizard Bank), Southwest Cay, Son Ca (Sand Cay), unnamed Cay, Sinh Ton (Sin Cowe), Hon Sap (Peerson Reef), Central London Reef, East London Reef, An-Bang (Amboina Cay) and Cuatoron Reef. The Chinese on the other hand, are occupying two reefs, i.e. Fiery Cross Reef and Louisa Reef, on two sides of the Spratlys. Taiwan's possession of the Spratlys is Taiping (Itu Aba), strategically located in the centre. Taiping is the largest islet spread across 100 acres, and it was the base for the Japanese submarines during the Second World War. On the other hand, the Philippines is in possession of Pag-Asa (Thitu), Kota, Parola (Northeast Cay), Likas (West York), Panata, Patag (Flat), Lawak (Nanshan) and Rizal Reef (Commodore Reef). Lastly, Malaysia is in possession of Turumbu Perahu (Barque Canada), Turumu Mantanani (Mariveles Reef). Turumbu Laya (Dalles Reef) and Turumbu Layang Layang (Swallow Reef).

Relative distances to the Spratlys include: about 650 kilometres east of the Vietnamese Coast, about 750 kilometres south of the Paracels, about 1,000 kilometres from Hainan Island to the northern-most edge of the Spratlys, about 250 kilometres west of the Sabah Coast, about 160 kilometres west of the Sarawak Coast and about 100 kilometres west of the Palawan Island.[3] Thus, compared to mainland China, all the occupants of the Spratlys are situated closer on its periphery. Their claims of jurisdiction over the Spratlys deserve to get international attention. But the Chinese diplomats have conducted their policies astutely in such a fashion that none of the claimants feel secure about their possessions. The Chinese rulers claim sovereignty over all the islands situated in the South China Sea. In order to fulfill its claim, China invaded the Paracel Island groups (Hoang Sa) in January 1974 and defeated the forces of the Republic of Vietnam (RVN). It occupied Hoang Sa on January 20, 1974, but did not go further. After a lapse of 14 years, it used its forces once again to capture the Spratlys in March 1988, but this time it could not defeat the forces of the Socialist Republic of Vietnam (SRV). Still, the Chinese are keen to drive out the Vietnamese from the Spratlys to fulfill their geostrategic interests. If Vietnam is forced to withdraw from the Spratlys, then Taiwan, the Philippines and Malaysia will have to follow suit. There is strong resentment of the

Chinese policy over the Spratlys in the ASEAN (Association of Southeast Asian Nations) countries also. Therefore, the conflict over the Spratlys is gradually assuming the status of a "most explosive" dispute with multiple ramifications. If left unresolved, it will become the most complicated dispute of recent times.

Location

Located at latitude 4° to 11° 30′ north and longitude 190° 30′ to 117° 50′ east, on the extreme south of the South China Sea, the Spratlys comprise a group of 500-600 islets, coral reefs and shoals. It is said that nearly 100 of the reefs in the Spratlys region are under water most of the time.[4] Spread over about 1,000 kilometres, the Spratlys form an irregular ellipse of islets, shoals and reefs extending from South Luconia Shoals, 100 miles northwest of Brunei, northeast-ward paralleling the Borneo and Palawan Coasts, but extending into the South China Sea half-way to the Vietnamese Coast.[5] Until 1960, much of this area was not even accurately surveyed, and was portrayed as "Dangerous Ground" on maps, and was generally avoided by commercial and military vessels.[6]

Whatever may be the nature of the geographical problems, this area is no longer treated as a "Dangerous Ground" in the geopolitical context. The American forces and international shipping generally use this waterway as the shortest route from the Pacific Ocean to the Indian Ocean via the Malacca Straits.[7] It has become strategically important for East and Southeast Asian nations. Any disturbance in the area is a matter of international concern and there is competition amongst several countries for more and more possessions in the Spratlys region.

Natural Resources

The Spratlys areas are not yet properly explored and exploited. There are indications of a number of natural resources in the area, i.e., oil, cobalt, copper, tin, phosphate and manganese nodules. This area is also rich in coral lime, high silicate sands, gem quality corals and natural pearls. The Spratlys areas are made up of sea mounts, probably volcanic, rising from the ocean floor. But the areas around An-Bang, Truong Sa, Rizal Reef, Hon Sap, Turumbu Perahu and Turumbu Mantanani are particularly made up of sedimentary depositions from the Mekong River and from another great river which flowed across what is now part of the South China Sea and the Gulf of Thailand.[8] Sedimentary depositions are very favourable territory for oil. In this context, it is noteworthy to point out that oil has been discovered off the Mekong in Vietnam, Jurudong in Brunei and El Nido in the Philippines.

There is an abundance of fish, i.e., black tuna, cuttlefish and trepang in the Spratlys. Coconut, bread fruit and tung oil trees have long been cultivated on many of the principal islets, and papaya, pineapple and banana plantations have been introduced in recent years. The Spratlys have also been a major nesting area for the migratory sea tortoise, the eggs, flesh and shells of which have been harvested for centuries. Most of the islets and reefs are covered with trees, grasses and mangrove swamps. As the islets are extremely tiny (less than 100 acres), the area has not been developed for massive agricultural production. But its climate is extremely favourable to raise guano, monkeys and giant lizards.[9]

People have not yet found the area suitable to settle down in, though fresh water is available at An-Bahg, Truong Sa, Pag-Asa and Itu Aba. Most of the people who visited this area in the historical past were either fishermen, businessmen or militarymen. They did not find the Spratlys region suitable to live in. But after the end of the Second World War, the importance of the area was understood and presently there is stiff competition amongst different countries to gain a strategic foothold there.

Strategic Dimension

The Spratlys waters connect the Pacific Ocean to the Indian Ocean. Any ambitious power on its periphery will remain ever entangled there to gain a strategic foothold. Again, the Spratlys have proximity to major shipping routes. As noted earlier, the international commercial ships from East Asia bound for Pacific, Indian, and Mediterranean shores pass through the Spratlys region and the western vessels also use these waterways. The Chinese, for example, are dependent on this route. China, therefore, wants the elimination of the presence of other powers inside the Spratly archipelago. The strategic analysis of the Chinese thinkers suggests that they will do anything to expand Chinese rule over the Spratlys. An analyst has said, "Spratly is an important piece of real estate in a much broader system of strategic links that would ultimately allow China to expand its maritime interests in the Indian Ocean."[10] A major objective for naval planners in Beijing is to build up an adequate naval force to secure China's interests all the way through to the Persian Gulf from what is seen in Beijing as a rising potential threat from India's Navy and from what is viewed as an ever-present Soviet threat.[11]

China is particularly concerned about the Soviet presence at the Cam Ranh Bay naval base (Vietnam). When the Chinese came on a "punitive mission" to Vietnam in February 1979, the Soviet Navy acted as a deterrent for any naval initiative by the Chinese Navy at the Hainan Island and the Paracels. In order to protect the Vietnamese interests, the Soviet Union sent Tupolev Tu-95 (Bear) reconnaissance planes near the Paracels and monitored the Chinese naval and air movements. In addition, the flagship of the Soviet Pacific fleet, the 16,000-ton-Sverdlov-class missile cruiser, *Admiral Senyavin* came to the Spratlys.[12] The Chinese were extremely annoyed at the presence of the Soviet Navy.

The above event exposed the vulnerability of the Chinese and since then they have been mounting diplomatic onslaughts against the Vietnamese. To achieve possession of the Spratlys is the objective in their heart of hearts. A Chinese naval officer has recently said, "The Spratlys cannot be seen in isolation, as not far away are the Straits of Malacca, then the Indian Ocean and, beyond, the Persian Gulf. This region is of critical importance to China's security because an increasing volume of China's trade passes through the area."[13]

There are reports that the Chinese leadership has a notion that in order to assert China as a dominant regional power, it is necessary to occupy the entire Spratlys. They believe that this will help them in improving relations with Southeast Asia, the earstwhile Soviet Union and Taiwan.[14] As they are trying to project China as a dominant regional power, they are not ready to tolerate any obstacle enroute.

China's adversary, the SRV, believes that the Spratlys, situated on its sea frontiers, are crucial for the maintenance of its security and independence. It believes that the Chinese endeavour to occupy the Spratlys is aimed at territorial expansion into the Southern Sea (Nan Hai). China's ambitions and expansionist designs in the South China Sea pose a threat not only to Vietnam but to the entire Southeast Asian region. A Vietnamese strategic expert has emphasised that "the Chinese efforts to take control of the Spratlys is a dangerous development of grave consequences. It violates territorial sovereignty not only of Vietnam but of the entire Southeast Asia."[15] The Vietnamese perception regarding the Chinese action in the Spratlys is a warning for the Southeast Asian countries. The *Vietnam Courier* has reported the Vietnamese perception in the following words: "The brazen Chinese encroachments on Vietnam's Truong Sa are premeditated acts which are part of a long-term Chinese scheme to control Bien Dong (East Sea) and expand into Southeast Asia. The danger posed by this scheme to the nations in the region has been further revealed by present Chinese actions with regard to the Truong Sa islands. From conducting naval exercises, reconnaissance and survey operations, planting markers, etc., the Chinese authorities have gradually proceeded to increase their naval presence in the area and engage in ever more serious actions. Such expansionist moves by China cannot but cause profound concern among the countries living on the rim of Bien Dong. ... It should be noted that by encroaching upon Vietnam's territorial sovereignty in Truong Sa, the Chinese authorities are deliberately running counter to the trend toward detente in the world, causing tension in the region, and seeking to block the trend toward dialogue aimed at peacefully resolving regional disputes, including the Kampuchean issue."[16]

Needless to say, the South China Sea, like the Indian Ocean, is of pivotal importance for the peace and progress of the Asia Pacific region. The South China Sea was considered so important for the success of American global policies that America had built two major naval bases on two fringes of the Spratlys. On the southwestern fringe, it had constructed the Cam Ranh Bay naval base and on the northwestern fringe, it developed the massive Subic Bay naval base. Thus, the US exercised a profound influence on the geopolitics of the region. But in 1975, the US withdrew from Vietnam and vacated Cam Ranh base. That base came under the jurisdiction of the Democratic Republic of Vietnam (DRV). Vietnam forged strategic relations with the Soviet Union and offered certain facilities to the Soviet Navy at Cam Ranh base. The DRV ignored the Chinese overtures for the Cam Ranh Bay naval base and sided with the Soviet Union, China's adversary. The presence of the Soviet Navy at the Cam Ranh Bay naval base boosted the security morale of the Vietnamese. The Soviet Union used the Cam Ranh Bay base for reconnaissance against the Chinese and American naval manoeuvers in the region.

The Soviet Union views the South China Sea as an important link between the country's European and Asian sectors. It did not have any access to that area till 1975. But when it was facilitated to use the Cam Ranh Bay naval base, the Soviets found it extremely strategic to balance the manoeuvres of the outside powers in that region. Influence over this area is considered essential for any Soviet plan to extend their sphere of influence in the Asia-Pacific region. Soviet submarines and surface warships are based at the Cam Ranh Bay and the base is used for communication facilities and intelligence data.[17]

On the other hand, the US has dominated the sea lanes of the region since the end of the Second World War. As a part of the global defence system, it is maintaining the Clarke air base and Subic Bay naval base in the Philippines. These bases have to perform different functions to maintain American strategic interests. It has been reported that the naval, air and communication facilities are pivotal to the US global defence system. Subic Bay's 55,000 acres of water and land encompass one of the region's best natural deep water ports, with repair yards capable of handling up to 27 ships simultaneously. The Subic Bay base can perform two-thirds of all the maintenance work, including work on aircraft carriers and nuclear submarines, required by the US Seventh Fleet. It also functions as a supply depot, handling millions of tons of commodities and petroleum products each year. An air station at Cubi Point, within Subic's perimeter, provides temporary refuge to carrier-based aircraft when their ships are in port. The P-3 Orion maritime surveillance aircraft cover large reaches of the South China Sea each day from Cubi Point.[18]

Just 70 kilometres from Subic, the Clarke air base serves as the Western Pacific hub of the US military communication and air transit system. In recent years, its 10,500 feet, all-weather runway has handled about 12,000 flights a month. It also serves as a massive depot for air-delivered military supplies. The home of the American 13th Air Force since the end of the Second World War, Clarke once encompassed 25,000 acres—larger than Washington, D.C. But since 1979, this has been reduced to 13,000 acres.[19]

Thus, both the superpowers are engaged in surveillance and other strategic activities to enhance their global interests. Both the superpowers are based at the two fringes of the Spratlys. Both of them consider each other their adversary. They know that the foothold around the Spratlys is important for the success of their East and Southeast Asian policies. The Chinese are interested in assuming a dominant role in the politics of the region and, therefore, China is trying to expand its maritime boundaries. They believe that strengthening their Navy in the Spratlys region is *sine qua non* to avoid being cut off by the Soviet or American forces.[20]

Southeast Asian countries—mainly the Philippines, Vietnam, Malaysia—also attach importance to the Spratlys for their own security. They consider their possessions in the Spratlys as their integral territories, and are very sensitive whenever the issue of the Spratlys is raised. But they have no joint action plan to deal with the external threat.

The Philippines attaches great importance to the Spratlys from a security perspective. The Spratlys was a springboard from where the Japanese forces came and occupied Luzon and other Philippine islands during the Second World War. The Spratlys was a base for the Japanese submarines during 1941-45. By occupying the Spratlys, the Japanese Navy was able to cut off Allied shipping in that region and neutralise the enemy forces. The Dutch, British and French Navies were ineffective against the Japanese and, thus, Japan conquered the entire Southeast Asian and South-Pacific region. Emphasising the importance of the Spratlys, Brigadier General Napoleon Angeles, head of the Kalayaan Command (Western Philippines Command) said, "The South China Sea serves as a buffer against any hostile activity by the communist neighbours on the Asian mainland."[21]

In order to protect its security interests, the Philippines has constructed a 1800-metre airstrip at Pag-asa. It is manned by the Philippine naval forces. On the other hand, Taiwan has a garrison force at Taiping, where a battalion of Taiwan's armed forces are based. Vietnam has also built a small airstrip, about 500 metres long on the Spratly Island to handle small aircraft such as CN 212 light transport planes. Compared to the forces of Vietnam, the Philippines and Taiwan taken together, the Chinese forces are greater in number. China has massive naval bases at Hainan and the Paracels and has 25 submarines, five destroyers and 200 coastal attack craft in the South China Sea.[22] The naval reinforcements are gradually increasing to take on menacing proportions.

China is applying maximum pressure on Vietnam to withdraw. Its security is regularly threatened on its eastern frontiers. Vietnam is confronted with the permanent Chinese threat. It has called upon the ASEAN states to take note of the potential threat to the region.

Though its call has elicited a sympathetic response from Indonesia and Malaysia, there has been no regional consensus on how to deal with the Spratlys issue. Vietnam's influence in the Southeast Asian region is limited because of its Kampuchean policy. It is because of Kampuchea that the ASEAN has worked towards isolating Vietnam since December 1978. The ASEAN took a serious view of Vietnam's military intervention against the Khmer Rouge government in Kampuchea. The process of Vietnam's rapprochement with the ASEAN can be workable only after Vietnam's total withdrawal from Kampuchea. The split amongst the Southeast Asian countries has prompted Beijing to pressurise Hanoi and have its say.

Genesis of the Dispute

In order to have a proper perspective of the Sino-Vietnamese dispute over the Spratlys, it is necessary to understand its brief history. The Chinese claims of sovereignty over the Spratlys date back to the Han Dynasty rule in the 2nd century B.C. They claim that the Paracels and the Spratlys were ruled by China for several centuries and were part of the Chinese empire during the Han, Tang, Song and Yuan dynasties. It was not until 1931 that the Chinese claims to those two island groups were seriously challenged. In that year, France sent a note to the Republic of China Legation in Paris, claiming Vietnamese sovereignty over the Paracels and the Spratlys. Both the island groups were subsequently occupied by France forcibly, without caring for the Chinese objections. France announced in 1933 that the Paracels and the Spratlys had been formally taken over and merged with the Vietnamese Kingdom. It is interesting to know that at that time Vinh Thuy (Bao Dai) was the King of Vietnam and Ngo Dinh Diem, his Minister of Interior. China has continued to reiterate its claims over the two islands ever since.[23]

The Vietnamese, on the other hand, trace the origin of their rule in the Paracels and the Spratlys during the reign of Gia Long (1802-1820). King Gia Long is believed to have incorporated the Paracels and the Spratlys into the Vietnamese Kingdom.[24] He had formed a company to make fertiliser from phosphate deposits in the Spratlys.[25] His successor, Ming Mang sent some of his subjects to the area in 1935 to build a pagoda and a stone tablet.

Vietnam's claims over the Paracels and the Spratlys were not properly understood before but when they were fully integrated into the Vietnamese Kingdom in 1933, they were immensely pleased. But the jubilation over the new possessions was short-lived. Japan emerged as a great imperialist power and started military campaigns against East and Southeast Asian countries. Japan conquered the Paracels in 1938 and the Spratlys in 1939. It developed a naval base at Itu Aba (Taiping) and from there came to Southeast Asia. Japan occupied the Spratlys up to 1945 and thereafter it came under the virtual trusteeship of the Allied Powers. At the time of the San Francisco Treaty in 1951, Japan renounced all rights, title and claim to the Paracels and the Spratly Islands. This treaty, signed on September 8, 1951, did not award the areas either to China or Vietnam outright. It ended in favour of a *status quo* vis-a-vis the sovereignty of the Paracels and the Spratlys.[26] The Republic of Vietnam continued to rule over part of the Paracels and the entire Spratlys after 1951.

To sum up the historical developments, it is necessary to point out that when Emperor Gia Long incorporated the Paracels and the Spratlys in his Kingdom, went on visits to the area and formed a company to make fertiliser from the manganese ores, there was no protest in China. This was possibly because he paid tribute to China.[27] But at the same time, it was impossible for a tributory ruler, particularly in Southeast Asia, to act without China's blessings or permission. Thus, it can be inferred that China then had no objection to Vietnam's efforts to expand its territories in the South China Sea. But soon China began to feel the loss. The western colonial powers began to come into the area in a big way. China was defeated in the opium war in 1842. The Franco-British colonial forces came to the area and dominated the South China Sea, and the threat of colonial aggression side-tracked regional disputes. The British and French Navies came to the area regularly and enhanced their commercial interests. The ownership of the Paracels and the Spratlys changed rapidly from one to another. It was under French rule from 1933 to 1939, under Japan from 1939 to 1945, under the Allied Powers from 1945 to 1951, under the Republic of Vietnam from 1951 to 1975, and so on. In the period 1945-56, parts of the Spratlys came under Taiwan, the Philippines and Malaysia.

China has been emphatic since 1951 that the Paracels and the Spratlys are Chinese territories. But because of its worldwide isolation during 1949-71, its voice could not be properly heard. But now the situation is entirely different. China is a regional power and wants to prove itself a great maritime power. On the other hand, its adversary, Vietnam is isolated. In the situation, China has accelerated its campaign to get back the Spratlys. It believes that every other ruler in the Spratlys is a tresspasser and has warned Vietnam to withdraw from the region. Though there are many reasons to motivate China to accelerate its campaign,[28] the historical factors are in the background. China had either directly ruled over Southeast Asia or exercised suzerainty through tributory relations. Vietnam, particularly, had been a Chinese colony. It had been annexed by the rulers of the Han Dynasty in 111 B.C. It was only after 1000 years that Vietnam became independent in 939 AD. But in order to protect their Kingdom from Chinese aggression, the various rulers of Vietnam continued to pay tributes to China. The rulers of other countries of Southeast Asia also paid regular tributes to China. The existence and unity of any Kingdom in the Southeast Asian region depended to a great extent on the Chinese goodwill. Thus, it is needless to point out that ancient China was a superpower and the states on its periphery, merely satellites. There was no one to challenge the predominance of the Chinese in the region.

In the wake of the nationalist movement in the Southeast Asian region, the main motivation of the respective countries was to gain political independence. The nationalists fought either against the French or British, or the Dutch or American colonial rulers. China too was fighting against western colonial powers. It ardently supported the freedom movement in the South and Southeast Asian region. China expressed solidarity and complete understanding with Southeast Asian national sentiments. On the eve of the departure of the respective colonial powers at the end of the Second World War, China was embroiled in internal turmoil and subsequently came under communist rule in 1949. At the same time, the communist movement in Vietnam had favourably touched the national sentiments. It was believed that the communists would come to power in Vietnam too. The Communist Parties of China and Vietnam had fraternal ties and they helped each other in their successes. The Vietnamese communists had to fight hard to come into power and they had to fight against the American forces till 1975. Thus, the Communist Party of Vietnam was in need of Chinese and Soviet assistance to face the American challenges. It did very little to take up any other issue except to maintain its survival and independence. The anti-communist forces in Vietnam had, however, the support of the Americans. They had taken up the responsibility to unfurl the Vietnamese flag in the Paracels and the Spratlys. They had pleaded the Vietnamese case over the Spratlys and the Paracels at the San Francisco Peace negotiations in 1951. RVN Prime Minister, Tran Van Huu issued a statement during the seventh plenary session (September 7, 1951) saying, "As we must frankly profit from all the opportunities offered to us to stifle the germs of discord, we affirm our right to the Spratly and Paracel Islands, which have always belonged to Vietnam."[29] The peacemakers of San Francisco, however, did not award the Paracels or the Spratlys to any one country and decided to maintain the status quo. Thus, a major point of discord was left which became complicated over the years.

France granted independence to Vietnam in July 1954. The country was temporarily divided into two parts. The northern part of the country came under communist rule and the southern part came under the anti-communists. The communist rule became known as the DRV and the anti-communist rule as the RVN. The Paracels and the Spratlys were given to the RVN. The anti-communists of Vietnam were the allies of the United States and, therefore, had little problem in accepting the naval capabilities and assistance of the United States to patrol the areas around the Paracels and the Spratlys. But the emergence of the National Liberation Front in South Vietnam in 1960 took up the shape of a mass movement in the following years and challenged the authority of the anti-communist rulers. The military action of the United States from 1964 to 1975 failed to contain the NLF activities and the Americans became tired of the Vietnam war. The ascendance of the Nixon-Kissinger team in the US in 1968 marked the change in the American policy towards Vietnam. The revelation of the Guam Doctrine and Vietnamisation (1969), Dr. Kissinger's secret missions to China (1971), President Nixon's visit to China (1972) and subsequent developments in the region shattered the morale of the RVN forces. The effort towards Vietnamisation was viewed as the announcement of American withdrawal from Vietnam. The process of Sino-US rapprochement and the change in American policy vis-a-vis Taiwan, the Paracels and the Spratlys were viewed with alarm by the government of the RVN. The first casualty of the rapprochement was indeed the RVN. Noting the favourable mood of the Americans, China invaded the Paracel Islands in January 1974. The RVN could not face the Chinese onslaught and was defeated at the Paracels. The RVN security forces were driven out and the Chinese occupied the entire island group of 130 islets—none larger than a square mile.

The Chinese action, though calculated, surprised the international community. The geopolitical climate was in China's favour as the Americans were so tired of the Vietnam war and so imbued with the euphoria of rapprochement with China that they allowed the latter to impose its will at the Paracels. Some commentators of American politics have revealed that there was serious bargaining between Chinese and American leaders before the signing of the Shanghai communique on the Vietnam question. One of them has written, "China agreed to contribute to maintaining the puppet regime in South Vietnan in exchange for the withdrawal of the US troops from Taiwan. China had also connived in the American blockade of the Vietnamese ports and its carpet bombing of Hanoi and Haiphong in exchange for US acceptance of China's entry into the United Nations and for allowing China to occupy the Paracels and the Spratlys."[30]

Another factor that motivated the Chinese action in the Paracels was the discovery of oil in the region. The RVN had entered into contracts for offshore oil exploration on July 20, 1973, with three American companies—Shell, Exxon, Mobil—and one Canadian company, i.e. Sunningdale. Shell officially announced that a well drilled in Block 08 had begun to flow at a rate of 2200 barrels a day. At the same time, Mobil also announced that a well drilled in Block 04 was flowing at a rate of 2400 barrels a day. Both finds were made after only a few days of drilling and both were on the western edges of the Spratly Islands.[31] But before annexing the Spratlys, it was necessary to annex the Paracels first.

All these factors prompted China to take action. But before doing so, the People's Liberation Army (PLA) encircled the RVN-held areas in the Paracels and issued a note on January 11, 1974, to reaffirm its claim to the Paracels, the Spratlys, and other South China Sea islands. The RVN refused to accept the claim the following day but by that time, PLA units had already penetrated the crescent group of the Paracels and planted Chinese flags on Robert and Drummond Islands. From January 16 to 20, the Chinese naval and marine units escalated their attacks on RVN garrisons at

Robert, Money and Pattle Islands. The units of the RVN forces based at the Spratlys were defeated and were compelled to withdraw. By January 20, China was in complete control of the Paracels and at the door of the Spratlys. The RVN forces retreated into the Spratlys with the assistance of the US Navy and the International Red Cross. This action cost the RVN the lives of 19 persons, injury to 43 servicemen, 48 prisoners of war (POWs) and about 101 missing.[32]

The US was in a position to prevent the fall of the Paracels but it chose to remain neutral. The Seventh Fleet monitored all Chinese air and naval movements but it had been ordered to observe strict neutrality. At the height of the fighting, all American personnel aboard RVN vessels and aircraft operating in the vicinity of the Paracels and the Spratlys were ordered to withdraw from their posts.[33]

Professor Marwyn S. Samuels while analysing the American behaviour in the Paracels has revealed that "despite the fact that South Vietnam was still an ally, the US played the role of an interested bystander. Ironically, the American position allowed (and perhaps even encouraged) China to exercise its will in the South China Sea."[34]

The Chinese did not proceed further to invade the Spratlys. There were some deterrent factors working against China. First, the action in the Spratlys could engulf China in war against the RVN, Taiwan, Malaysia and the Philippines. The Chinese leaders in those years were keen to normalise relations with the ASEAN countries. The war against the Philippines and Malaysia could impede the progress on this front and tarnish China's image. Moreover, Malaysia was also a member of the Five-Power-Defence-Agreement. Thus, to confront Malaysia, American neutrality was not the only prerequisite to be taken care of. Secondly, after the 1973 Paris Peace Agreement, the gradual withdrawal of the American forces from the RVN had already started. It was presumed that in case of a total withdrawal, the DRV would definitely try to capture it. Under that situation, the RVN would surely search for a new ally who could give security guarantees. The Chinese could openly come forward then against the DRV and offer security guarantees to South Vietnam. In return, it could bargain to take the Spratlys.

Whatever the calculations, the Chinese stopped at the door of the Spratlys. The RVN forces in the meanwhile came to the Spratlys and tried to strengthen reinforcements on the six major islets. The

RVN based its garrisons on the Truong Sa, Nam Yet, An-Bang and three others.[35] When the NLF, aligned with the DRV, captured Saigon, it annexed the Spratlys simultaneously. The DRV replaced the RVN security guards on the Spratlys on April 29, 1975, and quickly captured some more reefs and sand banks around An-Bang and Nam Yet and its jurisdiction ran over more than 22 islets and reefs. This was not appreciated by China but the time was not in its favour to march and "teach a lesson" to its fellow comrades in Vietnam. China reiterated its claim over the Spratlys and waited to see the emerging political developments.

In 1976, the two separate entities of Vietnam unified as the Socialist Republic of Vietnam (SRV). A new map of the SRV was published which not only showed the Spratlys but also the Paracels as its territory. In order to strengthen its security situation, the SRV gave permission to the Soviet Union to use the facilities at Cam Ranh Bay naval base. It ignored the Chinese overtures to fill the vacuum created by the American withdrawal at Cam Ranh Bay. In June 1978, the SRV became a member of the COMECON and in November that year, the SRV signed a Friendship Treaty with the Soviet Union. In view of the Sino-Soviet rift, the SRV overtures to the Soviets were ill received in China. But when the Chinese began to play the Khmer Rouge and Hoas against the SRV, the latter overthrew the Khmer Rouge from power in Kampuchea and made the lives of the Hoas in Vietnam very difficult. All these developments in the SRV irritated China deeply. In February 1979, China forgot its fraternal ties with the Vietnamese comrades and moved to take punitive action, "to teach a lesson" to the SRV. The Chinese were confident they could defeat the SRV and capture the Spratlys at least. But they failed in teaching a lesson to the SRV at the battlefront. However, China was successful in isolating Vietnam at the diplomatic front. On the other hand, Vietnam was forced to forge stronger security ties with the Soviet bloc.

The SRV could meet the Chinese challenges by virtue of its friendship with the Soviet Union. The SRV Navy was not in a position to face the Chinese Navy and, therefore, they could have lost the Spratlys. But the Soviet help prevented the fall of the Spratlys into the Chinese hands. The Soviet Union had sent a thirteen-ship Soviet flotilla including the flagship of the Soviet pacific Fleet, the 16,000-ton missile cruiser *Admiral Senyavin* and an aircraft carrier, to the South China Sea and the Gulf of Tonkin to warn China of the consequences.[36] Many of those vessels remained in the vicinity of Hainan and the Paracels for months, and some of them remained there on a semi-permanent basis. Thus, this dispute gave strategic access in the region to the Soviet Union.[37] Vietnam did not lose any territories in the war against the Chinese but it had to pay a great price for the same.

Today the Soviet Union is under the euphoria of glasnost and perestroika. It is attempting to restructure and review its earlier policies. It advocates detente in relations with China. A number of Soviet leaders have already visited Beijing in the course of attending "Sino-Soviet Ministers' Working Meetings" and a proper environment is emerging for normalisation. It is in this context, that the Chinese are willing to bring up the question of Vietnam and the strategy is to bargain in China's favour. The strategy of the Sino-US rapprochement allowed China the occupation of the Paracels. It is yet to be seen whether Sino-Soviet rapprochement will be able to give the Spratlys to China. The Soviet stand so far has been not to discuss the issue of the "third country," but recent developments in Sino-Soviet relations suggest that they are seriously discussing the third country issue, i.e., the Kampuchean problem.[38] The Vietnamese position on the dispute over the Spratlys is that it should be resolved through peaceful negotiations. The SRV leaders have visited several Southeast Asian capitals and expect the latter to take a reasonable stand. But the Chinese have consistently refused to talk about the Spratlys, and claim sovereignty over the entire archipelago. China's Foreign Ministry spokesman reiterated in April 1988 that, "Vietnam should revert to its correct position prior to 1975, drop its territorial claims over China's Xisha and Nansha islands and its harrassment of China in this regard, stop all its aggression aimed at occupying islands and reefs in China's Nansha islands and withdraw from the Chinese islands and reefs it has illegally occupied."[39]

There is no indication that China will negotiate its claims with any of the claimants in the Southeast Asian region. It has declared the Spratlys and Paracels as parts of the Hainan province. China seriously demands 90 per cent of the areas in the South China Sea. The latest map of the Chinese maritime border includes Taiwan, the Paracels, the Spratlys, the sea coasts off Vietnam and the Philippines coasts and up to 50 kilometres off the coast of the east Malaysian state of Sarawak.[40] It is not in a mood to moderate its claims and belligerent posture.

Conclusion

To sum up, it can be said that the contest for the occupation of the Spratlys is intense. None of the claimants will easily give way to a solution that can result in renunciation of their claims and occupation of that strategic area. The use of force in the past and the threat of aggression in the future to occupy the Spratlys are compelling the contestants to increase their armed presence and take security precautions. It is going to be a complicated dispute in the region.

Presently, China is in a stronger position to dictate terms on the Spratlys issue. It may get jurisdiction over Taiwan in due course of time. As soon as Taiwan comes under its control, Taiping (Itu Abu) will come under the jurisdiction of China. Situated in the middle of the Spratlys, Taiping will prove a spring-board to China to expand in the adjoining areas. It may create a situation that will compel Vietnam to vacate the areas. The present Taiwanese leaders have already expressed their solidarity with the Chinese leaders on the Spratlys and are ready for strategic cooperation. The final aim of the Chinese leaders is to convert the South China Sea into a "Chinese lake."

Vietnam can fight against the Chinese on the Spratlys issue with the help of the Soviet navy. Its indigenous capacity to face the Chinese challenges in the high seas is limited. Its economic situation is precarious. Michael S. Serrill has reported that "Vietnam is virtually bankrupt. Three Five-Year-Plans have failed. Unemployment is estimated at 33 per cent. In northern and central Vietnam, areas of chronic food shortage, the population is living on the edge of hunger. The currency, officially pegged at 368 dong to the US dollar, has effectively collapsed, with the black market rate plunging to 3,000 to the dollar a few weeks ago."[41] Thus, its potential to compete against China is minimum.

China is supporting American interests in the region, and has supported the existence of American bases, particularly in the Philippines. China is concerned about the Soviet presence in the Cam Ranh Bay. The Chinese are trying to neutralise the Soviet threat and the process of rapprochement is gradually changing the perceptions of the two adversaries. China is likely to give assurances to the Soviet Union that it will safeguard Soviet interests in the region in the same way that it has done for the Americans. In return, China might like to bargain that its vital regional interests, particularly in the South China Sea, should not be jeopardised. Vietnam is dependent on the Soviet support and is isolated at the international front. If the Chinese terms and conditions are accepted by the Soviet side, it will certainly have an adverse impact on Vietnam's territorial integrity.

Vietnam is earnestly trying to normalise relations with the US. It has agreed to cooperate in tracing out the MIAs (Americans Missing in Action) in Vietnam. The SRV is keen to revive the 1973 oil contracts of the three American companies in the Spratlys. But all these friendly gestures have not yet evoked the desired response from the US. The ignominous loss at the battlefront in Vietnam has psychologically affected the American decision makers. The US is still in favour of the campaign to "bleed Vietnam white." It is pouring arms and ammunition to the Khmer Rouge, KPNLF (Khmer People's National Liberation Front) and Moulinakas. These forces are engaged in guerrilla war against the Vietnamese forces. Vietnam has unilaterally announced its military withdrawal from Kampuchea by 1990. It has already started the pull-out process, but the Americans will take their own time to normalise relations. The Kampuchean imbroglio is about to be resolved and this should usher in a new era of Vietnam-US rapprochement.

The Spratlys dispute requires to be settled through negotiation and persuasion. The best forum to resolve this issue is the United Nations. Both China and Vietnam should respect international law and norms. If under international law, effective occupation of a particular area provides far better grounds for a land claim than mere prior discovery, this should not deter the contestants from accepting the international mediation. The occupation of the land is not the only criterion to decide the issue. In 1962, Phra Viharn Temple, then situated in Thailand's territory and under the effective jurisdiction of Thailand was awarded to Cambodia by the World Court. The historical documents, geographical contiguity and other aspects will also need to be taken care of while reaching a judgment.

Finally, it can be said that the Spratlys conflict and the resultant tension have contributed to the perpetuation of great power involvement in the regional politics. Though the name of Vietnam is mostly mentioned, the Philippines is equally endangered to lose its possessions in the Spratlys to the Chinese. If the Chinese mount pressure to capture Reed Bank areas (Pag-asa, Parola, Lawak, Likas and Kota), the Philippines will be compelled to compromise its present anti-nuclear postures and review of the base agreement with the United States. It will have no option but to seek the strategic cooperation of the US. In the same way, if pressure is mounted again against Vietnam, the latter will seek Soviet support to safeguard its national security. Thus, it can be said that China's militant postures to capture the Spratlys will ostensibly help the strategic interests of the superpowers.

The Southeast Asians should once again try to search for an indigenous solution of the crisis in the Spratlys. They have already resolved many conflicts in the past through peaceful means and they can do so in the case of the Spratlys also. If the three claimants of the Spratlys region—Vietnam, Malaysia and the Philippines—take a united stand and evolve a common policy to deal with the Spratlys question, it will have a salutory impact on the perception and attitude of China as well.

REFERENCES

1. The group of the Spratlys is known by different names in different countries. Vietnam calls it Truong Sa. The Chinese named it Nansha. But the Filipinos have known it as their Kalayaan. The situation is similar with different islets and reefs inside and the Chinese, Vietnamese, Malaysian and Philippine names are different.
2. A convoy of six Chinese warships had attacked three Vietnamese freighters near Sinh Ton Island, sunk one and damaged the other two. The Chinese also blocked Vietnam from rescuing 76 sailors from the burning ship. The Vietnamese have alleged that China grabbed some reefs in the process. For details see, *Nhan Dan,* Hanoi, March 17, 1988, *Indian Express,* New Delhi, March 18, 1988, *Rising Nepal,* Kathmandu, March 28, 1988, and "Details of Nansha Island Incident", *Views From China,* PRC Embassy, May 15, 1988, New Delhi, pp. 4-5.
3. Marwyn S. Samuels, *Contest for the South China Sea,* New York, Methuen & Co., 1982, p. 188.
4. *Asia Week,* Hong Kong, May 20, 1988, p. 26.
5. Martin H. Katchen, "The Spratly Islands and the Law of the Sea: 'Dangerous Ground' for Asian Peace", *Asian Survey,* Berkeley, Calif., Vol. 17, No.12, December 1977, p. 1169.
6. *Ibid.*
7. Jerry Cushing, "The Dragon's Long Reach", *Far Eastern Economic Review,* Hong Kong, Vol. 140, No. 18, May 5, 1988, p. 23.

8. That great river existed about 10,000 years ago, when the sea level was lower, see Katchen, n. 5, p. 1169.
9. *Asia Week,* May 13, 1988, p. 42.
10. Cushing, n. 7, p. 23.
11. *Ibid.*
12. *Hong Kong Standard,* February 26, 1979.
13. Cushing, n. 7, p. 23.
14. Harvey Stockwin, "Chinese Ambitions in South China Sea", *The Times of India,* New Delhi, 2 March 1988.
15. "Beijing's Designs as Revealed by its Recent Actions in Truong Sa," *Vietnam Courier,* Hanoi, Tran Hung Dao, May 1988, p. 11.
16. *Ibid.,* pp. 10-11.
17. Drew Middleton, "The US Alarmed at the Soviet Bases in Vietnam", *The Times of India,* New Delhi, February 2, 1984.
18. *Far Eastern Economic Review,* Vol. 140, No. 16, 21 April 1988, pp. 24-25.
19. *Ibid.*
20. "Another Spratly Spat", *Asia Week,* May 20, 1988, p. 27.
21. *Ibid.*
22. *Ibid.,* pp. 27-28.
23. For further details, see Hungdau Chiu and Park Choon Ho, "Legal status of the Paracel and the Spratly Islands", *Ocean Development and International Law,* Vol. 3, No. 1, 1975, pp. 9-12 and "Chinese Foreign Ministry's Memorandum on question of Xisha and Nansha", *Views from China,* PRC Embassy, New Delhi, May 15, 1988, pp. 4-5.
24. For details about this aspect, see *White Book on Vietnam's Sovereignty over the Hoang Sa and Truong Archipelagoes,* Hanoi, Ministry of Foreign Affairs, September 28, 1979.
25. S.K. Ghosh, "Rivalry in the South China Sea", *China Report,* New Delhi, Vol. 13, No. 2, March-April 1977, pp. 4-5.
26. For further details see, *Conference for the Conclusion and Signature of the Peace Treaty with Japan, Record of Proceedings,* Washington, DC, US Department of State, Publication no. 4392, December 1951.
27. Emperor Gia Long (Nguyen Anh) after ascending the throne in 1802 immediately sent an embassy to China asking for formal investiture. China granted the formal investiture in 1803. At that time, Kia King was the emperor of China who stipulated then that the tribute must be sent every two years and homage performed every four years. For details see: D.G.E. Hall, *A History of Southeast Asia,* London, Macmillan & Co., 1968, p. 431.
28. For this aspect, see, Alexander Woodside, "Nationalism and Poverty in the breakdown of Sino-Vietnam relations", *Pacific Affairs,* Vol. 52, No. 3, Fall 1979, pp. 380-88.
29. Samuels, n. 3, p. 79 and also see *White Paper on the Hoang Sa and Truong Sa Islands,* Saigon, Ministry of Foreign Affairs, RVN, 1975, p. 86.

30. Sushila Kaushik & R.P. Kaushik, *Back to the Front: The Unfinished Story in Vietnam*, New Delhi, Orient Longman, 1979, p. 50.
31. Leon Howell and Michael Morrow, *Asia: Oil Politics and the Energy Crisis*, New York, 1974, p. 126.
32. *Keesing's Contemporary Archives*, London, March 4-10, 1974, p. 26388.
33. George MacArthur, "US Seventh Fleet Keeps Chinese Forces Under Watch", *Manila Bulletin*, March 4, 1974.
34. Samuels, n. 3, p. 111.
35. Most of the writers have identified three islets only and have omitted mention of the other three, which were possibly Song Tu Tay (Pugad), Sinh Ton (Sin Cowe) and Hon Sap (Peerson Reef). For details see Katchen, n. 5. p. 1179 & Samuels, n. 3, pp. 101-02.
36. *Newsweek*, March 12, 1979, p. 11.
37. *Time Magazine*, March 5, 1979, p. 6.
38. The Deputy Soviet Foreign Minister, Igor Rogachev came to Beijing to attend the Sino-Soviet Vice-Foreign Minister's meeting in the last week of August 1988 and discussed the Kampuchean issue with his Chinese counterpart, Tian Zengpei. Rogachev is reported to have said in Beijing that a breakthrough in Sino-Soviet relations over Kampuchea was at hand. For details see *Xinhua*, Beijing, September 1, 1988 and *News from China*, PRC Embassy, New Delhi, September 7, 1988, p. 6.
39. *Xinhua*, April 24, 1988 and *News from China*, PRC Embassy, New Delhi, April 27, 1988, p. 8.
40. Harvey Stockwin, "Chinese ambitions in the South China Sea", *The Times of India*, New Delhi, 2 March 1988.
41. Michael S. Serrill, "Vietnam: Spoiled Fruits of Victory", *Time*, New York, August 8, 1988, p. 7.

9

The Politics of Perestroika in Vietnam, 1986-1990

The Socialist Republic of Vietnam, so far the nerve-centre of Communism in the Southeast Asian region, has introduced *doi moi*,[1] the Vietnamese equivalent of the Soviet *perestroika*, to develop and modernize living conditions in the country. The changes that have occurred in the Soviet Union, the end of the Warsaw Pact, the dismantlement of the Council for Mutual Economic Assistance (COMECON), and the complete transformation that has come about in the international environment have all prompted the leaders of that country to make changes in their political system and experiment with radical innovations in the different facets of the country's life such as agriculture, industry, the bureaucracy, the armed forces, the Party, the Press, and the Parliament. These experiments have yielded results in that they have helped in checking inflation and in raising production. In 1989 Vietnam exported as much as 1.5 million tonnes of rice to the world outside. The changes in Vietnam's traditional policies have reduced tensions in the region of Indochina and paved the way for the settlement of the Cambodian dispute. This article is, however, confined to an analysis of the factors which motivated the leaders to reform their political system. It also makes an appraisal of some of the important measures that they have already taken and their impact on the political system and the socio-economic outlook of the people of the country.

Genesis of the Reforms

The rulers in Vietnam have sought to reform their system by taking a number of non-traditional steps without disturbing the one-party system. The poor economic conditions in the country and the spiralling price rise were the first compulsion to reform the system. In the mid-1980s Vietnam was one of the poorest countries of the world. Its per capita income of $130 a year was lower than that of Bangladesh's $160 a year.[2] There were repeated devaluations and demonetizations to improve the financial position, but inflation continued to rise. The national currency, the dong, was devalued in April 1985 (from US $1.00 = 11.7 dong to US $1.00 = 100 dong).[3] The Deputy Premier, Tran Phuong, disclosed that the new rate had in fact been in effect for official transactions during the preceding two years but that the rate of exchange had not been announced to the public. He added that the exchange rate for the dong in the black market at the time was in the region of US $1.00 = 375 dong.[4] About five months later, in September 1985, Vietnam took the decision to demonetize. This completely shattered the process of economic growth. New currency notes were introduced, the value of one new dong being made equal to that of ten old dong. Fifteen new dong were considered to be equivalent to one American dollar.[5] According to a broadcast made over Radio Hanoi on 18 September 1985, the change was aimed at strengthening market management and stabilizing prices. These measures, however, proved to be disastrous. There was, therefore, a second devaluation a year later, in November 1986 (from US $1.00 = 15 dong to US $1.00 = 80 dong).[6] However, the black market rate for the dong at the time of this devaluation was in the region of US $1.00 = 430 dong.[7] The *Far Eastern Economic Review* commented on 11 December 1986 that the devaluation was aimed at combating an annual inflation rate of some 700 per cent.[8] This too failed to check the rate of inflation and tackle blackmarketeering.

Vietnam was confronted with budget deficits as well. From 1981 to 1984 the budget deficits averaged nearly 19 billion dong a year. The deficit increased further in 1985-86.[9] The rapidly deteriorating economic situation annoyed the people and the leaders alike. The situation became alarming; so much so that the then General Secretary of the Communist Party, Troung Chinh, remarked that the people had lost confidence in the leadership of the Communist Party and in the functioning of the state organs.[10]

The second important issue that bedevilled the Vietnamese system was rampant corruption. The traditional system of management, being autocratic, developed serious trouble particularly in the management of economic affairs. For instance, it was found that the state subsidies were being diverted to enrich the coffers of the state personnel. There were wide disparities between the official prices of the goods sold by the state and the free-market prices of the same goods. The prices of raw materials, electricity, and coal, which the state provided to the various enterprises under its control, were as low as one-tenth of the market prices. This was so because these prices were highly subsidized. The result was that the state personnel resold a large part of the supply to the people for profit.[11] Some state officials sold for profit even materials such as grain, clothes, and other consumer goods meant for distribution among the people. The officials concerned escaped punishment because of the understanding between them and the Communist Party bosses. It was common practice for candidates to use flattery to Communist Party officials in order to secure Government posts. The information media were censured for highlighting cases of omission and commission by Party officials. Whenever a top leader of the Party visited a province to acquaint himself with the problems there, the cadres accompanying him saw to it that the members of the local committees did not report the negative aspects of the situation there.[12] The result was that the leader never learnt of the actual problems confronting the people! No wonder, therefore, that the leadership became alienated from the people.

By 1986 the leaders were convinced of the need for drastic reform to fulfil the basic needs of the people. All those who would not brook any possible compromise with the traditional Communist framework were constrained to step down. General Secretary Truong Chinh, along with Premier Pham Van Dong and the Party ideologue, Le Duc Tho, resigned. Nguyen Van Linh, an advocate of radical reforms in the system, emerged as the topmost leader. He made his own assessment of the implications of Mikhail Gorbachev's *perestroika* and *glasnost* and of the rapid developments in the Southeast Asian region. He then chose to take his country towards a system of liberal democracy and market economy.

The Communist Party of Vietnam met for its Sixth Congress from 15 to 18 December 1986. The various participants made a critical appraisal of the political system and subjected the functioning of the bureaucrats and top officials to serious scrutiny. This resulted in a new awakening. There were new initiatives. Nguyen Van Linh became the new General Secretary of the Comunist Party of Vietnam. In that capacity he gave a call for wide ranging reforms in the name of what he called *doi moi*. Literally translated, the expression "*doi moi*" means renovation. As is well known, the idea of renovation was being extensively used in the various Communist countries of Eastern Europe to demand economic and political reform. It was used in the debates held in the various public forums to refer to reform in the policies towards prices and wages, a fair measure of autonomy for State enterprises, and the complementary roles of the State and private enterprise in the economy as a whole.[13] "Renovation" thus signified in Eastern Europe more than it normally means.

In Vietnam *doi moi* signifies a resolve to restructure Vietnam's Socialist system or, in any case, to throw some outdated ideas overboard. It is a means to social change and economic development, to the introduction of certain aspects of liberal democracy in the Communist system. *It is, however, against ending the dominant role of the Communist Party.* The leaders believe that their *doi moi* would make the Party strong politically, ideologically, and organizationally.

Nguyen Van Linh say that *doi moi* means a far-reaching, thoroughgoing revolution. It means renovation in thinking, in policymaking, in organization, and in the appointment of personnel. The road it has to travel, however, "is not a straight one. It is full of twists and turns."[14]

Under the stewardship of Nguyen Van Linh the country has carried out some vital reforms, including changes in the Constitution of 1980.

Agriculture

Reform of the system of agriculture received high priority under *doi moi*. In December 1986, immediately after the Sixth National Congress of the Communist Party, the Deputy Premier, Vo Van Kiet, submitted a report to the National Assembly suggesting reform, as well as offering his proposals for the socio-economic plan for 1987. Besides fixing the target for the production of grain, he recommended "incentive policies" to stimulate agricultural production. Farmers were to be given incentives to ensure the implementation of some reform measures. The Political Bureau of the Communist Party also decided in favour of important changes in the policy of land allocation that year. Earlier each household had some land allocated to it, the quantum depending on how many members it had. The allocation was made, however, in scattered fragments. This policy was now thoroughly reviewed. It was decided that the allocation should be made in terms of single parcels of land, with cultivation rights fixed for a period of fifteen to nineteen years. Farmers were thus given something approaching ownership rights to the land they were called upon to till and cultivate. Besides, the skill and efficiency of each household was taken into account in making allocations. The result of this reform was that land did not remain collectivized any more in any real sense of the term. In fact some people feel that the expression "agricultural cooperatives" has been a misnomer since then.[15]

The Communist Party introduced some further measures of agricultural reform at the Sixth Plenum of the Party Central Committee in April 1989. It decided to change thoroughly the concept of cooperatives in general and of agricultural cooperatives in particular. It felt that it was not necessary to collectivize all the means of production at the initial stages. Under the new policy it was for the members of a cooperative to decide on the scale and form of its contributions of capital and manpower, on the extent of the collectivization of the means of production, and on the managerial mechanism and the distribution of revenue. A farmer had the right to join or leave a cooperative of his own free will, and there was to be no coercion in any form. This readjustment of the relations of production and the longterm allocation of land to farmers transformed each family into a self-financing unit. Not only could a family work for a cooperative on contract, but it could also engage in some other trade or trades of its own choosing.[16]

These measures of reform in the agricultural sector have paid rich dividends. The total production has increased. In the Mekong delta the production of rice in 1989 was 7.7 million tonnes, which was a two-fold increase over the 1975 figure. Per capita output rose to 550 kilogrammes as against 230 kilogrammes in the northern provinces. Vietnam exported 1.5 million tonnes of rice and was ranked the third largest rice-exporter in the world after the United States and Thailand. The Mekong delta led in the production of certain other crops as well. It produced 40 per cent of the country's sugar, fruit, and pepper; and 50 per cent of its beans and tobacco; 40 per cent of its aquatic products; and 50 per cent of its pork.[17] Plans are now afoot to increase the area under fruit cultivation from 11 per cent to 20 per cent. The country's forest cover is to rise from 8 per cent of the total land surface to 20 per cent. Coconut, pineapple, and banana trees are being planted in every district with foreign collaboration. In 1989 Vietnam exported 4,000 tonnes of refrigerated pineapple, and from 4,000 to 5,000 tonnes of bananas, both dried and fresh, to the Soviet Union.[18]

Industry

After the unification of the two parts of Vietnam in 1975-76 there was little economic progress in the country. The standards of living were low. There was stark poverty everywhere. The country did not produce adequate consumer goods. Several factors were responsible for such a state of affairs, the most glaring being the faulty operation of the Central Planning Commission. The Commission was responsible for the production plans of the State-owned industrial enterprises, but these were mismanaged so that the production targets were never reached. The personnel concerned went about saying that as they were not involved in the planning and the management, they could not be blamed for any loss or mismanagement. They believed that if they had a say in decision-making or in the drawing up of production plans or in the formulation of procurement policies, there would be efficiency and a rise in production.

The new leaders saw that there was need to pay attention to private enterprises as well and to introduce "incentive policies" in them too.

The first thing to do was to develop a mechanism for improving the functioning of the State-owned industrial enterprises. At the same time it was necessary to evolve policies for the operation of private enterprises. The new leaders resolved to decentralize the process of decision-making in economic matters and to reduce the restrictions imposed on the various enterprises, whether private or public. They determined only three basic norms for the operation of any enterprise: total output value, total quantity of key products, and revenue contributions to the State.[19] The Government introduced what it called "Socialist business accounting", which consisted of measures to make the state bureaucracy more responsible in its behaviour. It also sought to ensure punctual and normal supplies of commodities to the different enterprises, both private and public.

The Communist Party noted in March 1989 that a beginning had been made in rebuilding the economic structure on the pattern of a multisectoral economy. Adjustments were made initially in the investments by concentrating on the targets set in the economic programme. The improvements made in the managerial apparatus gave a new impetus to production. Though there were difficulties in the state-owned economic sector, many units started operating effectively. The concept of "people's right to mastery", which was formulated and promoted while preparing for and conducting the Sixth Party Congress, was further developed: it became in fact the force behind *doi moi*.[20] All the measures taken in line with the concept of "people's right to mastery" have had a favourble impact on the management and on the attitude of officials. There has been a phenomenal development of the private sector; so much so that it plays a vital role in Vietnam's success today. The emphasis is on small-scale private enterprises. There is a campaign on to change the traditional thinking, which had overemphasized industrial and agricultural collectivization. Now it is accepted that the members of the Communist Party should possess adequate expertise in economic management. Foreign observers have commented that this makes the Communist Party "more expert and less Red".[21]

The new leaders feel that for a long time it would be necessary for the private sector (made up of those who own small, individual holdings and private capitalists) to function within the structure of a socialism-oriented commodity economy. They want private citizens to invest and engage in production in areas beneficial to the national economy and the people's life. They would allow the private sector to engage in production without limitation as to the scale or area of operations in all fields such as goods production, building, transport, and services—all except those forbidden to them by law for political or security reasons. As for private commerce, the Sixth Party Plenum said that capitalist traders on the domestic market might continue their business in lines not forbidden by law but under state control. It gave private citizens the right to deal in gold and silver but in accordance with state regulations. It, further, laid down that in the field of imports and exports, capitalist traders might not set up foreign trade companies. It, however, said that private enterprises producing goods for export which met the conditions required by law could deal directly with foreign partners and export their products and import the equipment and materials needed for production. It permitted participation by private citizens in banking and credit operations in a few places on an experimental basis.[22]

These concessions made to the private sector proved wise; for it was persuaded to produce goods in accordance with the needs of the market. Traditionally, enterprises set up in the private sector were under an obligation not to employ more than ten workers, but under the multisectoral economy plan, this restriction was lifted. It is reported that now there are some private industries employing as many as a thousand workers.[23] Vice-Premier Vo Van Kiet said on 6 February 1990 that Vietnam had already issued a hundred investment licences to foreign business organizations for projects worth US $800 million, mostly to those dealing in oil, gas and sea products or relating to tourism and the service industries.[24]

A serious handicap in the operation and functioning of private enterprises used to be the centralized socialist banking system. Radical steps have, therefore, been taken to reorganize it. Traditionally, the main bank of issue was the National Bank of Vietnam. The other bank was Vietcombank. In July 1988 there was a decree allowing new banks to come up. The banking system was divided into a Central Bank and a number of sectorial banks to promote trade and agricultural development.[25] In November 1989 a new bank known as the Vietnam Import-Export Bank was founded. Steps are being taken to facilitate the setting up of foreign banks as well. Efforts are being made to create the proper conditions, to provide for reserve requirements, to frame rules of operation, and to lay down management qualifications for the functioning of independent commercial banks.

The Bureaucracy

The Vietnamese bureaucracy had over the years turned into an instrument of the Communist Party, (operated) by the Communist Party, for the (benefit of the) Communist Party. Officials were by and large corrupt, and the bureaucracy as a whole was unpopular. It was grossly inefficient, and, being overstaffed, much of the revenue was spent on its maintenance. Corruption prospered under what was called the umbrella system, a system under which a high-level functionary of the Party made most of the lower-level official appointments and was responsible for promotions and salary increases. In fact he functioned as the patron of the lower-level Government officials appointed by him. If the lower-level personnel worked incompetently or indulged in corrupt practices, there was nothing anybody could do as their patron protected them. This system has been reviewed since the accession of Nguyen Van Linh to power. Many corrupt bureaucrats have been removed from office, and many more are on their way out. Following the Sixth Congress of the Communist Party, many well-entrenched leaders and officials have been summarily dismissed. Nguyen Van Linh has overhauled the apparatus of bureaucratic control over the management and the economy so as to promote efficiency and development. He has given responsibility and respectability to workers. Nobody now dare treat workers as mere robots as may were wont to do in the past.

Nguyen Van Linh has used the trade unions and the Press to make the bureaucracy more accountable and responsive. A number of trade unions, such as the Federation of Trade Unions, the Ho Chi Minh Youth Union, the National Peasants' Union (formerly the Collective Peasants' Union), the Women's Association, and the Fatherland Front, have been strengthened and encouraged to play an active role in the country's polity and keep a close watch on the bureaucrats and the management. By means of a decree passed in 1989 the regime has sought to create proper conditions for the functioning of the trade unions. It has asked the trade unions to organize independent bases for themselves so as to be able to carry out work on their own, i.e., independently of Government initiative. Elections to the unions are held by the unions themselves rather than by the Central Congress.[26] This frees the trade unions from their long subordination to the Communist Party. It is now widely recognized that the various unions have a duty to protect the interests of their members and to serve as an effective check on errant officials by exposing their acts of omission and commission.

The Press has an even more effective role to play in ensuring that the bureaucracy and the administration do not overstep their limits. There is a great debate going-on among members of the Communist Party on the freedom of the Press. The Government has given certain directives to journalists so that they reflect not merely "the voice of the party" but also "the voice of the people". Journalists are encouraged to investigate cases of alleged wrongdoing by prominent cadres of the Party and by officials, especially in the higher echelons of the Government, to make public wherever there is oppression of the people by the State apparatus, and to expose the unvarnished social and economic realities of Vietnamese life.[27] The *Christian Science Monitor* reported on 8 November 1987 that there was a Government directive granting more freedom for editors to print investigative articles about members of the Party. In fact the directive is said to have asked newspapers in each locality to take part in deciding which members of the Party were good and qualified.[28] A message from Nguyen Van Linh issued in this context deserves to be quoted at length. He said:

> I believe in any event you must not "bend your pens" in order to please people. As long as you cannot write as you wish, continue your research, continue to enrich your knowledge of life. But don't write opportunistic pieces. Today it is difficult to decide what to praise and what to condemn. Often, evils are found right among the people holding important posts in the Party and State apparatuses. The people who write about the seamy side are accused of "blackening the regime". Personally I think that in addition to writing about good people and good things, one must also portray bad people and bad things to arouse public indignation and censure. To do so is not to be critical of the regime. One just seeks to expose persons and practices that go against the noble ideals of Socialism. You must depict incisively and condemn severely all bureaucrats, bullies, thieves, hoarders, speculators, parasites, all superstitious practices, and all manifestations of moral degradation. You must make the whole of society hate evils, push them back, and avoid committing them. At the same time, you must paint faithful, convincing pictures of honest people engaged in manual and mental labour, people who in spite of privations and temptations are working with self-abnegation and courage for national construction and defence, in enthusiastic response to the Party's call for renovation.[29]

National Assembly

For long the National Assembly was regarded as a rubber stamp, but now the situation is changing. The deputies in the National Assembly debate bills and criticize Ministers for lapses and failures. A former Chairman of the National Assembly, Nguyen Huu Tho, made it clear in 1987 that the leadership would hereafter try to carry the Assembly by means of persuasion and that the views of the Party would no longer be imposed on the entire membership. He added that unanimity would no longer be required on substantive issues and that they would use secret balloting so that deputies might exercise their own judgement.[30] Nguyen Van Linh for his part was critical of the formalism and bureaucratism of the previous Assemblies. He said that elected bodies should no longer be presented with *faits accomplis* and that they should not be used as rubber stamps.[31] Vo Chi Cong, President of the State Council, was more forthright. He declared that it was necessary to allow the National Assembly to represent the people and to give it responsibility for solving important problems in the life of the people.[32]

Significant reforms have been made in the process of electing members of the National Assembly. The country has evolved a system called the "multi-candidate election system", which is in a way a challenge to the total monopoly of the Communist Party. It is not compulsory for anybody to be a member of the Communist Party to fight an election. People without links with the Communist Party or with any party for that matter may also contest. Candidates may, further, do some campaigning unlike under the previous system.[33] In 1987, when there were elections for the posts of deputies in the National Assembly, a number of candidates, not belonging to the Communist Party, contested. Twenty-six such candidates won; seventy-four seats went to the candidates of the Communist Party.[34] This was a unique development. Similar multi-candidate elections have been held for positions at the village, city, and provincial levels, and "independent" candidates have done fairly well.

Armed Forces

Since December 1986 Vietnam has sought to impress the world community with its peaceful intentions. It completely withdrew from Cambodia in September 1989 and decided to reduce its own armed forces drastically—at least by 50 per cent.[35]

It would be pertinent here to explain why Vietnam maintained a large army. It had to fight wars against France, the United States, and China in the past fifty years. Its rulers sensed a threat to the security of the country from all sides. They, therefore, chose to build their country's military might. Vietnam's armed forces were the fifth biggest in the world after the Soviet Union, China, the United States, and India. Its army numbered over a million full-time soldiers; there were as many as three million reservists.[36] Besides, there several special units and paramilitary groups. The total number accounted for 8 per cent of the total Vietnamese population. Vietnam could raise the strength of its armed forces further still any time because there was a provision in the Constitution which said that men between 18 and 35 years and women between 18 and 25 years were subject to conscription.

These arrangements are now a thing of the past. Vietnam has gradually reduced the size of its armed forces. According to Brigadier Nguyen Van Thai, the desire of the present rulers is to reduce the strength of the armed forces from 8 per cent to 1 per cent of the total population. He also disclosed that more than 300,000 soldiers would be retrenched in the near future. Yet another military spokesman, Lieutenant General Nguyen Quyet, stated that the military had undertaken a basic change in both direction and strategy. It was being streamlined into a defensive force consistent with peacetime needs, "an army numerically small but high in quality."[37]

The member countries of the Association of Southeast Asian Nations (ASEAN) appreciate the scaling down of Vietnam's military might. They are gradually getting convinced of the peaceful intentions of Vietnam. Consequently, there is a thaw in their relations with Vietnam. Indonesia has played a key role in getting the Cambodian question settled and in paving the way for a satisfactory and honourable settlement from the Vietnamese viewpoint. Singapore has allowed its entrepreneurs to explore possibilities of promoting joint ventures. It is, however, on Thailand that the changes in Vietnam have made the most impact. The former Prime Minister, Chartichai Choonhavan, has emphasized the economic potential of Vietnam and the benefits that may accrue to Thailand through collaboration and cooperation between Thailand and Vietnam. As both countries are major rice-exporters of the world, understanding between them would benefit both. Also, Thailand considers Vietnam a good market for its consumer products. The Thai leaders are already talking of "turning the Indo-Chinese battlefield into a market place."[38]

Monopoly of the Party

The biggest task of *doi moi* is to set limits to the power and the monopoly of the Communist Party. So far regarded as the vanguard of the people, the Communist Party had enjoyed a monopoly over the power structure till recently. The latest developments indicate that there is a demand for curbing the all-pervasive power of the Party and for ensuring that it has no chance of being criticized for abuse of power. The leaders are trying to give it a different shape to make it more disciplined, more sensitive, and more accountable.

The leaders, however, are not interested in establishing a multi-party system. Murray Hiebert say that the objective at present is political liberalization. There are moves to introduce more democracy in the Communist Party, separate the functions of the Party from the State, develop a more comprehensive legal system, and relax control on journalists and writers. The position of the Communist Party in Vietnam is often compared to that of the Chinese Communist Party.[39] Gareth Porter says that the thinking in the Communist Party in Vietnam is more in line with that of the Chinese Communist Party than with that of the Communist Parties in Eastern Europe with their pluralist tendencies. The demand for freedom from interference by the Communist Party and even for freedom for other parties to operate, in the context of the disturbing news coming in of happenings on the ideological front, constitutes a clear warning to the Communist Party in Vietnam.[40]

The Communist Party in Vietnam, however, has great influence on the people unlike its counterparts in Eastern Europe. It is not a party that was imposed on Vietnam. It emerged, when it did, as an indigenous development. It was under its leadership that the country fought for independence against France. It was also under its stewardship that the people fought successfully against the mighty United States. It was responsible for the unification of the two parts of Vietnam. It was in accordance with its blueprint that the foundations of the United Socialist Republic of Vietnam were laid. Nguyen Co Thach, a former Politburo member, explains it in the following words:

> Communism here is not a system that was imposed from outside, but it is a tool with which they fought for independence. Here there is a traditional Confucian desire for order, and harmony of authority accepted. Many would question [the wisdom of] changing to a multiparty system for which there is no tradition. They must avoid falling back into feudal provincialism and need something to keep the nation together. The party acts as a clamp for the country. Without it the old North-South conflict immediately comes up.[41]

The Communist Party of Vietnam has an illustrious history.[42] Its aim in the past was to fight foreign aggressors. According to Le Duan, it sought in those days to awaken the masses politically and organize them for the struggle to overthrow the domination of the exploiting classes and finally to seize power. Later it carried out the task of building up the State machinery.[43] When the country won freedom and the Socialist Republic of Vietnam was founded, a serious threat was posed to its security by the collusion between Cambodia (then Kampuchea) and China. Again the Party played a great role in resisting aggression.

However, the environment and the national priorities are changed today. The leaders feel that they can have a better security climate if there is peace and economic development. They are willing to adapt the Communist Party according to the priorities of the country's peacetime needs. They must, however, contend with some serious problems.

First, the educational curricula and the State media had inculcated certain cultural and ideological attitudes in the past, and it will take time for the people to understand the new environment and the new ethos.

Second, there are the practical problems. Serious discussions are now going-on for a change in the structure, role, and ideological moorings of the Communist Party. There is a growing demand for more democracy within the framework of the Constitution. On 1 February 1990 the newspaper *Nhan Dan* reported a symposium on the Communist Party organized by the Nguyen Ai Quoc National Institute in Hanoi. It said that at this symposium the participants debated emotionally the weaknesses of the Party. Some of the participants charged that the lapses of the Party were responsible for the erosion of the people's confidence in the leadership. Others referred to the bureaucracy, to corruption, to the isolation of the masses, to the infringement of the public services by the Party, and to the false notion that the party had the duty to govern. They even accused some Party members and executives of oppressing the masses. The delegates were unanimous that the Party should lead democratically within the framework of the Constitution and not place itself beyond the Constitution.

Results of *Doi Moi*

The impact of *doi moi* on Vietnam has been positive. *Doi moi* has proved useful at the domestic level. The availability of essential commodities has improved, and a number of consumer goods are now available. The rate of inflation has been checked. It was brought down from 700 per cent in 1987-88 to about 24 per cent in 1989.[44]

The currency system has stabilized; so much so that blackmarketeering has virtually disappeared. Many new houses are coming up. Japanese television sets and South Korean stereos are being marketed on street corners everywhere. Vietnam is in a position to export its agricultural produce. We may here point out that India is the largest buyer of Vietnamese rice. It bought 300,000 tonnes of rice (worth Rs. 2,100 million) from Vietnam in 1989.[45]

An appraisal of *doi moi* would show that it has helped in the process of development. In the words of a Soviet diplomat, "the liberal economic reforms in Vietnam are the most radical among the Socialist countries. Within two years Vietnam has brought down hyper inflation, established a stable foreign-exchange rate, and produced a big rice surplus."[46] International financial organizations like the International Monetary Fund (IMF) and the International Bank for Reconstruction and Development (IBRD) have also expressed their appreciation of Vietnam's economic development. The IMF has sent several teams to Vietnam to draw up a short-term economic adjustment programme to assist the country in fighting inflation. The IBRD and the Asian Development Bank have sent study teams to work out investment plans for the development of energy, engineering works, the infrastructure, and the production and processing of consumer and export goods. The IBRD has sent a delegation to draw up a credit plan too. During his visit to Vietnam in 1990 W.I. Kohl, the head of the IBRD delegation, remarked:

> We are surprised by the results of the new economic policy in Vietnam. It is impossible to conceive these without being here in the country. We have made suggestions to a number of countries whose economic reforms have been going on for over ten years. Vietnam has accomplished what those countries have failed to do, namely, the price reform and the change of exchange rates.[47]

The success of *doi moi*, however, has not prevented certain conservatives called Stalinists from opposing it. The leader of these conservatives is Mai Chi Tho, brother of the late Party ideologue, Le Duc Tho. He was formerly in the intelligence service and the secret police. He also served for a term as Interior Minister. Mai Chi Tho's is regarded as a major voice against radical reforms today. He states that the struggle against the imperialists and the reactionary forces continues to be a worldwide struggle on political, economic, cultural, and ideological fronts. To undertake an overambitious reform programme in favour of free enterprise and consumerism may, according to him, be a means of gathering intelligence on the disposition of the people themselves. The rapid rise in the crime rate is due to the implementation of reforms.[48] He suggests that freedom of worship, easing of travel restrictions, and greater access for foreigners within the country should, among other things, be the objective of reforms. He feels that the new policy of *doi moi* is leading the nation to disaster.[49] Some other prominent leaders are also opposed to rapid liberalization. These include the former Defence Minister, Van Tien Dung (who led the final assault to liberate South Vietnam), and the former Interior Minister, Pham Hung (the leader of the National Liberation Front of South Vietnam at the time of liberation).

The drastic reforms in the Soviet Union have pushed that country towards disintegration. The different federating republics have drifted apart because the Soviet leaders had failed to build a proper infrastructure before introducing momentous transformations in the form of *perestroika* and *glasnost*. Systemic changes cannot prevent fragmentation. In contrast the Vietnamese leaders, conscious of the dangers ahead of them, have sought to evolve ways and means of sustaining greater democratization. Though a country with a different history, culture, and religion, Vietnam has yet to be careful while transforming the system. The consensus, however, is in favour of structural changes and qualitative reforms.

REFERENCES

1. Gareth Porter says that *doi moi* includes "an endeavour of broadening of democracy through the revitalization—within the framework of firm Party control—of political institutions that had grown sclerotic and distant from the masses." See his article "Politics of Renovation in Vietnam", *Problems of Communism*, Washington, D.C., Vol. 39, May-June 1990, p. 73.
2. *International Herald Tribune*, Singapore edn, 21 March 1988. According to the *Statesman Yearbook*, London, the GNP per capita of Vietnam was $170 in 1978, $100 in 1984, and $300 in 1986. According to a survey published in *Asiaweek*, Hong Kong, 10 August 1990, it was $175. In contrast the GNP per capita of Bangladesh was $179.
3. *Nhan Dan*, Hanoi, 23 September 1985. Cited in *Keesing's Contemporary Archives*, London, Vol. 32, No. 1, January 1986, p. 34101.

4. *Ibid.*
5. *Ibid.*
6. *The Times*, London, 17 December 1986.
7. *Le Monde*, Paris, 11 November 1986.
8. Truong Xuan Le and The Duy say that during the period 1965-75, the budget deficit increased by about 10 per cent a year. In 1976 the rate of inflation was 21.6 per cent. It rose to 95.2 per cent a year in 1988. The price index was higher by 18.6 per cent in 1977 than it was in 1976. In 1985-86 it jumped to 369.7 per cent. See "About the Fight against Inflation in Vietnam", *Vietnam Courier*, Hanoi, No. 3, 1990, p. 10.
9. *Straits Times*, Singapore, 16 December 1986.
10. For Truong Chinh's address to the Sixth National Congress of the Communist Party, see *Vietnam Information Bulletin*, New Delhi, Embassy of the Socialist Republic of Vietnam in India, 23 January 1987, pp. 3–7. See also "VIth CPV [Communist Party of Vietnam] Congress in Hanoi", *Keesing's Contemporary Archives*, Vol. 33, No. 4, April 1987, pp. 35067-70.
11. See Porter, n. 1, pp. 72-88.
12. *Ibid.*, p. 75.
13. *Ibid.*, p. 73.
14. Nguyen Van Linh, "Let Writers and Artists Actively Contribute to Renovation", *Vietnam Courier*, No. 1, 1988, p. 11.
15. Porter, n. 1, p. 80.
16. "On Multi-Sectoral Economic Policy", *Vietnam Information Bulletin*, 14 July 1989, pp. 5-8.
17. "Prospect of Agriculture in Mekong River Delta", *ibid.*, 29 August 1989, pp. 7-8.
18. *Ibid.*
19. "The Communique of the VIth Party Plenum", *ibid.*, 29 May 1989, p. 2. See also *Nhan Dan*, 20 April 1989.
20. "The Communique of the VIth Party Plenum", *Vietnam Information Bulletin*, 29 May 1989, p. 1.
21. *Christian Science Monitor*, Boston, Mass., 8 November 1987.
22. "The Communique of the VIth Party Plenum", *Vietnam Information Bulletin*, 29 May 1989, pp. 1-6. See also "On Multi-Sectoral Economic Policy", *ibid.*, 14 July 1989, p. 8.
23. Porter, n. 1, p. 80; and *Nhan Dan*, 20 April 1989.
24. *Business Times*, New Delhi, 8 February 1990.
25. *International Herald Tribune*, Singapore edn, 21 April 1990.
26. "Draft Law on Trade Unions", *Nhan Dan*, 8 September 1989; and Porter, n. 1, p. 83.
27. Murray Hiebert, "Vietnam: Radical Political Reform Rejected by Party Leadership", *Far Eastern Economic Review*, Hong Kong, 12 April 1990, p. 12.

28. "The Hunt Is On in Vietnam's Party Purge", *Christian Science Monitor,* 8 November 1987.
29. "Speech by General Secretary Nguyen Van Linh at a Meeting with One Hundred Writers, Artists, and Cultural Workers in Hanoi on 6-7 October 1987", *Vietnam Courier,* No. 1, 1988, p. 12.
30. "Vietnam Urges Reforms to Forestall Discontent", *Straits Times,* 3 February 1990.
31. *Ibid.*
32. *Ibid.*
33. Clayton Jones, "Vietnam Trying a New Brand of Democracy", *Christian Science Monitor,* 16 November 1989.
34. "Members of the Eighth National Assembly, Socialist Republic of Vietnam", *Nhan Dan,* 22 April 1987. See also Porter, n. 1, p. 82.
35. Larry Jagan, "Vietnam Takes to *Glasnost* in a Big Way", *The Times of India,* New Delhi, 11 January 1989.
36. *Ibid.*
37. *Ibid.*
38. "Thai-Businessmen Delegation Visits Vietnam", *Vietnam Information Bulletin,* 29 July 1989, p. 6. Also see "Joint Press Statement of Vietnam and Thailand", *ibid.*, 23 July 1989.
39. Hiebert, n. 27.
40. Porter, n. 1, p. 85.
41. David Storey, "Vietnam Seeks New Political Model", *Bangkok Post,* 6 March 1990.
42. For a proper perspective on the role of the Communist Party of Vietnam, see Joseph Buttinger, *Vietnam: A Political History,* New York, 1968; Douglas Pike, *A History of Vietnamese Communism, 1925-1976* Stanford, Calif., 1978; Robert Turner, *Vietnamese Communism: Its Origin and Development,* Stanford, Calif., 1975; and Jean Saiteny, *Ho Chi Minh and His Vietnam: A Personal Memoir,* Chicago, Ill, 1972.
43. Le Duan, *On the Right to Collective Mastery,* Hanoi, 1980, p. 103.
44. Charles P. Wallace, "Vietnam Evolves Its Own Reform Model", *Deccan Herald,* Bangalore, 26 February 1990. However, Truong Xuan Le and The Duy say that the rate of inflation was markedly reduced, from 600 per cent in 1986 to 400 per cent in 1987. There was a slight increase in 1988: it went up to 480 per cent. It rose further by 25 per cent in 1989. For further details, see *Vietnam Courier,* No. 3, 1990, p. 10.
45. *The Times of India,* New Delhi, 13 September 1990.
46. Storey, n. 41.
47. Dang Duc Lan, "Vietnam Deserves Preferential Treatment", *Vietnam Courier,* No. 3, 1990, p. 11.
48. Alan Dawson, "Battlelines Are Drawn: Conservatives Opposed to *Doi Moi*", *Bangkok Post,* 13 and 15 April 1989.
49. *Ibid.*

10

Changes in Political System of Vietnam

The contemporary history of Southeast Asia has testified that the Vietnamese are dynamic in their approach and realistic in their policies. They are pursuing the policy of *Doi Moi* in their system and consequently political institutions are rapidly reformed to keep pace with the changing world. Hence, the role of the Party, National Assembly, Army, Bureaucracy and the Press have undergone transformations in tune with the democratic trends in the region. Though, the nature and function of the major political institutions are changing but the scrutiny of the changes suggest that the Vietnamese believe in continuity and change. One-party rule of the Communist Party remains but the evolving system has endeavoured to promote democratic way of life without diluting the principle of "dictatorship of the Communist Party".

Nobody can deny that Vietnam remains a communist country, but at the same time they cannot deny that they are cultivating democratic way of life by introducing the features of liberal society, i.e., decentralization, privatization, free trade, etc., to prove that Vietnam is an ideal partner of the Association of Southeast Asian Nations (ASEAN).

Socialist Republic of Vietnam occupies 130,000 square miles of the territory and has the population of 78.7 million. The annual birth rate is around 1.9 to 2 per cent and the family planning drives are not very successful. Though, there is a committee on Family Planning to minimise growth of population and policies have been adopted for late marriage and two-children families, etc., but they have yet to produce desired results.[1] The ethnic Vietnamese comprise the majority community, but simultaneously, there are ethnic Chams, Khmers, Tais, Hoas, Hmongs, Montagnards and heterogeneous tribal groups.[2]

Vietnam has a history of warfare against the Chinese for one thousand years from 111 B.C. till 939 AD. It emerged as a powerful Kingdom in the 13th Century AD after annexing Champa and subduing the Khmers. It lost its sovereignty only after the end of the opium war (1842), when France, as a colonial power, emerged on the Southeast Asian horizon. France colonised Vietnam in 1858, and expanded their rule over Cambodia, and Laos, but the Vietnamese did not accept colonial rule gracefully, and continued to struggle against it. Hence, it has a long and chequered history of struggle and warfare against colonialist forces.

The communists under the banner of the Indochina Communist Party (1930-42) and the Vietminh (1942-54) led the freedom movement and defeated the colonial powers.[3] The United States in pursuance of the policy of containment of communism, replaced the French to oppose freedom, and independence of Vietnam in 1954. Ignoring the nationalist nature of the communist movement, the Americans helped the process of temporary partition of Vietnam. It organised and aided anti-communist forces and sent its security forces to defeat communist guerrillas. The US involvement in Vietnam thus started growing and between 1964-75, 7 million tonnes of bombs, three times the tonnage used in World War II, had been dropped on Vietnam.[4] Besides, napalm and phosphorus bombs were also used. The tragedy of this phenomenon for the US was its defeat. It had to withdraw its forces lock, stock and barrel in April 1975. Besides, it had to accommodate thousands of Vietnamese refugees in the US. Vietnam war indeed proved very costly for the US, in which the US lost the lives of 56,559 servicemen and an expenditure of US $150 billion.[5] Though, millions of Vietnamese also died, but they were victorious finally in defeating the colonial forces and in uniting the two parts of Vietnam under a common political system. The communist ideology worked as a cementing force to unite the people of North and South Vietnam against external enemies.

The Communist Party of Vietnam (CPV) has special status because it led the nationalist movement against France and anti-colonial struggle against the U.S. successfully. Whether it was Indochina Communist Party (ICP) or National Liberation Front (NLF), their mobilisation and strategies were decided by the communist cadres. The role played by the communists were so much nationalistic that communism began to be equated with nationalism, and communist endeavours were projected as nationalist goals.

The victory over the US in 1975 boosted the morale of the Vietnamese. As it was under the stewardship of the CPV, the then leaders attached prime importance to it in the political system. Hence, they adopted one-party rule and the Constitution adopted in 1980, entrusted it with supreme powers of rule-making and rule-application. That did not work properly and therefore, there were some modifications when 1992, Constitution was passed. Now the attempt was made to separate the legislative, executive and judicial powers of the Government and thereby moderate the powers of the CPV. Though the consensus continues to be in favour of one party rule of the CPV, but the Constitution enacted in 1992, has definitely curtailed the role of the party to a great extent. Article four states that "CPV, the vanguard of Vietnamese working class, the faithful representative of the interests of working class, the working people and the whole nation, following Marxism-Leninism and Ho Chi Minh's thought, is the force leading the state and society."[6]

At the same time, the reforms are accelerated under the slogan of "we the people are fundamental". All party organisations including Communist Party, operate within the framework of the Constitution and the law. The people, therefore, exercise power through the National Assembly and the People's Councils.[7] The new Constitution, though, recognises the leadership of CPV, and guarantees that it is the one and only legitimate political party, but the overall situation is changing.

Mentioning the continued leadership of the Communist Party, however, is unique, because other socialist countries in the process of reorganisation and reform in the post-Cold War era, particularly in Eastern Europe left out the provisions dealing with the role of the Party, Vietnam has shown its courage by attaching importance to the CPV constitutionally even in the changed context and it continues to project it as a vehicle for development and modernisation.

The critics of the Vietnamese political system have been very active. They believe that Vietnam is unchanged as far as *Doi Moi* in political matters are concerned. They are unable to understand the rationale of one-party domination. They have been saying that the CPV conservatively clings to the right of leadership role and unless this situation is changed. Vietnam cannot evolve a democratic way of life. Notwithstanding, an objective assessment of Vietnamese politics that the leading position and role of the CPV has been agreed by the Vietnamese revolutionaries in the past five decades. The CPV leadership has been acceptable to the masses and without its leadership, it is difficult to promote nation building and at the same time promote reforms with efficiency and legitimacy. The CPV is relevant even in the changed context and plays its part in promoting liberalism and market economy.

Vietnam has accelerated the process of development and endeavoured to be a "market place". It wants foreign collaboration and investments and this factor was realized first by the CPV, which in its Sixth Party Congress, in December 1986, took momentous decisions that were beyond the scope of conservative communist thinking. The CPV, under the leadership of Nguyen Van Linh, adopted the policy of Doi Moi. This accelerated the reform process to open Vietnam to the outside world while projecting credentials of Vietnam as a peaceful country.

Doi Moi

Doi Moi is a unique way of bringing changes in the socio-economic life of socialist country and revolutionary in its own way. It is a means to social change and economic development, to the introduction of certain aspects of liberal democracy.[8] The various steps under Doi Moi have paved the path of development and the undergoing changes are appreciated at the global level.

Doi Moi has a wide meaning and it is being defined in various ways. Japan's Tetsusaburo Kimura analysed that Doi Moi has a wide range of contents, but it can be understood in three parts. The first is market opening measures including the abolition of the Central Government's monopoly of trade, encouragement of foreign investment and a shift to floating exchange rate system. The second part of Doi Moi is through which autonomy has been given to farmers, merchants, and enterprises in terms of manufacturing and sales. The third is the abolition of price control and use of interest as macro-economic variable.[9]

On the other hand Akie Ishida has said that Doi Moi is a legal reform in conformity with policy changes from a centrally planned economy to market-oriented economy. It is aimed at recognising multi-sector structure in the economy, operation of market mechanism and expansion of external economic relations.[10]

Ishida and Kimura both have stated that the emphasis of Doi Moi is reforms in the economic system, but its long-term impact on politics is a subject of speculation. Thus, Kimura says that Doi Moi is not to renovate everything in the short-term, but it is a process to study and experience trial and error. It is a repetition of an advance and retreat. It is different from *perestroika* and *glasnost* in meaning and texture, and a unique contribution of Vietnam under a communist order.

Doi Moi has proved advantageous in accelerating economic growth rate which has been around eight per cent since 1992. The measures under Doi Moi have enabled the government to control inflation rates and Vietnam is exporting 1.5 to 2 million tonnes of rice to the outside world. It has emerged as a third biggest rice exporting country. Besides, it is exporting crude oil, coal, tin and marine processed products. Agricultural exports also include groundnuts, wine, rubber, coffee, and tea. Again textiles and handicrafts production are rapidly rising. Thus, it has contributed to the factors for regional stability and prosperity.

While attending economic restructuring, Vietnam also looked towards some political institutions which have interconnections with management and economy. Hence, the role of the party, National Assembly, Army and the Press are changing. These transformations are complimenting the effectiveness of the economic institutions and helping the process of liberalisation and market economy. Here an attempt is made to analyse briefly the changes in the role of the Party, National Assembly, Army and the Press to prove that the political system too is in the transitional phase, and it is changing to cope with the challenges of economic development and globalisation.

Communist Party

Though, the new Constitution of Vietnam says that the CPV is the force leading the state and society, its powers have been reviewed as a result of the corresponding increase in the powers of National Assembly. Now it is not necessary to be a member of the Communist Party to be a member of the National Assembly. Nguyen Xuan Oanh, a member of Vietnam's National Assembly spoke to International Herald Tribune that the election for National Assembly in 1987, brought major change: 60 per cent of those elected were new to the legislature. They came from a variety of backgrounds. About 10 per cent of those did not belong to the Communist Party. Independent candidates are encouraged to fight and as they have opted for multi-candidate election, the electorates have choice of alternatives.[11]

The 1992, Constitution has attempted to define the limits of the role of the Party by stating that the people are the masters, the state is the manager and the party is the leader. While affirming the leadership in the CPV, the Constitution has pointed out its obligations to the state and society. For the party to lead does not mean, "try to impose its will", or "to do everything in place of the state bodies and social organisations". All party organisations should carry out activities in the framework of the Constitution and law.

The CPV has thus set for itself the reformative measures for the daunting tasks ahead. It has sought to raise the standard of its leadership and for building and developing an economy along the line of market mechanism. The party's guidance is designed to promote people's right of mastership, to raise the managerial skill and effectiveness of the state and role of the Front along with that of the people's organisations and social bodies, to mobilise the whole political system in society, thereby creating the strength of social democracy.

Though, the style of functioning of the CPV is changing, yet the demands for introduction of multi-party system have cropped up. This is because of the pluralist culture and historical legacies of Vietnam. Tonking, Annam and Cochin-China had three separate systems and there were cultural differences between the people inhabiting in the north and south. Saigon was the centre of business and trade during the Colonial period . The Americans propped up business culture of Saigon further and it was considered an ideal trading centre during 1954-75. When the two parts of Vietnam were united in 1975-76, Saigon (Ho Chi Minh City) had medium sized factories for production of consumer goods. It had a large service industry and an efficient commercial banking system. On the other hand, northern areas had communist infrastructure, where collectivisation of agriculture and a weak industrial base existed. With the unification, socialist drives started everywhere for integration of the economies as well. The CPV leadership ignored the ground realities in the process. Centralisation came in place of privatisation and collectivisation of agriculture was promoted in the south as existing in the north. It disturbed the entrepreneurial initiative of the people. Hoas, the business class of Chinese origin felt victimised so much so that they began to desert their homes to seek asylum elsewhere.

Vietnam soon became one of the poorest countries of the world. With rapid deterioration in the economy, people felt restless. They started questioning the leadership of the country and this tendency was witnessed at various forums of the government in due course. By 1986, the situation deteriorated to an extent that a number of leaders including Prime Minister Pham Van Dong resigned, to pave the way for reformists to take over. Hence Doi Moi process began.

Though, review of the existing rules and overhauling of the system have been promoted, Vietnam is not yet prepared to nurture a culture to tolerate dissent. Ross Range of *New York Times* reported in May 1995, that harsh sentences are meted out for the slightest show of dissent, such as, "15 years sentence" given to a man, named Phan Van Quang for waving the flag of the former South Vietnam during the Ho Chi Minh City international marathon in 1992. Ross Range, at the same time has reported that "although government-controlled, the press is relatively uppity, reporting all manners of corruption, scandal and general incompetence local television is heavily westernised. On my first night in the town, I was stunned to see 'Apocalypse Now' showing on the main channel followed by Operah, Popeye, The Master's tournament and the NCAA final etc."[12]

Thus, the western culture through media is welcomed and this would gradually influence the people. A number of westernised Vietnamese who have been doing business overseas are returning back. They have new thinking and new awakening and they symbolise new culture. They are interested in restoring Vietnam as an ideal trading centre and hence they would like to promote democracy and free trade. As multi-party system is an important element of democracy, it would naturally be encouraged advertently or inadvertently.

There are indeed some Vietnamese leaders who advocate the case for multi-party system and demanding more democratisation in the political process. Prominent amongst them are Tran Xuan Bach (former politburo member), Bui Trinh (former vice-editor, Nhan Dan), Phan Dinh Dieu (mathematician), Duong Thu Huon (novelist) and the Club of Resistance Fighters (an organisation of Veterans in the southern part of Vietnam). Again some pressure groups in the name of the Scientific Socialist Party (1990), the Form of Freedom (1993), the United Buddhist Church, and the Organisation of Catholic Church have time and again criticized the leadership and the system.[13] The influence of these groups are, however, confined to certain areas only and nationwide support is required to transform one-party rule to multiparty system.

National Assembly

Prime Minister Nguyen Van Linh and Vo Chi Cong strengthened the powers of the National Assembly. They believed that it was wrong to turn it as a rubber stamp and therefore while restructuring the system paid particular attention to make National Assembly vibrant and a strong institution of the government. Vo Chi Cong stated that "it is necessary to allow the National Assembly to represent the people and to give it responsibility for solving important problems in the life of the people".[14]

The powers and functions of the National Assembly have been effective in the Doi Moi era. Though, the old Constitution had also projected National Assembly as the highest organ of state power and the sole organ to legislate laws, it was virtually a rubber stamp till the adoption of new Constitution in 1992.

The new Constitution says that the National Assembly is the people's highest representative agency, and the highest organ of state power, exercising its supreme right of supervision over all operations of the state. It elects the President and Vice-President, the Prime Minister and senior judicial officers, and ratifies the Prime Minister's proposals for appointing members of the government. It decides the country's socio-economic development plans, national financial and monetary policies and foreign policy. The term of each legislature is five years. The National Assembly Standing Committee supervises the enforcement of laws and the activities of the government. Amendments to the Constitution may only be made by a majority vote of at least two-thirds of the Assembly's members.[15]

Again the Prime Minister has to be a member of the National Assembly, but this is not necessary for other ministers. The Prime Minister is responsible to the National Assembly and his term of office is the same as that of National Assembly. Again the term of office of the presiding judge of the Supreme People's Court corresponds to the term of the National Assembly and he or she is responsible to the National Assembly. The important point to be noted is that the National Assembly has started asserting its powers and this trend is encouraged.

The National Assembly before 1992, was ineffective because it was convened semi-annually merely for five days and its representatives merely raised their hands in favour of proposals made by the Council of Ministers. This practice was changed in 1993 and now each session continues for at least 29 days. As a result of the extended session, the time for discussion is longer and substantial. The representatives express their opinions and reservations freely and authorities have to answer their questions. If any bill is not discussed in the house, the representatives are empowered to reject it. The members of the National Assembly are also empowered to voice the concern of their respective constituencies and make important resolutions for consideration of the Government.

The changes in the nature of National Assembly is not only due to the powers that the new constitution has given but also because of the electoral reforms through which non-party and independent members depend on their performance in the National Assembly. So, they have to be vocal and fearless to voice the opinion of the people. They are not afraid to express their concern for the omissions and commissions committed by the government officials. They are playing important role in the nation building and modernisation processes.

Armed Forces

Vietnam is trying to impress that it is not chauvinistic as projected in the past. It has peaceful intentions. It fought wars in the past because it was compelled to fight. Now that there is crusade for economic development at the regional level and Doi Moi is the desirable goal, Vietnam abolished conscription under which men between 18 and 35 years and women between 18 and 25 years had to go compulsorily for military training. Vietnam also reduced the number of its armed forces by 50 per cent in 1987 and it further reduced it in conformity with peace time needs. In 1988, the strength of the Vietnamese armed forces comprised eight per cent of the total population, but the government endeavoured to reduce it to one per cent of the total population. The military spokesman, Lt. General Nguyen Quyet is stated as saying that the military have undertaken a basic change in both direction and strategy. It is being streamlined into a defensive force consistent with peace time needs. The ultimate aim is to have an army numerically small but high in quality.

Vietnam has thus succeeded in creating a new image and the world view regarding Vietnam has become positive. The Vietnamese no longer see the world in terms of two mutually antagonistic camps, but endeavouring to link Vietnam's economy with global economy. Foreign Minister, Nguyen Co Thach (1986-91), talked about interdependence in international matters and in May 1988, he was instrumental in passing a resolution which had deep-rooted impact on strategic thinking of Vietnam. The CPV politburo passed resolution 13 which officially accepted interdependence factor in international relations. While explaining resolution 13, Zachary Abuza says that it provided a new holistic paradigm for national security: One that included a strong economy, a peaceful international situation, "sufficient defence" and an increase in bilateral relations with countries in all three worlds.[16]

Thus, Vietnam adopted comprehensive security approach which included three components:

(*a*) to foster good bilateral relations with all countries, including former enemies, i.e., the U.S. and China,

(*b*) to have no alliances, nor a reliance on a superpower, and

(*c*) to maintain a peaceful external environment so that all resources can be spent on developing the economy.

The Press

The outlook of the Vietnamese press has changed in the past one decade. Though, censorship has altogether not been relaxed, the journalists are encouraged to report investigative articles and about wrong-doing of the officials. They keep a watch on bureaucrats and ministers, this development has irked some CPV stallwards. The government has given directives to the press to reflect not merely "the voice of the party" but also the "voice of the people". It has permitted the press to expose dark areas of socio-economic life and investigative pieces are given incentives.

Premier Nguyen Van Linh had set a new tone of the press by stating that they should not bend their pens in order to please officials. He said that "if a person is unable to write as they wish, they should do research and enhance their knowledge, till the suitable time comes for free and fair reporting."[17] He clearly said that the press should not write opportunistic pieces. His successors also promoted investigative articles and this has helped in the better performance of the government and better image of media.

Conclusion

The socio-economic and political developments in Vietnam are indicating that the changes are substantial and it would ultimately promote pluralism. Though, the people's faith in one-party rule remains, but the adoption of market economy do provide a choice between alternatives. Hence, alternatives to one-party rule also cannot be ruled out.

However, if we analyse the existing realities of the Southeast Asian Polity, we can easily predict that there is no immediate threat to the CPV leadership. Two neighbouring countires, i.e., China and Laos have one-party rule of the Communist Party. On the other hand, Indonesia with Golkar, Singapore with People's Action Party (PAP), and Malaysia with United Malay National Organisation (UMNO) have one-party rule, without the adoption of one-party system. All the above-mentioned parties have often been viewed authoritarian, yet they continue to remain in power. The notable reasons for their success is that they have performed well, and have led their countries on the path of modernisation and development. They are popular in their respective countries and the mere adjective of being "authoritarian" cannot destabilise them. Similarly, CPV may be projected authoritarian, but if it performs satisfactorily and so long as it contributes to increasing influence and affluence of Vietnam, it cannot be replaced. The political system is changing but the Vietnamese believe in continuity and change and hence, the process is gradual and substantial.

It is noteworthy that the changes in the political system have long-term implications on Vietnam's foreign policy and relations. It has been unique on the part of Vietnam to diversify its relationship from the erstwhile Soviet Union to the countries in Asia-Pacific. After the break up of the Soviet Union, with which it had cultivated intimate relations for decades, it adjusted astutely as a trustworthy partner of the countries in Asia-Pacific. Hence, the polemics of the cold war era was forgotten and realistic assessment of the international situation began. As trade with former communist allies declined, Vietnam was quick to forge new commercial links with Asian tigers. At the same time, initiatives were taken to promote trade links with the countries in the European Union and the United States. Murray Hiebert reported in *Far Eastern Economic Review* in May 1992, that Vietnam escaped the clutches of economic disaster by turning to its Asian neighbours to replace the collapsing Soviet Union, its major trading partner so far.[18]

Singapore, Japan and Hong Kong, which together accounted for half of Vietnam's trade in 1991, were the biggest beneficiaries of the Soviet collapse. Official Vietnamese statistics in mid-1992 showed that two-way trade with Singapore shot up from $111 million to $868 million, with Japan from $309 million to $709 million and with Hong Kong from $182 to $502 million.[19] Thus, Singapore emerged Vietnam's biggest trading partner in 1992, accounting for 26.7 per cent of imports and 33.7 per cent of exports. Vietnam and Singapore thus granted "most favoured nation" status to each other and signed a series of agreements to boost trade and investment relations. Other ASEAN countries also came forward to forge commercial links with Vietnam and subsequently became important trade partners and investors in Vietnam.[20]

Moscow, for decades, had controlled more than half of Vietnam's foreign trade and had provided Hanoi with more than $1 billion in aid and concessionary trade arrangements. It was difficult to envisage anything without the Soviet aid and assistance in Vietnam for decades, but it was smooth and admirable effort to diversify it. Vietnam succeeded in finding new markets, new allies and new donors in the post-1991 era.

The widespread changes in Vietnamese politics had implications on the attitudes of the US also. The Americans, which proved the stubborn enemy of Vietnam from 1945 to 1991, began to review its policies and adopted a favourable posture. President Clinton decided to remove the US veto on Multilateral lending to Vietnam in 1993 and paved the way for IMF, World Bank and ADB lending and operations. In 1994, the US lifted trade embargo and evinced interests in resuming diplomatic ties. In August 1995, Secretary of State, Warren Christopher initiated the resumption of diplomatic ties at the level of charge d'affairs and full diplomatic relations were established in May 1997.

Vietnam has earned the friendship of the ASEAN also due to changes in its system. This grouping, which had adopted anti-communist postures right since its inception, and had ostensibly worked for isolating Vietnam for decades, changed their attitudes rapidly. The ASEAN as a group was advertently supporting "bleed Vietnam white" policy ever since December 1978 and was critical of Vietnamese intervention in Cambodia. The Communist system was being ridiculed and they were projected as barbaric and monsterous. But changes in the Vietnamese political system, followed by the dissolution of the Soviet Union, changed the attitudes of the ASEAN countries. Hence, the ASEAN first offered observer status to Vietnam in 1992 and thereafter full membership in 1995. Though, Vietnam remains a communist country, but this reality does not inhibit its relations with the ASEAN partners.

The ASEAN leaders have very positive opinion regarding Vietnam and they admire the latter for worthwhile partnership. They are genuinely interested in Vietnam's locational advantages, mineral resources and its cheap and relatively well-educated labour force. Above all, Vietnam is considered important for ASEAN solidarity and regional consensus.

It is noteworthy that ideology, which perennially proved an irritant in Vietnam's interaction with the ASEAN and East Asian neighbours, is not considered a threat in the present context. The Communist Party of Vietnam is working as a facilitator to promote business and trade with the outside world. It is not at all interested in exporting revolution and does not talk of Indo-Chinese federation. Hence, it is unwilling to interfere in the affairs of Laos and Cambodia. It voluntarily withdrew its forces from Cambodia (1988) and is a silent spectator in view of the anti-Vietnamese rhetoric of the Khmer Rouge.

Vietnam now believes in peaceful resolution of the conflicts and is acting as a trustworthy and responsible neighbour. Above all, it has displayed good understanding of regional realities and simultaneously introduced structural changes to accommodate regional interests in tune with regional consensus. To conclude in the words of Vietnamese ambassador, Pham Sytam,

> the objective of reforms in Vietnam is indeed the policy of openness and integration into the world, selecting and adapting the world's essence with due regards to the trends and spirits of the present time. It is also a process in which whatever attained by modern science and technology is useful for his people and country would be taken in. The previous policy of "closed door" resulted in stagnation. International cooperation has become a common trend of the time now and an important condition for development too. The Doi Moi process is to befriend all nations for peace, independence, and development.[21]

REFERENCES

1. Nguyen Xuan Oanh, "Hanoi is moving towards more pragmatic socialism", *The Times of India*, New Delhi, 3 January, 1989.
2. For an understanding of Vietnamese society and politics, see Melanie Beresford, *Vietnam: Politics, Economics and Society*, London, 1988 and J. Buttinger, *Vietnam, A Political History*, London, 1969.
3. For an analysis of this aspect see William J. Duiker, *Rise of Nationalism in Vietnam, 1900-1941*, New York, 1976 and Nayan Chanda, *Brother Enemy: The War after the War*, London, 1986.
4. Nirmala Laxman, "Vietnam: Poised for a Boom" *The Hindu*, Madras, 25th April, 1993.
5. *Ibid.*
6. The 1992 Constitution continues to affirm leading role of the Communist Party of Vietnam, *Vietnam Information Bulletin*, New Delhi, Vol. 30, No. 6, 1992, pp. 1-3.
7. Tsutomu Murano, "Can the Communist Party Maintain its Dominant Position?", *Dynamic Vietnam*, Tokyo, June 1995, p. 27.
8. Ganganath Jha, "Politics of Perestroika in Vietnam 1986-1990", *International Studies*, New Delhi, Vol. 28, 1991, pp. 373-88 and; Gareth Porter, "Politics of Renovation in Vietnam", *Problems of Communism*, Washington, D.C., Vol. 39, May-June 1990, pp. 72-89.
9. Tetsusaburo Kimura, "Access to International Division of Labour", *Dynamic Vietnam, IDE Spot Survey*, Tokyo, June 1995, p. 2.
10. Akie Ishida, "Legal Aspect of Renovation Policy", *Dynamic Vietnam*, pp. 21-24.
11. Oanh, *The Times of India*, 3rd January, 1989.
12. Ross Range, "20 Year's on : Vietnamese are Looking Forward", *The Times of India*, 10th May, 1995.
13. Alan Dawson, "Battlelines are Drawn : Conservatives opposed to Doi Moi", *Bangkok Post*, 13th & 15th April 1989.
14. *Straits Times*, 3rd February, 1990.
15. *Constitution of Vietnam*, 1992.
16. Zachary Abuza, "International Relations Theory and Vietnam", *Contemporary Southeast Asia*, Singapore. Vol. 17, No. 4, March 1996, pp. 406-19
17. *Vietnam Courier*, No. 1, 1988, p.12.
18. Murray Hiebert, "Vietnam looks to Asia after Soviet Collapse", *Far Eastern Economic Review*, 14th May, 1992, p. 56.
19. *Ibid.*
20. *Ibid.*
21. Pham Sytam, "Vietnam: continuity and commitment to the Renewal". Paper presented in a seminar on Vietnam, India International Centre, New Delhi, 13 December, 1998.

11

Society and Politics in Cambodia

Cambodia has been known by different names in the past, i.e., Kambuja, Cambodge, Khmer and Kampuchea. Located in Indochina, it has 181,035 kilometers of territories, of which 10 per cent is covered with water.

Cambodia is bordered by Thailand to the west and Vietnam to the east and has Laos in the north and Gulf of Thailand in the south. It has mountain chains on three sides and they are rich in mineral resources. In the west, the granite Cardamom mountain rises up to 5000 feet and its steep slopes are densely forested. On the other hand, Dangrek mountain ranges form a sandstone terrace in the north and Moi plateaus are standing in the east. However, there is no natural barrier in some parts of the eastern and western frontiers through which Vietnamese and the Thais had been invading or trespassing.

The Mekong river running from north to south, comes through the Dangrek and its average width in Cambodia is two kilometers. The Mekong forms a great reservoir in the form of a lake, which is known as the "Tonle Sap". The water level in the river goes up to 40-45 feet high in the rainy season, causing the "Tonle Sap" to spread over an area of 770 square miles, but during the dry season the lake shrinks to 100 square miles only with a maximum depth of five feet. "Tonle Sap" is one of the most important fishing zones and account for half of Cambodia's production of fresh water fish.

Cambodia has a good alluvial soil and tropical monsoon climate without excessive rainfall. Besides timber, the country has wide variety of plants, i.e., palm, rubber, coconut, kapok, orange, banana, savannas, bamboos, pepper, tobacco, sugarcane and mulberries etc. The land is extremely fertile for producing rice and vegetables and the forest has elephants, rhinoceros, tigers, panther, bear and reptiles.

About 40 per cent of the territories are still covered with forests, but its volume is getting reduced. The rate of timber cut totalled 208,890 cubic metres in 1991 and 118,800 cubic meters in 1992. The situation was so alarming that at the end of 1992, the United Nations Transitional Authority in Cambodia (UNTAC) banned the exports of Cambodian timber.

Cambodia is also rich in natural resources, i.e., iron ore, jet, limestone and phosphates. Kompang Thom is potentially rich in copper, manganese and gold and the commercial production of jade, rubies, sapphires, garnets, conundrum and zircons are being explored.

Cambodia has 8.8 million population of which 85 per cent are ethnic Khmers, 5 per cent ethnic Chinese, 5 per cent ethnic Vietnamese and the remaining 5 per cent are comprised of Chams, Laotians, Thais and the tribal hill people, i.e., Rhade, Jarai, Kuoy, Stieng, Samre, Saoch and Pear etc.

Majority of the people have been the followers of Theravada Buddhism and according to David J. Steinberg, they comprise 90 per cent of the total population. It is interesting that Cambodian religion and culture have been influenced by various cults of Hinduism and their language, customs, traditions and architecture bears the stamp of Indian influence. Their epic, Ramakirti (Reamker) is based on Indian Ramayana and their religious edicts are in Pali language.

The origin of Cambodia is explained through a 10th century inscription, which says that the first founder of the royal family of Cambodia was born due to the marriage of a hermit, Kambu Swayambhuva with a celestial nymph Mera given to him by the God Shiva. The word Kamboj was derived from Kambu and hence Cambodge and Cambodia became popular. There are evidences to prove that the Khmers worshipped God Shiva before the advent of Buddhism.

History

Cambodia had a glorious past, which gave birth to Funan, Chenla and Angkor empires. Funan flourished from the first century A.D. to the sixth century and covered the territories of southern Cambodia and Cochin-China. Kaundinya, its founder is credited to have introduced the custom of clothing and hairdressing for women. According to the legend, Soma the daughter of the King of Nagas, wore no clothes when she encountered Kaundinya in the battlefield. When Kaundinya became victorious and Soma agreed to marry, he dressed her in a fold of cloth with a hole through which she could pass her head. He also asked her to tie hair in a knot and thus the system of clothing and hair dressing became popular.

Afte Funan, Chenla empire became very influential in the region. Based in northern Cambodia and Laos and earlier a Vassal state of Funan, Chenla conquered Funan and remained in power till the beginning of the Angkor empire. The rulers of Chenla promoted the worship of Lord Shiva and Lord Vishnu and further enriched Khmer civilization.

Both Funan and Chenla were integrated with the emergence of the Angkor empire (9th century A.D. to 14th century A.D.). It was very powerful which expanded its jurisdiction over the Mekong, the Menam Chaophraya, the Irravati and the Salween plains. It is stated that besides Cambodia, Jayavarman VII controlled parts of Malay peninsula and territories south of the Annamite chain including the state of Champa. One of the greatest contribution of the Angkor rulers, which presently attracts world attention is the temple of Angkor Wat. Another feature of Angkor period is that they introduced lots of socio-economic reforms particularly during the reign of Jayavarman VII (1181-1218) including the adoption of Buddhism as the state religion.

The downfall of Angkor started just after the death of Jayavarman VII. In 1238, the foundation of Thai Kingdom was laid when they defeated the Khmer commander at Sukhothai, then the Capital of the northwestern part of the Angkor empire. The Thais gradually expanded its influence and posed challenges to the Khmers. In 1253, Mongol emperor Kublai Khan conquered Nanchao and its repression caused large-scale transmigration of ethnic Thais towards down south. They came to Sukhothai and endeavoured to make their new kingdom strong and powerful. King Ramakhamheng (1270-1317) utilized their services to provide a strong foundation to his Kingdom and they continued to annex territories of the Khmers.

In 1353 another development took place in the Indo-Chinese region. Fa Ngum established the Kingdom of Lang Xang (Laos) in the region of the upper Mekong by uniting all the small principalities in the region. Though Fa Ngum was brought up at the court of the Angkor and was married to a Khmer princess, yet it is a fact that his newly found kingdom took control over a sizable chunk of the Angkor territories.

On the other hand, Vietnam, which became independent of the Chinese rule in 939 A.D., gradually developed expansionist ambitions. It conquered Champa in 1471 and looked beyond to annex Angkor territories to the extent possible.

By 15th century, Cambodia had to grapple with two hostile neighbours—Thailand and Vietnam—and they were helpless in subduing them on their own. The Han rulers in China and Majapahit rulers in Indonesia were zealous of Angkor glories and they liked to remain silent spectators and there were none to rescue the Cambodians from external invasion.

In fact, the internal situation and perpetual dispute in the royal family suited the neighbouring invaders. David P. Chandler has stated that Cambodian royal family, perennially riven by factionalism, was split along pro-Thai and pro-Vietnamese lines and they sought support from either of the two at different times to act against one another. The history of Cambodia in the 18th and 19th centuries, therefore, is one of almost continuous invasions from both Vietnam and Siam, preceded and followed by ruinous civil wars.

French Protectorateship

France after consolidating its colonial hold over Vietnam in the 19th century, looked towards Cambodia for further expansion of their rule. Cambodia then was under the domination of the Siamese but intended to assert her independence. The French understood the Cambodian perception and geared their diplomacy to influence the then King, Ang Duong who expressed the danger of Siamese invasion. The French expressed their willingness to help Cambodia if the latter could fulfil three conditions, i.e., (*a*) the freedom to move in the country, (*b*) the freedom to proselytize into Roman Catholic faith; and (*c*) the freedom to exploit teak woods for ship-building.

Doudart de Lagree, Francis Garnier, Jean Moura and Etienne Aymonier and others tried to influence Cambodia but French demands were considered sensitive. Though Cambodia wanted to get rid the Siamese suzerainty, but they were not sure that the French help could untangle it.

France tried to assure the King that they were capable of helping Cambodia to be free of Thai control and Vietnamese invasions. At the same time they had the potentials to assist Cambodia in regaining the territories that she had lost to the Thais and the Vietnamese in the historical past.

When momentous developments were taking place, King Ang Duong died (1860). The crowned Prince Norodom faced succession problems and he was opposed by the important sections of the Cambodian elites. Instead of seeking indigenous solution, he embraced the French in order to get the Crown. He expressed his readiness to fulfil French conditions, if his interests were properly protected. In August 1863, he signed the Oudong treaty with France through which the latter guaranteed protection against external invasion and supported Norodom's claim of the Crown. In return France was given timber concessions and mineral exploration rights. Cambodia also undertook not to entertain any foreign advisors without the consent of the Governor of Cochin China.

The French thus extended its colonial powers over Cambodia and the King Norodom acted as a pawn. He promulgated a series of rules in 1877 at the behest of the French which took away royal prerogatives in land ownership and tax collection.

Gradually the French endeavoured to establish de facto sovereignty and as a result Charles Thompson, the French Governor at Cochin China forced a treaty on King Norodom in June 1884 whereby the nominal sovereignty of the country was lost. King Norodom accepted "all the administrative, judicial, financial and commercial reforms which the French government shall judge in future, useful to make their protectorate successful."

The 1884 treaty affected personal prerogatives of the King to a great extent. Although he was permitted to retain his court ceremonies but had to transfer real governmental powers to the French Resident Superior. In addition each province received a Resident, whose task it was to supervise the hierarchy of native officers and councils forming its administration.

The French thus got a free hand to rule Cambodia and assumed full control over the royal administration, royal treasury and foreign trading. Cambodia was subsequently incorporated into the Indochinese union in 1887. The successors of King Norodom did not have courage to oppose the French till the beginning of the Second World War.

Japanese Occupation and Independence

Japan after occupying the Spratlys in 1939, moved towards Indochina states. In August 1940 it threatened General Catroux, the Governor-General of Indochina and demanded the right to free movement of the Japanese troops in Indochina, the free use of its ports and the free use of the available economic and military resources to serve Japan's war needs. The Vichy regime signed an agreement granting those rights to Japan as it did not have the potentials to face the challenges. Japan thus moved quickly and occupied Cambodia in July 1941.

Japan had earlier entered into a secret pact with Thailand through which it had assured the latter to regain the territories lost on the Cambodian and Laotian borders by virtue of the machinations of colonial France in the 19th century. Japan allowed Thailand to occupy Battambang, Sisophon and Siem reap. Thus Cambodia was naturally shocked and King Monivong felt emotionally perturbed to the extent that he died as soon as he came to know about it.

Prince Norodom Sihanouk succeeded King Monivong. He tried to promote the causes of Cambodian nationalism. He astutely manoeuvred propaganda machinery to advocate weaknesses of the colonial administration. The efforts were also made to highlight Cambodia's glorious past and existing potentials. When the Second World War was over, Cambodia got back the possession of Battambang, Sisophon and Siem reap and at the same time the French allowed him a degree of autonomy. France found nationalist upsurge in many parts of the country and therefore decided to grant independence on 9 November 1953, which was ratified by the Geneva Accord in July 1954.

Prince Norodom Sihanouk tried to introduce democratic polity with basic human rights. He wanted to stand neutral in the cold war of the two superpowers, but his policy of friendship and equidistance in relations with neighbours particularly with Democratic Republic of Vietnam irritated the US, advocating containment of communism. Thus Sihanouk was always criticized in the US and thus evoking bitter response in Cambodia.

Sihanouk opposed the formation of Southeast Asia Treaty Organization (SEATO) and disowned its "protective umbrella", thrust upon Cambodia. Thus Sihanouk was viewed pro-communist in the US and an enemy of the free world. It is believed that the

American Intelligence Agency (CIA) supported the coup d'etat of Marshal Lon Nol against Sihanouk in March 1970. Cambodia has remained unstable ever since and the return of Sihanouk to power after two decades have not changed the roots of instability that have grown subsequently.

Lon Nol after ousting Sihanouk from power, entered into a strategic alliance with the US and allowed the parts of Ho Chi Minh Trail in Cambodia to be bombed. He gave free access to American forces to crush communist guerrillas and allowed Vietnam war to expand into Cambodia. Sihanouk was unhappy with all these developments and therefore aligned himself with the Khmer Rouge to overthrow Lon Nol from power. Sihanouk's support gave legitimacy to the Khmer Rouge, so far known as bandits in the country.

The Khmer Rouge, led by Saloth Sar (Pol Pot) became victorious in overthrowing Lon Nol from power and assumed full governmental powers in April 1975. Pol Pot ignored Sihanouk now and tried to introduce socialist transformation in a revolutionary way. The new regime abolished the currency system and the private properties. It tried to abridge the gap between the rich and the poor and the urban and rural and in that endeavour supported resettlement plan. The regime fostered racist ideals and was harsh against the opponents. It is believed to be genocidal because during its tenure of three years, one million people died in Cambodia.

In the realm of foreign policy, Pol Pot supported pro-Chinese and anti-Vietnam policies. He ordered expulsion of 50,000 ethnic Vietnamese and claimed a chunk of territories on Vietnamese borders. He increased troops movements and made every efforts to antagonize Vietnam in liaison with the Chinese.

Vietnamese Intervention

Cambodia-Vietnam relations deteriorate rapidly during 1975-78 whereby Vietnam decided for a military solution. On 25 December 1978, Vietnam sent its forces to Cambodia to overthrow Pol Pot regime. Vietnamese forces had 200,000 troops, besides the volunteers of Kampuchean National United Front for National Salvation (KNUFNS). Vietnam occupied Phnom Penh on 7 January 1979 and installed Heng Samrin in power.

Heng Samrin government was recognised by Vietnam, Laos, India and the Soviet Russia but that was not enough. The neighbouring countries refused to recognise it. The ASEAN, China, Japan, the US, the UK and others did not provide diplomatic recognition and thus the UN also continued to recognise the Khmer Rouge regime. The Asian Development Bank, International Monetary Fund and the World Bank stopped lending loans to Vietnam and Cambodia, and environment was created to influence Vietnam to withdraw.

The ASEAN, the EU, China and the US actively supported the Khmer Rouge and other rebel forces, i.e., Khmer People's National Liberation Front (KPNLF), and Armee National Sihanoukiste (ANS) to fight against Vietnam's occupation forces. The Cambodian rebels formed a coalition government in exile in 1982, whose main task was to harass Vietnamese forces through guerrilla warfare. Thailand provided a sanctuary to all the rebels and became a conduit for supply of arms and ammunitions.

Vietnam was unhappy to be trapped in Cambodia. It decided to withdraw lock, stock and barrel in December 1986 and gave a deadline that they will withdraw before September 1989. They started the withdrawal process in phases and completely withdraw much before their deadline.

Vietnam cherished friendly relations with the ASEAN neighbours particularly after 1988, when its vulnerability vis-a-vis China were exposed in the Spratlys. It pursued confidence-building measures to convince ASEAN that they would abide by the regional consensus. It showed its earnestness to solve the Cambodian tangle and participated in the peace talks. Thus Jakarta Informal Meetings (JIM) and Conferences on Cambodia were held and the proposals for comprehensive solution started emanating.

The most significant proposal to resolve the Cambodian tangle came from Australia in November 1989. It suggested the installation of a UN caretaker administration in Phnom Penh, the deployment of a UN Peace Keeping Force in Cambodia to monitor ceasefire and the proposals of internationally supervised national elections.

The Australian proposal was finally accepted by all the participants in the peace talks. In August 1990, the Five permanent members of the UN Security Council endorsed the framework for a comprehensive settlement, i.e., the agreement for the UN supervision of an interim government, military arrangements for the transitional period, the holding of free elections and the provision of guarantees for the future neutrality of Cambodia.

Paris Peace Accord, 1991

The leaders of the four Cambodian factions—Khmer Rouge, Buddhist Liberal Democratic Party, Cambodian People's Party and Funcinpec—signed a peace agreement at Paris on 23 October 1991. This historic accord was also signed by the permanent five members of the UN Security Council and 12 other states involved in the Paris Peace Conference, namely Australia, Brunei, Canada, India, Indonesia, Japan, Laos, Malaysia, the Philippines, Singapore, Vietnam and Yugoslavia. Besides aforementioned 17 states, Secretary General of the UN also signed the Accord, which provided for the establishment of a United Nations Transitional Authority in Cambodia (UNTAC) entrusted with the task of demobilizing, disarming, and supervising the armed troops of the four factions, enforcing the ceasefire and arms embargo, administering key aspects of government (defence, foreign affairs, public security, finance and information) until the holding of elections in 1993 and ensuring the observance of human rights. At a projected cost of US $2000 million, it was planned the UNTAC would require 16,000 troops, 3,600 police personnel and 2,400 civilian administrators.

The peace makers were aware that if the indigenous regime would be withdrawn and the UNTAC would be the sole body to administer, the sovereignty of the country will be questioned. So they supported the installation of Supreme National Council (SNC) for the transitional period to cope with the sovereignty question. The SNC was to act as a neutral central authority and symbolize Cambodian sovereignty. The then Secretary General of the UN, Perez de Cueller expressed the hope that the SNC would go beyond being simply the embodiment of Cambodian sovereignty as provided for in the accords and help "fashion genuine national reconciliation" based on the higher interests of Cambodia and its people.

As desired by most of the actors in the peace talks, Prince Norodom Sihanouk became the President of the SNC and assumed powers as head of the state. Besides, SNC had 12 members of which six were from the CPP, 2 from the Funcinpec, 2 from the BLDP and 2 from the Khmer Rouge.

The SNC remained plagued from the outset by disagreements between the four factions. The Khmer Rouge dissented on most of the occasions, but that did not hamper the implementation of the Accord.

The UNTAC came to Cambodia in 1992 to implement the mandated tasks under the leadership of Yasushi Akashi. It succeeded in holding the election but could not fulfil the task of demobilizing and disarming all the factions. The election for the Constituent Assembly, which was converted to National Assembly, was held in May 1993 and 90 per cent of the registered voters took part in the poll. Funcinpec Party received 45 per cent of the votes, the CPP 38 per cent and the BLDP only 4 per cent. Accordingly Funcinpec got 58 seats, CPP 51, BLDP 10 and Molinaka one.

The first task of the Assembly was to approve the constitution but this act needed the deliberations of the deputies. So the first meeting of the Assembly declared 1970 coup "null and void" and bestowed on Sihanouk the "full and special powers" as head of the state, that he had held before he was overthrown. Sihanouk appealed to the Assembly members to work for national reconciliation and a definitive ceasefire, to restore agricultural prosperity and to regain territorial integrity.

Thereafter the Constituent Assembly completed the draft of the constitution and it was ratified by 113 votes to 5 on 21 September 1993 and on 24 September 1993, Norodom Sihanouk as head of the state signed it into law. Accordingly Sihanouk was sworn in as King of Cambodia. As envisaged in the Paris Accords, the Constituent Assembly was transformed into National Assembly. The SNC was immediately dissolved and UNTAC's role ended. Yasushi Akashi left Phnom Penh and the UNTAC began to dismantle itself and they completely withdrew by the end of 1993.

Another development after the May election was the decision of the FUNCINPEC, CPP and BLDP to work out a coalition government as none of the parties got absolute majority in the house of 120 members. Another compelling reason to form a coalition was to meet the threat of Khmer Rouge collectively, which remain outside to challenge the emerging political pattern.

The Khmer Rouge neither participated in the elections, nor joined in the coalition government. It is unwilling to compromise with the CPP and views it a pro-Vietnam party. It advocates anti-Vietnamese policies and demanding all treaties signed with Vietnam to be declared "null and void". It is engaged in spreading racial hatred against ethnic Vietnamese which is against reconciliation.

The Khmer Rouge is still a powerful organization and controlling 15 per cent of Cambodian territories, comprising

Kompong Thom, Siem Reap, Battambang and Preah Vihar, which inhabits 10 per cent of Cambodia's total population. It has adopted destructive and violent means and is considered major destabilization source for the government.

The Khmer Rouge is offending the government forces and trying to expand its influence. They have two main bases on Thai borders. First is at O'Trao, the intersection of Siem Reap and Kompong Cham and secondly at Trat, the intersection of Battambang, Pursat and Kampot. They are trying to encircle the areas between O'Trao and Trat for their fiefdom and procuring sophisticated weapons to threaten the government forces.

As the Khmer Rouge has refused to reconcile, there is civil war and Cambodians are killing fellow Cambodian. They are getting continued supply of weapons from Thai businessmen and the governments in Phnom Penh and Bangkok have so far failed to check the clandestine and illegal supply of weapons to the Khmer Rouge.

Political System

Though the communists came to power in Cambodia in April 1975, but they could not gain similar status and popularity as their counterparts in Laos and Vietnam. The Cambodians, by and large, continued to respect Norodom Sihanouk and his brand of politics.

Presently Cambodians are interested in supporting liberal democracy that can nurture their interests. They have shown their enthusiasm for the emerging system by massive participation in the elections. The rulers have adopted a democratic order, multi-party system, free press and independent judiciary. Now it will be in order to glance through some important provisions of the Constitution which have bearings on the emerging political system.

The Cambodian Constitution adopted on 24 September 1993 has 139 articles, which defines separation of powers into legislative, executive and judicial sections and enumerates a long list of human rights. The preamble of the Constitution at the outset has declared that "we the people of Cambodia, accustomed to having been an outstanding civilization, are determined to unite for the consolidation of national unity, the preservation and defence of the territory and precious sovereignty and the fine Angkor civilization, and the restoration of Cambodia into an "Island of Peace," based on a multi-party liberal democratic regime guaranteeing human rights."

The Constitution has provided for a system of constitutional monarchy, which has been explained in Part II of the Constitution. Article one has stated that the King shall rule according to the Constitution and to the principles of liberal democracy and pluralism, and the country will be permanently neutral and non-aligned.

Another interesting aspect of the Constitutional monarchy is that the King shall be chosen by the "Royal Council of the Throne" which will consist of the President of the National Assembly, the Prime Minister, the first and second Vice-President of National Assembly and also Somdech the Chief of the Orders of Mahanikaya and Thammayut. The King is not empowered to appoint heir to the throne and will continue to remain constitutional head only.

Chapter III from articles 31 to 50 have explained the rights and obligations of Khmer citizens. Every citizen shall be equal before the law, enjoying the same rights, freedom and fulfilling the same obligations regardless of race, colour, sex, language, religious belief, political tendency, birth origin, social status, wealth and other status.

Article 34 has stated that the citizens of either sex shall enjoy the right to vote and stand as candidates for the election. Citizens of either sex of at least 18 years, have the right to vote. Citizens of either sex of at least 25 years old, have the right to stand as candidates for the National Assembly.

As far as the legislature is concerned, it is unicameral. National Assembly is the sole body to formulate and review rules and regulations. The composition, powers and functions of the National Assembly has been explained in Articles 76 to 98. It is pointed out that the National Assembly will be comprised of 120 members, who will be elected by a free, universal, equal, direct and secret ballot. The tenure of the Assembly is five years and its members is to represent the entire Khmer Community and not only their constituencies. The Assembly's role as stated in Article 90 is that it will approve the national budget, the state planning, the loans, the lending and the creation, changes or annulment of tax, administrative accounts, etc. It has powers to approve the law of amnesty, treaties, international conventions and the law of the declaration of war.

Similarly the powers of the executive are defined in Articles 99 to 108 and of the Supreme Court from Articles 109 to 116.

Cambodia has adopted the system of multi-party system of which CPP, BLDP and Funcinpec are important. They are sharing the governmental powers. The Khmer Rouge on the other hand, is outside the government and playing the role of opposition. The government is showing reconciliatory gestures and has not banned it so far.

Foreign Policy

Foreign policy goals have been clearly defined in Article 53 of the Constitution, whereby it is stated that Cambodia will pursue a policy of permanent neutrality and non-alignment. It will follow the policy of peaceful coexistence with its neighbours and shall not join in any military alliance or military pact which is incompatible with its policy of neutrality. It will not permit any foreign military base on its territory and shall not have its own military base abroad.

Cambodia is trying to strengthen relations with all nations and intends to improve its regional image. The relations with Vietnam and Thailand however is crucial for its peace and prosperity. It is in that area that the Cambodians have been facing difficulties. Thai military businessmen have clandestine illicit relations with the Khmer Rouge. They are engaged in timber extraction and gemmining inside Cambodia with the support of the Khmer Rouge. In return they are supplying weapons to sustain Khmer Rouge activities.

On the other hand, improving relations with Vietnam is also faced with some hurdles. There is a feeling that the present border demarcation vis-a-vis Vietnam is unjust and edged in Vietnam's favour. They are demanding that the demarcation should be on the basis of the borders as prevailed in 1967. This is also a sensitive issue but the Cambodian government is trying to find out an amicable solution under the overall ASEAN framework.

The Cambodians have attracted global sympathies and the world community is eager to support her in reconstruction and development. However, they have yet to fight internal enemies and establish peaceful conditions in order to get international assistance and cooperation.

REFERENCES

Caldwell, Malcolm and Lek Tan, *Cambodia in the Southeast Asian War,* New York, Monthly Review Press, 1973.

Chanda, Nayan, *Brother Enemy, The War After the War,* San Diego, Harcourt Brace Jovanovich, 1986.

Chandler, David P., *A History of Cambodia*, Boulder, Colorado, Westview Press, 1983.

Chang, Pao-Min, *Kampuchea Between China and Vietnam*, Singapore, Singapore University Press, 1985.

Coedes, G., *The Indianized States of Southeast Asia*, Honolulu, Eastwest Press, 1968.

Findlay, Trevor, *Cambodia : The Legacy and Lessons of UNTAC*, SIPRI Research Report No. 9, London, Oxford University Press, 1995.

Kiljuen, Kimmo, ed., *Kampuchea – Decade of the Genocide*, London, Zed Press, 1984.

Leifer, M., *Cambodia – The Search for Security*, London, Pall Mall Press, 1967.

Majumdar, R.C., *Inscriptions of Kamboj*, Calcutta, The Asiatic Society, 1953.

Paliwal, O.P., *Cambodia : Past and Present*, New Delhi, Lancer International, 1991.

Pradhan, P.C., *Foreign Policy of Cambodia*, New Delhi, Radiant Publishers, 1982.

Reddi, V.M., *A History of the Cambodia Independence Movement, 1863-1955*, Tirupati, Sri Venkateshwara University Press, 1970.

Samphan, Khieu, *Cambodia's Economy and Industrial Development*, Ithaca, New York, Cornell University Press, 1979.

Steinberg, David J., *Cambodia : Its People, Its Society, and Its Culture*, New Haven, HRAF Press, 1959.

Vickery, Michael, *Cambodia : 1975-1982*, Sydney, Allen and Unwin, 1984.

Willmott, William E., *The Political Structure of Chinese Community in Cambodia*, London, University of London, 1970.

12

Security Concerns of the Emerging New Order in Cambodia

Cambodia, a country of 8.2 million people, endured one of the century's great tragedies—the slaughter of a million or more people during April 1975-December 1978. The Khmer Rouge under the leadership of Pol Pot was responsible for these misdeeds.[1] The unrealistic, immoral and genocidal policies in the name of socialism under the Khmer Rouge stewardship agonised the outside world.[2] The Socialist Republic of Vietnam was angered so much that it sent its military forces to overthrow this regime. Thus, on 7 January, 1979, a new government under the leadership of Heng Samrin, backed by Vietnam, was installed. This regime could not get international recognition and respectability. The neghbouring ASEAN countries proved hostile to it as they felt security concerns. They expressed their displeasure and viewed the Vietnamese action as interference in the affairs of the neighbouring countries. On the other hand, it was too late for Vietnam to retrace its steps.

The Khmer Rouge and other Cambodian rebels were provided a base and shelter in Thailand, depicted as a "frontline state." China, the US and the ASEAN countries aided the rebel forces and gave them logistics and weapons to fight against Vietnam and the Phnom Penh regime. It unleashed a chain of intermittent guerrilla warfare on the Thai-Cambodian frontiers. The Phnom Penh regime and the rebel forces led by the Khmer Rouge, Funcinpec[3] and Khmer People's National Liberation Front (KPNLF) became engrossed in the complex quagmire of conflict and perpetual tension. The Phnom Penh regime was supported by Vietnam and the Soviet Union. The rebels were supported by China and the Western world. This conflict gradually became intricate and polluted the security environment of the region. The ASEAN believed that a regime installed forcibly by outside help was illegitimate, and supporting the Heng Samrin regime was equivalent to supporting the case of overthrow and instabilities in the region. The ASEAN and the Western world were apparently unhappy with India because the latter accorded recognition to the Heng Samrin regime in July 1980 without assessing the ASEAN countries' apprehensions.

Cambodia subsequently became an arena of the Cold War where the two superpowers of that time experienced their strength and weaknesses. China was very happy with the situation, because these developments had shattering impacts on Vietnam's economy and thus its formidable adversary was unable to concentrate on modernisation and developments. Vietnam, on the other hand, was desperate to find out ways for an honourable pullout, but it was getting itself increasingly changed in the quagmire of Cambodia. But the global situation changed after the advent of Mikhail Gorbachev on the Soviet horizon in 1985. His zeal for implementing *glasnost* and *perestroika* and policies to befriend the United States had a statutory impact on the global political environment. The Soviet Union withdrew from Afghanistan and after the sixth party Congress of the Communist Party in Vietnam in December 1986, Vietnam also decided to withdraw from Cambodia. Those developments activated the brokers and peace makers to take initiatives and help in striking out an honourable settlement of the Cambodian dispute. The Jakarta informal meetings (JIM-1 and JIM-II) broke new ground to bring together the warring factions and enable them to talk to each other for a comprehensive agreement.[4] The diplomatic parleys and meetings at Jakarta, Paris, Beijing, Pattaya and New York were held from 1987 to 1991. The warring factions were told that their welfare, peace, progress and security would be assured only if they agreed to reconcile and cooperate. The outside powers supporting the civil war in Cambodia were convinced that a peaceful Cambodia would be an investment in stability for the region. The economic interaction with Indochina would reach its momentum in situations of relative peace and security. Japan, China, the United States and the ASEAN countries, willing to enhance their economic interests in Indochina, would find a better climate for the same if the civil war was terminated. The peace makers thus received an enthusiastic response from the international community.[5]

As far as the different warring groups in Cambodia are concerned, the Khmer Rouge was most reluctant to join, the peace talks if Hun Sen was invited there. But when China announced that it would no longer supply weapons to the Khmer Rouge, they changed their previous stances and joined the peace talks. Finally, the four factions agreed on the broad framework to resolve their disputes and agree to the ceasefire proposals.

Thus, the Cambodian Peace Accord was signed by 19 signatories in Paris on 23 October, 1991.[6] This paved the path for reconciliation and a new order in Cambodia. Along with the UN Secretary General, the representatives of the five permanent members of the Security Council, nine countries of Southeast Asia, India and four others were the signatories of that historic document. The accord was hailed as a landmark in the contemporary history of international politics and people interested in the welfare of the countries in Southeast Asia felt relaxed and cheerful.

The UN Secretary General Perez de Cuellar, the French President, Francois Mitterand, Chairman of the Supreme National Council (SNC), Prince Norodom Sihanouk, and others paid glowing tributes to diplomats involved in the peace negotiations.[7] They were emphatic in their remarks that the Accord had ushered in the beginning of a new chapter, new life and new order in Cambodia. The accord decided that the SNC will start working from its headquarters in Phnom Penh and it will symbolise Cambodia' sovereignty. The responsibilities to restore representative government, ceasefire, demobilisation of rebels, repatriation of Cambodian refugees and free and fair elections, etc. will be given to the United Nations' Transition Authority in Cambodia (UNTAC).[8] But before the dispatch of the UNTAC, the SNC will be assisted by the United Nations Advance Mission in Cambodia (UNAMIC). The UNAMIC team came to Cambodia as soon as the accord was signed. It will be in order to understand the composition and powers of the UNAMIC before analysing other aspects of the peace accord.

The SNC has to coordinate its activities with the UNAMIC till the arrival of the full-fledged UNTAC team. The Chairman of the SNC, Norodom Sihanouk, arrived in Phnom Penh from his exile in China on 14 November, 1991, and the cooperation with the SNC is in full swing. The UNAMIC originated as a result of a report to the Security Council, dated 30 September, 1991. The Secretary General, Perez de Cuellar, proposed that the UNAMIC would assist the

Cambodian parties in maintaining the present ceasefire and would also begin to clear out the landmines. In terms of staffing, the Secretary General estimated that the UNAMIC would require eight civilian liaison staff, 50 military liasion officers, 20 other military personnel for mine clearing, and about 75 international and 75 local civilian staff. In addition, a military communications unit of some 40 persons to be provided by Australia will be useful. The UNAMIC exercise would cost an estimated $19.9 million for six months.[9]

The Secretary General of the UN appointed Ataul Karim of Bangladesh as Chief Liaison Officer of the UNAMIC. The team of the UNAMIC came to Phnom Penh at the end of October. Australia immediately sent a military communications unit and France sent a contingent of planes. India also sent some civilian personnel to assist the UNAMIC.[10]

The UNAMIC was to merge with the UNTAC soon after its arrival in Cambodia. It was expected that the full-fledged UNTAC team will be able to come to Cambodia in February 1992. Thus, at that stage, the UNAMIC was to be there, but it was not mandated to take military actions to maintain law and order. This means that till the arrival of the UNTAC, maintenance of Cambodia's law and order were within the purview of the SNC. As there were old suspicious and mistrust amongst the components of the SNC, there was a serious threat to the establishment of peace and reconciliation. As the four important components of the SNC were competing for realignment and comparative advantages, there was a struggle for power. The coalition between the Cambodian People's Party of Hun Sen and Funcinpec of Prince Norodom Ranaridh was forged and abandoned. The coalition formation at this stage was perceived to prejudice the emergence of a neutral political environment. However, the attitudes of the leaders of these two parties were complementary to each other. The KPNLF, on the other hand, was seeking a neutral ground. But its leader Sonn Sann was more inclined towards the Sihanouk-Hun Sen groups than the Khmer Rouge. Sonn Sann personally was not a favourite of Sihanouk as he had taken the side of General Lon Nol in the 1970 *coup d' etat* to overthrow Prince Sihanouk from power.[11] Yet the efforts for reconciliation were being made by him. Sonn Sann was 80 years old in 1992 and he favoured the integration of his followers into the national mainstream before retiring from active politics.

The implications of these developments were that the Khmer Rouge was feeling isolated. This was the crux of the problem. This was indeed a matter of serious concern for the actors of conflict resolution. This issue had the potential to arouse internal and external foes and it was disturbing the implementation of the Peace Accord. This paper attempts to analyse these developments in depth and assess its overall impact on the emerging new order in Cambodia.

A survey of the ongoing Cambodian scenario indicated that the Khmer Rouge forces posed the major threat to the emerging political order. Disarming and demobilising its forces was difficult compared to other factions. Demobilising the Hun Sen followers was controversial and the Khmer Rouge was bound to criticise UNTAC for favouring it. Again, the repatriation and re-rehabilitation of Cambodian refugees in Thailand were contentious.

The Cambodian People's Party, Funcinpec and KPNLF were not perceived as a threat to the emerging new order, but there were widespread apprehensions against the Khmer Rouge. The Khmer Rouge did not stop completely its habit of flexing military muscles. It clinged to its past policies and linkages whereas the Cambodian People's Party of Hun Sen was trying to forget its past linkages with Vietnam and carve out independent and neutral policies. The KPNLF and Funcinpec also were trying to delink their bondage with the United States and become self-reliant. But the Khmer Rouge was not doing anything spectacular to indicate that it was reviewing its past linkages with the People's Republic of China.

It seems difficult for the Khmer Rouge to forget its ideology and past history. It still believes that "power comes out from the barrel of a gun." It has utilised every opportunity to mount an attack against the Phnom Penh government forces even after the withdrawal of the Vietnamese forces in September 1989. The change was only of tactics—the Khmer Rouge forces moved from guerrilla warfare to more conventional fighting.

The Khmer Rouge moved into populated areas to capture territories in October 1989. It was able to capture the gem-mining town of Pailin some 80 km from Battambang on 22 October, and Sam Lot, 35 km from Pailin on 28 October.[12] Taking advantage of the relaxed atmosphere, the Khmer Rouge militias showed their intentions to capture more and more areas around those districts.

The Khmer Rouge expeditions inspired KPNLF to intensify its attacks simultaneously and capture Phnom Sroc in Banteay

Meanchey province and some portions of the town of Svay Chek. By November 1989, it was assessed that more than 2,500 sq km of the Cambodian territory had gone out of the control of the Phnom Penh government.[13] In spite of these setbacks, the Phnom Penh authorities relied on self-reliance and indigenous capabilities. Despite debacles, they closed the option to ask Vietnam once again to help. Prime Minister Hun Sen tried to attract the attention of the international community and displayed diplomatic skills. He favoured negotiations for the reconciliation and settlement of the dispute. Initially he advocated only one condition, that there should be no place for the Khmer Rouge in the new dispensation. Speaking to correspondents on the eve of the second ministerial meeting of the International Conference on Cambodia in Paris in September 1989, he said, "The opposition Khmer factions and some countries are trying to obstruct the search for a political solution to the Cambodian conflict. They still cling to their absurd demand for the Khmer Rouge in the interim government in Cambodia, thereby to legalise the genocidal Pol Pot regime and avoid the discussion of measures to prevent the recurrence of such a brutal regime and the outbreak of the civil war in the country. No agreement can be reached if we fail to work out measures to prevent the return of the genocidal regime."[14]

Despite his misgivings regarding his adversary, Hun Sen proved to be accommodating towards the end. He agreed to the inclusion of the Khmer Rouge in the interim government and to share equal representations in the SNC, and after the signing of the Peace Accord, Hun Sen stopped the use of the term "genocide" for the Khmer Rouge. He took steps for reconciliation and establishing a neutral political environment.

On the other hand, the Khmer Rouge still believed in violent revolution. It was prejudiced against the Hun Sen group. There were apprehensions that it was supporting the armed insurrectionists against the Phnom Penh regime. On 22 December, 1991, some armed rebels joined by some youths marched through Phnom Penh demanding the release of jailed students. They created chaotic scenes and as a result three persons were killed and hundreds were injured. The government had to clamp a dusk-to-dawn curfew to deal with the situation.[15]

The Khmer Rouge controlled some areas on the Thai-Cambodian borders. It was believed to have at least 30,000 armed soldiers and huge stockpiles of arms.[16] It had its hardcore cadres inside and outside Cambodia. They had the potential to create problems in the implementation of the Accord. Again, the Khmer Rouge influence over the Cambodian refugees in Thailand was quite significant. The refugees estimated at 350,000 in Thailand were lured by the Khmer Rouge and they were aided and abetted to enter Cambodia in an unauthorised way to capture areas. The Khmer Rouge provided them logistics in the hope that these people will be loyal to them. These refugees were crossing the borders in Siemrip, Oddar Meanchey, Battambang and Kompong Thom provinces supported by the Khmer Rouge militias. Such a return and rehabilitation were illegal. The return of the Cambodian refugees was to be monitored and supervised by the United Nations High Commissioner for Refugees (UNHCR) through check-posts. The UNHCR had been issuing identity cards and other legal certificates to facilitate their return. But the refugees under the Khmer Rouge influence preferred to avoid coming through those check-posts because of the fear that they will be disarmed. There had been several cases of unauthorised crossing in the past few years and it was a matter of serious concern for the UNHCR.

The Khmer Rouge was under the shadow of the Pol Pot clique. It continued to believe in the tactics of intimidation and fear psychosis, and had little chance of gaining majority support in a free and fair election. There were assessments that the Khmer Rouge will gain not more than 10 to 15 per cent votes in the 1993 elections.[17] Therefore, the Khmer Rouge leaders were developing a sense of frustration. They had reasons to feel unhappy because China, so far their main supporter, had stopped supplying them arms and patching up their embittered relations with Vietnam. The Chinese no longer need to nurture a counter-balance or the support of Khmer Rouge to subdue Vietnam. Thus, the Khmer Rouge was faced with a predicament. It faced a dilemma when UNTAC took over Combodia and started taking initiatives towards demobilisation of militias.

The Khmer Rouge also faced a problem of image management also. Its image was spoiled not only because of the misrule during 1975-78 but also because it acted as a puppet of the Chinese. The Phnom Penh regime, on the other hand, contributed to the growing unpopularity of the Khmer Rouge. Ever since 1979, their leaders, the Press and media highlighted the misrule and atrocities of the

Khmer Rouge. Museums were established to explain the Khmer Rouge's genocide. The government media dug out the misdeeds and the stories of horrendous crimes. As a result, the general people in Cambodia felt revulsion for the Khmer Rouge. It was for this reason that when its ideologue, Khieu Samphan, returned from exile to take part in the SNC meeting in Phnom Penh in November 1991, he faced a hostile mob. The angry people broke into the Khmer Rouge headquarters, ransacked it and beat up Khieu Samphan after discovering him hiding in a closet near the bathroom. Prime Minister Hun Sen, who came to his rescue, proved incapable to prevent the ugly incident. Khieu Samphan received head blows. The people targetted him for attack because he was the primary author of the fanatical agricultural reform on which Pol Pot based his economic planning for Cambodia, and which ultimately resulted in hundreds of thousands of deaths.[18]

The developments leading to the physical assault on a leader of the SNC were embarassing for the Phnom Penh government and other SNC partners. It was embarassing for the Khmer Rouge also but they depicted this event as propaganda in their favour. The Khmer Rouge radio broadcast that Vietnam had organised the recent mob attack. The SNC leaders, however, refuted the allegation and said that Vietnam had nothing to do with it.

The SNC meeting of 3 December in Pattaya broadly discussed the Khieu Samphan issue and decided that the Khmer Rouge delegation to the SNC would be housed in the SNC building which accommodated in the residence once used by the French Governor during the colonial period. It is interesting that the office of the UNAMIC was also located in the same building. Phnom Penh police and Army patrolling also took security measures around the building. The communique of the SNC meeting in Pattaya clearly stated that "having received assurances from H.E. Mr. Hun Sen that the event of 27 November 1991, would never be allowed to recur. That a 300-500 metre primeter of security be established around the SNC members and their aides in their travel from their respective residences to the meeting place and to the airport, etc."[19]

The special arrangements for the security of the Khmer Rouge delegation had been made because unlike other delegations they felt more insecure. It is disturbing that they were not in a position to stay in their headquarters in Phnom Penh. It indicated their unpopularity. But these events gave them a feeling of deprivation and led them to resorting to strong-arm tactics. Other factions in the SNC were fully acquainted with the problem and they were making all efforts to prevent that possibility. Prince Norodom Sihanouk has postponed his scheduled visit to Vietnam in December 1991 and the Phnom Penh government was trying to maintain a distance in relations with Vietnam. Hun Sen ordered the demolition of the Victory Monument, a concrete memorial honouring the memory of the Vietnamese and Cambodian soldiers who fought against the Pol Pot forces in 1978. The monument has been replaced by a brass bowl, a repository for candles lit to celebrate Cambodia's freedom from French rule in 1954.

Prime Minister Hun Sen has also spoken about territorial disputes with Vietnam, particularly over Puolo Wai and Tang Islands.[20] He is trying to express his viewpoint and articulate Cambodia's national interests. Although these actions are geared towards neutralising the Khmer Rouge, at the same time, these endeavours are bringing public support to the Hun Sen leadership. Though the Phnom Penh regime is trying its best for a reconciliation, the Khmer Rouge is not reciprocating in the same manner. When the delegations of the SNC were discussing how to implement the Peace Accord at Pattaya, the Khmer Rouge forces were attacking Kompong Chhang. In a press conference, Hun Sen, after his return from Pattaya expressed his displeasure with the Khmer Rouge. He accused the Khmer Rouge of violating Cambodia's fragile Peace Accord by trying to enlarge the areas they control. He said, "Right now, the Pol Potists are in the process of extending their occupation very much. Three days ago, in the province of Kompong Chhang, taking advantage of our relaxed state of guard, the Khmer Rouge captured the village and dissolved its council, setting up the SNC at the village level."[21]

The Khmer Rouge endeavour to establish the SNC at the village level in the occupied territories at that stage was improper. The initiative for administrative reforms was under the domain of the UNTAC. The SNC components were required to act collectively and in coordination so that none of the parties or UNTAC could be prejudiced.

Here a few lines about UNTAC will be in order. The UNTAC was mandated to administer Cambodia during an interim period till 1993 elections were over. With the takeover of the UNTAC, the SNC was to act as a titular head. The UNTAC was to supervise the ceasefire and the cessation of outside military assistance and verify the withdrawal of foreign forces. It was also to be responsible for the regroupment and containment of all the armed forces for the Cambodian parties and ensure a 70 per cent level of disarmament and demobilisation. In addition, it will help to detect and clear mine-fields, which represent a daily danger for the civilian population and a barrier to the resumption of all normal economic activity.[22]

The UNTAC was also to be responsible for controlling or supervising, in various degrees, the activities of the existing administrative structures including the police, and for ensuring promotion of, and respect for, human rights, so that the Cambodian people will not again be exposed to the grave abuses of the past. The primary goal of these various measures was to encourage the establishment of a neutral political environment in which the Cambodian people can freely determine their future, within the framework of democratic elections organised and conducted by the UN.[23]

The UNTAC was also authorised to supervise the repatriation of refugees and displaced persons so that they can take part in the elections. The repatriation was to be undertaken in conformity with the principles outlined in the Paris Accords and in circumstances ensuring the requisite security and dignity. Lastly, it was planned, as a parallel measure, to launch an international programme for the rehabilitation and reconstruction of Cambodia which the UN has been called upon to develop and coordinate.[24]

The UNTAC was planning to send 20,000 soldiers besides civilian personnel to fulfil the mandate entrusted to it. The team was to arrive in Phnom Penh by February 1992. This exercise required at least US $2 billion for one year. The requisite funds for the operation of the UNTAC were being collected from a number of countries, particularly Japan, the United States, France, Australia and the ASEAN countries.[25]

There were two aspects of the role of the UNTAC that were bound to be controversial. First the demobilisation of the rebel forces. It was certainly a tough task. The International Institute of Strategic Studies, London, assessed the number of government military personal at about 100,000. The Khmer Rouge had 30,000-35,000 trained fighters. The KPNLF and Funcinpec have 10,000 each. However, the exact figures of the number of the armed forces were a matter of dispute. But nobody could say exactly who was a rebel and how many of them were still in the jungle and whether all of them were disarmed. The Pattaya meeting of the SNC in August 1991 had decided that the government and the three guerrilla forces will reduce their forces by 70 per cent. The remaining 30 per cent will be grouped in cantonments where they will surrender their guns to the UN forces. Nobody was allowed to fight. They were like civilians allowed with uniforms. The government police was to act under the UNTAC control, etc.[26] But in all these endeavours, there was a possibility of polemics and favouritism.

Secondly, the UNTAC was authorised to look after the massive repatriation of the Cambodian refugees. The bulk of the Cambodian refugees were based in Thailand and the United States. There were about 350,000 Cambodians in Thailand and 147,400 in the United States.[27] After the Communist takeover in April 1975, a great number of Cambodian refugees went to the United States and many of them had taken American citizenship. But those who were based in Thailand went there in phases during the Khmer Rouge tenure and particularly on the eve of its downfall in January 1979. How they were to return and how they will be settled and how they will be neutralised were to be a contentious issue. The Khmer Rouge wanted to push through its solutions and try to take advantage under the auspices of the UNTAC.

On the other hand, the international situation was changing very fast. The Soviet Union was no more and there was a quest for establishing a new order in which the United States might like to establish *Pax Americana*. China's ambitions to establish supremacy in the neighbourhood and take the position of a superpower might create problems for the UNTAC authorities. The ASEAN countries were already worried that the United States is going to reduce its presence in the region and might withdraw from the Subic Bay naval base in 1992. On the other hand, the Russians were committed to withdraw from Cam Ranh Bay naval base in 1992. Russia was seeking membership of NATO. The ASEAN apprehension, therefore, was that it will lead to a situation of a power vacuum which the ambitious powers of the region may wish to fill. Their indications were that the Chinese will force their way to fill the vacuum.

The Khmer Rouge was an old friend of China. Since 1975, it was shaping its policies in accordance with the wishes of China.

But in the present case, the Chinese were not likely to create any hurdles in the implementation of the Peace Accord. China was a signatory of the Peace Accord and tended to support peace, stability and security in the region. It was quite flexible in its support to the Communist Parties in Southeast Asia. It had forgotten the Burma Communist Party and was providing economic and diplomatic aid to the government of Burma. It stopped sending assistance and aid to the Malayan Communist Party (MCP) where the people of Chinese origin were fighting against the government of Malaysia. This resulted in an agreement between the MCP and Malaysian government on 2 December, 1990, through which the MCP agreed to return to the national mainstream and terminate the 41-year-old armed struggle. The MCP also agreed to surrender and destroy their arms and ammunitions. Subsequently, the North Kalimantan Communist Party also signed an agreement with the government and promised to get integrated into the Malaysian mainstream. The Chinese are interested in the larger business interests and not willing to nurture and promote liabilities. Moreover, if relations with Vietnam are given due importance, the Chinese will definitely try to forget the Khmer Rouge.

All these developments were not encouraging for the Khmer Rouge. It was feeling an increasing sense of frustration. It knew that if the constitutional processes are allowed to function uninterruptedly, it will have to compromise and thus will be the ultimate loser. It may try to gather courage to strengthen its position and challenge the authority of the Cambodian People's Party and in the process disturb the peace keeping role of the UNTAC. At the end, it can be stated that the internal threats to the emerging new order in Cambodia were substantial and the scope of external threat, namely of China and Vietnam, had been contained.

REFERENCES

1. For a study of this aspect, see *Documents on Democratic Kampuchea and the Current Struggle for National Independence*, New York, Kampuchea Support Committee, 1979 and Michael Vickery, *Cambodia : 1975; 1982*, George Allen and Unwin, North Sydney, 1984.
2. Valentin Shukin, *History Condemns Genocide Conducted under Pol Pot: Based on the Proceeding of the People's Revolutionary Tribunal of the People's Republic of Kampuchea*, Novosti Press, Moscow, 1985.

3. Funcinpec is a French acronym for National United Front for an independent, neutral, peaceful and cooperative Cambodia. This was also known as Sihanoukists.
4. Justus M. Van der Kroef. "Cambodia in 1990 : The elusive peace", *Asian Survey*, Vol. 31, No. 1, January 1991, pp. 94-102, and also see John Mcauliff and Mary Byrne Mcdound, "Cambodian stalemate: America's obstructionist role in Indochina", *World Policy Journal*, Winter 1989-90, pp. 71-106.
5. Stephen J. Solarz., "Cambodia and the International Community", *Foreign Affairs*, Vol. 69, No. 2, Spring 1990, pp. 99-115.
6. The signatories for the Cambodian Peace Accord in Paris were the United Nations, the United States, France, Britain, the Soviet Union, China, Japan, Australia, India, Yugoslavia, Thailand, Laos, Vietnam, Malaysia, Singapore, Indonesia, Brunei, Philippines and the four warring factions of Cambodia.
7. For speeches of leaders in Paris on Cambodian Peace Accord, see *BBC Summary of World Broadcasts*, Part 3, Far East, 25 October 1991, pp. A3/2 and A3/5.
8. For brief text of the accord, see *ibid.*, pp A3/1 and A3/2.
9. *UN Newsletter,* United Nations Information Centre, New Delhi, 12 October, 1991, p.1.
10. *UN Newsletter,* 16 November, 1991, p.1.
11. Rodney Tasker, "Cambodia: Watching brief", *Far Eastern Economic Review,* 21 November 1991, p.13.
12. *The Times of India,* 29 October 1989.
13. *The Hindu* (Madras), 30 October 1989.
14. *News from Cambodia,* Embassy of the State of Cambodia, New Delhi, Vol. 11, No. 14, 15 September 1989, pp. 5-6.
15. *The Times of India,* 23 December 1991.
16. Dilip Mukerji, "The fine Prince", *The Times of India,* 24 November 1991.
17. *Ibid.*
18. *The Times of India,* 28 November 1991.
19. *News from Cambodia,* 10 December 1991, p.3.
20. *Asiaweek,* 29 November 1991, p. 36.
21. *The Times of India,* 6 December 1991.
22. *UN Newsletter,* 2 November, 1991, pp. 1 and 3.
23. *Ibid.*
24. *Ibid.*
25. "Cambodia: Back in the hot seat", *Asiaweek,* 29 November 1991, pp. 34-36.
26. *Bangkok Post,* 28 August 1991.
27. *The Hindu,* 17 October 1991 and Rodney Tasker, n. 11, p. 13.

13

Vietnam, Cambodia and Laos: Political Development and Foreign Policy

Vietnam, Laos and Cambodia, comprised the territories of Indo-China and had been under the colonial rule of France (1852-1954). Vietnam, situated on the southern flank of People's Republic of China, became a centre of communist movement which influenced the developments in Southeast Asia. The spread of communism was opposed by the United States of America at the global level and Vietnam was no exception. Supporing the policy of "Containment" and "domino theory", the Americans believed that communism in Vietnam would be a security threat to the entire Southeast Asian region. Hence it advocated the formation of Southeast Asia Treaty Organisation (SEATO) in 1954 and sent its security forces to contain communist influence in Vietnam (1964). In the process of intervention it believed that Vietnamese communism cannot be contained unless Ho Chi Minh Trail is controlled. This trail indeed crossed through Laos and Cambodia but its location was dynamic and provisional. The United States was determined to destroy the illusory trail and therefore it bombed Laotian and Cambodian territories along with Vietnam. The issue of Ho Chi Minh Trail disturbed Americans, and it was for this reason that Cambodia and Laos were also involved in the Vietnam war. American bombing irritated public opinion in Indochina States and therefore communist influence in the region grew rapidly. As Communist Party was the only organisation capable of providing the healing touch to the people and fight against the U.S., it attracted popular support.

However, the war came to an end in April 1975 after the American defeat and withdrawal, and all the three countries of Indochina became communist countries. Cambodia came under the rule of the

Khmer Rouge and decided to adopt anti-Vietnam stances by forgetting the principle of communist fraternity. Laos and Vietnam remained friendly but Cambodia under Khmer Rouge ordered evacuation of citizens of Vietnamese origin. This irritated Vietnam because they had sacrificed their men and material in the war against invaders on Cambodian soil in the past. Vietnam was repeatedly annoyed by the Khmer Rouge's policies and nuances. When Pol Pot regime concentrated its armed forces on the Vietnamese frontier and provoked Vietnam, there was no alternative but to take military action in 1978. Vietnam's intervention in Cambodia was projected as an interference in the internal affairs of a neighbouring country. It was therefore, criticized and isolated at the international level in which the US, China, ASEAN and the Western World had colluded and displayed a consensus and they opposed Vietnam's occupation of Cambodia. The scenario changed only after the Vietnamese withdrawal from Cambodia (1988) and the regning of Paris Accord (1991).

In 1991 momentous developments took place at the global level. The Soviet Union was dissolved and the yearning for free trade, democracy and liberalisation became the important features of the emerging world order. This had wide ranging impact on Vietnam and Laos. On the other hand, Cambodia moved rapidly for a democratic framework under the care of United Nation's Transitional Authority on Cambodia (UNTAC). Vietnam accelerated the process of doi moi (renovation) and Laos evolved new economic mechanism (NEM) to introduce reforms in the economic sector to keep pace with the changing world. They introduced changes under the leadership of the Communist Party whereas Cambodia adopted democratic framework with multi-party system to promote liberalisation. All of them became the partners in Association of Southeast Asian Nations (ASEAN) and endeavoured to face the challenges of the new world order collectively.

Vietnamese Politics

Political developments in Vietnam has been a matter of interests at the global level because most of the affluent countries are in the race for trade and investment relations. The United States and the Western World, which opposed Vietnam for decades have established partnership and the level of Foreign Direct Investment (FDI) to Vietnam is increasing rapidly.

Vietnam has been transforming its political system and the National Assembly is being empowered to fulfil the demands of the general public. The constitution adopted on 15 April 1992 makes a provision for 450 member National Assembly in which there are also some representatives without the sponsorship of the Communist Party. They discuss the resolutions and emerging as the true rule making organ of the government. The Assembly is convened at least three times in a year and is assuming prominent role in the development processes. While explaining the political system, the constitution says that "all state powers belong to the people. The Communist Party of Vietnam is a leading force of the state and society. All party organisations operate within the framework of the constitution and the law. The people exercise power through the national assembly and the People's Councils." This is a new development compared to the experiences during 1975 to 1986 when National Assembly worked merely as the rubber stamp of the Communist Party.

The government is constantly reviewing its policies under the programme of doi moi which had started in 1986. Although doi moi were opposed by orthodox communists but the situation changed when Vietnam's economy started collapsing. The Soviet Union and East European countries were embroiled in their domestic matters and international agencies had stopped their aid programmes to Vietnam.

The Communist Party of Vietnam met for its sixth congress from 15 to 18 December 1986. The various participants made a critical appraisal of the economic and political system and subjected the functioning of the bureaucrats and top officials to serious scrutiny. This resulted in a new awakening. There were new initiatives. Nguyen Van Linh become the new General Secretary of the Communist Party of Vietnam. In that capacity he gave a call for wide-ranging reforms in the name of what he called '*doi moi*'. Literally translated the expression "*doi moi* " means renovation. As is well known, the idea of renovation was being extensively used in the various communist countries of Eastern Europe to demand economic and political reform. It was used in the debates held in the various public forums to refer to reform in the policies towards prices and wages, a fair measure of autonomy for state enterprises, and the complementary roles of the state and private enterprise in the economy as a whole. "Renovation" thus signified in Eastern Europe more than it normally means.

In Vietnam *doi moi* signifies a resolve to restructure Vietnam's socialist system or, in any case, to throw some outdated ideas overboard. It is a means to social change and economic development, to the introduction of certain aspects of liberal democracy in the communist system. *It is, however, against ending the dominant role of the Communist Party.* The leaders believe that their *doi moi* would make the party strong politically, ideologically, and organizationally.

Nguyen Van Linh says that *doi moi* means a far-reaching, thoroughgoing revolution. It means renovation in thinking, in policymaking, in organization, and in the appointment of personnel. The road it has to travel, however, "is not a straight one. It is full of twists and turns."

Doi moi has thus influenced the constitutional processes to a great extent. The 1992 Constitution has also explained economic system to be pursued in the country. It says that the state develops a multi-sectoral economy, in accordance with a market mechanism, based on state management and socialist orientations. All lands are under state management but the grip of the CPV is diluted. The state allots land to organisations and individuals for use on a stabilised long-term basis. They may transfer the right to the use of land allotted to them. Individuals may establish business and the state shall encourage foreign investment. Legal property of individuals and organisations, and business enterprises with foreign invested capital, shall not be subjected to nationalisation. Thus we find that the right to property has been restored in a modified way under the new dispensation. Reforms have been accelerated in agricultural, industrial and banking management, which is widely appreciated.

Foreign Policy

It is noteworthy that the changes in the political system have long-term implications on Vietnam's foreign policy and relations. It has been unique on the part of Vietnam to diversify its relationship from the erstwhile Soviet Union to the countries in Asia-Pacific. After the break up of the Soviet Union, with which it had cultivated intimate relations for decades, it adjusted astutely as a trustworthy partner of the countries in Asia-Pacific. Hence, the polemics of the cold war era was forgotten and realistic assessment of the international situation began. As trade with former communist allies declined, Vietnam was quick to forge new commercial links with Asian tigers. At the same time, initiatives were taken to promote trade links with the countries in the European Union and the United States. Murray Hiebert reported in *Far Eastern Economic Review* in May 1992 that Vietnam escaped the clutches of economic disaster by turning to its Asian neighbours to replace the collapsing Soviet Union, its major trading partner so far.

Singapore, Japan and Hong Kong, which together accounted for half of Vietnam's trade in 1991, were the biggest beneficiaries of the Soviet collapse. Official Vietnamese statistics in mid-1992 showed that two-way trade with Singapore shot up from $111 million to $868 million, with Japan from $309 million to $709 million and with Hong Kong from $182 to $502 million. Thus, Singapore emerged Vietnam's biggest trading partner in 1992, accounting for 26.7 per cent of imports and 33.7 per cent of exports. Vietnam and Singapore thus granted "most favoured nation" status to each other and signed a series of agreements to boost trade and investment relations. Other ASEAN countries also came forward to forge commercial links with Vietnam and subsequently became important trade partners and investors in Vietnam.

Moscow, for decades, had controlled more than half of Vietnam's foreign trade and had provided Hanoi with more than $1 billion in aid and concessionary trade arrangements. It was difficult to envisage anything without the Soviet aid and assistance in Vietnam for decades, but it was smooth and admirable effort to diversify it. Vietnam succeeded in finding new markets, new allies and new donors in the post-1991 era.

The widespread changes in Vietnamese politics had implications on the attitudes of the US also. The Americans, which proved the stubborn enemy of Vietnam from 1945 to 1991, began to review its policies and adopted a favourable posture. President Clinton decided to remove the US veto on Multilateral lending to Vietnam in 1993 and paved the way for IMF, World Bank and ADB lending and operations. In 1994, the US lifted trade embargo and evinced interests in resuming diplomatic ties. In August 1995, Secretary of State, Warren Christopher initiated the resumption of diplomatic ties at the level of charge d'affairs and full diplomatic relations were established in May 1997.

Vietnam has earned the friendship of the ASEAN also due to changes in its system. This grouping, which had adopted anti-communist postures right since its inception, and had ostensibly worked for isolating Vietnam for decades, changed their attitudes rapidly. The ASEAN as a group was advertently supporting "bleed Vietnam white" policy ever since December 1978 and was critical of Vietnamese intervention in Cambodia. The communist system was being ridiculed and they were projected as barbaric monsters. But changes in the Vietnamese political system, followed by the dissolution of the Soviet Union, changed the attitudes of the ASEAN countries. Hence, the ASEAN first offered observer status to Vietnam in 1992 and thereafter full membership in 1995. Though, Vietnam remains a communist country, but this reality does not inhibit its becoming relations with the ASEAN partners.

The ASEAN leaders have very positive opinion regarding Vietnam and they admire the latter for worthwhile partnership. They are genuinely interested in Vietnam's locational advantages, mineral resources and is cheap and relatively well-educated labour force. Above all, Vietnam is considered important for ASEAN solidarity and regional consensus.

It is noteworthy that ideology, which perennially proved an irritant in Vietnam's interaction with the ASEAN and East Asian neighbours, is not considered a threat in the present context. The Communist Party of Vietnam is working as a facilitator to promote business and trade with the outside world. It is not at all interested in exporting revolution and does not talk of Indo-Chinese federation. Hence, it is unwilling to interfere in the affairs of Laos and Cambodia. It voluntarily withdrew its forces from Cambodia (1988) and is a silent spectator in view of the anti-Vietnamese rhetoric of the Khmer Rouge.

Vietnam now believes in peaceful resolution of the conflicts and is acting as a trustworthy and responsible neighbour. Above all, it has displayed good understanding or regional realities and simultaneously introduced structural changes to accommodate regional interests in tune with regional consensus. To conclude in the words of Vietnamese ambassador, Pham Sytam,

> the objective of reforms in Vietnam is indeed the policy of openness and integration into the world, selecting and adapting the world's essence with due regards to the trends and spirits of the present time. It is also a process in which

whatever attained by modern science and technology is useful for his people and country would be taken in. The previous policy of "closed door" resulted in stagnation. International cooperation has become a common trend of the time now and an important condition for development too. The Doi Moi process is to befriend all nations for peace, independence, and development.

Laotian Politics

Laotian Politics is transforming. It has successfully retained friendship with the communist neighbours, and at the same time cultivated partnership with Thailand, Myanmar and other ASEAN countries admirably. Although it retains one-party rule of the Communist Party, but at the same time introduced reforms to promote democratic elements. It adopted reforms programme in the name of New Economic Mechanism (NEM) in 1986 to shift Laos towards a market economy. The market opening programme gathered momentum after the dissolution of COMECON and the Soviet Union. Laos is landlocked and its infrastructure is underdeveloped as some of its roads are waterlogged during the rainy season. The three main cities, Vientiane, Luang Prabang and Savannakhet very often become almost isolated islands during rainy seasons. Laos is striving to develop infrastructure with the help of NEM, which is aimed at decentralisation of economic decision-making, more accountability for public enterprises, fiscal and financial reforms, deregulation of prices, removal of trade barriers, implementation of new investment laws and overall greater reliance on market forces.

NEM has proved successful in the growth of industrial and agricultural output. Foreign investors are satisfied with the pace of reforms and attach importance to invest in tourism, textiles, mining, logging and hydro-electric power generation. Till 1995 total foreign investments were 600. An investment guidelines of the government allowed 100 per cent foreign owned investments, repatriation of capital and profit legal guarantees against nationalisation of private property and also pledged not to interfere with business or violate the principles of competition, it was sufficient to attract the investors from Japan, Korea and Hong Kong.

Laos adopted a constitution on 14 August 1991, which made a provision for ownership of private property. Article 15 states that as for the land which is under the ownership of the national community, the state guarantees the rights to using, transferring and inheriting in accordance with the law and Article 16 states that the economic management is carried out in line with the mechanism of market economy with the adjustment by the state, implementing the principle of promoting the centralised, unified management of the central branches in combination with the division of managerial responsibility for localities. The people have been granted equality before the law (Art. 22), equal political, economic cultural and social rights (Art. 24), freedom of speech, press and assembly (Art. 31) religious belief (Art. 30) and the right to education (Art. 25).

Chapter IV of the Laotian Constitution defines the structure, rights and duties of the National Assembly, which has the right to pass a vote of no-confidence in the government. The National Assembly is comprised of 85 members and national elections are held every five years for the new representatives. It is reported that the Assembly is taking active interests in the rule making. The representatives discuss the budget and has sometimes returned the bill for reconsideration (1993). The democratic ethos is being evolved but it will take years to tansform lifestyle of the people comparable to Thailand or Malaysia.

Foreign Policy

As Laos is a landlocked country, it has to take the route either throughThailand or Vietnam to transport its goods to the outside world. Its imports and exports are vitally linked with its relations with the two neighbours. Lao-Thai Friendship Bridge, which was constructed over Mekong River with the assistance of Australia in 1994, has indeed joined the two countries through land routes and traders on the two sides are vibrant with their activities. This phenomenon has been assisted by the Laotian government because of two reasons. Firstly the transportation system in Thailand is more efficient and roads are far better than in Vietnam. Secondly, Laos intended to eschew too much dependence on Vietnam for which it had no alternative at the time of Vietnam war.

Lao-Thai relations were boosted after Chatichai Choonhavan was appointed the Prime Minister of Thailand in 1988. He took several initiatives to improve relation with Laos while expressing his determination to transform Indochina from 'a battlefield into a market place'. He subsequently visited Vientiane for direct talks with Laotian government. The outcome of this meeting was the creation of a Joint Border Demarcation Committee, which completed aerial and land surveys of the disputed areas by May 1989. The two countries decided to improve economic relationships and forget past irritants which had arisen due to border conflict and past history. Thailand withdraw its forces from the disputed Sayaburi province and deicided to stop illegal activities of Lao exiles active on Lao-Thai borders. Thousands of Lao refugees were repatriated to Lao and relations started improving in the proper direction.

This did not adversely affect Laotian relations with Vietnam. They have been displaying solidarity with each other in the pace of reforms and partnership. In July 1992 both collectively signed ASEAN Treaty of Amity and Cooperation and endeavoured for wider regional cooperation. They have identical approach in the consensus-making for regional security under the stewardship of ARF.

Laos has gradually improved relations with China by restoring full diplomatic relations in 1988. China also restrained exiled Laotians operating from Chinese borders. When Kaysone Phomvihane visited China in 1989, agreements were signed for cultural cooperation, consular representation and the delineation of the border. In 1990 the Lao government and the provincial government of Laos signed an agreement providing for the promotion of economic development of two northern provinces in Laos. Chinese goods are crossing to the ASEAN market through Laos and mutual understanding and appreciation are growing.

Relations with the US are also improving rapidly. Laos cooperated fully in the search for US soldiers missing in action in Laos during the Vietnam war. In appreciation of the Laotian Coopertion, the US had given 5000 tons of rice to overcome the plight due to severe drought in 1987. When the US raised the issue of narcotics and opium production and smuggling, the two countries signed an agreement for a crop-substitution programme in Houaphanh province. The US and international agencies were satisfied with the cooperation and thus they resumed aid and assistance programme to develop Laotian economy. In 1989 Australia signed a new agreement to provide a programme of aid, which included a satellite communications project designed to improve international telephone links with Laos. Japan also agreed simultaneously to provide aid to promote tourism in the country.

Laos is presently the partner in ASEAN and endeavoured to promote ties with the ASEAN-10. Besides it is trying to cultivate ties with South Asia, by extending support to Ganga-Mekong Project and trans-Asian Highway linking Southeast Asia with Iran.

Cambodian Politics

Though the communists came to power in Cambodia in April 1975, but they could not gain similar status and popularity as their counterparts in Laos and Vietnam. The Cambodians, by and large, continued to respect Norodom Sihanouk and his brand of politics.

Presently Cambodians are interested in supporting liberal democracy that can nurture their interests. They have shown their enthusiasm for the emerging system by massive participation in the elections. The rulers have adopted a democratic order, multiparty system, free press and independent judiciary. Now it will be in order to glance through some important provisions of the Constitution which have bearings on the emerging political system.

The Cambodian Constitution, adopted on 24 September 1993, has 139 articles, which defines separation of powers into legislative, executive and judicial sections and enumerates a long list of human rights. The Preamble of the Constitution at the outset has declared that

> we the people of Cambodia, accustomed to having been an outstanding civilization, are determined to unite for the consolidation of national unity, the preservation and defence of the territory and precious sovereignty and the fine Angkor civilization, and the restoration of Cambodia into an "Island of Peace", based on a multiparty liberal democratic regime guaranteeing human rights.

The constitution has provided for a system of constitutional monarchy, which has been explained in Part II of the Constitution. Article one (1) has stated that the King shall rule according to the constitution and to the principles of liberal democracy and pluralism, and the country will be permanently neutral and non-aligned.

Another interesting aspect of the Constitutional monarchy is that the King shall be chosen by the "Royal Council of the Throne" which will consist of the President of the National Assembly, the Prime Minister, the first and second Vice Presidents of National Assembly and also Somdech the Chief of the Orders of Mahanikaya and Thammayut. The King is not empowered to appoint heir to the throne and will continue to remain constitutional head only.

Chapter III from Articles 31 to 50 have explained the rights and obligations of Khmer citizens. Every citizen shall be equal before the law, enjoying the same rights, freedom and fulfilling the same obligations regardless of race, colour, sex, language, religious belief, political tendency, birth origin, social status, wealth and other status.

Article 34 has stated that the citizens of either sex shall enjoy the right to vote and stand as candidates for the election. Citizens of either sex of at least 18 years, have the right to vote. Citizens of either sex of at least 25 years old, have the right to stand as candidates for the National Assembly.

As far as the legislature is concerned, it is unicameral. National Assembly is the sole body to formulate and review rules and regulations. The composition, powers and functions of the National Assembly has been explained in Articles 76 to 98. It is pointed out that the National Assembly will be comprised of 120 members, who will be elected by a free, universal, equal, direct and secret ballot. The tenure of the Assembly is five years and its members is to represent the entire Khmer community and not only their constituencies. The Assembly's role as stated in Article 90 is that it will approve the national budget, the state planning, the loans, the lending and the creation, changes or annulment of tax, administrative accounts, etc. It has power to approve the law of amnesty, treaties, international conventions and the law of the declaration of war.

Similarly the powers of the executive are defined in Articles 99 to 108 and of the Supreme Court from Articles 109 to 116.

Cambodia has adopted the system of multi-party system of which CPP, BLDP and Funcinpec are important. They are sharing the governmental powers. The Khmer Rouge on the other hand, is outside the government and playing the role of opposition outside National Assembly. The government is showing reconciliatory gestures and has not banned it so far.

Foreign Policy

Foreign policy goals have been clearly defined in Article 53 of the Constitution, whereby it is stated that Cambodia will pursue a policy of permanent neutrality and non-alignment. It will follow the policy of peaceful coexistence with its neighbours and shall not join in any military alliance or military pact which is incompatible with its policy of neutrality. It will not permit any foreign military base on its territory and shall not have its own military base abroad.

Cambodia is trying to strengthen relations with all nations and intends to improve its regional image. The relations with Vietnam and Thailand however is crucial for its peace and prosperity. It is in that area that the Cambodians have been facing difficulties. Thai military businessmen have clandestine illicit relations with the Khmer Rouge. They are engaged in timber extraction and gem mining inside Cambodia with the support of the Khmer Rouge. In returns they are supplying weapons to sustain Khmer Rouge activities.

On the other hand, improving relations with Vietnam is also faced with some hurdles. There is a feeling that the present border demarcation vis-a-vis Vietnam is unjust and edged in Vietnam's favour. They are demanding that the demarcation should be on the basis of the borders as prevailed in 1967. This is also a sensitive issue but the Cambodian government is trying to find out an amicable solution under the overall ASEAN framework.

The Cambodians have global sympathies and the world community is eager to support her in reconstruction and development. However, they have yet to fight internal enemies and establish peaceful conditions in order to get international assistance and cooperation.

To conclude, following observations are important :

(*a*) Vietnam, Laos and Cambodia support the policy of liberalisation to emerge important facilitator in the globalisation process.

(*b*) Vietnam and Laos retain one party rule of Communist Party, but they are evolving a system in which differing opinions, democratic ethos and pragmatism is promoted.

(*c*) Cambodia has not been able to resolve its internal problems. The Khmer Rouge guerrillas still create disturbances and the land mines have not been entirely removed. But the government is keen for reconciliation, reconstruction and development.

(*d*) Foreign Policy of the three Indochinese countries are bound to be in tune with the ASEAN-10. All of them have signed Treaty for Amity and Cooperation and all of them have supported ZOPFAN and nuclear-weapon-Free-Zone treaties.

(*e*) Vietnam, Laos and Cambodia oppose terrorism unequivocally and tries to remain neutral in regional matters. They intend to restrain themselves in flexing military muscles to resolve regional conflicts.

REFERENCES

Beresford, M., *Vietnam: Politics, Economics and Society,* London, 1988.
Buttinger, Joseph, *Vietnam: A Political History,* New York, 1968.
Chanda, Nayan, *Brother Enemy: The War After the War, A History of Indochina since the Fall of Saigon,* London, 1986.
Dommen, A.J., *Conflict in Laos: The Politics of Neutralisation,* London, 1964.
Ljunggren, Borje, ed. *The Challenge of Reform in Indochia,* Cambridge, 1993.
McNamara, Robert S., *In Retrospect: The Tragedy and Lessons of Vietnam,* New York, 1995.
Pike, Douglas, *A History of Vietnamese Communism, 1925-1976,* Stanford, 1978.
Prados, John, *The Blood Road—The Ho Chi Minh Trail and the Vietnam War,* New York, 1999.
Steinberg, David J., *Cambodia: Its People, Its Society and Its Culture,* New Haven, 1959.
Stuart-Fox, M., *Laos: Society, Politics and Economics,* London, 1986.
Thayer, Carlyle A. and Arnmer, ed., *Vietnamese Foreign Policy in Transition,* Singapore, 1999.
Vickery, M., *Cambodia, 1975-1982,* Sydney, 1984.

14

Society and Politics in Laos

Laos, also known as Lan Xang in the historical past, is the only landlocked state of Southeast Asia. It shares 4,700 kilometers common borders with five countries, namely China in the north, Myanmar in the northwest, Thailand in the west, Cambodia in the south and Vietnam in the east.

There are high mountain ranges in the north and lower in the south. Phou Luong range (Truong Son) is located in the north and Annamite ranges in the south. With an average altitude of 2000 meters, Phou Luong range is pierced by numerous passes from north to south, which facilitate geographical links with Vietnam.

The Mekong River running for more than 1875 kilometers in Laos, forms the western frontier of the country for much of its length. The various tributaries of the Mekong River—Nam Tha, Nam Ou, Nam Kham and Nam Ngum in the North, Nam Kading, Sebangfel and Sebangheu in the centre, and Sedone and Sekong in the south constitute the axial system of Laos, a link between the mountains and the plains, and has provided a convenient network of communication and abundance of hydroelectric power.

Laos has a tropical monsoonal climate and 45 per cent of its territories are still covered with forests. It has varieties of wood, i.e., timber, teak, trac, ebony, bamboo and rattan. Tigers, panthers, bears, deer, gaurs, and elephants are found in big numbers and the country is rich in flora and fauna.

Laos produces a number of agricultural products namely rice, maize, sweet potatoes, sugarcane, tobacco, coffee, groundnuts, garlic and soyabeans. It also produces opium poppy in the northern uplands, which form part of the so-called "Golden Triangle."

In 1993, Laos produced 1.5 million tonnes of rice 58,000 tonnes of maize; 48,000 tonnes of tobacco; 94,000 tonnes of sugarcane and

7,400 tonnes of coffee, and the production of these commodities are likely to be doubled at the turn of this century.

Despite centuries of colonial exploitation Laos has still some mineral resources and they are tin, gypsum, zinc, lead, coal, potash, iron ore, gold, silver and gems. Laos was also an important part of the Subarnabhumi (Golden Land) in the historical past and its natural resources are still plentiful to make it prosperous.

Laos has an estimated population of 4.4 million, of which 60 per cent are ethnic Lao and five per cent ethnic Chinese and Vietnamese. Remaining 35 per cent are comprised of different tribal groups, i.e. Hmong, Meo, Yao, Nung, Shans etc. The majority believes in Hinayana Buddhism, but one-third in tribal religion. Polygamy is an offence and Lao is the official language. However English, French, Thai and the Vietnamese languages are also spoken. Culturally ethnic Lao have similarities with ethnic Thais but politically they have more affinities with the Vietnamese.

History

The history of Laos began in 1353, when Fa Ngum, the son of Pha Nghien conquered Muang Swe and founded the Kingdom of Lan Xang (thousand elephants). He fought many wars to unite several scattered fiefdoms together and some of them were Muang Pak-Kop, Muang Kabong, Muang Fuan, Muang Noi, Muang Xieng–Sen and Muang Swe. Fa Ngum was very close to Angkor Kingdom, where he had studied in his childhood and he had restrained the expansion of Siamese and Annamite rulers in the area. His successors were not strong enough and therefore after a brief period of glory, the Kingdom of Lan Xang fell prey to expansionist neighbours. His dynasty however ruled Laos for two centuries.

Laos began to lose its power and prestige when Burmese, Vietnamese and Siamese rulers developed territorial interests over Laos. In 1570, the Burmese were the first to attack Laos and occupy Vieng Chan. Though this territory was restored by Laos when King Souligna Vongsa ascended the throne in 1637, but the Burmese rulers continued to pose security threats. The successors of Souligna Vongsa again were weak and they started taking assistance from either of the strong neighbours and began to cede territories in return. Siamese help were sought against the Burmese, Vietnamese help against Siamese and vice versa and in the process Laos lost its inner strength.

Burma attacked Laos once again in 1760 and captured Vieng Chan and Luang Prabang. Thus Siamese help were taken to throw out the Burmese, but now Siam developed its own territorial interests while pushing out the Burmese. It occupied Vieng Chan in 1778 and established its domination over Luang Prabang.

Laos under Prince Chau Anou, tried to be free of Siamese domination during 1827-28. Chau Anou secretly tried to secure Vietnamese assistance against the Siamese, but his efforts failed miserably. He was caught, arrested and insulted in Bangkok and he died in captivity. He is however regarded as a symbol of Laotian nationalism by the historians, besides Fa Ngum and Souligna Vongsa.

In mid-1870s, China too attacked Laos to occupy northern territories of Tran Ninh, but Siamese forces foiled it. Now Siam established a virtual protectorate over Laos in 1885-86, but this did not prove propitious. The French colonial forces had started coming and had already established its colonial rule over Vietnam and Cambodia. They were exploring monopoly over Mekong route to China and also for natural frontiers of their colonial domain. The Mekong river, dividing Indochina with rest of Southeast Asia, was viewed to be the best demarcation line and thus Laos became a subject of colonial interests. The French displayed gunboat diplomacy and pressurized Siam to vacate areas east of the Mekong river for the French, and the Siamese rulers were compelled to sign a treaty in 1893, to cede all the territories lying east of the Mekong river. Thus Laos became a part of "Union Indochinoise", and got protectorate status.

Nationalist Upsurge

The Laotians have been extremely nationalistic, but effective articulation of their patriotism were displayed only after the formation of Indo-China Communist Party (ICP) in 1930. The ICP was determined to wage war for independence and free Indochina states from the grip of French colonial masters. Laotian leaders under the banner of ICP, sought to cultivate fraternal ties with Vietnam, and mobilized its masses against French colonialism.

During the Second World War, the communist forces in Laos fought against French and Japanese aggressors and was in control of northern areas at the time of Japanese surrender. The royal family however was divided on the question of support to the communist endeavours or on continued allegiance to French. In the beginning, King Sisavang Vong welcomed Japanese protection but after its surrender in August 1945, he expressed his allegiance to the French. He refused to abide the proposal of complete independence, as suggested by his son, Prince Phetsarath. The crowned Prince Savang Vatthana moved in the footsteps of his father and the overall situation was disturbing.

Prince Phetsarath was unhappy and tried to distance himself with the king by starting Lao Issara movement in April 1946. He advocated complete independence for Laos and fought against the French colonial forces. His endeavours were strongly backed by Viet Minh. Lao Issara tried its best to prevent the return of the French colonial forces but could not succeed. The French forces came back and got all those areas which were occupied by the nationalist forces.

The domestic situation in Laos compelled Phetsarath to go to Bangkok to live in exile along with his close followers, including Prince Souvanna Phouma and Prince Souphanouvong. The latter was more revolutionary who adopted uncompromising stance on the question of independence and revolutionary means. He differed with Souvanna Phouma and some other followers of Prince Phetsarath and therefore he chose to leave Bangkok for Hanoi.

The Viet Minh was enthusiastic to welcome Prince Souphanouvong and promised to provide strategic facilities to fight war for independence. Souphanouvong thus formed Lao Patriotic Front (Pathet Lao) and proclaimed Laotian independence by announcing the formation of Democratic Republic of Laos in August 1949. He gave inflammatory speeches against France and exhorted Laotians to fight. With a strong foothold at Phong Saly and Sam Neua and strongly backed by Vietnam and China, he made it extremely difficult for the colonial forces to rule.

Geneva Accord, 1954

The Geneva agreement was signed on 21 July 1954 and thereafter Indo-China states, including Laos, Cambodia and Vietnam were liberated and the colonial forces departed. Laos, which became a constitutional monarchy, chose Souvanna Phouma to be its Prime Minister. He tried to pursue the policy of neutrality, but at the same time tried to maintain some distances with the communist forces. The pro-communist Pathet Lao, however had seized two important provinces of Laos under their control. Those two provinces—Phong Saly and Sam Neua—were located at the Vietnamese frontier and were inaccessible to the Vientiane forces for effective control.

Souvanna Phouma was determined to reunify Sam Neua and Phong Saly and he tried to enlist the cooperation of International Control Commission (ICC), which suggested dialogue with the Pathet Lao for a lasting solution. In 1956 Pathet Lao agreed for reunification of those provinces with their government in Vientiane and the agreement was signed for common administration. It was also agreed that Pathet Lao forces would be integrated into the royal army and they would share governmental powers.

However the royal forces and Pathet Lao continued to remain apprehensive of each other and therefore honest implementation of the Accord was difficult. Though Sam Neua and Phong Saly were placed under the jurisdiction of the central government and Souphanouvong included in the Central Cabinet in November 1957, the Accord failed subsequently. The rightist forces began to treat Pathet Lao supporters as untouchables and the conflict continued.

The Pathet Lao tried to extract maximum benefits out of this coalition. It increased its power base and won more seats in the election for National Assembly in 1958. The right wing parties united to oppose Pathet Lao and the situation deterioted. Prime Minister Souvanna Phouma resigned and there was a Coup d'etat in Laos to crush Communism. During 1960-62, Phoui Senanikone, Kong Le, Phoumi Nosavan and Boun Oum, all rightwing supporters came into power to check the momentum of Pathet Lao movement, but all these endeavours only helped in the consolidation of the Pathet Lao power base. By 1961, Pathet Lao was in control of Nam Tha, besides Sam Neua and Phong Saly. It was difficult for the government forces to contain Pathet Lao, because the latter symbolised Laotian nationalism and had popular support.

The civil war started in Laos because of the belligerency of the rightist who after facing reverses called the outside powers to intervene to protect their so-called neutrality. Thus the 14-nation conference on Laos started in May 1961, in which the United States, the Soviet Union, the United Kingdom, China, France, North Vietnam, South Vietnam, Cambodia, Burma, Thailand, Poland, India, Canada and Laos participated. Though the expressed aim of this conference was to establish Laotian peace and neutrality, but the apparent objective was to neutralize Pathet Lao.

The conference discussed several issues and an agreement was signed in 1962 through which the participants declared that they would refrain from all direct and indirect interference in the internal affairs of Laos. They also assured not to establish military bases, not to introduce foreign troops or military personnel in Laos. Thus both rightists and leftists decided to work together in a coalition and promised not to enter into military alliance with any of the superpowers. Another achievement of this agreement was that the "protective umbrella" of SEATO, which had been forced upon Laos in 1954, was withdrawn.

Despite these agreements Pathet Lao did not get due recognition, and this was the major cause of the conflict. The United States was involved in the containment drive. It had signed Southeast Asia Treaty Organization (SEATO). It had declared to fight against communism at the global level and had targetted Pathet Lao and Viet Minh as their major enemies and were exploring all avenues to contain them.

The US treated Laos strategically important as it was a gateway to both China and Vietnam. They were interested in turning Laos as an anti-communist bastion. D.G.E. Hall has clearly stated in his book, *History of Southeast Asia,* that "American policy was seeking to build Laos as an anti-communist bastion. American aid per head of the population in Laos was higher than any other country in the world."

The American involvement in Laos grew steadily to contain communism in the region. The Central Intelligence Agency (CIA) had established its regional headquarters in Laos, which trained special ground forces, such as the army of Hmong tribesmen under the command of General Vang Pao. There were 30,000 irregular troops under his command. There were at least 6000 "Thai irregulars" formed in 15 battalions of 400 each in Royal Army of Laos, and they were also trained by the CIA.

Laotian territories were also used by the US for reconnaissance and bombing raids over Vietnam. The US believed that Ho Chi Minh Trail, the supply route of arms to National Liberation Front (NLF) of South Vietnam passed through Laos. The US tried to disrupt or destroy the NLF. The US bombers based in Thailand indulged in bombing communist held areas in Laos ever since 1965. But the most ferocious American attack was in February-March 1971, when it moved towards north eastern borders and indulged in massive bombing, using its military and airforce. They had even captured the town of Tehepone before retreating. It was surprising that the government of Souvanna Phouma did not raise its voice against American action this time and allowed the situation to deteriorate.

Assertion by the Pathet Lao

All attempts to isolate Pathet Lao failed and their influence continued to grow. In January 1973, Paris Peace Agreement was signed to end the Vietnam War. This agreement was also signed in Laos on 21 February 1973 for restoration of peace and reconciliation between warring factions of leftists and rightists. It made a provision for provisional government of National Union, consisting of the representatives of the Vientiane government side and Pathet Lao in equal number. On 5 April 1974, the King of Laos, Savang Vatthana legitimated that agreement by signing a decree, which proposed coalition government with the Pathet Lao.

Thereafter Prince Souphanouvong returned to Vientiane to share equal powers with the Royalists. Though Souvanna Phouma remained the Prime Minister, it did not create difficulties for the Pathet Lao to assert its position. The rightists and royalists became increasingly unpopular and their leaders started seeking asylum in the Western World. After NLF victory in Vietnam (1975), the royalist forces deserted their ranks in great numbers and Pathet Lao started replacing them. King Savang Vatthana realized the situation and abdicated in December 1975. Now under the guidance of Pathet Lao, constitutional monarchy was abolished and in its place Lao Peoples Democratic Republic (LPDP) was installed.

The communists thus came into power and elected Souphanouvong as the first President and Kaysone Phomvihane as the Prime Minister. The new regime endeavoured to implement Marxism-Leninism at the domestic front and cultivated close relations with Vietnam, Cuba and Soviet Union. Thus Laos was identified as an integral part of the communist world and Pathet Lao was named Lao Peoples' Revolutionary Party (LPRP).

Laos pursued policies to cultivate special ties with Vietnam by signing a Treaty of Friendship in July 1977 whereby the latter promised to assist Laos in security, economic and political matters. Vietnam sent 40,000 troops to protect Laos on the eve of intervention of Cambodia in December 1978 when Pol Pot was overthrown and Heng Samrin was installed in his place. Cambodia,

Laos and Vietnam decided to unite strategically and their foreign policy goals became common. In 1980, the Foreign Ministers of the three countries of Indochina met in Hanoi and expressed their determination to forge solidarity with one another. They collectively opposed the Chinese and gave an impression of forging an alliance. This did not go well with the regional ethos as the ASEAN countries and China became apprehensive of this alliance and worked together to oust Heng Samrin regime from power. However the situation started changing after Vietnamese withrawal from Cambodia and ultimately with the termination of the Cold War.

New Economic Mechanism

The economic liberalization in Laos started with the policies, known as new economic mechanism (NEM), and this term has special significance in Laos. The genesis behind adopting this policy cannot be understood in proper perspective unless we know the developments in the Soviet Union, which was the biggest donor for communist countries, including Laos.

M. Gorbachcv came to power in 1985 and started restructuring Soviet society in the name of perestroika and promoted openness in the name of glasnost. He cared little about the opinion of the Soviet allies and rapidly moved for rapprochement with all its adversaries at the global level. He gave a clear impression that he was not bothered about the future of communist allies, and would surely reduce the quantum of aid so far given to Vietnam and Laos. These developments alarmed Laos and began to review its policies to cope with the emerging challenges.

Laos had other domestic compulsions in the mid-eighties to evolve NEM, and they were its deteriorating economy, inflation, devaluation and corruption. The leadership understood the realities of the socio-economic situation and decided to introduce reforms to arrest its weaknesses.

In October 1986, President Souphanouvong stepped down voluntarily and encouraged younger leaders to come at the helm of affairs. Thus Phoumi Vongvichit was appointed acting President and Sisophon Lovansai, the President of the Supreme Peoples' Assembly. Those two were advocating reforms in the past and now they were authorised by the party to embark on a series of reforms to check inflation and devaluation and promote the path of economic development. This was the genesis of market-oriented reforms in the name of NEM, which was endorsed by the fourth Party Congress of the LPRP in November 1986. It is noteworthy that Laotian decision for economic reforms was taken a month earlier than Vietnam, which also adopted policies for economic reforms in the name of Doi Moi (renovation) in December 1986.

The NEM was indeed aimed at decentralization of economic decision-making, more accountability for public enterprises, fiscal and financial reforms, deregulation of prices, removal of trade barriers, implementation of new investment laws and overall greater reliance on market forces. In short Laos took a decision for opening up its economy to the outside world.

The advocates of NEM also implied a more outward-looking development strategy. The state's monopoly on the import and export of a wide range of commodities was removed in 1987 and the official currency (Kip) was devalued from the official rate to free market rate.

In 1988, a new foreign Investment Law was adopted, and in the same year, the government published a range of new decrees covering reforms in the financial and fiscal sectors. In 1990, the government initiated a privatization (disengagement) policy with respect to state enterprises. The fifth Party Congress (1991) reiterated party's support for the transition to "multi-sector" market economy through which the private sector was acknowledged to have a key long-term role to play. The Lao government sought to attract the return of professional people and the other skilled Laotians living in exile.

Though the NEM stands for economic liberalization, and it is against ending the dominant role of Communist Party simultaneously, the market forces have its impact on the political environment also. Laos at present supports one-party system, similarly on Vietnamese model. It has been sensitive to demands for multi-party system. But the opposition to the existing policies continues. In October 1990, Tongsuk Saisangkhi and Latsami Khamphoui, both former vice ministers were arrested because they were actively campaigning for the introduction of multi-party democracy. In March 1991, LPRP pledged to continue reforms aimed at replacing the centrally planned economy with free market principles, but denied the need for political pluralism. However the most important was the change in the wording of national motto, whereby the word "socialism" was substituted by the words "democracy and prosperity."

The NEM has given priority to boost agricultural and industrial production. It has taken decisions towards privatization of land ownership. In 1993 Laos passed three land related laws, which were published in a multi-lingual monthly gazette. The first part established rules surrounding ownership and use of land, second was regarding land taxation and third was about land licences. Though the law affirmed that the state owned the land, but the farmers were allowed to have the right of lease, sale and inheritance etc.

As far as industries are concerned, the government is attracting the foreign investors and various projects in agro-business, garments and wood-based industries have been approved. The foreign investors initially liked investments in tourism and textiles, but now the number of investments have grown. The number of projects approved by the government of Laos gives a fascinating picture, i.e. 69 new projects were approved in 1991, followed by 102 in 1992 and 79 in the first half of 1993. Foreign companies are encouraged to make investments in mining sector also. Australia's **CRA Exploration** and the US **Newmount Mining** have signed gold mining contracts. Thailand has signed new agreements for hydroelectric power and China for air services. The ASEAN countries and East Asian tigers are exploring avenues for investment relations and some of them have already established collaborative relations.

The foreign investments are having positive impact on the economy. The change in Laotian policies have generated economic clout and the average growth rate which is 7 to 8 per cent at present, is rising. The stabilization of financial and monetary sectors are satisfying. The inflation rate has been reduced from 85 per cent in 1988 to 6 per cent today. The quality of garment production have improved and its exports in 1992 fetched US $30 million for Laos. Total exports from Laos in 1993 rose by 20 per cent over 1992 and 66 per cent over 1991 figures.

Political System

Laos had a long history of monarchy till the advent of the French rulers. The colonial France retained the institution of monarchy in Laos without sovereignty. That was the situation during 1893 to 1954. In the post-independence era, Laos opted for the system of constitutional monarchy. The role of the constitutional monarch, Savang Vatthana proved dubious and therefore when the communists came to power in December 1975, they abolished the system of constitutional monarchy.

When Laos became a communist state, the dictatorship of the party in power prevailed. They had socialist agenda and the ideologies of Marxism and Leninism were given paramount importance. But that could not benefit the interests of the majority. Laos became one of the ten poorest countries of the world.

Thus Laos started introducing democratic reforms under the guidance of Communist Party, LPRP. The rapid changes in the existing polity suggest that Laos is passing through a transitional phase. It is difficult to analyse the characteristics of the political system, yet some landmark developments are analysed.

The political system in Laos might be compared with that of Vietnam, which is also passing through a transitional phase. Both Laos and Vietnem have opted for economic liberalization but resisted political liberalization.

Laos adopted a new constitution on 14 August 1991 through which one-party rule has been legitimated. LPRP has been declared the "central nucleus" of the people's democracy. The Constitution explicitly recognises the role of the private sector in the economy, and provides specific guarantees to woo foreign investments.

The constitution also makes provisions for an elected 85-member National Assembly to act as an important governmental organ for the rule-making. The National Assembly was also empowered to elect Laotian President to exercise executive powers. The Constitution also endeavoured to improve the judicial organ of the government to ensure fairness and justice in considering legal issues in conformity with the provisions of the Constitution. All these arrangements indicated that the consensus was in favour of the division of powers.

In 1991 Constitution also removed the terms "socialism" and "working class" from the preamble and replaced it with peace, independence, democracy, and prosperity. Again the Constitution guaranteed private ownership of prodution along with state ownership, and discussed the provisions of its transfer and inheritance.

Rule three of the Constitution enshrined rights and obligations of the citizens, which included freedom from arbitrary arrest, freedom of speech, press and assembly, freedom to form association and stage demonstration. These rights however are limited by a sublaw that any demonstration or a demand for multi-party system would be illegal and considered punishable. Despite limitations, the provision for human rights in the Constitution was a great achievement as it did not find any mention in the past when LPRP assumed full command of the country in 1975. The governance of the country then was mostly based on decrees and decisions of the party Congress.

The new Constitution also introduced important changes in the name and nomenclature of government positions. Thus the designation of "Chairman" was replaced by the Prime Minister, and "General Secretary" was termed President. Again the Supreme People's Assembly, which exercised the power of the Parliament so far, was named, National Assembly.

Though the President is to be elected by the National Assembly, but Prime Minister and his Council of Ministers are to be appointed by the President, which is again subject to approval by the National Assembly. The overall attempt of the leaders are to arouse legal political consciousness and democratic framework.

Lastly the Constitution has also enshrined election rules. LPRP used to be the most powerful body to conduct elections, but now the situation is changing. The Constitution has allowed private candidates side by side the official candidates to fight in the elections and private candidates are winning the elections to make their presence felt under the new dispensation.

The National Assembly in Laos has the potentials to be vibrant and active. The first election for the composition of the National Assembly took place on 20 December 1992. There were 154 candidates for 85 seats. It is reported that only 70 per cent of the victorious candidates were from the LPRP and remaining 30 per cent from outside.

The National Assembly, which is unicameral, has started debating various bills and corruption cases. In 1993, it raised objection to fiscal budget, 1993-94 and asked for its resubmission in the next session. Again it rejected a new foreign investment law on technical grounds. This shows that they are asserting their rights and acting as an effective rule-making branch of the government.

However, the maxim of one-party rule has not yet been diluted. It is because Laotians still view LPRP as a successor of Pathet Lao, which symbolized nationalism during the colonial struggle. Again the introduction of multi-party system in Cambodia have not proved successful and what happens in Cambodia can have implications on Laos also. Also it is always useful to go slow in a transitional phase. The criticism against Laos in the west is that it is one of the closest societies in Asia in terms of access to information. They do not allow foreign newspapers and their own media is secretive. Some observers have pointed out that many personnel changes at the top level of government are not publicly gazetted and the officials are secretive even on those matters which are not sensitive. These criticisms may be serious but Laotians have developed their own style of politics and diplomacy.

Foreign Relations

The economic liberalization generated modes of foreign capital and modern technologies which could not be fulfilled by the communist world. The western aid and assistance were essentially required. Laotian leaders understood this reality and were realistic in changing the course of its foreign policy. They adopted NEM and attached due importance to cultivating relations with the United States, European Community, Japan, Korea and the Association of Southeast Asian Nations (ASEAN). The overall change in the course of Laotian foreign policy had positive impact on the opinion of international community and bilateral relations were reciprocated by all the nations with whom it was sought.

Relations with United States

Laos viewed the US to be hostile during Cold War years, but now it is projected very friendly. In 1992 the two countries upgraded their diplomatic relations to ambassadorial level and opened a new chapter for their cooperative relations. Laos has agreed to cooperate on two issues that the US has been demanding. First is the search for remains of the US soldiers "missing in action" (MIA) in Laos during the Vietnam war, and secondly the narcotics control.

Laos has already returned the remains of several MIA's to the US and has intensified its efforts to search the remains of more MIA's if still left out. As far as opium production and trafficking of narcotics are concerned, the government is trying to exercise more effective control. However this issue is subject to regional cooperation. If the countries of the golden triangle, i.e. Myanmar, Thailand, Laos along with Vietnam prepares a collective strategy that may check this illegal trade. Laos is doing its own efforts and the US is apparently satisfied. If the communication system in the golden triangle areas are improved, the situation would definitely change.

Relations with China

China is the immediate neighbour with which relations had deteriorated when Laos signed friendship pact with Vietnam in 1977. Now after the changes in international environment, Laotian relations with China have improved. They re-restablished their diplomatic relations in 1988 and delineated their boundaries. China is developing two northern provinces of Laos for commercial purposes and the Accord on Sino-Laos economic relations are signed. The Chinese goods are coming in increasing quantities through the ancient route on the common border and the two countries are evolving strategies to promote security cooperation also.

China and Laos are directly linked after the construction of Friendship Bridge over the Makong River. There is booming economic activity under the Greater Mekong Subregion (GMS) project, especially Northeast Economic Corridor is emphasing greater level of cooperation amongst Cambodia, Laos, Myanmar and Vietnam (CLMV) with solid support from China. Vientiane is closely linked to Kunming (China) by roadways and the volume of trade and investment between the two are rising rapidly.

Relations with Vietnam

Both Laos and Vietnam both under the Soviet sphere of influence were friendly. Both had signed a friendship pact (1977) and as a result Vietnam had sent 40,000 troops to Laos in 1978 to boost security morale. When Vietnam militarily intervened in Cambodia in December 1978, Laos was the only Southeast Asian country to demonstrate support for Vietnam. Both cooperated with each other in economic, security and foreign policy matters, but both became internationally isolated due to that friendship.

The situation started changing after the withdrawal of Vietnamese forces from Cambodia and the 1991 Peace Accord. Both adopted policies to break their isolation and integrate into the global economy. Both gave emphasis on economic liberalization and agricultural and industrial developments. Both attracted foreign investments and collaboration and introduced momentous changes in their polity.

Despite changes in their foreign policy priorities, both Laos and Vietnam are trying to ensure that their relations remains at the same level as it was in the past. They are exchanging ministerial visits and expressing their solidarity with one another. As the two countries are bound together geographically with one another, the relations cannot be diluted, but it is showing downward trends. The relations with Thailand are given much more weightage and economic considerations are given importance in the foreign policy decision-making.

Relations with Thailand

There has been phenomenal rise in Lao-Thai relations in the recent past. In 1988 Thai Prime Minister, Chatichai Choonhavan visited Laos with some agenda on co-operation, i.e., a bridge over the Mekong river to link Laos and Thailand by roadways, opening up of trading points on their common borders, the production of hydro–electric power and tourism, etc. He was extremely successful in confidence-building and striking a rapport with Laotian leaders. While in Vientiane, he announced his determination to transform Indochina from a "battlefield" into a "market place."

Chatichai's visit was extremely successful and as a result Laos decided to cooperate more closely with Thailand. Thus a series of agreements have been signed between the two in the years following, which shows an attempt for revival of friendship that existed in the historical past.

In 1988, both countries established joint border demarcation committee (JBDC) for settlement of border disputes and withdrawal of troops from the disputed areas. Thai government also assured that it would suppress subversive activities of Lao exiles in Thailand and as a part of the confidence-building measure, Thai police arrested 11 Lao exiles in Thailand in 1992, who were alleged to be planning subversive activities against LPDR. Again JBDC delineated the common frontier to the satisfaction of both sides in 1993 and the troops of the two sides were withdrawn.

There has been growing collaboration between the two to promote economic ties. Thailand is an important partner in producing hydro-electricity and the two signed major agreements on this collaboration during the visit of Thai Prime Minister, Chuan Leekpai to Vientiane in 1993. Thus Xeset dam had been planned to be constructed. In this connection, it is important to know that the first phase of Nam Ngum dam (1971), generating 30,000 kw, provided a surplus of energy that were purchased by Thailand. Its second phase (1987) had a capacity to generate 150,000 kw, which exported 90 per cent of the output to Thailand. As and when the new dams start production, it has a ready market in the neighbouring countries.

Thailand is ranked topmost as a foreign investor in Laotian economy, which also acts as conduit for capital inflows from third parties. Thai currency (Baht) is acceptable in Laos and between 1988-93, about 112 Thai firms pledged US $150 million for various projects. In 1993 Thailand invested $20 million to collaborate in the brewery sector, in which it has got monopoly.

Thailand has also collaborated in improving communication network on lengthy Lao-Thai borders and 13 border checkpoints have been opened. Thailand is supporting regional efforts to improve roads and bridges in Laos with the support of China and Vietnam, and this endeavour is backed by the Asian Development Bank (ADB). The proposal is to build a road linking northeast Thailand, Laos and Vietnam with one another. Again the construction of another road is planned in the "golden triangle", at the confluence of Lao-Thai-Myanmar and China border.

The road communication between Thailand and Laos have improved tremendously with the inauguration of Lao-Thai friendship Bridge on 8th April 1994. This 1,170 metre long bridge built by the Australians at the cost of US $30 million, facilitates Lao-Thai commercial and cultural ties. This bridge directly links Vientiane to Nongkhai.

The developments in the region suggest that Laos is a responsible member of the ASEAN. It has already signed ASEAN Treaty of Amity and Cooperation (1992) and improved its image in the ASEAN capitals. Some of the ASEAN partners, notably Thailand, Singapore and Malaysia have already made sizable investments in Laos, and its "observer status" was raised in 1997 to full membership of the association. It is noteworthy that after Vietnam's inclusion in the ASEAN in 1995, polarisation of Southeast Asia along communist and anti-communist camps were diluted and efforts for regional cooperation and harmony were intensified.

REFERENCES

1. Anna Louise Strong, *Cash and Violence in Laos*, Calcutta, Cardinal Press, 1975.
2. A.J. Dommen, *Conflict in Laos: The Politics of Neutralization*, London, Pall Mall Press, 1964.
3. G. Evans and K. Rowley, *Red Brotherhood at War*, London, Verso, 1990.
4. Kayson Phomvihane, *Revolution in Laos*, Hanoi, Foreign Language Publishing House, 1988.
5. P.F. Langer and J.J. Zasloff, *North Vietnam and the Pathet Lao*, Cambridge, M.A, Harvard University Press, 1970.
6. LPDR, Report on the Economic and Social Situation Development Strategy and Assistance Requirements, Vols. 1 & 2, prepared for the Asia-Pacific Round Table Meeting, Geneva, 1983.
7. F.M. Le Bar and A. Suddard, *Laos, Its People, Its Society, Its Culture*, New Haven, C.T, HRAF Press, 1960.
8. *News Bulletin*, Lao People's Democratic Republic, Embassy of the Lao People's Democratic Republic, New Delhi.
9. Ratnam Perala, *Laos and the Superpowers*, New Delhi, Tulsi Publishing House, 1980.
10. Fox M, Stuart, *Laos : Politics, Economics and Society*, London, Francis Printer, 1986.
11. P.K. Tiwari, "Determinants of the Foreign Policy of Laos: A Study of its Relations with Neighbours, 1975-1988", Unpublished M. Phil. Dissertation, Jawaharlal Nehru University, 1993.
12. Viravong Maha Sila, *History of Laos*, New York, Paragon Reprint Corporation, 1964.
13. J.J. Zasloff, *The Pathet Lao: Leadership and Organization*, Lexington M.A. Heath, 1973.
14. Laos was included as a member of ASEAN in 1997.

15

Indonesian Profile

Indonesia situated at the crossroad of the Pacific and the Indian Ocean, is the largest country of Southeast Asia. It covers about 5,193,250 square kilometers of the territories, of which 2,027,087 sq. km. are landed and 3,166,163 sq. km. are sea territories. Again it is the largest archipelago of the world with 17,508 islands and 210 million population. Formerly under the Dutch colonial rule, it declared its independence on 17 August 1945 and became a Republic. Though the founding fathers tried to evolve a system in which all the three branches of the government, the executive, legislature and judiciary were to be equally vigilant, but Presidential system emerged and powers of the legislature and judiciary were eroded. First two Presidents, namely Sukarno (1945-65) and Suharto (1966-98) were extremely powerful and dominating. They increased the powers of the Presidency enormously and the mechanism of checks and balances were diluted. After getting independence, Indonesia tried to be assertive in the politics of the region in particular and Third World in general. President Sukarno was vocal against the western world and opposed US policy of containment. He endeavoured to nurture a system, which could prove ideal and indigenous by Asian standards. Thus the word Panchasila, also pronounced as Pancasila was popularised for the political system. Panchasila became the ideological and philosophical foundation of the Republic and its ideals were incorporated in the constitution declared on 18th August 1945.

Panchasila is a Sanskrit word, which was also considered the philosophical foundation of Indian Foreign Policy, but for India this word was incorporated in the document much later. Indonesia wanted to incorporate the ideals of Panchasila, both in foreign policy and domestic matters right since its inception. The

Constitution of 1945 explained five principles of Panchasila as the following:[1]

- Belief in the one and only God.
- A just and civilised humanity.
- Unity of Indonesia.
- Democracy guided by the inner wisdom of deliberations of representatives.
- Social justice.

The Articles of the 1945 Constitution enumerated the ideals and goals for which the nation was born. The founding fathers were inspired by the use for unity, common goals and democracy built upon the age-old Indonesian concepts of Gotong Royong (mutual assistance), of deliberations of representatives (Musya Warah) and consensus (Mufakat). Preceded by a preamble including Panchasila, the Constitution had 37 Articles defining the role of the Chief Executive (President), Legislature (MPR and DPR) and the Judiciary. The founding fathers envisaged the foundation of a unitary state with sovereignty vested in the legislature. However, the subsequent developments favoured the adoption of a Presidential system in which the President was very powerful. The President was projected as *primus interpares* and his council of ministers always looked to him for guidance and support. Both Sukarno and Suharto believed in the personality cult and strengthene the powers of the President enormously.

The sovereignty of the people was symbolised by Madjelis Permusjawaratan Rakjat (MPR), also known as people's consultative assembly. The number of members and the role of the members of the Dewan Perwakilan Rakjat (DPR) augmented with the representatives of the regions, political and Karja (functional) groups. The total number of appointed members to MPR was fixed at one-third of the total number of MPR members and the number of MPR members were to be twice the total number of the members in DPR. Accordingly the members of the MPR had been fixed at 1000 out of which 425 were elected, 75 appointed by the armed forces and the remaining 500 were government appointees.[2] MPR met every five years to elect and re-elect President and the latter was legally accountable to this House.

The legislative powers are in fact vested in the Dewan Perwakilan Rakjat (DPR) also known as the House of People's Representatives. According to 1969 Act, the number of members of

DPR had been fixed at 460, of which 360 were elected and 100 nominated. However this figure was increased in 1975 to 500 of which 400 were elected and 100 were appointed members. Each member of the DPR pledged that they will always uphold the message of the people's sufferings, that they will adhere to and defend Panchasila as the basis and ideology of the state, the 1945 Constitution and all existing laws and regulations in force in the Republic of Indonesia, that they will endeavour to the best of their ability to promote the welfare of the Indonesian people and be loyal to the country, nation and the state of Indonesia.[3] They, however, proved a rubber stamp during 1965-99, but they started emerging as an important institution of rule-making when Abdurrahman Wahid came into power.

The most striking feature of Indonesian politics is that it has not declared any state religion. Although the Muslims are in overwhelming majority and most of its neighbouring states have declared their state religion in order to maintain their national unity, Indonesia has abstained from doing so. Malaysia and Brunei, the two immediate neighbours, have declared Islam as the state religion but Indonesia preferred to remain secular. The Preamble of 1945 Constitution assures religious freedom by declaring protection and promotion of faith in the God Almighty and endeavoured to create a just and civilised humanity. The various governments have been pursuing a religious policy, which respects the right of every religious groups and takes into account the feelings of all religious comunities. They have officially recognised religions namely, Islam, Protestantism, Catholicism, Buddhism and Hinduism. As a result, there are 26,769 Protestant churches, 13,361 Catholic churches, 34,408 Hindu temples, 2552 Buddhist *Viharas* and 537,837 Muslim mosques.[4] The break up of the different religious communities in Indonesia in mid-nineties indicated that Muslims comprised 87.2 per cent, Protestants 6 per cent, Catholics 3.5 per cent, Hindus 2 per cent and the Buddhists 1 per cent.[5]

Indonesia gives emphasis on "Unity in Diversity", to unite the people in a common fold. It has heterogeneous ethnic and linguistic groups. More than 300 languages are spoken and their culture and lifestyle differ. The majority is of Malay stock, split into dozens of smaller sub-groups, with varying family structures and social systems. The prominent ethnic groups are the Javanese, the Sundanese, the Minhasans, the Bugis, the Makassars and the

Balinese. Again there are the Dayaks, the *Bataks* and *Dani* and the *Asmat* of Melanesian stock.

There is sufficient impact of Sufism on art and culture, namely the *Wayang*, myths and folklores, poems and songs, the Islamic calendar, ceremonies and festivals, etc. Sufi saints understood that Javanese were very fond of art, so they inserted Islamic teachings in the stories of *Ramayana* and *Mahabharata* to be played in *Wayang*. They created new myths, stories, poems and songs, which had local name, local languages but Islamic teachings. A Sufi saint, Walisongo led the Sufi movement in the 15th century and became very popular in Java with Islamic ideologies. His strategy of adopting local stories, local heroes and myths were adopted by the Sufi saints in other parts of the archipelago.

Threats to the Republic

Indonesia is faced with numerous problems of different types but here an attempt is made to point out outstanding political problems. The archipelagic concept as enunciated by the founding fathers are losing its importance and Panchasila doctrine, especially its third principle "Unity of Indonesia" has been endangered. The separatist movement in Aceh and Irian Jaya are too serious to be ignored. East Timor which had been annexed after a military action in 1975 has already become an independent state in 1999, and similar demands are articulated by separatists in Aceh and Irian Jaya.

Aceh, situated at the northernmost region of Sumatra, have a distinct culture and history. Its 4.5 million population has been strong supporter of *Darul* Islam movement and views the authority of Central government un-Islamic. This is because the government is dominated by Javanese, who are *Abangans*. The people of Aceh has been struggling for its own identity and separate nationhood because the government of Indonesia has not been sensitive to their grievances. The government gave them autonomy in religious and educational affairs after a long struggle in 1959 but it was withdrawn without any rhyme or reason. Though it is rich in iron, oil, gas and coal, it is not given any share in the benefits. At the same time, the government has supported migration and transmigration of population to that area which has been disliked. The people in Aceh have opposed the presence of new migrants and they have been agitating. The continuing conflicts over economic and demographic issues have fuelled separatist movement. In 1976,

Hasan Di Tiro established *Gerakan* Aceh *Merdeka* (Free Aceh movement) and subsequently declared independence. But this movement was suppressed and Tiro fled to Sweden. It was from Sweden that he announced the formation of Aceh government in exile. The unrest mounted enormously in Aceh in 1989 when National Liberation Front Aceh Sumatra (NLFAS) was established. They mounted onslaughts on the government forces and Amnesty International claimed that 2000 people were killed during 1989-93, and the casualty number have been increasing every year.

Similar is the situation in Irian Jaya, where Organisasi Papua Merdeka (OPM), also known as Free Papua movement leads separatist movement. There has been lot of bloodshed in that province also and the cases of human rights violations are reported. Irian Jaya is rich in timber, gold and silver. Indonesia is trying to exploit the natural resources of the area, but the indigenous people are resisting it. They have not yet been fully integrated with the national mainstream as their outlook and culture are different. They have not accepted their integration so far and they display much in common with the people of Papua New Guinea. It is a fact that Dani, Asmat and other ethnic groups of the province are of Melanesian stock and they are entirely different in their customs and traditions compared to Javanese Malays. Some of the tribal groups gave procured weapons to kill transmigrants and foreigners. The army, on the other hand, has been vindictive while assuring law and order.

The separatist tendencies in both Aceh and Irian Jaya have religious dimension. As far as Aceh is concerned, it is Muslim dominated area. They believe that the government of Indonesia is under the control of the Javanese, and a Javanese cannot be a true Muslim. The Javanese leaders have reciprocated such a feeling regarding the nationalism of Acehnese as well. There has been persecution of the leaders in Aceh and mass graves have been found. Some of the dissident leaders have left their homeland to seek asylum elsewhere. Their participation in the government has been nominal and guerrilla warfare continues. On the other hand, Irian Jaya has 83 per cent Christian population. The Church is the main centre of social congregation. They know that the province had not been handed over to Indonesia along with other provinces by the Dutch colonial masters on ethnic and religious grounds. Their projection is that given the situation in which they are, their identity is bound to be lost forever in Indonesian state.

The socio-economic factor is the root cause of trouble in Ambon also. History says that majority of the pro-Dutch elements and militias inhabited in that area especially on the eve of independence. They had struggled against their integration with the Indonesian Republic and had fought for their independence. Known as Amboina in the historical past, Ambon has a number of people with Dutch descent. There are some people with Portuguese origin. On the other hand, there are some Chinese traders, who have prospered in business and trade. Although the government statistics claim that 55.8 per cent are Muslims, 38.2 per cent are Protestants and 5.3 per cent are Catholics, but this figure needs to be verified. A study of social life in Ambon shows that it is a Christian dominated area. There is disparity in the lifestyle of the Muslims and Christians. Catholic Christians are relatively better economically than their Muslim counterparts.

There has been violent clashes between the Muslims and Christian communities especially after Indonesia was gripped by the economic crisis (1997-98). Hundreds of people have lost their lives. Militant groups have emerged to protect the lives of their people and communal virus has engulfed the area. Islamic outfits such as Islamic Defender's Forum have given a call for *Jehad* and such a call is appropriately reciprocated. It is believed that the government was lackadaisical in their attitudes about the happenings in the area in the post-1998 period and did not act swiftly to stop rioting.

The development in Aceh, Irian Jaya, and Ambon clearly suggest that the concept of *Bhineka Tunggal Eka* (Unity in Diversity) is endangered. We find that there are growing threats to minorities. The Chinese for instance have felt traumatic experiences. Anti-Chinese riots have taken place in Jakarta also on one pretext or the other.

The ethnic Chinese are feeling threatened in all parts of the country. The Chinese, who have traditionally been involved in business and trade, and who have prospered economically are made victims of looting, arson, rape, riots and humiliation ever since the beginning of *Habibie* era in 1998. Anti-Chinese riots have been taking place and the worst affected areas are Medan, Titipatan, Solo and Samarinda. The hooligans involved in rioting argue that the Chinese are responsible for spiralling price rise and the economic crisis. In February 1998, the riots in Medan were serious enough to compel some ethnic Chinese to leave their houses. Twelve Chinese owned shops had been torched and dozens of buildings damaged at Kendari in Sulawesi. The looting of Chinese stores and shops have been occurring ever since.[6]

Again the communal life has been tense ever since religion and ethnicity were used as weapons in politics. President Suharto, who had secular credentials ever since he came into power, felt the need to establish *Ikatan Cendekiawan Muslim* Indonesia (ICMI) in December 1990. Though B.J. Habibie is given credits for establishing this ICMI, but in reality it was born with the support of Suharto. The ICMI objectives were to face the challenges of the Islamic parties and provide ideological and philosophical support to Panchasila democracy. It was made essential for every Islamic academics and intellectuals to be a member of ICMI and work for it. As a result, other religious groups also started activating their associations and the problems started complicating with the dawn of Habibie era (1998-99). The Christians were targeted by the Muslims and they are not feeling safe as riots have taken place against them at Ambon and other cities. The *loompens* are let loose with the tacit support of the Islamic fanatics.

Again the religion had come in the path of *Megawati Sukarnoputri's* candidature as President of Indonesia. Though she is a popular leader and daughter of Sukarno, the Father of the Nation, her credentials to uphold Muslim values are questioned because of her genealogy. When her candidature for Presidency was considered, there were lots of debates that her mother and grandmother were Hindus and therefore her Muslim heritage is diluted. The military supported Golkar Party made allegation that *Megawati* was secretly praying at a Hindu temple in Bali. Another criticism was that she had chosen a majority of non-Muslim Candidates for her party, and if appointed the President, her conduct would be identical. Finally since she is a woman, she can't be appointed the head of state of a Muslim dominated country. All these opinions prevailed in the deliberations of the MPR in 1999. Though Abdurrahman Wahid had won only 54 seats compared to 153 of *Megawati Sukarnoputri*, but his support grew rapidly in MPR. Besides other factors, religion played significant role in mobilising support for him. He got 373 votes in the race for Presidency, whereas *Megawati* secured only 313. The result was so surprising that the politicians started demanding the system for directly elected President on the pattern of the U.S. in Indonesia.

Needless to say that religion is assuming center stage and the use of Islam is increasing in the struggle for power. Nahdlatul *Ulama*

(NU), Muhammadiyah and Syarikat Islam (IS) have a feeling that they would lose their popular support if they ignore importance of Islamic religion in socio-economic life. They may be right that Islam is the single most important factor in the unity of the community, but overemphasis is counterproductive as Indonesia has multi-ethnic and multi-religious society. If the religion is used for power politics, it can generate force of destabilisation and disintegration and this logic is particularly relevant in Indian and Indonesian context. *Darul* Islam in Indonesia, for instance, has been advocating *Jehad*, Islamic purity, and violence. They are influential in Aceh and the result is social tension which is disastrous. Indonesia indeed has been facing challenges through religious groups but its beginning can be traced ever since its independence. Masjumi Party (*Majlis Sura Muslim Indonesia*) influenced by the teachings of Mohammed Abduh of Cairo University, which had mobilised support of the Muslims in Sumatra, South Sulawesi and West Java, was highly critical of Marxist-oriented socialism of Sukarno. It had posed serious problems to Sukarno administration, particularly when guided democracy was declared. Masjumi leaders argued that a renewed Islam was capable of providing a religious and philosophical base for rapid social and economic development. It believed in replacing Panchasila-based Indonesia to one founded on Islam. Mohammad Natsir, a Masjumi leader pleaded that since Islam was the religion and philosophy of most Indonesians, the Islamic majority should not accept a state based on secular Panchasila, because secularism is an alien concept. This Party was advocating the inclusion of *Shariat* laws in the constitution and their activities created serious problems for Sukarno administration. Hence his government moved to ban this organisation. Though this party was officially banned, its appeal continued to exist.

In fact, the role of religious groups and missionaries cannot be overlooked in the context of Indonesia because of their constructive role in the freedom struggle. It was *Hajis* (visiting Mecca on pilgrimage) who worked for anti-colonial struggle. Whenever they returned after their pilgrimage, they felt the need of indigenous, Islamic political order, purification and even outright assertion against the colonial master. They began to express their critical views about the political system. They began to evaluate and review the role of their social and religious institutions which helped the colonial rulers to perpetuate their rule. It was common for *Hajis* and their circle of followers to express critical views about *Adat*, (customs and traditions of Islam) which were making them subservient to the colonial rulers. One of them, name Haji Muhammad Rifangi who led Buduah movement among the rural population of Pakalongan and Kedari advocated religious reforms. He tried to mobilise public opinion to boycott official rituals in the Kalisalak mosque. The Dutch colonial government was annoyed so much so that Rifangi was exiled to Maluku.

Another *Haji* who became a national figure was Haji Abdul Karim of Banten. He established a Pesantren School in Banten and tried to evolve Islamic Political thinking. He travelled throughout Banten holding puification rights, *Ziki* and holy processions. He was regarded very devout possessing divine powers. He was one of the first, who had predicted inevitability of *Jehad* (holy war) for the survival of Islam, the arrival of Mahdi and subsequently the ushering of a new era.[7]

Hajis had always played significant role in the nationalist upsurge. Whether it was Boedi Oetomo or *Sarekat* Islam, they were born with the support and insight of the *Hajis*. Boedi Oetomo established by Indonesian intellectuals in 1908 for educational purposes, started working for political consciousness. Subsequently *Sarekat* Islam was born in 1912 under the leadership of *Haji* Samanhudi. Though the apparent objective of *Sarekat* Islam was to strengthen business relations with the Dutch empire, it turned out to be a political party under the leadership of H.O.S. Tjokroaminoto, Haji Agoes Salim and others. *Hajis* had played significant role in the establishment of Muhammadiah also in the same year under the leadership of K.H. Ahmad Dahlan in Jogyakarta. Again Partai Indonesia was formed by Setiabudi, Tjipto Mangunkusumo and K.I. Hajar Dewantoro in the same year.

The religious groups in Aceh made great contributions in the freedom struggle and the pursuit of revolution against the colonial masters. The Pesantren and the Ulemas mobilised training centres for freedom fighters.[8] One of the famous leaders of Aceh was Tengku Cik Tiro, who contributed new insights in the nationalist upsurge by advocating that the Dutch psyche understands the language of violence and war only. The negotiations and dialogues are redundant to gain nationalist goals. Tiro was educated and trained in Pesantren. He advocated self-rule for the Indonesians and was extremely critical of the Dutch colonial system. He argued that the

Dutch regime was exploitative and opposed to Islamic ideas. He established links with reformist Muslims and anti-colonial forces in Java to arouse anti-Dutch sentiments. His followers in Aceh had taken up arms to fight battles against the Dutch colonial forces. Tiro propagated guerrilla warfare and preferred jungles and mountains to confront the enemy. He was successful in igniting the nationalist forces and intermittent warfare became the outcome of his efforts in Aceh.

The followers of Tiro preached that blessings of the Allah are unlimited for those who serve for the community and fight for the Muslim nation. All those who are ready to serve and sacrifice, are dear to the Allah, who gives name, fame and wealth to dear and devouts. He blesses paradise full of lights to martyrs. Their appeals had long-term implications. The Dutch colonial forces were unable to cope with the challenges, but independence in 1945 did not bring an Islamic state. The new rulers thought that unity of the country was more important and accepting Islam as state religion would have adverse reactions on Christian dominated areas.

In short, it can be stated that the interplay of religion with society is key to understanding Indonesian politics. Japanese invaders knew this and nurtured the activities of Islamic institutions to neutralize the Dutch interference. Islamic leaders were anti-Dutch in their activities and temperament and therefore they supported the Japanese as friends to throw out the Dutch colonial rulers. Sukarno, the father of the nation, however was not in favour of establishing an Islamic state. He astutely manoeuvred the support of the members in the Constituent Assembly to dilute this proposal. He stimulated his people to evolve other revolutionary ideas while assuring that he will protect religious interests of the Indonesian people. Panchasila became the preamble of the 1945 constitution and equal status was offered to five religions. Muslim clergies who continued to grumble disliked this.

Though the downfall of Sukarno is attributed to several factors but one of them was the opposition of important Islamic groups. They were critical of his socialist rhetorics, land reforms and dependence on communist forces. His successor, General Suharto initially cultivated the Islamic religious groups and indulged in *Jehad* of the communists, but did not do anything to alter the constitution to suit their demands. The Muslim groups remained suppressed and ultimately felt cheated. They gradually started supporting Nahdlatul Ulama and Muhammadiyah to fulfil their interests. These organisations subsequently became vocal critics of the Suharto regime, which forced Suharto to counter them at the intellectual level. He thus supported his information and technology Minister, B.J. Habibie to float ICMI (Ikatan Cendikiawan Muslim Indonesia) in 1990.

ICMI stands for improvements in all aspects of life. Habibie said: "ICMI is not a political organisation. Its main objective is to make a real contribution to ever-increasing challenges to the way of life of whole Indonesian population, especially the Islamic community".[9] Notwithstanding the government patronage, ICMI became controversial. The main Muslim organisations viewed it as an instrument of the government, bent on relieving the role of Islam in Indonesian politics.[10] They proved right and subsequently when Suharto resigned in 1998, ICMI lost its appeal. However, the reality is that Suharto felt the need to cultivate religious groups in order to survive politically which underlines the importance of religion in contemporary politics of Indonesia.

Abdurrahman Wahid's selection as Presidential candidate at the cost of Megawati was inspired by religious groups. Though a product of Pesantren and innovative, Wahid as a politician could not deal with serious challenges posed to him by some other religious groups. The situation in Aceh and Irian Jaya are disturbing where the separatist movement is mainly based on religious and economic grounds. East Timor became independent because differences between Islam and Christianity remained unabridged. Religion is an important weapon available to political parties and if it can get the support of religious leaders and the innovators of mysticism, it can prove deadly. Though Wahid excelled in strategy, mission and vision, the paradigm of power politics generated upredictable forces. He could not stand trial for corruption charges. He was forced to resign and Megawati Sukarnoputri was appointed the President. As the daughter of Sukarno and an activist for democracy movement, she has secular credentials. Her predicament is to balance her politics regarding the Armed Forces, Islamic and Christian associations and her own followers in order to survive and provide example of good governance and stability. Growth rates are to be accelerated and transparency in administrative decisions are to be displayed.

Indonesia is on the democratic path and it is not easy to harmonise religion with development, order and secularism to the satisfaction of all its citizens. It is a fact that Indonesians believe in mysticism and nobody can stop its impact at the community level. How it will evolve and affect the system, the leadership and broader politics are unpredictable. However, it is important to give vent to the grievances of the people necessary for the stability and prosperity of the nation.

The leaders of the present order have to review the role of the Armed Forces in the politics of the country. Their intrusion in administration and politics had been legitimated with the acceptance of *dwifungsi* (Dual Functions).[11] The meaning and significance of *dwifungsi* were aimed at perpetrating army rule. It was argued that the concern of the armed forces were not simply to look after national defence, but also the actual conduct of the government in the interest of good administration. A powerful propaganda was made that the armed force had played the principal role in securing independence, that it had done so in the face of obstruction and betrayal by the civilian authorities, and it therefore retained a special right and duty to supervise and take charge of the government. Under the stewardship of Suharto, *dwifungsi* principle became operational and accordingly serving and retired army officers took a wide variety of posts, from that of a cabinet minister down to a village head.

Though the leading role of the army in the freedom struggle is a historical reality, but the fact that it played some negative role subsequently, cannot be overlooked. They had assumed a major role in the economy as the managers of the Dutch enterprises, which had been nationalised in 1957. They took major part in the administrative system and their performances were not satisfactory. They did their best to suppress democratic ethos, which had been cultivated at the time of freedom struggle. The increasing importance of *dwifungsi* resulted in turning democratic institutions subservient to promote army rule and thus political parties, pressure groups, media and information channels had limited freedom to express their viewpoints. The number of appointed members grow enormously in the House of Representatives (DPR) and the MPR (People's Consultative Assembly) was made almost redundant. MPR used to be convened at the end of every five years to appoint a President, whose candidature were decided by the armed faces. The legislature was treated as a rubber stamp and it was difficult to speak anything against omission and commission of the officials. The intelligence network to monitor the activities of the civilian population were outrageous and Indonesians could reflect their opinions about their political system only after much persuasion. But when they realised that restoration of democracy is imminent, they began to articulate their viewpoints.

When Suharto resigned on 21 May 1998, there were jubilation, but it ushered into an era of political uncertainty and instability. Even though democracy was restored, anarchic situation prevailed. The ethnic disputes erupted and riots abetted. The violence, riots and vandalism at Aceh, Ambon and Irian Jaya as highlighted to the outside world through internet and media are reprehensible. The democratic leaders have to perform their tasks more astutely and prove their management skills. The armed forces should not feel neglected at the same time. They exercise enormous clout in the socio-economic life and command prestige. They have vested interests in politics and economics. The leaders in the present government have to be highly sensitive to their opinion, without which the task of nation-building, stability and development cannot be promoted. Instituting inquiry committees, special courts and open hearings against the armed forces might not yield the desired results. The special investigation implicating some Generals in East Timor massacres proved to be contentious. The report assumed political colour when the name of General Wironto was mentioned. It was a pretext to demand the resignation of the General from the cabinet and he had no choice but to resign. In retrospect, it was found that the conviction was not convincing. General Wironto was honest and widely respected and his ouster had been disliked by a section of the people and the armed forces. If the armed forces are offended, it can prove very costly for evolving democratic experiments.

Indonesia is also known for corruption and cronyism in high places. Former President Suharto supported his children to develop business connections, based on privileged access to government contracts, licenses and subsidies. Hutomo Putra Mandala (Tommy) had obtained exclusive rights for the purchase of cloves from farmers. He extracted benefits from monopolies over flour and tin plates. He also got the coveted authorisation to produce Indonesian car (*Pt Timor Putra Nasional*) and establish Sempati Air. Suharto's daughter, Siti Prabowo got the share in a $10 million project linking Malaysia and Indonesia over the Malacca Straits. Likewise his two other sons Bambang and Sigit Harjojudanto had greatly benefited in business matters because of their genealogy and the President knew it. The Economist (London) had reported that the members of the Suharto clan could walk into any State Bank and demand a loan at favourable terms. The government always awarded the juicy contracts to Suharto family in the areas of power generation, telecommunications and toll-roads.[12] The corruption and cronyism had become an important part of his administration and the socio-economic life had started feeling too much pressure. The political and economic situation had deteriorated because most of the monitoring agencies—the legislature and judiciary—had become subservient to the executive. The political parties were either banned or if they survived they had to observe a code of conduct favourable to the armed forces. They had to express their faith in Panchasila, which had been declared a national ideology, which was treated sacred for every Indonesian.[13] The Suharto regime was named Panchasila democracy and the government was responsible for formulation of ideas and interpretation of the Panchasila. The meaning of Panchasila had been stretched too far aimed at prescribing a society modelled on the traditional family, in which parental authority was respected and in which individual interest was subordinate to the community. The government came forward with some laws under its framework like Panchasila labor relations, which implied that there could be no conflict of interest between workers and management and that the strikes were inherently anti-social. The dissent or opposition to the dictates of the government was not allowed. The Presidency had assumed all the powers of the government advertently or inadvertently, and under the system the maxim that "power corrupts and absolute power corrupts absolutely" became a reality.

Political reform has been on the agenda of the government in the post-Suharto era. They have decided to lift control over the political parties and thus multi-party system have emerged. All parties are given financial aid from the government and the amount depends on the number of votes received in the elections.[14] They also want to activate MPR and DPR by reducing the number of appointed members and increasing their power in rule-making. For instance, although the MPR was declared supreme power through Article I of the 1945 Constitution, vested with three important tasks, namely approving the constitution, deciding the guidelines of state policy and election of the President and Vice-President, its authority has been eroded. It was authorised to convene a special session whenever necessary but it met only once in five years. MPR indeed had abdicated all its responsibilities except ritually appointing the President after five years. Now there is a growing demand that it should play an active role in decision making. The first step in that direction has been the reduction in the numbers of appointed members and according to 1999 Act of the government, the members of the MPR are reduced to 700 only, instead of 1000. However, the most important aspect of the reform process is that they have decided to restore Article 28 of the 1945 constitution in letter and spirit, which guarantees "the right of free assembly and association, of expression of opinion, orally or in writing" to the Indonesian citizens.

Human Rights

The issues concerning human rights of Indonesian people have assumed importance as it is an important element of civilised society. It has been suppressed in many countries of the Third World and Indonesia is no exception. It has assumed significance in the New World Order as the United States is the ardent advocate of assuring it at the universal level. Though the United Nations General Assembly proclaimed the Universal Declaration of Human Rights in 1948 itself and emphasised that all human beings are born free and equal in dignity and rights, and endowed with reason and conscience, and should act towards one another in a spirit of brotherhood, this has been ignored very often in course of drives for nation-building and modernisation. Indonesia has signed the covenants for the Universal Declaration but it has been found lacking in implementing it. Amnesty International published "Indonesia: Shock Therapy Restoring Order in Aceh: 1989-93", and revealed many cases of omission and commission committed by the government. Similarly, there were numerous reports about excesses committed in East Timor, which broke away from Indonesia in 1999. If we go into the genesis of the conflict, we find logic on both sides.

Indonesia gave priority to economic development in the era of new order (1965-98) and that was in tune with international covenant on economic, social and cultural rights (*Unga Resolution 2200*). In accordance with the Universal Declaration of Human Rights, the ideal law of free human beings, enjoying freedom from fear and want, can only be achieved if the conditions are created whereby everyone may enjoy his economic, social and cultural rights, as well as his civil and political rights. The removal of poverty is essential in order to promote human rights. Indonesia adopted development programmes for its impoverished population in 1967, when Suharto signed the documents of declaration of world leaders on population. In view of this policy, national family planning programmes were supported and the schemes proved successful in limiting the increase of population, which are below 3 million population growth annually. Total fertility rate came down to 50 per cent as desired by the government and Indonesian expertise was appreciated in most of the neighbouring countries. But the policy, which proved controversial, was regarding transmigration of the people from densely populated areas to less populated zones.

Java and Bali inhabit 65 per cent of Indonesian population. Java alone has 100 million people. This island however occupies only 6.8 per cent of the total land of the country. Sumatra, which is comparatively bigger in size, has 41 million, Sulawesi 13 million, Nusatenggara 11.5 million, Maluku 11.9 million and Kalimantan has 11 million population.[15] It is known that only 992 out of 17508 islands are mainly populated zones. But Haryati Soebadio says that 5000 islands are inhabited.[16] There has to be a better management of the inhabited and uninhabited islands to accelerate the pace of development. There is abundance of natural resources in all parts of the country and their exploitation can be facilitated only when there is availability of manpower. Indonesia endeavoured to diversify its population from densely populated areas to new zones. They passed relevant rules in that direction in 1960 and 1973 and transmigrated people from Java to other islands. Initially, 17116 families were settled in Irian Jaya and 8155 in Maluku but a number of people were also transmigrated to Kalimantan, East Timor and Aceh.[17] Joan Hardejono said that the number of transmigration were 49772 in 1979-80, 108081 in 1980-81, 123846 in 1981-82, 167477 in 1982-83 and 86298 in 1983-84.[18] As the government supported it, transmigration continued but it has not resolved the problem of population density in Java. As job opportunities are available mostly in Java, poor and impoverished people continue to come and the problem remains the same.

There has been some omission and commission, while transmigrating the people as alleged by Aceh Merdeka, OPM and some other opposition groups. They stated that the alien population is arbitrarily introduced to change the demographic complexion and this is a matter of intrusion in matters of their human rights. They understand that the transmigrants would alter the indigenous character of their socio-economic life and usurp their properties. The Javanese speak an alien language and have faith in Islamic religion. But the people in Irian Jaya and Ambon have significant number of Christians. The indigenous people are unhappy that their distinct identity would be diluted in due course if the arrival of transmigrants are not stopped. They allege that Javanese migrants are arrogant with a sense of superiority. They assume that they are unwanted people thrust upon them, who may be interested in colonising the entire area. The new migrants generally search jobs in oil exploration, mining and forestry department and the local people project this behaviour contrary to their interests saying that ultimately the new transmigrants would deprive them of their resources and wealth.[19]

Indigenous people in Irian Jaya, Aceh and Ambon are alarmed by the activities of the ethnic Javanese. They observe that the Javanese migrants have excellent rapport with government authorities. They are trusted by the government and offered all types of facilities at the cost of the indigenous people. Hence, they are demanding that the transmigration should be scrapped with immediate effect. Thus transmigrant population are faced with a dilemma in coping with the situation and the human rights of transmigrated have been threatened. The opposition to government policies remained suppressed under the authoritarian rule, but now the situation is changing very fast. Although transmigration has been stopped, the present government has to cope with the challenges of transmigration policies of Suharto era. With restoration of democracy, it is natural that the issue of transmigration is politicised and it would be more complicated in due course.

It may prove more suitable and less controversial if the transmigration is directed towards those islands where there are no population at all and such areas as assessed by the government sources are more than two-thirds of the inhabited islands. The people might not be interested in inhabiting in new areas because of poor living conditions and necessary infrastructure, but the government should take the assistance of the international financial institutions to create necessary conditions for settlement on uninhabited islands of Indonesia.

Besides human rights, the issue of environment have assumed importance in Indonesia in the past few years. The increasing denudation of forests and logging have to be stopped completely. The forest fires creating smoky haze have to be contained. But Indonesia has the shortage of fire-fighting machines. It was due to this that the forest fire in Sumatra and Borneo in 1997 engulfed a large part of Southeast Asia for months. The fire had reached Malaysia, Brunei, Singapore and Australia as well. The smoky haze generated a number of health problems and disrupted tourism and transport systems. A forest fire at Sumatra in March 1999 caught Malaysia and Singapore as well. The neighbouring countries are alarmed by the recurring forest fire in Indonesia. These developments have grave implications on Indonesian image outside, and therefore the government has to evolve a sound policy to check fire in its jungles and co-operate more closely with the ASEAN regional task force to monitor and put stop to it.

Although environmental problems are serious, they can be resolved with the support of the ASEAN, the APEC and UN. What is more difficult and complicated is to maintain territorial integrity of Indonesia. The independence of East Timor has opened floodgates for disintegration. There is separatist movements in Aceh, Irian Jaya and Ambon. The Christians are unhappy with their Islamic counterparts. The terrorist groups have emerged to protect their ethnic groups. Islamic outfits are clamouring for *Jehad* and similarly the Christians have taken up arms in vengeance and there is bloodshed. Although Aceh is intra-Muslim conflict, Irian Jaya and Ambon present a different scenario. In both these cases, the conflict is between two religious groups, i.e. Muslims and Christians. There is a history behind these conflicts which cannot be overlooked. The Ambonese in Maluku had embarked on separation on the eve of independence of the Indonesian Republic. On 25 April 1950, Ambonese leaders, J.H. Manuhuttu and A. Wairisai had proclaimed the establishment of the state of South Moluccas. Indonesian government felt great concern, but projected the conflict as a family quarrel.[20] But when the Ambonese, who had served in the Dutch army, started fighting against the government, the separatists took the control of Ambon and adjoining islands, and it was not easy for the government to resolve this problem for quite some time. The government had to organise sea blockade by the Indonesian navy to contain dissident activities. As Ambon is dependent on other islands for its food supply, the sea blockade crippled them. It was only thereafter that troops were dispatched to take control of Ambon and adjoining islands. Ambonese leaders did not give up their idea of independence even after the defeat. Some of them fled to Holland and continued to oppose their integration with Indonesia.

The history of Irian Jaya is more or less similar. The Dutch government had retained it while transferring sovereignty of other islands to Indonesian leaders. The Dutch colonial masters viewed that Irian Jaya was much different in culture, religion and ethnicity to be integrated in Indonesia. Another dimension of the Dutch policy was to create a homeland for the people of Dutch-Indonesian descent on that island, where a sizeable section of the indigenous people opposed their integration with Indonesia.[21] The government of Indonesia, on the other hand, invoked the principle of archipelagic concept and fought for the control of the island. Irian Jaya became a part of Indonesia only after the intervention of the United Nations in 1963 but it continued to remain isolated and backward. When East Timor became independent in 1999, it had its impact on political developments in Irian Jaya as well. What is striking is that the church and the Christian associations have played important role in the freedom struggle of East Timor. Hence the role of Christian institutions and associations are gaining new meaning in the context of Irian Jaya and Ambon and counter developments are taking place. It is a matter of concern that Islamic groups are alarmed and advocate *Jehad* for an Islamic state. The development activities are opposed by the natives. If there is logging or mining, it is resisted by the separatists on various grounds. The separatist leaders argue that their natural resources are exploited for the benefit of the Javanese and they cannot get justice under the present dispensation. The Armed Forces, which ruled the country from 1965 to 1998, have committed atrocities and suppressed dissidents. Now that democracy has dawned, they have started articulating their grievances in public. It demands lot of courage and wisdom to involve them in the decision-making and make them feel secure as distinct ethnic groups in the respective areas. The principle of "unity in diversity" has to be implemented in letter and spirit, and ethnic leaders are to be promoted in national decision making.

To conclude, it can be stated that the problem of national integration is complicated and there is threat to unity of Indonesia. Irian Jaya, Aceh and Ambon are disturbed and solution to their grievances are not in sight. Although the dissidents would welcome referendum on the pattern in East Timor, it is difficult now. When Habibie had announced referendum, it was without taking the consent of the DPR, which is the supreme decision-making body. His successor, Wahid also announced referendum for Aceh without discussing it in the DPR, which is the proper forum where such resolutions should first be discussed. Naturally there was immediate opposition to the proposal, and when the issue was referred to DPR it was opposed. The representatives of the people in the Assembly rejected Wahid's proposals and established an expert panel to suggest measures to resolve the dispute. In December 1999, the expert panel on Aceh recommended policy alternatives, which did not include a referendum on Acehnese independence.[22] It is known that the secession of any one province would encourage fragmentation of the Indonesian republic resulting in political instability in the region. The Indonesian legislature (DPR) might be ready to discuss autonomy proposals. For instance, DPR representatives are suggesting that Aceh might be allowed to decree radical Islamic Laws in place of Panchasila. It may be apportioned up to 75 per cent of the revenues on account of its oil, besides the right to generate other sources of revenues.[23] Similarly Irian Jaya, which is the largest and remotest province of Indonesia, can think about autonomy. The DPR might discuss apportioning the share of that province in the profits due to mining of gold, logging of timber, etc. They may be allowed to declare Christian laws, but the secession of the province cannot be entertained.

To sum up, there are some issues which demand immediate attention. First, Article 1 of the 1945 constitution states that "sovereignty is vested in the people to be fully exercised by the elected MPR vested with supreme power". This house is meant to voice the social and political aspirations of the people and the President is made accountable to it. However its powers were eroded and it was summoned for ceremonial occasions only. It was convened only after the gap of five years to elect a new President. Thus it became a rubber stamp under the stewardship of Sukarno and Suharto. The role of the MPR has to be reviewed in the light of political developments since 1945 so that it is enabled to check and balance the political system. The President should be compelled to feel accountable to it and there should no dilution of the separation of powers of the three branches of the government as enunciated in the constitution.

Secondly, the ideals of Panchasila although became the philosophical foundation of the Indonesian republic, it became very controversial during the stewardship of President Suharto. When Sukarno was overthrown and Suharto assumed control of the political power on 11 March 1966, the latter period was projected as ushering into an era of Panchasila democracy. In fact, the military dictatorship under which millions of PKI supporters were killed, *dwifungsi* was evolved and opposition suppressed, Suharto took the support of Panchasila to legitimize his actions. Hence trade unions faced restrictions in the name of Panchasila and political parties were suppressed in the name of Panchasila. A situation developed in which Panchasila became synonymous with military dictatorship. Hence the elan of Panchasila for unification of the country was lost. Indonesia, being multi-ethnic and multi-religious, have to search a new symbol and concept which can substitute Panchasila to maintain the unity and solidarity of the nation. The archipelagic concept has to be reinforced in conjunction with Panchasila philosophy to promote integrationist forces.

Finally, although democracy has dawned, authoritarianism has prevailed in Indonesia for centuries. Whether in Dutch or post-Dutch political order, the opposition to the establishment has not been tolerated. President Sukarno started with democracy but ended with crushing it with an iron hand. Suharto presided over a military rule and so there was less scope for dissent and discussion. The cultural ethos is to obey and not to question the wisdom of the leaders. However, democracy is the only form of government, in which aspirations of the people can be fulfilled and unity and solidarity of the people can be enhanced to the satisfaction of the majority. Nevertheless the threat of authoritarian rule cannot be ruled out if there is continued threat to the unity of the country by the dissident groups. The turmoil and instability in Indonesia generates grave implications for geo-politics of the region. Whatever happened in East Timor, have been reverberating on the security environment of Irian Jaya, Mindanao and Kashmir. If constitutional means prove ineffective, authoritarianism is bound to evolve.

REFERENCES

1. Indonesia, 1997, *An Official Handbook*, Jakarta, Department of Information, Republic of Indonesia, pp. 37-40.

2. *The Composition and the Status of the MPR, DPR and Regional House of Representatives*, Jakarta, Department of Information, Republic of Indonesia, 1996, pp. 9-10
3. *Ibid.*, pp. 19-20
4. *Indonesia Handbook*, Jakarta, Department of Information, 1989, p. 196.
5. Indonesia, Information Section, Embassy of the Republic of Indonesia, New Delhi, 1995, p. 64.
6. *The Times of India*, New Delhi, 20 February 1998.
7. For details, see Zuhri, K.H. Saifuddin, *The History of Islamic Resurgence and Development in Indonesia*, Bandung, 1979.
8. For better analysis of this aspect see Noer Deliar, *The Modernist Muslim Movement in Indonesia, 1900-1942*, Kuala Lumpur 1973.
9. Adam Schwartz, *A Nation in Waiting, Indonesia in the 1990s*, Melbourne, 1994, p. 179.
10. *Ibid.*
11. General Edi Sudradjat, *The Dual Function of the Indonesian Armed Forces*, Indonesia, New Delhi, Embassy of the Republic of Indonesia, 1995, p. 32, and also see Nrugroho Notosusanto, *The National Struggle and the Armed Forces in Indonesia*, Jakarta, Department of Defence and Security 1982.
12. "Indonesia: Dear Daddy", *The Economist*, 13-19 December 1997, p. 61.
13. "Panchasila, the State Philosophy", *Indonesia: An Official Handbook*, Jakarta, Department of Information, 1997, p. 41.
14. "Political Reform", *Image of Indonesia*, Jakarta, July 1998, p. 3.
15. Juwono Sudarsono, "The Challenges to Indonesia's Unity", *Indonesia: 50 Years*, Embassy of the Republic of Indonesia, New Delhi, 1995, p. 51.
16. Haryati Soebadio, ed., *Dynamics of Indonesian History*, Amstardam, North Holland Publishing Company, 1978, preface.
17. Soewartoyo, "Internal Migration between Java - Bali and Eastern Indonesia", *Indonesia Quarterly*, Vol. 24, No. 3, 1996, p. 130.
18. Joan Hardjono, "Transmigration: Looking to the Future", *Bulletin of Indonesian Economics Studies*, Vol. 22, No. 2, August 1986, p. 29.
19. Michael Richardson, "Making Irian Jaya Pay its Way", *Far Eastern Economic Review*, 13 June 1975, p. 15.
20 Harja W. Bachtiar, *The Indonesia Nation: Some Problems of Integration and Disintegration*, Singapore ISEAS, 1976, pp. 29–30.
21. *Ibid.*, p. 31
22. P.S. Suryanarayana, "Wahid talks tough on Aceh", *The Hindu*, 5 December 1999.
23. *The Hindu*, 28 November 1999.

16

Indonesian Politics: Debates for Rethinking

Indonesia, the greatest archipelagic nation of the world, with more than 17508 islands and 221 million population, is at the threshold of great political transformations. The political culture and political behaviour are changing rapidly to suit democratization and the public shows sudden awareness of their political rights. There is increasing demands for more freedom, equality and human rights. The various islands (the provinces) are articulating their problems and there is a debate for better centre-state relations. These demands are not always articulated in a peaceful manner but emphasis is given on violence and revolution by fanatic elements. There is bloodshed in Aceh, Ambon and West Papua and their demands for provincial autonomy and referendum on the pattern of East Timor are disturbing. It is clear that if all the demands of all the provincial leaders are accepted, Indonesia would be divided into several parts, and it is naturally a matter of great concern of the political masters not only in Indonesia, but all the countries in the neighbourhood.

Indonesian republic had been established with great sacrifices of patriots and freedom fighters. The Dutch political masters were unwilling to withdraw without dividing it. They had occupied the territory step by step and they wanted to liberate them step by step by creating several independent nations out of the territories of the Dutch East Indies. However their tactics failed before the collective onslaughts of Indonesian freedom fighters. Sukarno, Hatta and Sjahrir were astute enough to understand the Dutch designs and mobilised public opinion to oppose the Dutch policies. They organised revolutionary army to fight against the colonial forces and were successful ultimately to throw out the colonial rule and keep the country united.

Here it is in order to mention that whenever the country was integrated, whether at the time of Srivijaya, Majapahit or the colonial periods, it had been possible through the use of the armed forces, wherein Indonesians had made great sacrifices. During the freedom struggle, Indonesian revolutionary army played the decisive role and therefore it had been assigned the task to maintain unity and territorial integrity in post-independence era. Whether it was Sukarno or Suharto, they made use of the armed forces to maintain unity of the Republic and protect law and order. Suharto went a step further by expounding and promoting the idea of dwifungsi (dual role of the armed forces).

Dwifungsi enabled the armed forces to play their role in politics of the country besides their traditional functions. The use of the armed forces in politics of the country proved ominous and unpopular. But this policy was difficult to be rolled back. When Suharto strove to roll it back towards the end of his stewardship, he failed and resigned. Now the same armed forces, which helped the integration processes of the republic, were projected as hostile in East Timor, Aceh and Ambon. Thus their role was not in tune with the spirit of national integration. A study of the troubled areas in Indonesia, indicates that besides ethnic, religious or political differences, they have been sensitive to stationing of the armed forces in those provinces. They are opposing the use of the police force and demanding greater autonomy to protect their culture, customs and traditions. They articulate that they must get share in the profits generated through their resources and they must have total monopoly over their local administration. They are concerned about their democratic rights and sustainable development. Some of their demands are reasonable but their objectives are the subject of speculation. An understanding of the Indonesian politics suggest that the consensus is for a federal system, although their articulation differs. It is clear from their arguments that "resilience" and Bhinekka Tunggal Ekka (Unity in Diversity) which was the essence of Indonesian politics in the beginning still remains important and is of greater relevance in maintaining territorial unity and archipelagic nature of the Republic.

It is a subject of introspection today is as to what measures should be considered appropriate in promoting integrative nature of the Republic. Common language, history, literature, dance, epics, architecture, etc., are in the background but they are not sufficient to harmonise the nation. Though Bahasa Indonesia is the national language of the country, but more than 10 per cent population are unable to understand it. Though they have common history of Srivijayas, Shailendras, Majapahit and common struggle of nationhood to inspire, but there are a few leaders in the country who admire defiant regional/local warriors, who contributed to the downfall of either Majapahit or Srivijayan rulers. Their epic differ in details and national symbols do not compliment each other. These diversities are the realities of Indonesian life and cannot and should not be altered. However, serious attention needs to be paid to the following four issues:

(*i*) Education,
(*ii*) Religion,
(*iii*) Economic Development, and
(*iv*) Mass Media

Education System

Education system in Indonesia needs thorough overhauling. There must be a fusion of Christian missionary and Islamic Pesantren Curriculum of education. Madrasah or the Church are for the people's welfare, for better life and discipline. Their efforts in supporting schooling have been to promote the interests of their co-religionists. They have been working for centuries and in the process have been politicized. It is here that the students are taught to hate the people of other faiths. On the other hand, there are lot of disparities in the standards of education given by different schools in the country. Although synchronising them may be a sensitive matter and a difficult task, but it is of primordial importance. These matters cannot be simply brushed aside and kept under the carpet. The efforts should be made to bring consensus amongst the leaders, intellectuals and opinion leaders for a quality modern education which may be relevant for all Indonesian citizens from Aceh to Ambon. The education should be of universal application and in this respect, lessons may be drawn from the experiences in People's Republic of China. People may differ on the salient features of Chinese political system but the education system is admired. Its school curriculum are common in all parts of the country. The standard of education and curriculum are framed in such an order that the quality of schooling in Beijing, Shanghai or Tibet do not differ. The education in the remotest rural area and the modern urban centres have similar standards. India on the other hand, have lot of qualitative differentiation in the schooling patterns. Here we have municipal and village schools which is cheaper and missionary and public schools which is expensive. Their contents and curriculum are different. Constitutionally, the education is placed in the state list and therefore different states have different yardsticks. The medium of instruction, workloads and appointment of teachers are decided very often on political basis and hence superior education is a privilege of a few. Indonesia is also following a similar path. It has a feeling that education should be a provincial subject and the central government should not interfere with it. Such an idea may be liked by the western world, but it is not propitious for nation-building of a large state. The reforms in the education system in Indonesia at present is aimed at providing greater authority to school managements to decide the contents and the techniques of curriculum so that the students become a person of good character, who is healthy, knowledgeable, creative, aesthetic and democratic. The National Education Commission under the stewardship of Arief Rachman, has been advocating decentralisation of education with a view to proposed autonomy plans for different provinces. Although such a decision is democratic, but the possibilities and projections cannot be much different from what we witness in India.

Religion

Indonesia has the majority of Muslim population but it inhabits a large number of Buddhists, Hindus and Christians. There has been intra-communal conflict for decades and they have been simmering right from Sukarno era. These differences were suppressed with a heavy hand for years, but emerged hydra headed after the downfall of Suharto in May 1998. Christians are in majority in Ambon and West Papua and there are differences in the rituals and customs of the Islamic people in Aceh, Kalimantan and Java. A number of religious groups are influenced by the Islamic fundamentalism ever since Ayatollah Ruhollah Khomeini's Islamic revolution in Iran in 1970s. It is a reality that Islamic leaders had attempted to declare Islam as the state religion of Indonesia in 1945, but could not succeed. But after the success of Ayatollah revolution in Iran, the scenario changed in Southeast Asia too in places where Muslims were in dominating position. Risalah, Al-Rabitah, Sedah and Dakwah groups became active and advocated the relevance of Islam in the political life. Some of the best educated and articulate Muslims were associated with the religious groups and hence the number of hardcore Islamic activists began to grow. This had adverse impact on other communities and they also began to take offensive steps by countering it with their own brand of fundamentalism. In this endeavour they used their separate history, ethnicity, traditions and culture besides religion, to express their identity different from Islamic demands. Hence there is friction and rioting in certain areas.

The constitution (1945) recognise the existence of Islam, Buddhism, Hinduism, Catholicism and Protestantism in Indonesia. It has allowed religious freedom to all its citizens, but political ethos is edged in favour of Islam. Different political parties have emerged to protect the interests of Islam and some of them are supported by Saudi Arabia, Libya and Iran. Reports are coming that Indonesia has Al Qaida network also. This is a matter of concern not only for Indonesia but for the entire Asia-Pacific region. These developments are bound to complicate religious differences and the political leaders have to address this problem with new thinking and new doctrines in right earnest. The religion makes a person more humane. If the concept of jihad was propagated in Quran, it was to protect community interest at the regional level. It was not endeavoured to promote it at the international scale, but the fundamentalists are trying to apply it at the global level. They are unwilling to understand the beauty of "Live and let live."

Economic Development

Economic development of Indonesia is a pre-requisite for prosperity and stability of Asia-Pacific region. The developments so far has been Java-centric but other provinces have very slow growth. There is lot of gap in the life-style of the rich and poor and therefore the requirement is to uplift the living standards of the poor section of the society. The socialism of the Sukarno era failed and capitalism of Suharto era had no equitable application on all the provinces. Western Papua, Nusa Tenggara and Kalimantan remained least developed. However, there is a need of balanced and sustainable development and for that purpose a new version of

"Berkeley mafia" are required. The government under Megawati Sukarnoputri attaches importance to "reformasi", which connotes reform in political, economic and legal order complimentary to democratisation and development. She perhaps does not believe that Malaysian type of the system might be most suitable. The political trends are showing that the situation is more or less similar to India where the level of politicisation is very high on all the levels. More than 26 million people live below the poverty line and there are some backward tribal areas living in the primitive age. This demonstrates that the accumulation, allocation and distribution of resources have not been balanced and in that endeavour macro-structural change and micro-transformation are suggested. The legacy of Suharto regime is that it attached dominant role to private sectors in capital market growth, but the economic crisis of 1997-98, exposed it as bankrupt. Some economists began to remember the virtues of the socialist era and some started criticizing conditionalities of the World Bank and IMF for the economic mess. The problems for the economic crisis were multifaceted and its genesis could not be generalised and focussed on one factor. The overall reading of the crisis suggest that it had occurred due to several factors. Portfolio investment rules, rampant corruption, crownism, authoritarian governance, unpopularity of Suharto and negligence of the "Berkeley mafia", etc., were responsible for the currency crisis and subsequently it had a shattering impact on Indonesian economy. Though the situation has been improving now, but the budget deficit in 2002 stands at Rupiah 5.6 trillion. Innovative steps are required to bring the economy on fast track and sources of income have to be increased. Besides oil and natural gas, tourism, textiles, sugar, coffee, paper, palm oil and fishing industries, etc., should be attached importance, and latest technologies must be procured to remain globally competitive. How these policies can be evolved, who will monitor their progress and how it will suit the democratization process are issues to ponder about by the political leaders in coming years.

Mass Media

Propaganda of certain activities create public opinion and it is an important aspect for the success or failure of a policy. Although Indonesia had censorship of the press for decades, but it is open now. Radio, television and newspapers are not the only media of information but internet and e-mail provides instant service. The media in general stimulates a growing awareness of citizens for their rights and duties, to deepen the sense of responsibility and national discipline, to enrich national cultural values and to fortify national identity. At the same time, media contributes to the improvement of general intelligence level, to social communication and articulation of popular aspirations so that the citizens are inspired to participate in development activities. All those involved in the dissemination of information should be dedicated to professional responsibility and should be free and objective to channel popular aspiration, social communication and participation. In fact, media plays an important role in both nation-building or destruction. The western world have privatized the information media and their systems work perfectly in promoting their national interests but the situation in Asia is far different. The reporters here can be purchased cheaply resulting in biased reporting and misleading. Indonesia is facing turmoil in different parts of the country and reports about looting, arson, rape and sabotage are regular. One religious group or the other are blamed for such activities and counteraction is taken in revenge. There should be a strong monitoring system of the information media and its personnel should be trained to understand the ethics of journalism.

There is lot of emphasis on democracy and democratization in the post-cold war era. The urge for right to freedom, equality and property can be fulfilled under the democratic system. Democracy, however should be indigeneous and reflect the realities of the society that it represents. For centuries before the colonial period, Indian or Indonesian societies were governed by several Kings or Sultans, whose civil laws were mainly based on religion. Hinduism or Islam taught great amount of discipline to their adherents. Their religion taught to pay respects to elders. It also taught them ethics of life-style and they tried to display their behaviour, culture and way of life on the basis of religion. They knew the best of human values and respected each other. If any of them would commit mistakes, the society would punish or excommunicate them. It was seldom that the culprits ere produced before the King for justice. However, when the colonial period started, alien rules and regulations were imported. After gaining independence, very few countries tried to revive their old indigenous system. Most of them tried to implement constitutions on the basis of Great Britain or the US models and miserably failed. The western model may be excellent in western conditions and environment but it does not suit the interests of the Afro-Asian world. The political system as evolved in Malaysia, China and Singapore may be criticized as undemocratic, but they reflect the realities of social life in those countries. That system have proved useful for development and those models with certain modifications may be cultivated for other countries in the region. However this is a difficult task now, because the level of politicization is so high and so complicated that consensus is difficult.

Strange developments are taking place in Indonesia. Suharto is generally projected as a devil and institutions of governance built by him are rapidly disowned. As was the process of perestroika in the Soviet Union, the reformasi in Indonesia is moving rapidly in the same direction. The changes should be slow and gradual. Abrupt changes can bring untold miseries which may not be easy to comprehend at the outset.

Indonesia is setting new paradigm for its democratization. It has adopted multiparty system and there are more than hundred political parties. The two houses of Parliament (DPR and MPR) are becoming strong at the national level and provincial assemblies are becoming powerful. The threat of "recalling" from DPR no longer haunts and all its members are elected. It is a reality that whosoever adopted an independent and critical stand in the parliament, were disliked by Suharto and he had the powers to get them recalled. The powers of the Armed Forces which were exalted at the time of the Suharto era, have been minimised and their special prerogatives are getting eroded. The bureaucracy is being revamped and attempts are made to decentralise government powers. The provinces are likely to get shares in the profits generated through their resources and thus a number of proposals are considered which would result in the structural changes in the political system. They are also thinking about affirmative action, for the deprived and weaker section of the people. How these measures are to be evolved and with what implication are various issues of conjectures and projections. But every political party and pressure groups are coming out with new proposals in the name of reformasi which may not be universally acceptable.

Indonesia is facing insurgency and terrorism in different parts of the country. The main genesis of the crises differs from one region to another. If religion and economic factors are responsible for turmoil in Aceh, ethnic, geographical and religious factors are important in the crises in Irian Jaya and Ambon. It is simplistic to suggest that the solution for Aceh would be equally suitable to Ambon. Yet there is a dialogue for a federal system wherein autonomy is proposed to be given to different provinces. Indonesian realities are different from the United States and to suggest that the American federal laws or constitutional system would be a guide to resolve ethnic and religious crises in different parts of the country, needs to be properly scrutinized and probed.

Indonesian realities are strikingly similar to India but Indian model cannot be considered ideal. Although when Indonesia became independent, it had accepted some important characteristics of Indian constitutionalism for Indonesia, i.e., mixed economy, Pancasila, non-alignment and multi-party system, but their performance were not satisfactory. In matters pertaining to union-state relations, there were more similarities. India had declared that it "would be a Union of States", wherein the union exercised important powers through the Governor who were appointed by the central government. In Indonesia too, the central government exercised control over the provincial administrations through the office of the Governor, who were appointed by the central government. There has been friction in the provinces as a result of the omission and commission committed by the governors on the advice of the central government. India has friction in Kashmir, Mizoram, Nagaland, Manipur and some other areas whereas Indonesia is facing problems in Aceh, Ambon, West Papua, Nusa Tenggara, Kalimantan and some other areas. These instances suggest that the existing arrangements are faulty and there should be amendments in the constitution for better administration in the provinces and for cordial central-state relations. However, any amendment in the constitution should not be hasty. President Suharto hastily decided to change the policy of mixed economy with privatization and had to repent when the economic crises gripped the region in July 1997. There should be a thorough dialogue before bringing out a resolution for fundamental changes. I have a feeling that constitutions are not bad, but leaders are indeed bad. When they don't try to understand the letter and spirit of the constitution, when they interpret it to suit their narrow personal interest and when they make it as mere tool of power politics, the political system is eroded and diluted. The beauracratic corruption and dishonest leaders promote economic backwardness. Hence, a number of people start arguing that the constitution is outdated and it should either be amended or revoked. If the quality of leadership is corrupt and if they think only in terms of power without ethics, political environment becomes polluted. All the virtues of the constitution becomes meaningless, if it is in the hands of undesirable elements or bad leaders.

The issue of structural changes in the constitutional order may be relevant, but the most important aspect of the changes very often neglected, are regarding credibility of leaders and voters. The study of the political system in India, Indonesia, Malaysia or the Philippines do establish a theory that the problems in the political system are due to the mistakes and eccentricities of both leaders and voters to a great extent. The decision makers must attach importance to minimum qualification of the candidates who intend to contest in the elections. Every candidate must have secondary school certificate, a good track record in social service and a commanding knowledge of the problems in the constituency. The candidates should be at least 30 years of age with good health and temperament. Every contesting candidates should talk about their manifestoes in open debates. If possible, the debates must be telecasted with an institutionalised attempt to assess public opinion. A proper scrutiny of the legislators at the outset would surely improve the performance of the government. I will also suggest review of the concept of universal franchise. The voters too must be educated with minimum source of property. If a voter is totally illiterate and impoverished, he cannot be free and fair while exercising right to franchise. The history of constitutional developments in Great Britain and the US say that they did not offer right to universal franchise in the beginning. The Great Britain offered women the right of franchise after the end of the First World War. On the other hand, a section of the people, projected as slaves, had no right to vote in the US till recently. We, in the Asian region, are adopting democratic system and proper institution and environment are yet to be evolved. Of course, denying right to universal franchise to illiterates and downtrodden are against universal declaration of human rights, but in view of problems in Indonesia, it is incumbent and need of the hour. The Government of India Act (1909) and the Government of India Act (1919) are relevant in connection with the criteria for contesting candidates and voters through which the right to vote had been restricted. Although the Act had been framed by the colonial masters to promote colonial interest, it was pertinent for good governance. It was through this act that unwanted leaders and voters were eliminated. It is necessary to shortlist voters list and bring forward good and devoted leaders. This would have qualitative and quantitative impact on the election processes as it would surely reduce the danger of poll-related violence, rigging, and loompenism. By curtailing voting rights to illiterates, the message will be clear that education is of primary importance in exercising the right of franchise. Everyone would be prompted to send their children to schools so that they may be considered good citizens when they are grown up.

Indians are debating electoral reforms in the past one decade to make it more free and fair. The proposals are coming that the candidates should not be a convicted person, that he should explain the known sources of income and also that he should not have more than two children etc. All these suggestions arc good but not to be implemented in letter and spirits. It seems redundant to link family planning with electoral reforms and other issues cannot prove relevant in the present context. The problem of poverty, illiteracy, backwardness, and unemployment do affect electoral behaviour adversely and if those issues are to be attended, we must have good and honest leaders and in that endeavour structural changes in the existing laws must be introduced. The implementation of full universal franchise should be made conditional to universal literacy and prosperity in society.

The rise of multi-party system in Indonesia have simply raised the level of politicization. There are more than one hundred political parties and most of them have either religious, ethnic or regional manifestoes which is not in tune with the ethos of national interests. Java-bashing has been on the agenda of opposition elements outside Java. They do allege that "Java is the only island, which have prospered at the cost of all other islands". These allegations help in the spread of disgruntlement of have-nots.

Indonesia is also facing problems of the shortage of manpower on many of its islands. It is understood that only 6000 islands are properly inhabited and others are empty. In this context, the policy of transmigration as adopted during Suharto era needs to be resurrected in the modified way. In order to accelerate development everywhere and bring them at par, the presence of manpower is required. The policy of transmigration had earlier been adverently aimed at transforming the demographic balance in certain sensitive areas and therefore it became unpopular. That policy is suspended for the time being, but it is the need of the hour to resurrect it for positive purposes. All those islands, where there is no inhabitation, must get manpower. While transmigrating, the care should be taken to inhabit persons from more than one island, so that it is not projected as Javanese aggression.

The ethnic Javanese are indeed superior in terms of culture and they rightly feel themselves as the inheritors of Majapahit legacies. They have their different life-style and idioms of understanding. Some of them do feel that the people outside should understand and imbibe Javanese cultural values in the country. But all major ethnic groups in Indonesia are trying to retain their own cultural identity. The Javanese, though tolerant and gentle, becomes violent when they find their opponent adamant and volatile. The Javanese behaviour may be compared with ethnic Hans, but the latter are in majority in all the provinces of China. They are better organised and mobilised, but Javanese on the other hand, are not in majority in all parts of the country. They are localised and therefore they can't prove as much assertive as their Han counterparts in China. Hence there is a need for tolerance and consensus for greater good of the society.

Finally it may be stated that as Indonesia is multi-religious, multi-lingual and scattered in a vast area, its problems are also multifaceted. They may be endeavouring to have democratic order or reviewing their 1945 constitution, but any new arrangement cannot prove suitable universally or equally for all sections of the society. Authoritarian rule may not be liked by the majority, but mere democracy without development, would create anarchic situation. Obedience to laws and discipline are required for stability, modernisation and nation-building in Indonesia. This is not to suggest that the political system of Suharto era should be revived but modus operandi must be evolved to fix reasonable targets, accountability and management. Civil and criminal laws must be suitably amended to punish the guilty and rewards and incentives must be given to all those whose performance excells in their respective areas.

17

The Question of Indonesian Unity

Indonesia is faced with a plethora of internal challenges to its territorial unity ever since the exit of President Suharto from power on 21 May 1998.[1] The financial crisis (1997-98), the referendum in East Timor (1999), anti-Chinese riots, militancy and demand for autonomy in some parts of the country have exposed the vulnerability of the Republic. The archipelagic concept as enunciated by the founding fathers are losing its importance and third doctrine of Pancasila (unity of Indonesia) has been endangered after the secession of East Timor. The continuing unrest in Indonesia is a cause of concern not only for Indonesian leaders but for the world outside. The unrest in Indonesia have adversely affected the pace of ASEAN boom and the ethos of regionalism.

The separation of East Timor have symbolic impact on champions of secessionism at the regional level. The insurgents have raised their voice and violent activities in Aceh, Irian Jaya (West Irian), Ambon (Moluccas), Kalimantan (Borneo) and Nusa Tenggara (west Timor) are disturbing. The unity of Indonesia for which there was a national consensus, is facing the greatest challenge in the new millenium. It is necessary at the outset to know its genesis and understand the rationale of unrest in different parts of the country. Professor Robert Scalapino of California University while speaking about Indonesia in a seminar in JNU on 15 March 2001 remarked that Indonesia was never unified and its integration was fragile from the beginning. Dutch scholars in International Institute of Asian Studies in Leiden, also express similar views. They speak about the identity of different ethnic groups scattered all over the country and their quest for identity. Indonesians, on the other hand, accept the heterogeneity, but speak about various unifying elements, such as common language (Bahasa Indonesia), common literature, epic and architecture etc. They also articulate the spirit of togetherness evolved at the time of freedom struggle, when all ethnic groups displayed a consensus to fight against the Dutch colonial rulers. Geographyically scattered into 17508 islands, their problems and habits have similarities. If the Javanese with 65 per cent of the population comprise the majority, and if they are assertive, it is not designed. Every country have their majority and minorities. Han and Hindus have been the dominant majorities in China and India respectively but that should not be the cause of their disintegration.

The problem in Indonesia has socio-economic and religious dimension. All the provinces had not developed equally during the new order era of President Suharto, and some ethnic groups were unhappy for different reasons. Suharto was targeted as soon as economic crisis began. Anti-Chinese riots in Jakarta, anti-Suharto slogans and demonstrations were ostensibly supported to remove Suharto from power. Financial crisis ultimately caused not only the resignation of Suharto but it also finished the role of military in politics. Later developments were ominous. The shattered economy and demoralization of the armed forces affected the national cohesion. People's anger and violence were sporadic. The ethnic groups, who had been nursing grievances against their central government sensed success in the removal of Suharto and began to articulate their own agenda in the changed situation. They felt that it was the appropriate time to press for their autonomy or independence. It is in order here to discuss about some troubled areas where violence and bloodshed have raised questions about territorial integrity of Indonesia.

East Timor, 27th province of Indonesia till 1999, had been in turmoil because of intra-ethnic conflict ever since it was annexed by Indonesia in 1975. The ethnic Timorese, under the leadership of Jose Ramos Horta, was preparing the grounds for independence from Portugal, when Indonesia intervened militarily on the pretext that Timor was under the jurisdiction of Indonesian archipelago. Fretilin did not accept Indonesian claims and started guerrilla warfare and argued their case on ethnic and religious grounds. Timorese leaders were critical of the Indonesians and projected that Indonesians being hegemonistic had replaced the Portuguese as colonial rulers and hence independence struggle would continue.

Indonesia felt otherwise. The success in the military exercise had generated confidence. As it exercised control over West Timor, it felt that it was its natural right to exercise sovereignty over East Timor also. It evolved its integration drive, which was resisted by the Fretilin and the United Nations. The Indonesian army was tyrannical while implementing the integration drive. Hence one-sixth of the population of East Timor, numbering about one lakh, were killed. The East Timor military command was established by the government to maintain law and order with enormous powers. Their activities were insensitive while exercising their duties and hence a wide vacuum emerged in the attitudes and perception of the government vis-a-vis ethnic groups. The military resorted to shooting at the slightest provocation and carnage at Santa Cruz Cemetry in Dili in 1991 had been condemned internationally. It was reported that 115 people died on the spot and hundreds were injured.[2]

In fact, the Timorese are of Malanesian descend, and they have a distinct culture and traditions. They opposed Indonesian domination from the beginning and when Indonesian President B.J. Habibie agreed for a referendum, panicky situation developed in the area. Thousands of those people who had transmigrated from Java to East Timor felt threatened in East Timor. They decided to leave their new homes. Thus there were influx of Javanese refugees on neighbouring islands. On the other hand, the armed forces who had developed vested interests in the area felt threatened. They indulged themselves in violence before their return and thus there was a civil war. East Timor finally became an independent state on 30 August 1999, and it was a welcome development. However, this event gave rise to irredentist and secessionist activities in other parts of the country. J.A.C. Mackie had rightly prophesied long ago that "I doubt that if there is currently as much risk of secessionism or territorial disintegration of Indonesia as is often suggested, for the centralizing tendencies of the last two decades have seen very powerful. But it is probably true to say that Indonesia's national unity is still rather brittle creation, which might not stand up to any serious blow to the authority of the central government. If any part of the archipelago is able to defy Jakarta's authority on a major issue and get away with it, the chain reaction elsewhere could be quite disastrous".[3]

Another disturbed area is Aceh, situated at the northern tip of Sumatra. Acehnese had fought against the Dutch to protect their distinct culture and history. Its 4.5 million population has been strong supporter of Darul Islam movement and views the authority of Central government un-Islamic. They argue that the Javanese, who dominates the government cannot be a true Muslim. The people of Aceh have been struggling for their identity and separate nationhood because the government has not been sensitive to their grievances. The government gave them autonomy in religious and educational affairs after a long struggle in 1959 but it was withdrawn without any rhyme or reason. Though it is rich in iron, oil, gas and coal, it is not given proper share in the benefits. At the same time, the government has supported migration and transmigration of population to that area which has been disliked. The people in Aceh have opposed the presence of new migrants and they have been agitating. The continuing conflict over economic and demographic issues have fuelled separatist movement. In 1976, Hasan Di Tiro established Gerakan Aceh Merdeka (Free Aceh movement) and subsequently declared independence. But this movement was suppressed and Tiro fled to Sweden. It was from Sweden that he announced the formation of Aceh government in exile. The unrest grew enormously in Aceh in 1989 when National Liberation Front Aceh Sumatra (NLFAS) was established. They mounted onslaughts on the government forces and Amnesty International claimed that 2000 people were killed during 1989-93, and the casualty number have been increasing every year.[4]

Similar is the situation in Irian Jaya, where Organisasi Papua Merdeka (OPM), also known as Free·Papua Movement leads separatist movement. There has been lot of bloodshed in that province also and the cases of human rights violations are reported. Irian Jaya is rich in timber, gold and silver. Indonesia is trying to exploit the natural resources of the area, but the indigenous people are resisting it. They have not yet been fully integrated with the national minstream as their outlook and culture are different. They have not accepted their integration so far and they display much in common with the peole of Papua New Guinea. It is a fact that Dani, Asmat and other ethnic groups of the province are of Melanesian stock and they are entirely different in their customs and traditions compared to Javanese Malays. Some of the tribal groups have procured weapons to kill transmigrants and foreigners. The army, on the other hand, has been vindictive while assuring law and order.[5]

The separatist tendencies in both Aceh and Irian Jaya have religious dimension. As far as Aceh is concerned, it is Muslim dominated area. They believe that the government of Indonesia is under the control of the Javanese and a Javanese cannot be a true Muslim. The Javanese leaders on the other hand are apprehensive of the nationalism of Acehnese and have used force to bring them into national mainstream. There has been persecution of the Acehnese and their mass graves have been found.[6] Some of the dissident leaders have sought asylum elsewhere. Their participation in the government have been nominal and guerrilla warfare continues. On the other hand, Irian Jaya has 83% Christian population. The Church is the main centre of social congregation. They know that the province had not been handed over to Indonesia along with other provinces by the Dutch colonial masters because of ethnic and religious grounds. Their projection is that given the situation in which they are, their identity is bound to be lost forever in the present dispensation.

The religion and ethnicity are the root cause of trouble in Ambon also which is the capital city of Maluku. History says that majority of the pro-Dutch elements and militias inhabited in that area especially on the eve of independence. They had struggled against their integration with the Indonesian Republic and had fought for their independence.[7]

Known as Amboina in the historical past, Ambon has a number of people with the Dutch and Portuguese descend. There are some Chinese also who have prospered in business and trade. Although the government statistics claim that 55.8 per cent are Muslims, 38.2 per cent are Protestants and 5.3 per cent are Catholics, but this is the figure of Maluku province in general.[8] A study of the social life in Ambon presents a different picture. The Christians are in numerical majority and they are relatively better economically than their Muslim counterparts.

There have been violent clashes between the Muslims and Christian communities especially after Indonesia was gripped by the economic crisis (1997-98). Hundreds of people have lost their lives. Militant groups have emerged to protect the lives of their people and communal virus have engulfed the area. Islamic outfits such as Islamic Defender's Forum have given a call for Jehad and such a call is appropriately reciprocated.[9] It is believed that the government was lackadaisical in their attitudes about the happenings in the area in the post-1998 period and did not act swiftly to stop rioting.

The development in Aceh, Irian Jaya, and Ambon clearly suggest that the concept of Bhineka Tunggal Eka (Unity in Diversity) is endangered. We find that there are growing threats to minorities. The Chinese for instance, have felt traumatic experiences. Anti-Chinese riots have taken place in Jakarta also on one pretext or the other and they are feeling threatened in all parts of the country. The Chinese, who have traditionally been involved in business and trade, and who have prospered economically are made victims of looting, arson, rape, riots and humiliation ever since the beginning of Habibie era in May 1998. Anti-Chinese riots have been taking place and the worst affected areas are Medan, Titipatan, Solo and Samarinda. The hooligans involved in rioting argue that the Chinese are responsible for spiralling price rise and the economic crisis. In February 1998, the riots in Medan were serious enough to compel some ethnic Chinese to leave their homes. Twelve Chinese owned shops had been torched and dozens of buildings damaged at Kendari in Sulawesi. The looting of Chinese stores and shops have been occurring ever since.[10]

The role of the ethnic Javanese in anti-Chinese riots are alleged but they too are targeted in certain areas. They have been hunted and killed in Kalimantan (Borneo) in the recent past by Orung Gunug (Mountain People), the head hunters. Also known as Dayaks, they too are of Melanesian descend and traditionally they have been nomadic. They believe in animism and have distinct culture and traditions.[11] They are unhappy with Javanese and Madurese transmigrants whose number is more than one lakh. The indigeneous people have a feeling that the new migrants are unfriendly and a threat to their customs and way of life. Orung Gunung are using blowguns and blowpipes (Sumpit) to fight against their adversaries. Sumpit is a narrow tube about two to three meters long made of hardwood or bamboo, fitted with iron sights, and shot darts. The tip is lashed with deadly poison and the death is instant if it hits. The Dayaks are fierce people who display the skulls of their victims on their doors. They also burn the body of the victims on occasions and distribute body parts for eating. The literacy rates are low, but they are gradually becoming aware of the resources in the area, which like Aceh have huge oil reservoirs and timber.

In fact, the problems that agitate the minds of the ethnic leaders are mainly associated with their socio-economic life. Java island has prospered more than other provinces. Javanese are big land owners on other islands too. They dominate in politics and civil administration on other islands as well. The ethnic groups are very sensitive to their separate identity and feel that identity can be protected under an autonomous regime whereby there is no interference by Jakarta in day-to-day administration. As they were under authoritarian regime for decades and as there was censorship of the press, little was known about their activities. But the situation changed with the dawn of democracy, when right to speech and expression (Article 28) and multi-party system was restored. They have started demanding autonomy, and at the same time targeted Javanese and Madurese transmigrants who are settled in their areas. It would be in order here to explain the genesis of transmigration policy, which have become a subject of controversy at present.

Transmigration policy had been evolved to balance population distribution from densely populated to less populated zones. It is true that Java and Madura inhabit 65 per cent of Indonesian population. Java alone has 100 million people. This island however occupies only 6.8 per cent of the total land of the country. Sumatra, which is comparatively bigger in size, has 41 million, Sulawesi 13 million, Nusatenggara 11.5 million, Maluku 11.9 million and Kalimantan has 11 million population.[13] It is known that only 992 out of 17508 islands are mainly populated zones. But Haryati Soebadio says that 5000 islands are inhabited. There has to be a better management of the inhabited and uninhabited islands to accelerate the pace of development. There is abundance of natural resources in all parts of the country and their exploitation can be facilitated only when there is availability of manpower. Indonesia endeavoured to diversify its population from densely populated areas to new zones. They passed relevant rules in that direction in 1960 and 1973 and transmigrated people from Java to other islands. Initially, 17116 families were settled in Irian Jaya and 8155 in Maluku but a number of people were also transmigrated to Kalimantan, East Timor and Aceh.[14] Joan Hardejono said that the number of transmigration were 49772 in 1979-80, 1080 in 1980-81, 123846 in 1981-82, 167477 in 1982-83 and 86298 in 1983-84.[15] As the government supported it, transmigration continued but it did not resolve the problem of population density in Java. As job opportunities are available mostly in Java, poor and impoverished people continue to come and the problem remains the same.

There has been some omission and commission, while transmigrating the people as alleged by Aceh Merdeka, OPM and some other opposition groups. They stated that the alien population is arbitrarily introduced to change the demographic complexion and this is a matter of intrusion in matters of their human rights. They understand that the transmigrants would alter the indigenous character of their socio-economic life and usurp their properties. The Javanese speak an alien language and have faith in Islamic religion. But the people in Irian Jaya and Maluku have significant number of Christians. The indigenous people are unhappy that their distinct identity would be diluted in due course if the arrival of transmigrants are not stopped. They allege that Javanese migrants are arrogant with a sense of superiority. They assume that they are unwanted people thrust upon them, who may be interested in colonizing the entire area. The new migrants generally search jobs in oil exploration, mining and forestry department and the local people project this behaviour contrary to their interests saying that ultimately the new transmigrants would deprive them of their resources and wealth.[16]

Indigenous people in Irian Jaya, Aceh and Ambon are alarmed of the activities of the ethnic Javanese. They observe that the Javanese migrants have excellent rapport with government authorities. They are trusted by the government and offered all types of facilities at the cost of the indigenous people. Hence they are demanding that the transmigration should be scrapped with immediate effect. Thus transmigrant population are faced with a dilemma in coping with the situation and their human rights have been threatened. The opposition to government policies remained suppressed under the authoritarian rule, but now the situation is changing very fast and the present government is bound to review transmigration policies. With restoration of democracy, it is natural that the issue of transmigration is politicized and complicated.

One of the important reasons for differences with the centre have been the unequal distribution of income. It is known that Aceh gets only two per cent of the revenues that it generates through the sale of its oil.[17] Irian Jaya and Ambon are getting far less and Kalimantan has remained primitive in terms of modernisation. This situation has been complicated after the financial crisis wherein Indonesia has been subjected to observe IMF conditions.

Indonesia could not cope with the problem of financial crisis which started in Thailand in July 1997 and engulfed Indonesia finally. Though President Suharto felt great concern but he was unable to tackle it satisfactorily. He became increasingly dependent on IMF to resolve the crisis and accepted the reform agenda. He distanced himself from the economists who had been the pillars of his success since 1966. He removed the Governor of Bank Indonesia and sought advice elsewhere. When he was reappointed as the President in 1998, most of the advice tendered by the IMF was implemented, except the establishment of Currency Board System as advised by Professor Steve Hanke of John Hopkins University. Suharto felt that the IMF programme by itself was not going to resolve the problem because when he signed an agreement with the IMF on 15 January, the Rupiah had lost another 40 per cent of its value. With a total depreciation of some 80 per cent, the private sector of the economy was bankrupt.[18] Suharto was most anxious at this juncture of the inflationary effects if the devalued currency could not be resuscitated. There were rough estimates that if the currency stayed at the 10000-12000 level against US $1, inflation would build up over 200 to 300 per cent over a year.[19] When there was rioting over price rise and shortages, the question was what would happen if prices doubled and kept on going up while more businesses folded and household incomes shrank in many cases. Indonesia had presented a case of market failure, where there was a massive flight of capital goods and foreign currencies. As a result, Jakarta stock exchange collapsed.[20] There were unforeseen fall in the value of the Rupiah and rapidity of the capital flight was traumatic. The availability of the foreign currency become scarce and the banking system failed. Sixteen banks were closed at a stretch and the work on many foreign sponsored projects were stopped. The IMF came out with certain new conditions to provide bail out funds and tension was visible at the socio-economic level.

The price rise was so rapid and painful that people's faith in the system started vanishing.[21] The cases of looting, arson and intermittent firing caused unrest. The resignation of Suharto did not improve the situation. Habibie, his successor, had neither the support of the public or the armed forces. He was unable to curb the growing violence. Although he had no mandate of popular support, he ordered referendum in East Timor and the results were predictable. The independence of East Timor opened floodgates for disintegration. The separatist activities in Aceh, Irian Jaya and Ambon picked up momentum. The Christians expressed unhappiness with their Islamic counterparts. The terrorist groups emerged to protect their ethnic groups. Islamic outfits clamoured for Jehad and similarly the Christians took up arms in vengeance.

Although Aceh is intra-Muslim conflict but Irian Jaya and Ambon presents a different scenario. In both these cases, the conflict, is between two religious groups, i.e., Muslims and Christians. There is a history of their conflict, which cannot be overlooked. The Ambonese in Maluku had embarked on separation on the eve of independence of the Indonesian Republic. On 25 April 1950, Ambonese leaders, J.H. Manuhuttu and A. Wairisai had proclaimed the establishment of the state of South Moluccas. Indonesian government felt great concern, but projected the conflict as a family quarrel.[22] But when the Ambonese, who had served in the Dutch army, started fighting against the government, the separatists took the control of Ambon and adjoining islands and it was not easy for the government to resolve this problem for quite some time. The Indonesian government had to organise sea blockade by its navy to contain dissident activities. As Ambon is dependent on other islands for its food supply, the sea blockade crippled them to withdraw. It was only thereafter that troops were dispatched to take control of Ambon and adjoining islands. Ambonese leaders did not give up their idea of independence even after defeat. Some of them fled to Holland and continued to oppose their integration with Indonesia.

The history of Irian Jaya is more or less similar. The Dutch government had retained it while transferring sovereignty of other islands to Indonesian leaders. The Dutch colonial masters viewed that Irian Jaya was much different in culture, religion and ethnicity to be integrated with Indonesia. Another dimension of the Dutch policy was to create a homeland for the people of Dutch- Indonesian descend on that island, where a sizable section of the indigenous people opposed their integration with Indonesia.[23] The government of Indonesia, on the other hand, invoked the principle of archipelagic concept and fought for the control of the island. Irian Jaya became a part of Indonesia only after the intervention of the United Nations in 1963 but it continued to remain isolated and backward. When East Timor became independent in 1999, it had its impact on political developments in Irian Jaya as well. What is striking is that the Church and the Christian associations have played important role in the freedom struggle of East Timor. Hence the role of Christian institutions and associations are gaining new meaning in the context of Irian Jaya and Ambon and counter developments are taking place. This is a matter of concern that Islamic groups are alarmed and advocate Jehad for an Islamic state. The natives oppose the development activities which benefits the Centre. If there is logging or mining, it is resisted by the separatists on various grounds. The separatist leaders argue that their natural resources are exploited for the benefit of the Javanese and they cannot get justice under the present dispensation. The Armed Forces, which ruled the country from 1965 to 1998, have committed atrocities and suppressed dissidents. Now that democracy has dawned, they have started articulating their grievances in public. It demands lot of courage and wisdom to involve them in the decision-making and make them feel secure as distinct ethnic groups in their respective areas. The principle of "unity in diversity" has to be implemented in letter and spirit, and ethnic leaders are to be promoted in national decision-making.

The main issue to ponder about is that there is substantial threat to unity of Indonesia. Irian Jaya, Aceh and Ambon are disturbed and solution to their grievances is not in sight. Although the dissidents would welcome referendum on the pattern in East Timor, but it is difficult now. When Habibie had announced referendum, it was without taking the consent of the DPR, which is the supreme decision-making body. His successor, Wahid also announced referendum for Aceh without discussing it in the DPR, which is the proper forum where such resolutions should first be discussed. Naturally there was immediate opposition to the proposal, and when the issue was referred to DPR it was opposed. The representatives of the people in the Assembly rejected Wahid's proposals and established an expert panel to suggest measures to resolve the dispute. In December 1999, the expert panel on Aceh recommended policy alternatives, which did not include a referendum on Acehnese independence.[24] It is known that the secession of any one province would encourage fragmentation of the Indonesian republic resulting in political instability in the region. The Indonesian legislature (DPR) might be ready to discuss autonomy proposals. For instance, DPR representatives are suggesting that Aceh might be allowed to decree radical Islamic Laws in place of Pancasila. It may be apportioned up to 75 per cent of the revenues on account of its oil, besides the right to generate other sources of revenues.[25] Similarly Irian Jaya, which is the largest and remotest province of Indonesia, can think about autonomy. The DPR might discuss apportioning the share of that province in the profits due to mining of gold, logging of timber, etc. They may be allowed to declare Christian laws, but the secession of the province cannot be entertained.

Besides invoking some features of the federal system, it is also important to pay attention on the armed forces, who has been demoralised in the post-Suharto era. Both Habibie and Wahid have contributed to the diminution of their dual role in the politics of the country and both have blamed Armed Forces for omissions and commissions in the past. But it can't be brushed aside that the armed forces exist for protecting sovereignty and territorial integrity of the nation and this role cannot be exercised by others. If they feel demoralised they can't exercise their role properly. The civilian leaders might have several grievances against some generals loyal to Suharto, but security situation demands that they should be strong and effective.

The civilian leaders are trying to curb the role of the military in politics of the country and inadvertently have done certain things, like instituting enquiry committees, to highlight negative points which is not in tune with national interests. History says that military role in administation and politics had been accepted with the acceptance of *dwifungsi* (Dual Functions) concept in government and politics.[26] The meaning and significance of *dwifungsi* were aimed at perpetrating army rule. It was argued that the concern of the armed forces were not simply to look after national defence, but also the actual conduct of the government in the interest of good administration. A powerful propaganda was made that the armed forces had played the principal role in securing independence, that it had done so in the face of obstruction and betrayal by the civilian authorities, and it therefore retained a special right and duty to supervise and take charge of the government. Under the stewardship of Suharto, *dwifungsi* principle became operational and accordingly serving and retired army officers took a wide variety of posts, from that of a cabinet minister down to a village head.

However, the situation have changed now. There is democracy and rulers are to be elected. The two houses of parliament—MPR (Madjelis Permusjawaratan Rakjat) and DPR (Dewan Perwakilan Rakjat) are becoming vibrant and effective. The civil service system is being revamped and democratic institutions are strenghened. Although the armed forces, who guided the destiny of the nation for decades, are feeling deprived, but ways and means should be evolved to keep them satisfied. Their role in maintaining the unity and integrity of the country should not be overlooked.

Notable worries to the nation is the rise of fundamentalism supplemented with the armed militant forces to protect territorial nationalism. Indonesia has officially recognised five major religions, namely Islam, Protestents, Catholics, Hindus and Buddhists, Muslims comprise 87.2 per cent, followed by Protestents 6 per cent, Catholics 3.5 per cent, Hindus 2 per cent and Buddhists one per cent. But the realities suggest that Christians are in majority in certain territories, namely in Ambon and Irian Jaya. The Hindus are in majority in Bali. Again the Islamic community is not monolithic and it is divided along several ethnic groups namely, the Javanese, the Madurese, the Sundanese, the Minhasans, the Bugis, the Makassars and the Acehnese. History says that there were different kingdoms in the archipelago when the Dutch colonial masters had come in 1605 and they had hostile relations. The Dutch supported one group against another and thereby established herself as the colonial master. It was under the Dutch that the different islands in the archipelago was unified. So the unification was not through consensus, but it had been imposed by force. All these issues were relevant at the time of freedom struggle, but all the leaders joined together to fight unitedly against the colonial rule. The religion was given a new meaning and made an important instrument to promote nationalism. The Wayang (shadow plays), the symbols (Garuda), the national flag etc. reflected religious fervour and mysticism which spread in tune with religion and superstitions. These factors mobilised public opinion against the colonial rulers. The role of all the religions were equally important in evolving Indonesian nationalism and therefore when they framed their constitution in 1945, they did not declare one religion of the state. It stated that the state shall be based upon belief in the one supreme God. The state shall guarantee freedom to every resident to adhere to his respective religion and he perform his religious duties in conformity with that religion and that faith. (Article 29).[27]

President Sukarno, who was secular in his thought and behaviour and who had marrid a Hindu girl, began to think like Jawaharlal Nehru that if economic factor is stressed, religious differences would recede into the background. He undertook several socio-economic programmes for nation-building and was assertive in regional politics. He also adopted militant policies to assume sovereignty over West Irian and Malaya, but his policies could not divert the opinion of religious fanatics. His successor Suharto allowed freedom to religious groups under the framework of Article 29 but opposed the idea to declare Islam as the state religion. Indonesian leaders tried to prove themselves unique as the only Muslim dominated society where Islam as state religion is not declared.

However, the existing realities show disturbing trends. There are some Islamic groups advocating religious revivalism.[28] They want to prove themselves as much religious in temperament and behaviour as their counterparts in Iran or Saudi Arabia. They are keen to show that they are equal to their co-religionists in the Muslim heartland in terms of applying Islamic ethos. They are reflecting their opinion to implement Shariat laws and enforce the routine of daily prayer, circumcision rite, Ramazan fast and pilgrimage on state level. Koranic exigencies, dogmas, jurisprudence and eschatology are highlighted for nation-building. They also advocate jehad for the perceived enemy in the society. It is thus pertinent to know as to why such a phenomenon is occurring in a society, which had been tolerant and human for centuries.[29]

The quest for Islamic resurgence in Indonesia is a new phenomenon.[30] It has been caused due to several reasons. First and most important is the external factor particularly the Arab world. The Islamic world and Muslim Ummah faced peculiar challenges in the beginning of 1970s. The Islamic revolution in Iran under Ayatollah Khomeini, the Soviet invasion in Afghanistan, the shooting incident at Masjidil Haram (Saudi Arabia) and Arab-Israel war drove the Muslim world to forge greater solidarity with one another at the global level. The countries in West Asia took advantage of its conflict with Israel and raised the price of oil and natural gas exorbitantly. This enriched them to exercise power at the international level. They started aiding and abetting Islam at the global level. Libya, Saudi Arabia and Iran started taking interests in rejuvenating Islam internally and externally and it was natural for them to pay attention on Indonesia, the largest country of the Muslim world. As a result, some Islamic groups, in Indonesia started advocating Islam as all encompassing way of life (al-din), superior to other religions. They began to display assertion in espousing Islamic fundamentalist values, ideals and solutions, and emphasized on the role of the organization to make them more organised and effective at the state level.[31]

There is a trend towards Islamic resurgence at the Southeast Asian level also. The religious groups through their theological and intellectual publications, namely, Pesantren in Indonesia, Risalah in Malaysia, Al Rabitah in Thailand and Sedar in Singapore, have highlighted the case of Islamic resurgence, and the impact of their writings are deeprooted on a section of Muslim elites. They aspire the formation of a state that would resort to the Koran and Sunnah as the sources of law and place the Alim-Ulama at the apex of the state leadership. Thailand has a sizable Muslim population in Patani areas and the Philippines have in Sulu and Mindanao. Being dominant in certain areas, they are demanding autonomy or independence to maintain their Islamic identity. There has been serious violence in those areas led by Muslim fanatics in the past few decades.

Again Brunei Darussalam and Malaysia which have the majority of Muslims and which have declared Islam as the state religion, also witness the movement for Islamic resurgence. Although Islamic laws are applied in regulating family matters such as marriage, divorce and inheritance, but fundamentalists believe that the government is not doing much for Islam and the Muslims. They want reflection of Koran and Sunnah at the apex of state leadership. Their influence are increasing and as a result more and more Muslims are attending religious classes. The Muslim students are easily distinguishable from others by their dress and address. Their popular dresses are Songkok, Julbab, Sarban, Telekong—Mini and Purdah (Burka) and their style of addressing (greeting) is Assaamulaikum.

The fundamentalist ideas are getting support through Muslim missionary activities, called the Dakwah, which is generously supported by the oil-rich West Asian countries. Dakwah missionaries have succeeded in influencing urban population in Malaysia and inculcated Islamic consciousness on a scale never witnessed in the past. The Sultenate of Brunei is very sensitive to Dakwah activities, and has been compelled to prove that it protects Islamic interests. It has been making bigger financial allocation to build Mosques and Madrasah. It has been generously aiding the upgradation of Islamic lessons and textbooks in the school curriculum. However, these measures are not sufficient to dilute the appeal of the Dakwah.

Malaysia, with a contiguous border with Indonesia, is facing the upsurge of fundamentalist ideas. The Dakwah activities led by Abim, Darul Arqam, Jamaat Tabligh and Perkim are critical of the government policies. Their appeal under the patronage of PAS (Islamic Party of Malaysia) and ABIM (Malaysian Islamic Youth Movement) have increased. The government is concerned about it and Prime Minister, Mahathir Mohamad has been taking several measures to cope with the situation. He has been announcing some policies and perspectives supporting greater Islamization. Yet his credentials as an Islamic leader is questioned. His administration has established Islamic Banks, Islamic Insurance, Islamic Economic Foundation, Special Islamic Enforcement Group, International Islamic University, Islamic Medical Centre, Puset Islam (the nerve centre of Islamic Bureaucracy) and the government has made official declaration of "Islamization of the government machinery".[32] These steps are apparently to refute the allegation that Mahathir government is not doing much for Islam and the Muslims. It is trying to convince its Muslim population that his administration would always safeguard Muslim interests and also that it is committed to promote Islam at the national and international levels.[33]

Malaysia is indeed facing problems in its Islamization process. It is multi-ethnic society, where ethnic Chinese have a sizable population. Though ethnic Malay Muslims dominate politically and their dominant rights are reserved constitutionally, it is not easy for them to find out a common identity acceptable to all the three important ethnic groups, i.e. Malays, Chinese and the Indians. All of them may be patriots but when the question comes to foster and promote Islam as the foundation of national culture and identity there is no unanimity. The country since its independence, have nurtured democratic institutions, secular norms, pluralism and humanitarian ethos and it is not easy to impose Islam on others arbitrarily. The Muslims might be more assertive, but that may prove counter productive in due course.

It is, therefore, that there are differences in attitudes and opinions of Islamic leaders and intellectuals on the question of Islam in politics and Islamic fundamentalism. There are differences on details governing the principles of faith in Islamic concepts such as Aldin, Tawheed and Aqeedah as well as the modus operandi of the Islamic state in the modern environment. However the quest for unification and globalization of Islamic world and the endeavour to link "peripheral" Muslims with their counterparts in the Muslim "heartland" in letter and spirit, are motivating factors for the fundamentalists to work for Islamic assertion is Southeast Asia.

The situation in Indonesia is more or less similar on the pattern of Malaysia. There is a quest for assertion of religious values and symbols and Harakah groups are active. They have been arguing for the establishment of Negara Islam Indonesia and replacement of Pancasila with Islam as the foundation of state philosophy. The attempts towards revitalization of the Islamic spirits have been accentuated through some organizations, namely Darul Islam, and Ikhwanul Muslimin. These organizations have sought to transform their modus operandi from ordinary organizational activities into that of an Islamic movement. They draw their inspiration from the life and practices of the Prophet Mohamad, the Koranic Generation of the Sahbahs (Prophet's close companions) as well as from the ideas and programmes of more recent Harakah (cause oriented) movements like Jamate Islami. They have given attention on their planning, methodology, operations and special training to display their militancy. They are committed to sacrifice their lives to attain their objectives. They attach importance to education (tarbiyah and Usrrah) under the supervision of alimulama (pious Islamic scholars), with a message that goes beyond rituals to generate special identity. The leaders of Islamic movements are mostly graduates of secular Western Universities and they tend to operate more from the cities than from rural areas.[34]

Thus Indonesia has been facing challenges through religious groups but its beginning can be traced ever since its independence. Masjumi Party (Majlis Sura Muslim Indonesia) influenced by the teachings of Mohammad Abduh of Cairo University, which had mobilized support of the Muslims in Sumatra, South Sulawesi and West Java, was highly critical of Marxist oriented socialism of Sukarno. It had posed serious problems to Sukarno administration particularly when guided democracy was declared. Masjumi leaders argued that a renewed Islam was capable of providing a religious and philosophical base for rapid social and economic development. It believed in challenging Pancasila based Indonesia to one founded on Islam. Mohammad Natsir, a Masjumi leader pleaded that since Islam was the religion and philosophy of most Indonesians, the Islamic majority should not have to accept a state based on secular Pancasila, because secularism is an alien concept.[35] This Party was advocating the inclusion of Shariat laws in the constitution and their activities created serious problems for the administration. However, those issues are matters of historical relevance. Now it is joined with new issues and new challenges.

Indonesia is presently facing a transitional phase from dictatorship to democracy when institutional faith in the government of the people, for the people and by the people is yet to percolate down in the political system. The threat of the military rule has not been dissipated as the social unrest and economic deterioration continues. No country in the region would like to see Indonesia embroiled in the crises for too long, because their stability and boom is linked with Indonesia, the largest state in Southeast Asia. The ASEAN countries, whether civilian or military, can support any group, if they are able to put Indonesia on the development track. However, it is difficult to find a ready-made solution for the gigantic problems of Indonesia, which has been complicated in recent years.

To be brief, there are two issues, which apparently, are major threats for the evolving political system. First is the rise of fundamentalism under Darul Islam and Masjumi, demanding the declaration of the Islamic state. They are opposing Pancasila as the state philosophy, and believe that the adherents of other religions are infidels. They are strongly preaching the ethics of holywar (Jehad) and are involved in organised crime in Aceh, Irian Jaya and Ambon. Their roles in communal riots have generated ethnic tension in all parts of the country.

Secondly, the separatist movement has shaken the foundation of the Indonesian republic. There is intense struggle for autonomy or independence in Aceh, Ambon and Irian Jaya. There is disturbances in West Timor (Nusa Tenggara) after the separation of East Timor as an independent state. Besides these areas, we have found incidents of rioting and violence in other parts of the country as well. In fact, there are hundreds of ethnic groups and all of them would like to preserve their separate identity. Sukarno, the father of the nation, nurtured and cared for all the ethnic groups, in order to promote common nationalism. But when he was ousted from power, anti-Sukarno campaign was launched to tarnish his image and contributions, Suharto, his successor, remained in power with the support of the armed forces. He was authoritarian and suppressed the opposition for 32 years. It was difficult to diagnose the simmering dessent, which exploded massively in 1998. The unrest continues and the prevailing situation can come under control only by dialogue, persuasion and progress.

A glimpse of the ethnic disputes show that the situation is disturbing. Timorese for example, are of Melanesian stock, whose claim for territoriality is spread over both parts, but one of them is an integral part of Indonesia and another has become independent. There has been massive exodus of the population from East Timor of Javanese and Bugis, numbering about 50,000, who had transmigrated in that area after 1976. It is understood that 100,000 Timorese had been massacred in 1975 and similar thousands were killed in 1999 when the referendum for independence took place. An overwhelming majority of the people are Christians and Islam never went on this island. Most of the indigenous people are dark skinned and light built and their 36 distinct ethnic linguistic groups. However there are no link between Bahasa Indonesia and the languages of the Timorese. Some of the Melanesians still believe in animism. The farmer still spills blood before tilling the soil, and accordingly to their traditional system, they worship crocodile (the fertility god), and the figure of a crocodile is used in Timorese weaving motifs. Their integration into the national mainstream is difficult indeed, particularly after the separation of East Timor as an independent state. The exodus from East Timor to West Timor and now from West Timor to other provinces has posed serious threat to national integration.

Another group, the ethnic Chinese, numbering about 6.5 million population are unhappy. The Chinese are comparatively well off and they have excelled as a businessmen, bankers, professionals, traders, shop-keepers, mechanics, tour-guides, plantation owners and overseers in Indonesia and have generated jealousy of the native population. They control the economy and they are targeted as the main enemy for the economic crisis. There have been anti-Chinese riots since 1998. Their shops have been looted, women have been raped and properties damaged. More than 70,000 people left Indonesia in 1998 and they feel insecure in the country. Hence the pertinent question is whether Indonesia will survive economically without the Chinese entrepreneurs and their capital?

Again Aceh is burning where there has been a call to massacre government troops stationed there. Aceh Merdeka under Mustafa Abubakar, believes in religious extremism. As Aceh was one of the first part of the archipelago to be converted to Islam, it is the bedrock of Islamic religion and culture. Numbering about three million people, they are highly Islamic. Most of them read and write Arabic and pray in Arabic. Their language, Acehnese, have lot of words from the Cham language and they are different from Bahasa Indonesia. They have been demanding autonomy or independence and in order to press their demands have formed free Aceh Movement, which believes in guerrilla warfare. Indonesian troops have tried to suppress them and indulged in massacres but that have not changed the ground realities. Acehnese have become very active after the separation of East Timor, and forced President Abudurrahman Wahid to announce referendum on the pattern of East Timor, but subsequently he had to withdraw the offer on one pretext or the other.

Yet another ethnic group, which draws our attention are the Ambonese in Maluku province. The Ambonese, also called "black Dutch", were the Dutch minded people, who had been trained by the Dutch colonial masters to fight Indonesian revolutionaries in the post-1945 era. The Ambonese are generally the people of mixed race of Portuguese, Alfuros, Malays, Javanese and Dutch descend. The mixed blood is most obvious in the lighter-skinned coastal villages. The people in the countryside have darker complexion and more pronounced Melanesian features. Ambonese speak a dialect belonging to Melayo-Polynesian groups. Religionwise most of them are Protestants. It has been the famous spice-island, where there is an excellent harbour. They are also interested in establishing a Republic Maluku Selatan and have been critical of the central government.There was a serious riot in January 1999 between Christians and the Muslim population in Ambon. The riots started after three Mosques and three Churches were torched on the occasion of Id-ul-Fitr. Over 88 (eighty-eight) homes were burnt and many were set on fire. *Guardian* (London), reported that 24 Christians were massacred in the Church by the Muslim mobs on 12 August 1999 and equally some Muslims were also killed. A spokesman for Ambon's Al-Fatah mosque confirmed that at least 60 Muslims were killed and 50 others were wounded. The situation became so serious that there has been exodus of thirty thousand people from Ambon to other areas and the communal life remains disturbed. Radical Muslims are preaching that there should be a Jehad to take revenge and the conflict remains unresolved.

Lastly, we have to examine the problems in Irian Jaya where the separatist movement is strong. The indigenous people of that island, the Melanesians integration into the national mainstream is still a distant dream. Their voice is articulated by the Free Papua Movement (OPM), since 1960 and they have been waging a low level guerilla war. Situated on the border of Papua New Guinea and far away from Jakarta, this area has been very sensitive and vulnerable.

Needless to say that the government policy of unity in diversity needs infusion of new spirits to make intra-ethnic and inter-communal life harmonious. The spirit of tolerance and accommodation needs to be enforced and growth of all sorts of fundamentalist ideas curbed. There is a need to spread the gospel of "live and let live". No community should be given an impression that a "big fish will eat smaller ones". Indonesia is very rich in natural resources. It has gold mines and great reservoir of oil. It has also got timber, rubber, coffee, sugar, copper besides a huge manpower. For its prosperity, it simply needs a good governance, political stability and efficient economic management. As it is a mosaic of different culture and ethnic groups, Indonesia is naturally endowed to articulate the voice of Asia at the global level.

As far as political system of the country is concerned, the 1945 constitution is enforced, but there has been no amendments. There has been lot of transformations in the country at the social and political level, and amendments are needed to cope with the challenges. Islam has to be given due importance in the polity because that is the religion of the overwhelming majority, but other religions cannot be bulldozed. They have tolerated Hinduism and Christianity for long and they have evolved a distinct Indonesian culture. Their social and religious organizations are formidable and there is a need to evolve a system in which they feel secure and prosperous. As the low profile of Indonesia helped ASEAN to grow, so the low profile of the Javanese can help the trends towards national integration.

REFERENCES

1. For understanding Indonesian society and politics, see Douglas E. Ramage, *Politics in Indonesia : Democracy, Islam and the Ideology of*

Tolerance, London, Routledge, 1995 and Lee Khoon Choy, *A Fragile Nation: The Indonesian Crisis*, Singapore, World Scientific Publishing Co., 1999 and Clifford Geertz, *The Religion of Java*, New York, The Free Press, 1960.

2. For detailed analysis of this aspect see Ganganath Jha, *Ethnic Politics in Southeast Asia and Quest for Identity*, New Delhi, NBO, 1998, pp. 42-67, and also see Jill Joliffe, *East Timor: Nationalism and Colonialism*, St Lucia, Queensland, 1978.
3. J.A.C. Mackie, *Konfrontasi: The Indonesia-Malaysia Dispute, 1963-66*, Kuala Lumpur, 1974, pp. 75-76.
4. Amnesty International, *Indonesia: Shock Therapy, Restoring Order in Aceh, 1989-1993*, London 1993, pp. 1-25, and also see Baulch Emma, "The Human Rights Debate", *Inside Indonesia*, Jakarta, 1992, No. 32, pp. 5-15.
5. For a comprehensive understanding, see Carmel Budiardjo & Soi Liong Liem, *West Papua: The Obliteration of a People*, London, 1988 and Ralph R. Premdas, "The Organisasi Papua Merdeka in Irian Jaya", *Asian Survey*, Berkeley Calif, Vol. 25, No. 10, October 1985, pp. 1055-74.
6. *The Times of India*, New Delhi, 28 May 2000.
7. Harja W. Bachtiar, *The Indonesian Nation: Some Problems of Integration and Disintegration*, Singapore, ISEAS, 1976, pp. 28-33.
8. Indonesia (1997), *An Official Handbook*, Jakarta, Department of Information, pp. 37-40.
9. *Jakarta Post*, 14th May 1998 and 29 July 2000.
10. *The Times of India*, 20 February 1998 and *Bangkok Post* 20 & 21 February 1998.
11. *News From Indonesia*, Embassy of the Republic of Indonesia, New Delhi, January 2001, p.16.
12. Juwono Sudarsono, "The Challenges to Indonesia's Unity", *Indonesia: 50 years*, Embassy of the Republic of Indonesia, New Delhi, 1995, p. 51.
13. Haryati Soebadio, ed., *Dynamics of Indonesian History*, Amstardam, North Holland Publishing Company, 1978, preface.
14. Soewartoyo, "Internal Migration between Java—Bali and Eastern Indonesia", *Indonesia Quarterly*, Vol. 24, No. 3, 1996.
15. Joan Hardjono, "Transmigration: Looking to the Future", *Bulletin of Indonesian Economic Studies*, Vol. 22, No. 2, August 1986, p. 29.
16. Michael Rechardson, "Making Irian Jaya Pay its Way", *Far Eastern Economic Review*, 13 June 1975, p.15.
17. Manoj Joshi, "Aceh in Indonesia is Kashmir to India", *The Times of India*, 12 January 2001.
18. Rawdon Dalrymple, "Indonesia and the IMF", *Australian Journal of International Affairs*, Vol. 52, No. 3, Deaklin, November 1998, p. 234.
19. *Ibid.*, pp. 234-35.
20. *Ibid.*, p. 236.

21. Leekhoon Choy, *A Fragile Nation: The Indonesian Crisis,* Singapore, 1999, preface.
22. *Ibid.*, pp. 348-64.
23. *Asiaweek*, 7 July 2000, p. 29.
24. *Ibid.*, p. 34.
25. Harvey Stockwin, "Wahid: New Indonesian President", *The Times of India*, 21 October 1999 and P.S. Suryanarayana, Wahid Talks tough on Aceh, *The Hindu*, 5 December 1999.
26. General Edi Sudradjat, *The Dual Function of the Indonesian Armed Forces*, Indonesia, New Delhi, Embassy of the Republic of Indonesia, 1995, p. 32, and also see Nrugroho Notosusanto, The National Struggle and the Armed Forces in Indonesia, Jakarta, Department of Defence and Security, Jakarta, 1975.
27. Text of the 1945 Constitution and Article 29.
28. For details, see Zuhri, K.H. Saiffuddin, *The History of Islamic Resurgence and Development in Indonesia*, Bandung, 1979.
29. For better analysis of this aspect, see, Noer Deliar, *The Modernist Muslim Movement in Indonesia, 1900-1942*, Kuala Lumpur, 1973.
30. Adam Schwartz, *A Nation in Waiting; Indonesia in the 1990s*, Melbourne, 1994, p. 179.
31. Mutalib Hussein, *Islam and Ethnicity in Malay Politics*, Singapore, ISEAS, 1990, pp. 9-10.
32. Hassan Laggulung, "Philosophy of Islamic Education: The Indonesian and Malaysian Experiences", in Mutalib Hussain, ed. *Fazar Islam*, Vol. 2, Singapore, 1989, pp. 71-72.
33. Anwar Zainah, *Islamic Revivalism in Malaysia*, Petaling Jaya, Pelanduk, 1987, p. 74.
34. Nawaz B. Mody, *Indonesia Under Suharto*, New Delhi, 1987, p. 152.
35. For better understanding of this aspect, see Lik Arifin Mansurnoor, *Islam in an Indonesian World: Ulama of Madura*, Yogyakarta, Gadjah Mada University Press, 1990.

18

Fight Against Terror in Indonesia

A new history of terror and bloodshed began in Indonesia after the fanatics of *Jemaah Islamiyah* (JI) bombed tourist resorts at Bali on 12 October 2002. The bombing of Kuta, Renon and Manado in Bali shook the international community and they were alarmed. The government of Indonesia recovering from the economic crisis and the problem of political instabilities (1998-2002), faced with a greater threat of Islamic terrorism. Bali blast caused the death of 190 and injuries to more than 300 people. Press statement accepted the death of 182 and injuries to 132 persons.[1] *The Times of India* reported the death of 187 and injuries to 300. Most of the victims were foreigners from Australia, Britain, France, Germany and Sweden. Almost half of them were from Australia but the other half were from Britain (30), France, Germany, Sweden and Indonesia.

Bali is regarded as a paradise on earth and world's most popular tourist destination. It attracts holiday makers, jet setters and backpackers at global level. October bombing turned the throbbing strip of bars and discotheques into a scene of bloody carnage. There were two explosions at Kuta—a small one in the Paddy's discotheque—followed by a far more powerful one outside Sari. Another bomb went off 50 meters from the US consulate in Sanur, also a tourist spot.[2]

President Megawati Sukarnoputri felt traumatised and instantly flew to Bali to express her condolences. She said that Bali blasts were a warning that terrorism was a threat to national security. She inspected the site of the bombing and spoke in general terms about how terrorism violates the fundamental values of all religions. She, however, was not clear on how she and her government would tackle terrorism in Indonesia. Indonesian forces were instructed to beef up security around oil and gas installations particularly operated by foreign multinationals like Exxon Mobil, for fear of further terrorist attacks. Indonesian press statement on 13 October expressed condolences and deep sympathy to the bereaved families by reiterating that "Such a brutal and inhuman acts of violence contravenes laws, religious teachings and moral standards of Indonesian people".

British Prime Minister Tony Blair expressed his horrors and Australian Prime Minister, John Howard while expressing his frustration that Jakarta was the weakest link in the battle against Islamic militants, urged Indonesia to crack down on terrorists. Howard felt great concern about the carnage wherein hundreds of Australian tourists died. This was bound to have repercussions on Australian public opinion and thus Howard while expressing his anguish went a step further by threatening pre-emptive strikes against any country in the region, which Canberra saw as a base for an actual or potential terrorist attack. He defiantly asserted that Australia had the right to pre-emptive action.

The United States was equally concerned at the developments in Indonesia. It had been warning the Indonesian government in the past that a group linked to Al Qaida was planning to kill Americans and other Westerners but it was not given much attention. Ralph Boyce, the American ambassador in Jakarta had himself conveyed this information to top officials. The US had come to know about the operation through Omar al-Faruq, linked to terrorist group in Indonesia. It had been made clear that the attack would not necessarily have on official American site as its target, but also those areas, which attract American civilians. Ralph Boyce had spoken to Megawati "to wrap up the terrorist cells, block it and demonstrate that you are serious about eliminating the threat against us". Indeed the US signalled that Indonesia was a terrorist heaven after the carnage in Bali and ordered 350 Americans connected with the US Embassy—about 100 diplomats—to leave the country.[3]

The US denounced bombing by calling it a "despicable act of terror". It believed that Osama bin Laden's Al Qaida network was trying to establish a foothold in the world's most populous Muslim nation. Although none of the terrorist groups in Indonesia claimed responsibility for the bombing, but it was clear that the terrorists linked to Al Qaida had planned and executed the heineous crime at Kuta. The *Jemaah Islamiyah* is indeed responsible for the bombing. The Indonesian police for investigations summoned Abu Bakar

Bashir, projected main suspect of the crime. Bashir was also summoned under an article in the criminal code on treason, which is theoretically punishable by death.[4] But his lawyers, Mahendradatta and Ahmad Khalid believed that summons against Bashir were not justified. Mahendradatta said. " We can only say that we are sad that the government has succumbed to international pressure to arrest *ustadz* (the teacher)."

The US and Australia subsequently circulated a report blaming *Jemaah Islamiyah* for deadly bombings and pleaded with the United Nations to declare *Jemaah Islamiyah,* a terrorist group. The US State Department added the group to its own list of terror groups on 23 October 2002. It was declared that it would be a crime to contribute funds to *Jemaah Islamiyah.* The members of this terrorist group were debarred from entering the US. Both countries hoped that a UN Declaration would help them launch an international campaign to isolate it and cut its financial support. Singapore and Japan expressed solidarity with the Americans in approving the proposed declaration to support the campaign against terrorism in the region.

The UN Security Council on 14 October strongly condemned the attacks on Bali and urged the international community to work together and help Indonesia see that justice was done and the perpetrators punished swiftly. Reaffirming the need to combat terrorism in accordance with resolution 1373 (2001), the council unanimously adopted resolution 1438 which essentially calls for the Indonesian government to allow other countries to come and investigate the attack and combat terror by all means.

The intelligence document made available through CIA, details a confession made by Omar Faruq, regarded as bin Laden's envoy in Southeast Asia, who was arrested in Indonesia in June, and handed over to CIA subsequently. It revealed that Abu Bakar Bashir the spiritual leader of *Jemaah Islamiyah,* received $74,000 from bin Laden's account.[5] This amount was for purchase of explosives to be distributed to Islamist groups. Bashir was questioned for terrorism in relation to a series of bombing of Christian Churches, treason for plotting the assassination of Indonesian President, immigration offences and destruction of property. Faruq revealed a series of plots to kill Westerners, Indonesians and Israelis.

Indonesian police started looking for the culprits of the Bali bombing and came to know that Imam Samudra was the mastermind of the blast. He along with two of his body guards—

Rauf and Yudi—were arrested. Indonesian Police Chief, Dai Bachtiar said that Samudra having six aliases, was a leading member of the *Jemaah Islamiyah.* He chaired meetings to plan the October 12 night-club terror bombing which killed 190 people, identified the targets and gave the order to carry it out. It was after the arrest of Samudra that the name of another terrorist came into the picture. Hambali, an Indonesian whose real name is Ridnan Isamuddin, is the chief of operations group of JI and is also believed to be a leading member of Osama bin Laden's *Al Qaida.* He has escaped to Pakistan, but is being wanted by five countries in Southeast Asia. He has been linked with terror operations in different countries of Southeast Asia. It is indeed very difficult to arrest the terrorists because they have meticulous network to escape. If Imam Samudra was arrested, credit must be given to a mobile phone technology operated by joint investigation team of Australian and other foreign agencies. Indonesian police arrested him aboard a bus that was about to cross the Sunda Straits by ferry to Sumatra.

It was only after Bali bloodshed that Indonesian government accepted possible link between local militants and *Al Qaida.* The administration used to deny any links of the terror groups with *Al Qaida* in the past and when Lee Kuan Yew said that Indonesia is a favourite ground of *Al Qaida* after September 9/11, there were hostile reactions in Indonesia. Many top officials expressed their disagreement with the observations of Lee Kuan Yew and Singapore was projected unfriendly. When an Indonesian General Hendropriyono said that *Al Qaida* agents were present in Indonesia, it was taken as a false information. Some leaders even demanded that Hendropriyono be dismissed from the services. When Paul Wolfowitz, Deputy Secretary of Defence in Washington said that after Afghanistan, the US target will be South Philippines, Malaysia and Indonesia, there were widespread reactions. The ideologues of radical Islam were angry with the observations of Wolfowitch. Their reaction was that Western "infidels" have conspired to tarnish Islam's image. Any demand to fight terrorism was criticised and projected as anti-Islamic. However, when Abu Bakar Bashir and Imam Samudra were arrested, it was clear that they had definite links with *Al Qaida.* The terrorist organisations have made an effort to divest regional reactions after Bali outrage by saying that the CIA is responsible for the blast because this could force the administration to crack down on Islamic groups.[6] There are many people who disagree with such rhetorics but at the same time there are some who attach importance to such observations.

The influence of Islamic groups are spreading and they are not neglected. Indeed they are increasingly used by politicians and ambitious leaders to promote their interests in power politics. They know very well that the terrorists propagate militant *Jehad* for the establishment of a theocratic state. They also know that Islamic radicals are striving for implementing *Shariat* laws against the existing constitution (1945) and drop *Panchasila* as the guiding principles of the state, yet they are trying to appease them to extract political advantages. The number of Islamic radicals may be small but their views are properly highlighted in the recent past because there are many who believe that Islamic terrorists are fighting for dignity of the Islamic people and for their resurgence. The fight against Western supremacy is their fundamental right, and the US and the Western world must be taught a lesson for their support to the zews against Arab Muslims. The US policy towards *Al Qaida,* Taliban and Saddam Hussain are projected as a threat directed against the Islamic World. The terrorists have supporters in the administration. Vice President, Hamzah Haz has openly supported radicals like Abu Bakar Bashir of JI and Jafar Umar Thalib of Laskar *Jehad* (LJ). He has been visiting pesantren (boarding schools) run by JI and LJ and delivering lectures to provide them support and legitimacy.[7]

Indonesian politicians are generally reluctant to publicly criticise the ideology and strategies of radical Islam. They do not want to be seen as un-Islamic as their eyes are fixed at coming general elections in 2004. They advocate that Islam is the only thing left in Indonesia to feel proud of. Islamic groups on the other hand, are trying to project Islamic religion as the most important element of Indonesian nationalism. They argue that if there is proper assertion of Islam, Indonesia will be the unquestioned leader of the Malay world. Sukarno had indeed envisioned the leadership role of Indonesia in the Malay world but his policies were disowned by his successors. Now those ideas are being resurrected in the framework of radical Islam. There are no leaders now to counter the ideology of terrorists, and presently most of the political leaders are grooming pressure groups based on religion to promote their electoral prospects.

This is not to suggest that the administration is not doing anything to cope with the threat of terrorism. When the trade towers had been bombed in New York, President Megawati had personally visited the US to express her concern and solidarity. She expressed co-operation in establishing an international front to tackle terrorism. Indonesia along with other ASEAN partners held a meeting with the US in New York to build a consensus to combat terrorism. Accordingly the partners agreed on three points of co-operation—the exchange of intelligence information, improvement of potential to deal with the question of terrorism and also to evolve mechanism against terrorist attacks.[8] Thai Prime Minister Thaksin Sinawatra later visited Indonesia and talked of concerted efforts to battle terrorism, including exchange of intelligence.[9] Hasan Wirajuda, Indonesian Minister of Foreign Affairs, spoke that the administration was ready to round up the terrorists and bring them to justice. He agreed to destroy their cells and their networks and deny them their ill-gotten financial and other resources. Let us see that there are no safe heavens anywhere for any of them.[10] Indonesia introduced anti-terrorism bill on 3 October 2002 which defines terrorism as an illegal act carried out intentionally that endangers people and their belongings or sparks widespread destruction, fear or causes death. Terrorism, therefore, can be directed to damage a range of targets, including national assets, the environment, state secrets, culture, education, the economy, technology and industry. [11]

The bill threatens terrorists with a minimum three years in jail and a maximum sentence of death. Capital punishment will also be imposed on terrorists who commit attacks using airplanes, or those who misuse chemical, biological or nuclear materials. Those who have the intention to carry out such attacks could be sentenced to a maximum of 15 years in jail.

Anyone who smuggles in and out of Indonesia or manufactures, receives, hides or uses weapons, ammunition or explosives with the intention to terrorise others will also face death. A company convicted of organising a terrorist act will be fined one trillion Rupiah (US $111 million) and will be dissolved and declared a banned organisation. The bill also says that investigators, prosecutors and judges can order banks to block and disclose accounts and other properties of suspected terrorists. While investigating terrorism, the bill stipulated that bank secrecy laws do not count.[12] These measures complimented the law about money laundering and ratification of the International Convention on the Suppression of Financing for terrorism, the convention against Trans-national crime and the convention on the Suppression of Terrorist Bombings ratified by the President of Indonesia in April 2002.

After the Bali blast, the government took vigorous steps to empower the police and security authorities to act more decisively to thwart terrorist activities. The President issued a Regulation on the eradication of terrorism and Presidential Instruction mandating the co-ordinating minister for political and security affairs to co-ordinate measures in combating terrorism, and another Presidential Institution giving the head of the National Security Agency the authority to co-ordinate all intelligence activities.[13]

Although various steps have been taken and mechanisms evolved to fight against terrorism, it is not regarded sufficient. The biggest problem with the present system in Indonesia is that whenever they pass any resolution, it is viewed as dictated either by the World Bank, IMF or the United States. In case of fight against terrorism also, the impression generated is that it is done with a view to appease the United States. The political leaders and the national media have failed to project the losses incurred due to terrorist activities. After the bomb blast in Bali, the country is projected as a failed state and the confidence of the foreign investors are losing.

It is understood that the cost of terrorist attacks are greater than September 11 attacks in the US (US $10 billion). Michael Schuman says that psychological shock waves surging outward from Kuta Beach are bound to intersect with the nation's fragile social and political ecosystem in unpredictable ways, testing the allegiances and resilience of an ineffective government, and dealing a body blow to a sputtering economy that has yet to fully recover from Asia's 1997 economic crisis. The bomb blast in Bali hurts a situation that is already bad.[14]

The business community has to cope with random violence. A bomb had earlier exploded in the building housing the Jakarta Stock Exchange, killing 15 people. But Bali blast is more serious. In the week following that blast, the US athletic gear giant Nike stopped ordering sneakers and thus a factory on the outskirts of Jakarta was closed. The country's $5 billion tourism industry—contributing three per cent of GDP—was devastated. The Mandarin Oriental Hostel in Jakarta saw 700 room cancellations. Again a High School soccer tournament scheduled to take place in Jakarta was moved to Malaysia. Tourism was affected adversely so much so that 12 million Indonesians felt jobless. Again foreign direct investment (FDI) came down because the investors felt hostile environment in Indonesia. They are relocating their factories in China and Vietnam. They are finding operational risks in oil and gas sectors also. Caltex Pacific Indonesia has been forced to turn over management of an oilfield in Sumatra and they are unhappy with social unrest, militant unions and rapacious local business. Many foreign companies have fled from the mining industries and new explorations have stopped.[15]

The country is facing a crisis and Al Qaida network is spreading. Driven by the ideal of a universal *Jehad*, it has been able to politicise, radicalise and mobilise Muslims. *Jemaah Islamiyah*, *Abu Sayyaff* and Moro Islamic Liberation Front (MILF) have been supported to mobilise Muslim opinion in Southeast Asia. Telephone intercepts indicated that in early 1999 at the request of *Al Qaida*'s head of external operations, Abu Zubaida, the MILF opened special camps for training foreign recruits. These camps were located in Abu Baker complex, which was later overrun by the Philippine military.[16] Simultaneously Lashkar Jundullah established a facility in Poso in Sulawesi. JI established its cells in Singapore and Malaysia for internal subversion and the downfall of Taliban regime in Afghanistan did not alter the situation in Southeast Asia. *Al Qaida* operates in a framework that is deceptive. In addition to despatching its operatives to target countries, it provides experts, training and resources to other Islamist political and military organisations to advance a common goal. It has influenced JI, a regional organisation with overground and underground networks extending from Southern Thailand to Australia.[17] Other Southeast Asian Organisations that *Al Qaida* has influenced are Kumpulan Mujahidin Malaysia, Laskar Jundullah Indonesia, and MILF. When JI wanted to destroy the US, British, Australian and Israeli diplomatic targets in Singapore, *Al Qaida* despatched four Afghan trained Arab suicide bombers to Southeast Asia. Striving for establishing Darulah Islamiah Raya, comprising Malaysia, Singapore, Brunei, Indonesia and Mindanao, Islamic ideologies are spreading in the Malay world against the existing order.[18]

Regarding Islamic radicals, James Hookway of Far Eastern Economic Review reported that for any new operation they attach emphasis on new converts to Islam, who are prepared to kill and die for their new found faith.[19] The phenomenon of tapping converts is strategically conceived. Initially Abu Sayyaf group in the Philippines was encouraged to enagage new converts in terrorist activities, but now JI and others have picked up that methodology. Briton Richard Reid tried to blow up a US airliner flying from Paris by smuggling explosives aboard in the soles of his running shoes. In the US, Jose Padilla of Chicago tried to procure materials for constructing a radiation for a bomb. Ramzi Yousef credited to bomb World Trade Centre, had earlier come to Manila to assassinate Pope John Paul II. *Al Qaida* believes that these converts are ideal terrorists who prove more dangerous than established Muslim guerrilla groups. The new converts are often more zealous and eager to prove themselves worthy of their new faith.[20]

There is a sizeable section of population of Arab Origin, known as Hadrami, which has been supporting the rise of radical Islam in Indonesia. Their population is estimated at 5 million and they have maintained connections with the Arab World.[21] They are respected in Indonesia, because it is understood that they introduced Islam in that archipelago. They have been sending their children to study in the Arab World and therefore their knowledge of Islamic ideology and ethos are better than others. Abu Bakar Bashir is a Hadrami and his role in growing radicalisation of Islamic politics in Indonesia has been enormous. Hadrami radicals and moderates calls for the adoption of *Shariat* laws for governance of the country. Hadrami have Al Irsyad organisation which has been funding the establishment of several schools and colleges and their existence in Solo, Central Sulawesi and Maluku have attracted headlines, because some of the militants interrogated in recent years are the products of these schools and colleges. Al Irsyad operates 140 missions and several hospitals nation-wide and their positive role in the social life of the country are also significant. However problem arises because some of the Hadrami elites consider it as their duty to correct Indonesia's syncretic brand of Islam.[22] They have traditionally tended to be more conservative than their counterparts in Indonesia and indeed holier than Santri and Abangans in Java. Habib Abdul Rahman Al Habsyi, a noted Hadrami cleric, has been drawing large number of young students to classes in a mosque in Jakarta and sending hundreds to Yemen every year to study in religious schools. Airline Yemenia started twice weekly flights linking Sanaa and Jakarta directly to facilitate the movement of the people in 2002.

Indonesian Muslims are taught Salafism, a school of Islam that preaches Puritanism. Alwi Shihab, a Hadrami and former foreign minister, however says that an Islamic education in Yemen should not be equated with militancy. He says that there are more fundamentalist schools in Saudi Arabia and Egypt supporting Puritanism in Islam.[23] Radical Islam is thus getting an indigenous touch and there is absence of clear consensus on how to tackle them.

Senior leaders are unable to articulate the view that extremism is a serious threat to the future of democracy and pluralism in the country and that the existence of moderate Islam are in tune with the Malay ethos. If the clerics in Solo display the sign "No prestige without *Jehad*", or if they echo the seven words of Abu Bakar, "I am a Muslim. They are infidels", or if they promote the sale of Osama T. shirt, it should be tackled at the ideological and religious levels. We are citizens of a civilised world and should not preach bloodshed deliberately against it. The founding fathers of Indonesian constitution promoted Bhinnekka Tungul Ekka (Unity is Diversity) and unity of the nation is related with maintaining diversity of the archipelago. If *Shariat* laws are to be adopted, it is for the elected representatives to decide, and if they have to offer *Namaz* (Prayer) five times a day or observe a code of conduct, they are educated and civilised enough to decide their course of action. No sect, race or groups have any right to impose their will on fellow citizens, and thus terror groups should understand the limitations of their operations. National leaders should articulate the issues of national development and promote integrationist ideas.

Amien Rais, Chairman of the Indonesian People's Assembly, has been an influential leader for propagating moderate Islam in Indonesia. According to him, "all Muslims have to respect the invaluable existence of human beings. *Al Quran* says that when a soul happens to be pure and clean, and has never caused any earthly corruption, whoever kills the innocent soul without any reason has committed a grave crime against humanity, as if he has killed all human kind. But whoever saves a soul has done a noble act, as if he has saved the human kind".[24]

Amien Rais further stated that "here and there, now and then, there are some offensive, xenophobic statements made by Muslim teachers in the mosque. But, I can assure you that they are very small, insignificant pockets. When Taliban regime collapsed after the American attack, all people in my country were happy and excited. Why? Because to us, Taliban is a very bad advertisement for Islam. It is anti-Islamic. Islam does not prohibit a women to be educated. Islam does not order women to stay in the houses, covering all the body except the two eyes. Islam does not teach us to grow our beard whereby the beard becomes a symbol of religiosity and piety. The wonderful, noble teachings of the Prophet were reduced absurdly by the Taliban".[25]

The bloodshed in Bali has tarnished external image of Indonesia. The national moral movement—a forum of religious leaders and public figures—issued a statement on 12 November 2002 expressing their support to the government to fight against terrorism. They emphasised that no religion recommends the use of violence and the statement was signed by Hasyim Muzadi, (Chairman, Nahdlatul *Ulama*), Syafi Ma'arif (Chairman, Muhammadiyah), Cardinal Darmaatmadja (Chairman, Indonesian Bishop's Council), Roeslan Abdulgani (Freedom fighter), and Nurcholish Madjid (Muslim Intellectual). The government observed November 15 as a National day of Silence and Prayer for the Victims of Bali blast. Thousands of Balinese Hindus performed a ritual cleansing at the site of the blast and at the sea to release the souls of victims and plead for the blessings of heaven to bring spiritual and economic recovery.[26] The pictures of the victims were placed at the bomb site surrounded by incense. This was attended by ministers, ambassadors, the families of the victims and thousands of Balinese.

The national leaders by and large do not approve the actions of radical Islam advertently but they are neither vocal against them. So their silence and sophisticated opposition are considered support for the terrorist groups inadvertently. President Megawati is more careful in making statements against them because of her personal experiences. Although her party had secured the largest number of seats in the DPR, she could not be elected the President in 1999 on the basis of her genealogy. It is known that she had a Hindu mother and if she becomes aggressive against radical Muslims in her country, she will be projected anti-Muslim once again. It will be very difficult for her to come back to power. But as a Javanese, she is determined to fight against terrorism slowly and effectively. She is in search of a new vision and strategy for reforms and this will take care of various problems in the country.

Although *Al Qaida* and JI have their foothold and their followers claim allegiance of many, it is a established fact that moderates are in majority. Indonesia for centuries have been influenced by world's major religious systems, namely Hinduism, Buddhism, Islam, Christianity and Confucianism. Indonesian Islam has engaged with other faiths, adapting and adopting the cultural traditions of diverse people.[27] Islamic expression is very different in Indonesia compared to puritanical brand that has been nurtured in the Arab world. It has been moderate, tolerant and progressive for centuries. Karim Raslan has explained that this modernisation is because of geography and history. Being closer to Indian subcontinent geographically and located en route Lombok, Malacca and Sunda Straits—it tended to remain syncretic. Historically, Islam's spread in Indonesia was through peaceful means, by Arab and Indian traders and preachers. It spread peacefully and there was no Jehad for conversions. Indonesia emerged as a unique centre of Islam when one could find the amalgam of the essence of major religions of the world. Indonesian Islam also contributed new chapters in the existing philosophy of Islam, the concept of ijtihad—the spirit of questioning, self criticism and renewal—that placed Islam at the vanguard of science, technology and civil society.[28] Ijtihad is ignored in the Arab world but it is an important subject of understanding in Indonesia. Santri and Abangans are devout and conversant with the *Koran*, familiar with classical Islamic works and trained in fiqh (Islamic jurisprudence). They have the confidence to debate and confront their own ultra-conservative co-religionists on anything from Jehad to women's rights.[29] These Muslims are humble and compassionate and they know what is decent and what is rubbish and brutish.

To conclude, it may be observed that although the number of Islamic radicals have increased and terror groups activated, the moderate elements have potentials to promote resilience, pluralism and democracy. They know their history and realities of social life. They draw inspirations from the heroes of the Srivijayan, Majapahit and colonial periods. Though they went to battlegrounds intermittently in the past, it was never for forcible conversions. There had been widespread bloodshed in Indonesia during 1965-69 to contain communism, but it was motivated politically. Some observers projected this phenomenon as *Jehad* but this had nothing to do with the spread of Islamic religion. Anti-communist crusades simply strengthened the foundations of military rule under the stewardship of General Suharto. This *Jehad* simply proved retrogressive, the manifestations of which became transparent in due course. Indonesia does not need bloodshed but peace, resilience and good governance to establish themselves as a secular model amongst the Islamic world. It has to reflect the essence of Malay culture in order to remain united and strong.

REFERENCES

1. Press statement issued in Jakarta, 13 October 2002.
2. *The Times of India*, 14 October 2002.
3. *Ibid.*, 17 October 2002.
4. *Ibid.*, 18 October 2002.
5. *Ibid.*, 22 October 2002.
6. Ulil Abshar-Abdalla, "Silent Witness", *Time*, 28 October 2002, p. 45.
7. Andrew Marshal, "The Rage Culture", *Time*, 28 October 2002, pp. 52-57.
8. *Antara in News from Indonesia*, Embassy of the Republic of Indonesia, New Delhi, No. 24, December 2001, p. 5
9. *The Jakarta Post in News from Indonesia*, January 2002, p. 5.
10. *Ibid.*, No. 9, September 2002, p. 3.
11. *The Jakarta Post*, 3 October 2002 and 7 October 2002.
12. *Ibid.*
13. Yusril Ihza Mahendra, "Shared Responsibility in Combating Terrorism: Post-Bali Tragedy", *News from Indonesia*, November 2002, No. 11, pp. 26-27 .
14. Michael Schuman, "A Failed State", *Time*, 28 October 2002, p. 46.
15. *Ibid.*, pp. 46-50
16. Rohan Gunaratna. "Al Qaida in the Asia-Pacific", *IIAS Newsletter*, Leiden, 14 June 2002, p. 4.
17. *Ibid.*
18. *Ibid.*
19. James Hookway, "How a Terrorist Proves his faith", *Far Eastern Economic Review*, 14 November 2002, pp. 14-15.
20. *Ibid.*
21. Dini Djalal, "Where Terror is Taught", *Ibid.*, p. 18.
22. *Ibid.*
23. *Ibid.*, p. 19.
24. Amien Rais, "The War Against Terrorism in Indonesia", *IIAS Newsletter*, No. 28, 20 March 2002, p. 1.
25. *Ibid.*, p. 3.
26. *The Jakarta Post*, 16 November 2002.
27. Karim Raslan, " The Moderate Majority", *Time*, 28 October 2002, p. 57
28. *Ibid.*
29. *Ibid.*

19

Indian Diaspora in South and Southeast Asia

The Encyclopedia of Social Sciences defines that "diaspora is a Greek term for a nation separated from its own state or territory and dispersed among other nations but preserving its national culture". In the idea of dispersal and fragmentation and in much of the presumed relationship between the diasporic community and the country (motherland), which they left, the possibility of return remains. This may be true in the context of Jews but the possibility of return is a complex issue in the context of Indian diaspora in South and Southeast Asia.

Indian diaspora is spread in different parts of the world and its number is around 20 million. It is the third largest in the world after the British and the Chinese diaspora. Such persons are prosperous in the US, Mauritius, Singapore and Thailand but struggling very hard in Myanmar, Fiji, Malaysia and Sri Lanka.

Indian diaspora became important for India when the policy of command economy was replaced by market economy. India became sensitive about the challenges of the new world order and evolved the policy of "Look East" to promote strategic and economic ties with Asia-Pacific. In that endeavour, it was found that Indian diaspora had immense potential to support Indian contacts with East Asian neighbours. As the Chinese diaspora greatly contributed to the development of new economic zones in China, so it can be similarly expected from the Indian diaspora if the necessary infrastructure is evolved. Indian diaspora in the ASEAN region (a region of the "Association of South East Asian Nations") is resourceful and capable of facilitating India's connections with the countries of their adoption.

Understanding Indian Diaspora

Indians have gone overseas as travellers, labourers and businessmen in the past, but in the wake of partition of the country in 1947, millions went from one part of the subcontinent to another. There was exodus of Indian Muslims to Pakistan, where they are known a Mohajirs. Despite having a common religion,.their integration with the native population remains a distant dream. There was exodus of Hindus from Pakistan to India and they also faced problems in adjusting with the new environment. India, which emerged as a secular state and stood against the "Two-Nation Theory" provided religious freedom to all its citizens and tried to rehabilitate displaced persons without discriminating against their ethnicity and religious affiliations. All those who migrated from India to settle elsewhere were projected as its diaspora.

Hindus who migrated from Pakistan to India and Muslims who migrated from India to Pakistan are nostalgic about their ethnicity and place of origin. Both of them are in the category of diaspora and it is a sensitive matter to project them whether they are Pakistani diaspora or Indian.

Dilemmas about Diaspora

There are outstanding issues and dilemmas about the diasporic community in the South Asian context. For instance, East Bengal became Pakistan after independence, and it emerged, as a new nation of Bangladesh in 1971. The people of Bangladesh are known as Bangladeshis but Bengalis in general parlance. They have migrated to Assam and other parts of India in recent years. It is debatable to project them Indian diaspora, but Bengalis are an essential part of Indian civilization. There has been exodus of Kashmiri Pandits from the Kashmir valley. They have been dispossessed of their properties and they are struggling for their shelter. Can they be projected as a diasporic community even if they inhabit the same country?

There are groups of Punjabis, Sikhs and Gujaratis who have migrated in different directions of the world more than once. Fijians of Indian origin have migrated to Australia and New Zealand after Lt. Col. Sitiveni Rabuka staged a coup d'etat in 1987. Sindh is an important part of Pakistan and Sindhis are proud of claiming their

Indianess outside. A large number of Indian diaspora in the region have emigrated from one country to another and they have forgotten their native language also. For instance an Indo-Fejian emigrating to Australia to Canada tend to forget their indigenous cultural touch. The section of Indian diaspora, which is "twice migrant" have lost touch with India. For the host country, they may be projected as Indians, but they are fragmented and have very little to share especially with those groups, who are "twice migrant" from two or three countries respectively.

They do not speak the same language, or visit the same temple and hardly intermarry. As a supporter of "Unity in diversity", India may project them as Indian diaspora, but it is difficult to categorise them as an India-centric homogenous group.

Diaspora Affluence

The Indian diaspora is affluent not only in the US, Mauritius and the Caribbean, but they are also influential in Singapore, Thailand and the Philippines. There are two types of diaspora in the ASEAN region of which one is affluent and another is striving to be affluent. They need interaction with the motherland for business, trade and religious purposes. It is also felt that if India has to play a constructive role at the international level, the feedback of the diasporic community and their support is solicited. Indian diaspora is playing an important role in the ASEAN economy and they are trusted by the local leaders. It was the Indian diaspora with whose mediation various indigenous groups in Southeast Asian region were supporting the Indian National Army (INA) of Netaji Subhas Chandra Bose. They had kept affiliation with Indian National Congress and supported the anti-colonial struggle. However when India became independent and pursued a non-alignment policy, it was not within their framework to support the diasporic community more openly. Its socialistic drives and nationalization policies deterred the investors, but the situation started changing in the post-liberalisation era. The influence of the diaspora on Indian decision-making could not be ignored and overseas Indians were ready to reciprocate. The Indian diaspora are applauded for developments in India for science, technology, human resources, and for extending support to bring together business network to forge closer linkages with the country of their adoption.

Diaspora Policy in the Past

India had been very circumspect regarding its policies towards its diaspora in South and Southeast Asia. From Prime Minister Jawaharlal Nehru to Prime Minister Rajiv Gandhi, the advice to Indian diaspora was to integrate in the mainstream of national life of the countries of their adoption. It could not exercise its diplomatic influence to deter democratic Burma under U Nu from its anti-Indian crusades. The Citizenship Act (1948) was tailor-made to deprive Indians of Burmese citizenship. Naturally when General Ne Win usurped power in 1962 and nationalized the properties of Indians, India was unable to restrain military rulers. There was turmoil and unrest in Bangladesh and Pakistan, but the Indian Government viewed these developments as too sensitive to express its opinion. The political developments in Burma had wide-ranging repercussions. Indians, who were affluent in business and trade, were evicted and subsequently Burma turned from a rich to a poor country of Southeast Asia.

If Burma was compelled to embrace friendship with the Chinese, it was because of its poor economic situation. The Chinese have filled up the vacuum created after the eviction of Indians and today they are powerful element in the politics and economy of Burma.

India has overlooked the plight of the Indian diaspora in its neighbourhood in the post-independence era. As India's unity was challenged on regional, linguistic and religious considerations it was engaged in putting its own house in order. It believed that if it supports the integrative drives of its neighbours, others would also reciprocate the gesture. It was one of the reasons that India decided to support Singalese in Sri Lanka against militant Tamils in 1987. India dispatched its troops to fight against Tamils (LTTE). These steps proved counterproductive. It neither subdued the Tamils nor did it create any goodwill for India in the neighbourhood. Pakistan's crusade for Kashmir was intensified and external agents of destabilization became active against India.

India's "inaction" in Burma (1948-1962) and its "Pro-active" role in Sri Lanka (1987-88) vis-a-vis its diaspora lacked vision and rationality. India was criticized for its inaction in Burma and it was condemned for its action in Sri Lanka. These events gave wrong signals and complicated the process of conflict resolution.

India began to attach importance to its diasporic community with sensivity and care in the era of liberalization. When India opened its markets and the economic situation and global competition became matters of concern, it became necessary to review its perspectives and policies in the light of new developments. India needed infrastructure and in that endeavour "Foreign Direct Investment" (FDI) was required. It was only thereafter that the importance of overseas Indians was emphasised and high-powered committee under L.M. Singhvi was established to understand the problems and perspectives of Indian diaspora.

India overhauled its economic policies to create an attractive economic environment. It offered tax holidays and removal of tariff barriers. It assured its support for free trade and promote economic integration with Asia-Pacific. Prime Minister Atal Bihari Vajpayee offered special incentives to the Indian diaspora and assured them he would create special economic zones for their project of dual citizenship facility and full solidarity. He gave the idea of celebrating Pravasi Bharatiya Diwas every year, which has proved useful in establishing rapport and understanding with the diasporic community.

The changes in the economic policies and friendly gestures for the diaspora were widely appreciated. India, which was welcomed as the dialogue partner of ASEAN, and partnership with ARF ("ASEAN Regional Forum") was happy to cultivate its diaspora. It was believed that with the assistance and support of NRIs in the ASEAN region, the objectives of Mekong-Ganga project and BIMST-EC ("Bangladesh, Bhutan, India, Myanmar, Nepal, Sri Lanka, Thailand Economic Co-operation") would be achievable. In all those endeavours and to assure fruitful partnership, the feedback and support of diaspora are crucial.

Categorising Indian Diaspora

Indian diaspora is of different types. In order to understand it, we need to understand various categories of Indian diaspora. They are known as Non-Resident Indians (NRIs). Persons of Indian Origin (PIO), Persons Resident in India (PRI) and Overseas Indians and each term has a different legal connotation.

NRIs & PIOs

According to the Foreign Exchange Management Act (FEMA) 1999, which came into effect from 1 June 2000, an NRI is an Indian Passport-holder who stays outside India on employment, business or vocation or for any other purpose for more than 182 days in a financial year. The 182 days need not be continuous. On the other hand, a PIO is a person, who while not being a citizen of Pakistan or Bangladesh, shall be deemed to be of Indian origin if he or either of his parents or any of his grand parents was a citizen of India by virtue of the Indian Constitution or Citizenship Act of 1955. Foreign wives of Indian citizens are treated as PIO, though they don't have Indian parentage. Indians who emigrated as indentured labourers during the British colonial period also come under this category. The concentration of PIOs is high in countries like Malaysia. An NRI will become a PIO if he acquires the citizenship of another country. Because there was no provision for dual citizenship under the Indian Constitution before 2004, they were unable to get Indian citizenship. But now the situation has changed and the facility of dual citizenship can be attained.

PRI & Overseas Indians

The next category is the PRI. Persons Resident in India are those Indian citizens who go to foreign countries for higher studies, educational training, medical treatment or any other purpose indicating their intention of not staying outside the country for an uncertain period. Indian students abroad who take up jobs on completion of their education abroad would attain the PRI status from the day of joining the employment.

The concept of Overseas Indians emerged during the 20th century when the plight of the Indian emigrants overseas kindled a strong political protest in India against the British Indian government's attitude towards them because India was then a part of the British empire and all in India and overseas were said to be the British Subjects.

Generally speaking, the term PIO and NRI have been used interchangeably by the Government of India (GoI) in Parliamentary debates and other official literature as well as by the Indian Press. There are different categories of migrant Indians; this includes emigrants under the British colonial system including indentured labourers and free passage migrants to Southeast Asia and the Caribbean countries. Free passage/commercial emigrants are those who left India after independence for higher education and better jobs in the U.K., the U.S. and Australia and the labour migrants in the Gulf countries to this day.

The Problem about Indian Diaspora

The problem of the Government of India is that it tries to group the Indian diaspora under one definition. This is the principal reason why the debate on dual nationality has stagnated. If a PIO has the inherent right to apply for Indian citizenship and is allowed to maintain his or her other nationality, it would also by default allow Pakistanis or Bangladeshis to seek Indian citizenship.

From time immemorial, Indians have migrated from India to different parts of the world. Indian diaspora comprises persons who migrated both involuntarily and voluntarily, namely, the PIOs, NRIs and the stateless persons of Indian origin. The present government's classification of the Overseas Indian communities into Indian citizens, PIOs and stateless persons can be collectively referred to as the Indian diaspora. Therefore, a multi-layered, broad and all encompassing definition is required. An accurate definition or acronym for the Indian diaspora is difficult to come by.

In the Southeast Asian region, the Overseas Indians invited their families to their countries of settlement and started family-owned shops. They built railroads and involved in development of port facilities. PIO constituted a significant number in Burma where they were involved in money-lending and bureaucracy. They also worked as watchmen, prison officers, school teachers, etc.

In South Asia, Sri Lanka accounts for a large number of PIO. Here, they are called Indian Tamils. In Nepal, the skilled and unskilled labourers are called Madhesias. In West Asia, Kuwait has a large number of Indian emigrants, who are involved in skilled and unskilled labour. They also work as drivers, nurses, and housemaid. Bachelors alone can stay on temporary contracts. They cannot bring their family. They are not allowed to settle permanently.

Indian Diaspora in South Asia

India encompasses a vast territory inhabiting a large number of ethnic groups. The Punjabis, Nepalese, Gujaratis, Sindhis, Biharis and Marwaris are spread into different parts of South Asia. Their ethnicity and primordial loyalties are not monolithic, but they are Indians in temperament and outlook. The British colonial masters had facilitated the movement of Indian diaspora through indentured labour system, Kangani or Maistry system and finally when they transferred sovereignty to the natives, various nationalities took their shape in different countries. India, Pakistan, Bangladesh, Sri Lanka, Bhutan, Nepal and Maldives emerged as separate independent nations. The regions of Bengal and Punjab, the main Center of India's nationalist movement is divided and is the constituent units of Pakistan, India and Bangladesh. Though all the nations have tried to establish separate identities, it is difficult to bifurcate their culture from Indian civilization, if they are outside the sub-continent, they are an essential component of Indian diaspora. Although it is debatable but people of the sub-continent have similarities and the people of South Asia, outside the territory of India, may be called diasporic.

Burma had been a part of British India from 1824 to 1937 and ruled from Calcutta and New Delhi, respectively. The Britishers encouraged Indian farmers and labourers to go to Burma for farming and trade. Indians found this venture profitable. There was large-scale emigration of Indians to Burma. Subsequently they ultimately preferred to settle down in that country. But when Burma became independent Indians were projected as foreigners and their properties and businesses were nationalized. Similarly Sri Lanka had been governed from Madras during the colonial period till 1802. There were frequent movement of the people from Madras to Colombo and a large section of Tamils stayed back in that country. Sri Lanka discriminated them from Sinhalese and projected them as illegal immigrants. Similarly a large number of population in the Tarai region of Nepal are considered alien. Indians treat Himalayan mountain ranges as sacred and sacrosanct on religious grounds and have been visiting Nepal from time immemorial. The socio-economic interaction with Nepal is so deep-rooted and overwhelming that isolation of Indians from Newaris or Gurkhas and vice versa is impossible. Moreover the Janakpur and Birat Nagar regions are inhabited by Madhesiyas and they play an important role in the national life of the country.

Indian diaspora in South Asia have been influenced by the Indian way of life and they are sensitive about their culture, religion and ethnic genealogy. Their marriages with other groups, especially of tribal descent, are abhorred. Indians endeavour to maintain their separate ethnic identity and therefore their patriotism towards the country of their adoption are questioned. Moreover, it has been a common trend in South Asia to criticize India at various forums to project their own separate identity. Indian diaspora in South Asia has suffered because of irrationality in nation-building and integrationist drives pursued by the governments in Bangladesh, Nepal, Pakistan and Sri Lanka. In all those countries, a particular ethnic or religious group, which wants to establish their preponderance in the political system, comes out with parochial ideas of discrimination, on religious, caste and ethnic considerations. The Sinhalese versus the Tamils, Hindus verses Muslims and Newaris versus Madhesias etc. are the endeavour of assertions of one community over another.

India has tried to convey that its diaspora should forge harmonious relations with natives of the country of their adoption, without demanding any special rights and privileges. It wanted that the Indian diaspora should evolve a practical approach to be integrated in the mainstream of national life. It never spoke about any guarantees of support if its diaspora was discriminated at the political and economic levels in the countries of their adoption. In fact, it remained silent when Indians faced discrimination vis-a-vis the natives in Burma, Malaysia and Fiji. This was in sharp contrast to the Chinese attitudes, which support their diaspora more openly. When Vietnam discriminated against and persecuted Hoas (ethnic Chinese in Vietnam), China displayed its disapproval by dispatching its troops, to teach a lesson to Vietnam. India has merely used its moral and diplomatic influence to support its diaspora, which is insufficient and too little to make any significant impact to address the problems of diaspora.

The attitude of Indian government is changing in the post-cold war era. Indian diaspora is viewed as an important asset in enhancing its economic interests. A new policy towards Indian diaspora takes into account their economic contribution to India. According to the Economic Survey 2000-2001 and Reserve Bank of India's Annual Report 2000-2001, the NRI deposit during April-September 2000 in India was 1,362 million US dollars.

Indian Diaspora in Southeast Asia

Southeast Asia, known as 'Subarnabhumi' ('golden land' or 'land of gold') in the ancient past was frequently visited by Indians for business, trade and missionary activities. Indian culture is prevalent in art and architecture, language and literature, religion, customs and traditions of most of the countries. The famous temples of Angkor Wat (Cambodia), Borobudur (Indonesia), Emerald Buddha (Thailand) etc. prove our connections and the epic of Ramayana and Mahabharata in different versions in the region indicates our cultural influence and interaction from that region from time immemorial. Streams of Indians have been going to that area but some of those who went under indentured labour system or Kangani system, stayed back. These people played crucial role in the production of sugar, tea, coffee, cocoa, rice, tobacco and rubber. Since Southeast Asia is located at the doorstep and labourers were getting different types of incentives by the colonial rulers, Indians were very enthusiastic to go there for their bread and butter. During 1852 to 1937, about 2 million Indians went to Malaya and nearly 2.5 million went to Burma. Besides Malaya and Burma, thousands of Indians went to Siam, Sumatra, Java and the Philippines especially after the economic depression of 1929. A number of people from Uttar Pradesh, Punjab, Gujarat, Madras and Bombay transmigrated. The Marwaris from Rajputana, Chettiyars from Madras, the Punjabis from Gujranwala went towards Rangoon, Bangkok and Singapore respectively and they played important roles in the economic spheres of those countries. Although they faced stiff competition from the Chinese business circles but the hurdles did not deter them. The bulk of Indian diaspora are located in Malaysia, Singapore and Thailand as their contribution in the national economy have been regarded positive by their political masters.

There are three types of Indian diaspora in Southeast Asia, namely NRIs, PIOs and stateless Indians. The largest number of NRIs are in Singapore (90 thousand), followed by Malaysia (15 thousand), Thailand (15 thousand), Brunei (7 thousand), Myanmar (2 thousand), the Philippines (2 thousand), Indonesia (500), Vietnam (320), Cambodia (150) and Laos (107). The number of PIOs is largest in Myanmar (25,00,000) followed by Malaysia (16,00,000) Singapore (2,17,000), Thailand (70,000) and Indonesia (50,000). The number of stateless Indians is largest in Myanmar (4,00,000) and Malaysia (50,000). The citizenship laws in Myanmar and Malaysia are difficult especially for Indians. The knowledge of language, customs, traditions and residential criteria are difficult to be fulfilled and there are ethnic lobbies to work against them.

As far as Indo-China is concerned, the number of Indian diaspora is small. Although India was very close to all the three countries, Vietnam, Laos and Cambodia during the cold war years, yet Indians did not prefer to stay there for long. The total number of NRIs and PIOs in Vietnam are 320, followed by Laos 115 and in Cambodia 300. In fact, that area was a battleground between communist and anti-communist forces. All the three had been supporting nationalization campaigns for decades and business opportunities were limited.

Singapore, Thailand, Malaysia and Indonesia on the other hand, offered business opportunities. Indians found it profitable to go there for trade, investments, and jobs. In Brunei, the number of Indian doctors, engineers and teachers is around 3000 and they are famous for their hard work and professionalism. On the other hand, Indians have been associated with textile industries in Indonesia. The bulk of investors in textile business is Sindhis whereas the Sikhs are engaged in the sports goods business. The contribution of Indians in IT, medical, accounting and law are appreciated and incentives are offered to take their services. Such professionals are also in demand in Malaysia, but a majority of the diaspora are engaged in rubber and palm plantations. Their economic situation and literacy rates are low compared to Indian diaspora in other parts of Southeast Asia.

The position of the Indian diaspora in the Philippines is encouraging. The Sindhi community is engaged in trade and manufacturing whereas Punjabis are dealing in money-lending. Manila has been treated as an important conduit to immigrate to the United States and services of Indian professionals are appreciated. However, Singapore is the most favoured destination of the Indian diaspora despite Singapore's prohibitive immigration laws. Tamils, Malayalis, Sindhis, Gujaratis and Punjabis are the major components of the Indian diaspora and they are involved not only in business and trade but also in civil services, the judicial system and educational institutions. Besides traditional business, Indians are contributing in the advancement of knowledge in IT, medical sciences and pharmaceutical research. Their role in transforming Singapore, as the economic hub has been recognised and their professional inputs are widely appreciated.

Indian diaspora in Thailand is respected for its knowledge and skills. The largest number of Indian diaspora in Thailand is Sikhs followed by Sindhis, Punjabis, Tamils and Purabias. They have been traditionally engaged in textile business. Some of them are also dealing in real estates and jewellery sectors. On the other hand, the services of Indian professionals, IT experts and skilled personnel are in great demand in international financial institutions and MNCs based in Bangkok. Indian diaspora feel at home in that country and some of them have assumed Thai names and a Thai way of life. Intermarriage between Indian and Thai nationals, which was not allowed in the past, is permitted now. The level of socio-economic interaction with the natives is ideal.

Evolving Perspective

Indian diaspora has a mature perspective to co-exist in the countries of their adoption. If they had a weakness to look towards India in the past, it was because most of them had emigrated with the support of the Britishers and Britain was the common colonial master. The Congress Party was a nationalist party to act as a safety valve to articulate the grievances of the people and the diasporic community wanted to express their grievances through that party. The Congress party under Mahatma Gandhi had effectively argued the case of the Indian diaspora in South Africa, Fiji and Burma during the colonial era. Indian diaspora was indebted to Mahatma Gandhi for what he had done against apartheid in South Africa and indentured labour system in Fiji. It was for this reason that they were politically affiliated with developments in India. But when the Britishers transferred sovereignty to India and other countries in the region, the situation started changing. Although, it took some time, gradually they de-linked their political affiliation with the parties in the motherland.

When India became independent, it could not fulfill the expectations of Indians in Burma, Malaysia and Fiji. India advised its diaspora to adjust and co-exist with the natives and evolve indigenous solution to resolve their problems. It was made clear to the diaspora that Indian government will not mediate and if they have to survive in the countries of their adoption, they have to seek political and economic affiliation with the natives. This proved painful in some cases, but it also helped integrationist drives. Indian diaspora in the ASEAN region have thus changed their perspective and evolved professional values, to play a useful role in the culture and economic life of the countries of their adoption.

The post-independence era has witnessed the struggle for national identity and ethnic assertion. The nation-building activity, which began with the dawn of freedom, is continuing. India with a plural society supported "Unity in diversity" and tolerated ethnic, religious and linguistic diversities. Its own problems were gigantic in proportion and its advice was not solicited in the politics of the region.

After 1947 Prime Minister Nehru suggested that the overseas Indians should identify themselves with the aspiration of the local population. The assumption was that such a course would facilitate the building of bonds between the overseas Indians and native population and contribute to healthy relations between the two. India's policy since 1947 has been determined by this very assumption. To summarise the issues regarding Indian diaspora in the ASEAN region, the following observations can be made :

- The number of Indian diaspora in the ASEAN region are estimated about 2 million, but their figures for South Asia are difficult to be mentioned. Most of the new nations in South Asia are trying to carve out a separate identity for themselves, which may prove different from India.
- Indian diaspora is fragmented along caste, religion, region and ethnic lines. A Sikh in the ASEAN region or a Muslim or a Sindhi or Gujarati have their own separate cultural and political affiliations.
- Most of Indian diasporic community is inhabited in the capital cities of ASEAN. Bangkok, Singapore, Manila, Kualalumpur Bandar Seri Begawan and Jakarta have been their favoured destination and they are connected with business and commerce.
- Indian diaspora have played important role in the ASEAN boom. Their contribution in IT sectors, construction, business, textile industries and human resource develop-ments are appreciated.
- The diasporic community has supported the transformation of India from command economy to market economy. It is in the economic area that they are willing to cooperate and coordinate contacts between India and the countries of their adoption.
- ASEAN region have proximity with India. We share common maritime borders with Indonesia, Thailand and Myanmar. We also share common land frontiers of 1600 kilometres with

> Myanmar. We are willing to establish growth areas on the common frontiers and develop Andamans as an important trading centre. Indian diaspora can provide important input in those directions if the proposals are mutually beneficial.

Presently the world is changing rapidly in view of globalisation. The countries of Asia-Pacific have to evolve a common strategy and the diasporic community can act as a facilitator in that process. Indian diaspora in the ASEAN region is inadvertently endowed to play the diplomatic role of a facilitator so that the countries of Asia-Pacific comes closer to face the challenges of the new world order and contribute to the emergence of an "Asia Century" in the near future.

Conclusion

In short, most of the Indian diaspora in the ASEAN region are skilled people, who are gradually integrating with the mainstream of national life. They are no longer disliked even in Myanmar and Malaysia now. Their role in the economic life of the countries of their adoption are substantial and they have proved themselves relevant for the countries in the region.

Indians remain a heterogeneous group with their loyalty and allegiance towards their own ethnic community, religious institutions, customs and traditions in conjunction with the customs and traditions of the countries of their adoption. They are no longer India-centric. Sikhs or Muslims or Buddhists identify themselves with their respective religions. On the other hand, Sindhi, Tamil, Bengali or Bhojpuri communities differ in their life-style, culture and rituals. They have affiliation with their ethnic groups and they have proved themselves assimilative, permissive and accommodative in recent years.

REFERENCES

Chakravarthy, N.R., 1971, *The Indian Minority in Burma: The Rise and Decline of an Immigrant Community*, London, Oxford University Press.

Jain, R.K., 1970, *South Indians on the Plantation Frontier in Malaya*, New Haven, Yale University Press.

Kurian, George and Srivastava, Ram P. (eds.), 1983, *Overseas Indians: A Study in Adaptation*, New Delhi, Vikas.

20

The Struggle for Democracy in Southeast Asia—A Study of Myanmar

Dr. Radhakrishnan said "democracy means rule of law and of reason. It means rule by consent—We should try to achieve for all our policies as much consent as possible. The consensus should be with us. Democracy means humility. No sense of infallibility and a spirit of give and take."

The democracy stands for the rule by the people based on free and equal participation by all enfranchised adults, the election of public officers by the majority of the citizens voting with

(*a*) Freedom to nominate alternative candidate.
(*b*) The right of citizens to form political parties and present their candidates.
(*c*) Freedom to conduct campaigns, and
(*d*) The right of defeated candidate to continue their propaganda.

Southeast Asia in general, has faced the struggle for establishing democracy in the past few decades. Malaysia, Singapore, Indonesia, Thailand, Cambodia and the Philippines have succeeded in establishing democracy. Vietnam and Laos have communist system, but they too are adapting to features of democracy in the post-Cold War era. However, the case of Brunei and Myanmar are different. Brunei has absolute monarchy and Myanmar has military dictatorship. The people of Brunei feel proud of their Sultan and Sultanate but Myanmar is a different case. National League for Democracy has been working for the restoration of democracy but they have been suppressed. The NLD have made sacrifices for it, but failed in their endeavors. This paper will try to examine the compelling urges for democracy, emerging hindrances and future prospects for democracy in Myanmar.

Myanmar shares 1600 km long border with India and both were associated with each other during the British colonial period. India and Burma fought together against colonial rulers. Both had urges for establishing a state practicing "government of the people, for the people and by the poeple" which may represent and articulate their aspirations. Both had evolved democratic institutions during the colonial period and had identical views on domestic and foreign policies. India and Burma framed their constitutions, which was secular, balanced and effective to promote ethos for participatory democracy. They felt that there should be no discrimination between majority and minority ethnic groups. In view of the multi-ethnic and multi-religious societies, India and Burma tried to promote the policy of "unity in diversity". It was in that endeavor that Burma failed. A section of Burmese leaders were adamant in pronouncing "Burma for the Burmese", in which ethnic Karens, Shans, Rohingyas, Chins and Kachins etc. wanted autonomy. Due to the slogan of "Burma for Burmans", the minorities felt deprived of their traditional rights. The ethnic groups raised the demand for autonomy and they were ruthlessly suppressed. Although the civilian rulers were sympathetic to consider the case of autonomy, the military thought otherwise. The situation worsened during 1958-62, when ethnic disputes turned into civil war. The military usurped power in 1962, solely for establishing law and order and unitary structure of the state. The military rulers categorically announced that they will not discuss autonomy or cessation for territories for ethnic minorities in the country, and ruthlessly suppressed all types of opposition for decades. The military under leadership of General Ne Win systematically destroyed the institutions of democracy. Multi-party system was abolished and constitution was abrogated. However, the urge for democratic system, parliamentary democracy and quest for unity in diversity remained relevant and these are the issues to be attended to in the present context.

Myanmar is geopolitically closer to India than any other neighbours. Thailand, Laos, China and Bangladesh also share contiguous frontiers with Myanmar but culturally and politically the Myanmarese population have more affinities and attraction for India. Having been linked to India administratively during the colonial period and having experienced the common political system, party politics and struggle during the freedom struggle, it was natural for both to be attracted towards each other, but political masters guided them in different directions. Military leaders in Myanmar cultivated special relationship with Communist China after 1962 and nurtured one-party rule of Burma Socialist Programme Party (BSPP) with socialist orientation. The evolving partnership between Myanmar, China and Pakistan subsequently affected the democratic ethos at the domestic level and promoted authoritarian values in the country.

Myanmar is under direct military rule, which is presently called the State Peace and Development Council (SPDC). Military has been ruling by various decrees after abrogating the constitution and persecuting democracy leaders. The martial laws for certain regions are imposed frequently. Military has complete command with its Commander-in-Chief designated as the Supreme Commander. There is a law that the Supreme Commander would assume state power in a national emergency if there is danger of disintegration of the union, national solidarity as well as the loss of national sovereignty. There is no check on the powers of the Supreme Commander and he is the Supreme authority.

Military representation in civil services is overwhelming. Active and retired military officers are appointed as officers and executives in ministries, corporations and economic enterprises. The Chief Executives are appointed with the approval of the military junta only. Political role of military has been legitimated through the doctrine of Tatmadaw, which projects military as the most disciplined cohesive and enduring institution. Evolution of the military force during the freedom struggle was through patriotic volunteers who made sacrifices for the nation and who had legitimate rights to play their role in national politics also. The military had played important role in maintaining law and order during the democratic rule of Prime Minister, U Nu, during 1958-60, and thereafter the civilian administration had almost become dependent on the military to protect national sovereignty and ethnic distrubances.

Tatmadaw doctrine is similar to the doctrine of Dwifungsi (dual role of the armed forces) in Indonesia. Military in Indonesia also advocated that the army was the only disciplined, honest and dynamic element in Indonesian society and therefore they had their legitimate role to play in politics. But after the resignation of President Suharto in May 1998, this doctrine was disbanded and military leaders were asked to go back to the barracks. Indonesians preferred a parliamentary system in the post-Suharto era and presently the parliament and judiciary have become important branch of the governmental powers. They have also decided now that their President (Chief Executive) will be elected directly by the people on the pattern of the United States for a period of four years.

In Myanmar also Tatmadaw doctrine is contentious. The NLD is struggling to disband it. When General Ne Win resigned in the wake of student-led demonstration in 1988 and succeeded by Maung Maung, the consensus was to abolish Tatmadaw, but Maung Maung could not survive in power. General Saw Maung staged a coup d'etat and assumed power in the name of State Law and Order Restoration Council (SLORC). Under his leadership general election were announced which was held on 27 May 1990. In that election, which was free and fair, democratic forces led by National League for Democracy (NLD) got 80 per cent seats. To be precise NLD got 392 seats out of 485 seats whereas the military's National Unity Party got merely 10 seats. This development clearly indicated that the general people in Myanmar disapproved the doctrine to Tatmadaw. However, SLORC did not allow civilian leaders to assume power. The new parliament was not convened and military tried to stay in power on one pretext or the other. The military called for a national convention to draw up the principles of the new constitution and said that only after the new constitution is framed there will be a new election to elect the members of Parliament for power sharing. NLD leader Aung San Suu Kyi was kept under house arrest and other elected NLD members were either persecuted or jailed. So far there is no consensus on the provisions of the new constitution because the intention of the military rulers is not to transfer power to the civilians. They insist on asserting Tatmadaw in the politics of Myanmar permanently. Although General Saw Maung stepped out of power in 1992, there was no change in the system.

There are serious restrictions on the activities of pro-democracy leaders. Madam Suu Kyi has been under house arrest and freedom of speech and expression are curtailed. Civil society norms and human rights situation are deplorable. The UN human rights commission (UNHRC) has repeatedly called for cessation of human rights violation and the UN Secretary General has deplored human rights situation in Myanmar. The UN has sent a special envoy to Myanmar on several occasions to impress the military leaders for democratisation and liberalization in the country. Rights and freedoms of the people are marred by sporadic political violence and the government has freely resorted to the Sedition Act, Public Order Preservation Act, the Official Secrets Act and the Unlawful Association Act against the opposition. There are restrictions on trade unions, student unions and political parties. Although business groups and NGOs have been given some space in the new dispensation, but there is no constitutional guarantee and the efforts are made to promote the interest of military in all walks of life.

SPDC has been assuring the international community that it will support democratization process. They have assured to take step-by-step approach to normalize the situation for reconciliation and democratic restoration. Some of the steps which have been envisaged by the military and which has been discussed through the media are the obligations of the military towards the people of Myanmar. The elected leaders should exercise their powers under the guidance of military rulers. For those who were elected in 1990 had been assigned certain tasks. The SLORC assigned the task to elected representatives to constitute election laws (Pyithu hluttaw), the second was the drafting of the new constitution, the third was the national convention and fourth step was to put the draft of the new constitution for national referendum.

The national convention to frame a new constitution was convened by the military in 1993 in which there were 702 delegates. Although the convention for drafting the new constitution was called, NLD members were not given due importance for expressing their opinion. It is understood that only 88 NLD members were invited and their opinion were rarely noted. They felt themselves neglected in the convention and therefore decided to remain outside. The consensus is yet to emerge on the nature of the Constitution. The deliberation of National Convention indicates that military intend to play dominant role in politics. When NLD walked out of the national convention in December 1995 and opposed the dominant participation of Tatmadaw in future politics of the country, no serious efforts were made to bring them back on the constitutional process.

SPDC is trying to legitimate the role of military through the new constitution. It is striving to make a provision to reserve the post of executive head for the military, which rules out the possibility for Suu Kyi to be the head of the executive branch of the government. The judiciary will have no jurisdiction over the armed forces and will adjudicate on matters concerning the civilians only.

The evolving constitution as published in the newspaper, "New Light of Myanmar", indicates the role of Tatmadaw in all the branches of the government. Accordingly the chief of the staff of the Defence Forces will be the most powerful person, beyond the control of the civilians. The chief of staff of the Defence Forces will be entitled to nominate 25 per cent of all members of the Peoples Assembly, the National Assembly and the State and Regional Assemblies. Again it will be the chief of staff who will appoint the Minister of Defence, the Minister of Interior and Minister for Border Affairs and Vice President of the Union. The draft constitution has attracted the attention of the international community. Burma Lawyer's Council has criticized the draft constitution and stated that the National Convention has been a farce and a shame to camouflage a constitution drafted by the military to entrench its own role in the future political affairs for Burma. The objectives of the national convention were the following :

(*a*) Non-disintegration of the Union (*b*) Non-disintegration of the national solidarity (*c*) Perpetuation of the national sovereignty (*d*) Flourishing of a genuine multi-party democratic system (*e*) Further flourishing of worldly values-justice, liberty and equality in the nation (*f*) Participation of the *Tatmadaw* in the national political leading role of the future State.

Thus the last line of the stated objective of the convention reveals the real intentions of the military rulers. The military has abused the constitutional drafting process to cling to power while progressively dismantling the democratic opposition within Burma.

The NLD and like-minded groups argue that the ultimate goal of democracy movement in Myanmar is the establishment of genuine Federal Union. They refer the utility of Panglong agreement, which had been concluded between ethnic groups and Bogyoke Aung San in 1947. This was an agreement for autonomy for some states. The national convention on the pattern of Panglong conference is required to establish a true democratic federal union in the country. The national states should be constituted on the basis of ethnicity rather than geographical basis and at least eight states should be created on the basis of ethnicity, namely Chin, Kachin,

Karen, Kaya, Mon, Shan, Rakhine and Burmans are major ethnic groups with distinct culture and lifestyle.

The arguments of the NLD and others are not given due consideration in the country because the rulers are apprehensive that those measures would have adverse impact on national unity and sovereignty of the country. But the opinion of NLD are given due importance in the United States and the European Union. Aung San Suu Kyi, the Nobel laureate, has a number of supporters at the global level. National coalition Government of the Union of Burma, formed after the military refused to transfer power in 1990, has not been given diplomatic recognition but the Voice of Democratic Burma is regularly broadcasted from Oslo. The UN is monitoring the developments and Burma cell in the Pentagon has been sympathetic to democratic movement in Myanmar. Americans are continuing with their trade sanctions against Burma and express their concerns through international forums. They had opposed the membership of Myanmar in the ASEAN and raised the issue of human rights violations.

China and ASEAN are the two important factors as far as the stability of military rule in Myanmar are concerned. China's geo-strategic and economic connections are so deep-rooted with the SPDC that they are restrained to support any resolution for restoration of democracy. However, ASEAN as a regional grouping has to articulate regional response to developments within the region. The oppressive government of the military, their efforts to carve out a permanent role in national politics, and their systematic efforts to crush democratic ethos are against the norms of civil society. The ASEAN is keen to support the issues of democracy, human rights and environment and in that endeavor Myanmar record is to be made satisfactory. Mahathir Mohammad spoke against the military rule in Myanmar before his exit from power in Malaysia and urged for initiating steps for restoration of democracy. Thai Prime Minister, Thaksin Shinawatra, too expressed his concern about developments in Myanmar and similarly other members of ASEAN have displayed their concern for constitutional processes in Myanmar.

Prime Minister Khin Nyunt knew the importance of ASEAN for external image of Myanmar and in response to Prime Minister Thaksin's initiative he agreed to participate in an international meeting in Bangkok on 15 December 2003. In this meeting, the representatives from 13 countries attended which included UN special envoy to Myanmar, Indonesia, Australia, Japan, China, India, Singapore, Italy, Austria, France and Germany etc. Khin Nyunt had come to the meeting with a Roadmap, a blueprint of the future constitution for finding out a solution for reconciliation and democratization. The participants in the Bangkok process discussed a political solution of the Myanmar crisis and for the norms of establishing civil society. Main points of the roadmap were controversial, yet it was regarded as a positive development.

The evolving constitution has 104 principles and 6 guidelines. The framework is suggesting a Presidential system and not the Federal system. The Fundamental Rights are not guaranteed and while mentioning the composition of the states there is preponderance of only one ethnic group. Parliament will have 25 per cent non-elected members appointed by the President of the Union. The President will not be answerable to Election Commission or any authority and he will have absolute right to appoint Chief Ministers, Chief Justice and Attorney General. There is no commitment or timetable for restoring democratic order. The Bangkok process is an endeavour of ASEAN countries to impress that a National Convention should be held again in which NLD, ethnic minorities, farmers, military, civil servants and workers should participate. ASEAN has given an impression that the military should make an effort towards reconciliation and accommodation with democracy leaders and in that endeavour dialogue should be encouraged. It also conveyed that if ASEAN feels satisfied with the initiative of the military junta, they would extend full support to the military to synthesize the divergent opinion and facilitate the understanding and meeting between NLD leaders and the government. Although SPDC assumes that the issue of the democracy is an internal affair of Myanmar and outsiders have no role to play, it is difficult for them to ignore the opinion of ASEAN partners.

Thai foreign minister Sukakiart has stated that the Myanmar issue has come out in the international forum now and Myanmar has to defend itself in the process is something noteworthy. Myanmar sent its foreign minister to give testimony before the representatives of 13 countries in Bangkok and for the first time demonstrated its commitment to break the deadlock. It was for the first time that the international community was the jury and SPDC in the dock. The issue of democratic transition has been thus internationalized.

ASEAN has been supporting a global resurgence of democracy. They have respect for Asian values, which supports a cultural predisposition towards stable leadership and collective welfare. The Asians in general have intuitive respect for authority and social harmony. They like to build a consensus to live and let live. They do avoid confrontation with the adversaries. In short, Asian values tend to support economic dynamicism, political stability, social discipline and cultural conservationism. Mahathir Mohammed and Lee Kuan Yew have articulated features of Asian values vis-a-vis Western values and established the democracy in Asia is different from democracy in the western world. The democracy in ASEAN region has to reflect the social and religious values for the countries concerned. It was the respect for Asian values that the ASEAN countries did not give due attention to western opinion for democratization in Myanmar. For ASEAN, Myanmar area is an important segment for constructive engagement. It is in the economic and security interests of ASEAN countries to delink the dependency syndrome of any of its partners. In order to evolve common concern and similar outlook, they have to accelerate integration process towards Myanmar because that will open the road for trade and investment in South Asia. Most of the ASEAN members have incorporated virtues of Asian values in their political system. Most of them have liberalized in view with globalization, and rulers in Myanmar do not have potential to stop the trends in the international arena. They have to cope with the challenges of globalization, democratization and trends in the neighbourhood.

India, Burma and Malaya were having the similar political arrangement during the colonial period. They had developed similar views and fought together against the colonial rulers. Any solution to the continuing crisis in Myanmar can be found within the perview of the political system existing in the three countries. On the other hand, there is an effective political model in Thailand where civil democracy has been able to establish their role in the politics of the country. Military was in power in Thailand from 1932 onwards but now they have gone back to the barracks in 1990's. The role of military elites in restoring democracy in Thailand in 1973 and again in 1992 was substantial. In 1973, General Kris Sivara opposed the oppressive ways of Thanom Kittikachorn and again in 1992 a section of the military disapproved the action of General Succhinda Kraprayoom. At present the military and bureaucracy have provided a momentum to economic growth and they had left the political domain for the civilians.

Myanmarese junta have not displayed any major differences regarding the horrible state of affairs in the country in their outlook so far. They remain united against restoration of democracy. However there are external pressures to start the constitutional processes. Major concern of the military has been to protect the unity of the nation. They are apprehensive that if the democratic process are accelerated and if the ethnic minorities located on border areas are given freedom and choice, the tendency for fragmentation will be substantial. NLD leader, Madam Suu Kyi, who has been under house arrest is severely criticized because she has attracted global support. Military argues that Myanmar is a nation of ethnic Burmans and the SPDC is the only way through which their interests could be guaranteed and promoted.

The estimated population of Myanmar is about 52 million of which ethnic Burmans comprise 68 per cent, Shans 9 per cent, Karens 7 per cent, Arakanese 4 per cent, Chinese 3 per cent, Mons 2 per cent and others 5 per cent. The Burmans are dominating the plains and urban centers while minorities are concentrated in regions bordering India, China, Laos and Thailand. Burmans are mostly Buddhists, the Karens are Christians and Arakanese are Muslims. Buddhists constitute over 89.3 per cent of Myanmar's population. Religious beliefs have played important role in determining the cultural pattern. Although the population in general, respect the authorities, but they aspire minimum rights of civil society. In 1988, when there was a demonstration against the governance of General Ne Win, Buddhist monks had been in the forefront to demonstrate. They had solidly supported the campaign against military in 1990 elections. However the opposition was arbitrarily suppressed along with the elected MPs. Most of the elected NLD members were forced out of the country and they sought refuge in Thailand, India or the United States. Some MPs who stayed back in the country were persecuted or jailed. The Buddhist monks once again came out for peaceful demonstration against the military in 2007 but it was suppressed once again. The military rulers felt so uncomfortable that they clamped martial law and draconian measures to stop dissent in any form.

Democracy leaders have good rapport with ethnic leaders because they have together spent years in Myanmar jails. They have a consensus of opinion against the military rule. They do not argue the reservation of special rights of ethnic Burmans in the future political system. They aspire to restore democratic norms, equal opportunity and federal union for their country.

To conclude, it can be stated that there is a consensus in the entire ASEAN region for democratization. Indonesia under Suharto had placed military in all branches of government. It was difficult to envisage that the political system could ever change. But now Indonesia has a vibrant democracy. In the Philippines, there were martial laws for decades under Ferdinand Marcos but now the country has a democratic structure. The emergence of peoples' powers changed the authoritarianism of the Marcos era. Thailand embraced democracy and it was buoyant, but due to certain lapses committed by Prime Minister Thaksin Shinawatra, the military usurped power. However, national elections are due in December 2007 and there are every possibility that military will go back to the barracks. Thus changes in Myanmar also can be delayed but cannot be stopped. The silver lining since 2003, regarding Myanmar is that it is monitored by the ASEAN very closely. Although the parties supporting the movement for democracy are fragmented, scattered and divided but as and when the conditions for restoration of democracy will be ready, the political system will change. The majority of the people will surely support parliamentary form of government.

BURMESE AGONY

India and ASEAN countries are facing a typical problem regarding their policies towards the military regime in Burma. They tend to support democratic aspirations of the people but at the same time they advocate the policy of non-interference in the internal affairs of their neighbours. Although they advocate non-violence and negotiated settlements, but they have no consensus on how to deal with those countries who are violent, tyrannical and unpopular.

Burma is witnessing tragic situation today. The Buddhist monks and civilians, who gathered courage to come out of their homes and demonstrated with folded hands and prayers against the misrule of the military, are arrested, persecuted torchered and killed. The icon of the democracy movement, Aung San Suu Kyi is kept under house arrest. The important leaders of NLD are arrested and situation is grim.

General Than Swe's politics goes around the thesis of the military, for the military and by the military. The NLD leaders are projected anti-nationals, and opinion about ethnic Shans Karens, and Rohingyas are similar. Any opposition to military rule have been mercilessly crushed since 1962.

The Burmese military believes that they have divine right to rule. They used to draw inspiration from Dwifuncti principle of General Suharto in the past that military had a duel role in security and politics of the country. However the popular movement for reformasi saw the downfall of Suharto in 1998 and dwifuncti policy was abandoned.

In retrospect, we find that although dwifungsi asserted the powers of the military, but Indonesians were holding general elections after five years regularly to elect their President. Suharto always tried to pay utmost respects to popular sovereignty and sought his political legitimacy through elections. Burmese military on the other hand have failed to conduct any elections ever since 1990, when they were massively defeated. The NLD had swept the polls but military did not respect the popular mandate of the people and pursued repressive means to govern.

The Burmese military is not conducting the elections on the ground that the consitution of the country is not ready. The constitutional roadmap that they are discussing are to convince the outside world that they are evolving framework for peaceful transfer of power to elected representatives. Seventeen years have passed since drafting the constitution and certainly it is an unending process.

The military wants to remain in power by delaying the process of constitution making and the people of the country are feeling betrayed. At the same time they are facing difficult time because of the spiraling price rise. The market exchange rate for one US $ is 60 times more than the government exchange rate of Kyat.

Burma has a population of 56 million of which majority is believed to live under the poverty line. The regime almost doubled the price of fuel last month, which had devastating impact on the economic situation. The prices of palm oil, chicken, drinking water and other essential commodities increased substantially and survival of the ordinary people became difficult. Thus the unrest and protest became imminent.

According to latest reports more than 200 people have been killed in the crack down process. The military has adopted repressive means. The foreign reporters are not allowed to enter into Myanmar. The media is gagged. The government has closed internet access, cut phone landlines and confiscated mobile phones. On top of all their misdeeds, they do not hesitate to forcibly occupy religious places for prayer and congregation. They have trespassed into monasteries and locked the gates. The key intersections near monasteries in Rangoon and Mandalaya are sealed by barbed wire.

The domestic situation in Burma is turbulent and the military remains adamant and coercive. They are unwilling to do anything for reconciliation and peace. Hence there is a need of actors to activate peace initiatives to change the hard line perspective of the military.

The UN is concerned about tragic developments in Burma and has sent its envoy, Ibrahim Gambari to express its concern and convince the military rulers to end brutal repression. This may not resolve the crisis as Singapore's Foreign Minister, George Yeo has rightly remarked "we are not very hopeful from this mission, but it is the best shot we have."

China and India have different strategic objectives in Burma. Although both share common frontier with Burma and trade and energy are important contents in their agenda of cooperation, but Chinese influence on military rulers in Burma are stronger compared to India. The Chinese strategic presence at Coco, Hanggyi, Sittwe and Naypitaw has been massive. The military rulers express solidarity with the Chinese leaders.

On the other hand, Burmese people have attraction towards India. They aspire democratic governance and they have a growing dislike for the Chinese because of their nexus with the military. It is the Chinese weapons and technologies that has been used for crushing the democracy movement. As and when democracy will be restored, it will have serious consequences on Chinese business and strategic interests. It is therefore that the Chinese are arguing for stability and status quo in Burma.

India is exhorted to take initiatives for reconciliation and peace in Burma. Different opinions are coming. The suggested policy options are (a) to "wait and watch" till political developments in

Myanmar takes a concrete shape, (b) to engage military leaders for constitutional solution in coordination with and support of the ASEAN, (c) as suggested by George Fernandes to severe all ties with military junta and work out diplomatic pressures through the UN to declare military rule a pariah state.

India is interested in political development in Burma but it is very cautious to take any redical initiatives. The past experiences have been bitter. It had faced diplomatic reverses after upgrading full diplomatic recognition to communist Vietnam (1972), Heng Samrin regime in Cambodia (1980) and dispatching troops to Sri Lanka (1987).

India did not like the ushering in of military dictatorship in Burma in 1962 or 1988. It kept herself aloof from engaging military rulers for political and economic relations for decades, which facilitated the emergence of China-Pakistan-Myanmar axis. Thus Indian policy-makers were roundly blamed for sacrificing its national interests in that area.

When India evolved "Look East Policy", engagement with Burma became a pre-requisite and hence trade and investment ralations were given importance. When Burma became a member of ASEAN in 1997, India became an important partner of Burma through ARF, BIMST-EC and Mekong-Ganga project.

However, India cannot remain a silent spectator of the simmering political crisis in Burma. It is looking for appropriate response. Suitable initiatives will be taken to suggest solutions. The military rulers cannot always, ignore the opinion of the UN, ASEAN and other neighbours. The regional consensus is in favour of democracy movement and international opinion have abhorrence for the enemies of "open society". The reign of terror is against the norms of civilized society, and political changes in Burma cannot be stopped by repressive measures.

Seven steps of Roadmap for Political Reform are the following :

(1) Reconvening of the National Convention that has been adjourned since 1996.

(2) After the successful holding of the National Convention, step by step implementation of the process necessary for the emergence of a genuine and disciplined democratic system.

(3) Drafting of a new constitution in accordance with basic principles and detailed basic principles laid down by the National Convention.

(4) Adoption of the constitution through national referendum.

(5) Holding of free and fair elections for Pyithu Hluttaws (Legislative bodies) according to the new constitution.

(6) Convening of Hluttaws attended by Hluttaw members in accordance with the new constitution.

(7) Building a modern, developed and democractic nation by the state leaders elected by the Hluttaw; and the government and other central organs formed by the Hluttaw.

REFERENCES

B.K. Sen, "Road Map or Road Trap?" *Legal issues in Burma Journal*, Bangkok, No. 16, December 2003.

Burma: The Military and its Constitution, Bangkok, 1999.

Josef Silverstein, ed., *Independent Burma at Forty Years: Six Assessments*, Ithaca, Cornell University Press, 1989.

Kanishka Jayasuriya, ed., *Asian Regional Governance*, London, 2004.

Lian H. Sakhong, "A Two-Fold Path: The Transition to Democracy and Federalism in Burma", *Burma Debate*, Summer Fall, 2001.

Maung Maung Gyi, *Burmese Political Values, The Socio-Political Roots of Authoritarianism*, New York, 1983.

Martin Smith, *State of Fear: Censorship in Burma, 19 country Report*, New York, 2001.

Nawrahta, *Destiny of the Nation*, Yangon, 1995.

Robert H. Taylor, "The Constitutional Future of Myanmar in Comparative Perspective" in Peter Carey ed., *Burma: The Challenge of Change in a Divided Society*, London, 1997.

Index

Super